Agnieszka Bron, Michael Schemmann (Eds.)

Social Science Theories in Adult Education Research

Bochum Studies in International Adult Education

edited by

Agnieszka Bron and Michael Schemmann

Editorial Board

Joachim H. Knoll
Agnieszka Bron
Michał Bron Jr
Linden West
Edmée Ollagnier
Anja Heikkinen
Paul Bélanger

volume 3

LIT

Agnieszka Bron, Michael Schemmann (Eds.)

Social Science Theories in Adult Education Research

LIT

Managing Editor: Marcus Reinecke
Cover-Layout by Ramona Čačić

Manuscripts for publication may be submitted directly to the Editors,
Prof. Dr. Agnieszka Bron and Dr. Michael Schemmann.

Lehrstuhl für Erwachsenenbildung
Institut für Pädagogik
Ruhr-Universität Bochum
Universitätsstr. 150
D-44780 Bochum

Printed with support of the Ruhr-University Bochum

Die Deutsche Bibliothek – CIP-Einheitsaufnahme

Social Science Theories in Adult Education Research / Agnieszka Bron, Michael
Schemmann (Eds.). – Münster : LIT, 2002
  (Bochum Studies in International Adult Education ; 3.)
  ISBN 3-8258-5787-5
  ISSN 1617-3287

© LIT VERLAG Münster – Hamburg – London
Grevener Str. 179 48159 Münster Tel. 0251-23 50 91 Fax 0251-23 19 72
e-Mail: lit@lit-verlag.de http://www.lit-verlag.de

Distributed in North America by:

Transaction Publishers
New Brunswick (U.S.A.) and London (U.K.)

Transaction Publishers
Rutgers University
35 Berrue Circle
Piscataway, NJ 08854

Tel.: (732) 445 - 2280
Fax: (732) 445 - 3138
for orders (U. S. only):
toll free (888) 999 - 6778

Contents

THEORIES AND PERSPECTIVES IN ADULT EDUCATION RESEARCH
AN INTRODUCTION 7
Agnieszka Bron / Michael Schemmann

PART ONE: KEYNOTE

SHAPING SOCIOLOGICAL IMAGINATION
THE IMPORTANCE OF THEORY 21
Piotr Sztompka

PART TWO: THEORIES AND PERSPECTIVES

POSTMODERNISM AND THE CHANGING 'SUBJECT' OF ADULT
LEARNING 41
Linden West

REFLEXIVE MODERNISATION IN ADULT EDUCATION RESEARCH
THE EXAMPLE OF ANTHONY GIDDENS' THEORETICAL APPROACH 64
Michael Schemmann

ON THE 'GENDER' PERSPECTIVE IN ADULT EDUCATION
METHODOLOGICAL NOTES 81
Bettina Dausien

CONSTRUCTIVISM
AN EPISTEMOLOGICAL CHANGE 109
Horst Siebert

A CONSTRUCTIVIST APPROACH TO ADULT LEARNING 130
Etienne Bourgeois

SYMBOLIC INTERACTIONISM AS A THEORETICAL POSITION IN
ADULT EDUCATION RESEARCH 154
Agnieszka Bron

ON THE THEORY OF TRANSFORMATIVE LEARNING 180
Lena Wilhelmson

LIFELONG LEARNING AND 'BIOGRAPHICITY'
TWO THEORETICAL VIEWS ON CURRENT EDUCATIONAL CHANGES 211
Peter Alheit / Bettina Dausien

LEARNING ORGANISATION IN THEORY AND PRACTICE
ONGOING ORGANISING AND COLLECTIVE LEARNING IN TEACHER TEAMS 242
Jon Ohlsson

LIFE HISTORY APPROACH IN ADULT EDUCATION RESEARCH 270
Edmée Ollagnier

RECOVERING A CRITICAL HISTORY OF ADULT EDUCATION
THE ROLE OF INTELLECTUALS IN SOCIAL AND CULTURAL FORMATIONS 293
Barry J. Hake

PART THREE: EPILOGUE

CONCEPTUALISATION
ON THEORY AND THEORISING USING GROUNDED THEORY 313
Barney Glaser

AUTHORS 337

Agnieszka Bron / Michael Schemmann

THEORIES AND THEORETICAL PERSPECTIVES IN ADULT EDUCATION RESEARCH
AN INTRODUCTION

The relationship between adult education and theory is one of tension. This tension can be described on various levels. First of all, there is the fact that adult education does not have much theory that can be considered originating in the scientific discipline. It depends very much – probably more than any other scientific discipline – on borrowing theories from other disciplines such as the social sciences, pedagogy and philosophy. However, this also leads to friction within the community of adult educationists, since an understanding of the discipline shifts depending on whether it is more closely aligned to social sciences or to pedagogy and philosophy. Looking at the various national, but also international discourses it seems that positioning the discipline of adult education closer to social sciences has gained the majority of support. This, however, does not change the fact that adult education does not have many theories that can be considered originating in the discipline.

The second level which causes tension between adult education and theory is that many adult educationists, maybe because of the difficulties mentioned above, do not often engage in theoretical discourse and in theory building. The small number of publications dealing with adult education and theory underline this point. There are of course differences between national discourses. What is astonishing when considering the above points is the frequent complaint from within adult education that the discipline suffers from a lack of theory building.

A third level can be discerned when looking at adult education practice. The theoretical discourse is of particular importance for adult education practice because it helps to keep or establish a critical distance from the action of the practitioner, it reveals alternative solutions and innovations and it points to the dangers of instrumentalisation of adult education. However, it seems that practitioners tend to lose interest in theoretical discourse and certainly the current developments within the field of adult education – like increased competition and marketisation as well as the withdrawal of the state from the funding of adult education (Tuijnman 1996) – do not increase the willingness of adult educators to embark upon reflection processes.

While not an issue that can be exclusively attributed to the discipline of adult education, a fourth level can be discovered in the actual usage of theory in adult education research. The problem here lies in the discrepancy between theory and empirical studies. On the one hand, there are several empirical studies carried out without any theoretical guidance. On the other hand, there is theorising and theory building taking place without any empirical support. This is exactly the point where this book connects to the problem of theory and adult education research. It pleads for the importance of the combination of empirical and theoretical work in a symbiotic way. Good empirical studies need theoretical guidance and good theory building needs a solid empirical basis. Thus the book aims at exploring and displaying several theories and theoretical perspectives and their potentials for adult education research. But before presenting the contents of the book and the *raison d'être* for the selection of presented theories we intend to make some comments on what is understood by theory and theoretical perspective.

Theory, Theoretical Perspective and their Differences

The terms theory and theoretical perspective are referred to in various ways within theoretical discourses. As such, some researchers use the terms synonymously and make no differentiation at all. Others make the following distinction: On the one hand, there is a tendency to understand a scientific theory as a much more logically built set of propositions, which are related to each other and accurately defined, whereas a theoretical perspective, while also giving a basis for understanding and explaining social reality, is understood as being much less formally organised. On the other hand, it seems that theoretical perspective is considered as a more general and broader term than theory. As such it is referred to as, for example, a positivistic science perspective or as a phenomenological or ethnographic perspective. Within one theoretical perspective, several theories can be distinguished. Thus theoretical perspective serves as a generic term.

Before going any further, what is usually meant by theory should first be established. The Oxford Dictionary of Sociology defines theory as "an account of the world which goes beyond what we can see and measure. It embraces a set of interrelated definitions and relationships that organises our concepts of and understanding of the empirical world in a systematic way" (Oxford Dictionary of Sociology 1994, 532).

The meaning of the term 'theory' therefore very much depends on the researcher's goals of a particular study and what kind of research questions the researcher is posing. Two Norwegians, Föllesdal and Walloe, (1977) write that a theory is "a set of propositions whose inter-relatedness is made explicit. It is therefore characteristic of a theory that it makes clear how the different propositions which are included in it depend upon each other" (translation taken from Karlsson 1995, 21). The use of this meaning of theory is typical when the researcher attempts to verify an explicit hypothesis. The researcher is working with a prejudiced, or explicit, idea which must be tested and then verified or falsified. But there is another meaning of the term 'theory' (Karlsson 1995, 21). It goes back to the so-called '*Weltanschauungen*' philosophers of science (e.g. Hanson, Kuhn, Toulmin) who were in opposition to positivism. This approach determines how one views and describes the world, thus establishing an umbrella philosophy or a general world view. According to '*Weltanschauungen*' philosophers, observations and facts are imbued with conceptual organisation. In other words, they are influenced culturally, historically and linguistically. Thus, we cannot speak about objective observation that is free from such influence (Karlsson 1995, 21).

Generally speaking, it is possible to distinguish three conceptions of theory in social sciences. According to the first, theory is seen as a generalisation that allows us to classify the social world. The extent of generalisation, however, differs and includes both theorising about a specific range of phenomena, as well as the creation of far more abstract theories about society and its development.

The second concludes that theoretical assumptions should be transformed into propositions that are empirical and observable and, as such, should be systematically examined. Such an approach is often called positivism. Finally, the third concept of theory attempts to explain phenomena by identifying casual mechanisms and processes via their consequences even if they are not directly observable. The Marxist approach serves as an example, where the so-called contradictions between the forces and relations of production, which are unobservable, are used to explain fluctuations in the development and the levels of class struggle, which are observable.

We can also speak about social theory in order to understand the most general level of societal theory. In this case, it can refer to perspectives such as structural functionalism, phenomenology, or Marxism. Such perspectives involve or accept most or all of the social sciences. Some scholars, however, refer to this type of theorising as 'social philosophy'.

Grand, Middle-Range and Grounded Theory

When using the term theory, it is often connected with different adjectives. To these belong grand theories, formal or abstract theories, as well as grounded theory and middle-range theories.

The term grand theory was predominantly shaped by C. Wright Mills in his book *The Sociological Imagination* (1959) and refers to a highly abstract and conceptualised theoretical structure that explains the social world by a quite formal and logical framework using ordering concepts. Mills referred to Parsons' system theory as an example of grand theory (Mills 1959, 206). Another example could be Giddens' theory of reflexive modernisation.

The term middle-range theory was coined and advocated by Robert Merton in his attempt to bridge the gap between empirical studies that were not anchored in any theory and grand abstract theory that was not supported by any empirical studies. He suggested to develop a theory that is located between the set of hypotheses that we usually acquire in the research process and the systematic effort to formulate a unified theory that has as its aim the explanation of all observed similarities of social action, institutions and social change.

Both grand theory and middle-range theory are formal and abstract theories which are logically structured. They are developed through a process of deduction (according to logical rules) that follow Merton's idea to use hypotheses from the research observation to contribute to the formulation of a theory. This way of developing a theory was criticised by Glaser and Strauss on the grounds of discrepancy between empiricism and theory. Hypotheses that develop from this kind of formal theory are tested against observation. As a counterbalance in their book *The Discovery of Grounded Theory*, published in 1967, Barney Glaser and Anselm Strauss introduced the term grounded theory. According to them, theory can be developed and discovered from close observation of the social world. Thus, they argue for inductive theory-building wherein one develops theoretical ideas on the basis of collected empirical data. Here the skills of conceptualisation are necessary. To construct either substantial or formal theory 'sensitising concepts' are necessary to be developed from the close observation of data and than compared with other linked areas of inquiry. Development of concepts are useful for theory building in the sense that they link data with an emerging theory. The constant comparison of data and theory are also typical for a grounded theory approach. The sample is never chosen on representative but on theoretical grounds (for example by sampling critical cases). The methodological basis of using this approach can be symbolic interactionism or analytical induction.

Glaser and Strauss advocate for using the grounded theory approach to develop either substantive or formal theory. Substantive theory, the first stage of discovering a theory, means being able to conceptualise and theorise about one empirical or substantial area, but not being able to generalise to other settings or phenomena. In other words, it explains a specific studied phenomenon and cannot be generalised. Formal theory is much more abstract and allows one to generalise into other areas of inquiry. More formal theories are less specific to place or to particular demographics and can be applied to a wider range of concerns and problems in the studying discipline (Strauss, Corbin 1998, 23-24).

Norman Denzin (1989) also advocates for formal theory grounded in data, contrasting it both with middle-range theories and grand theory. He distinguishes between Merton's middle-range theories and formal theory which is discovered from data, as e.g. proposed by Goffman (1964, 1968, 1969). According to Denzin, formal theory is "any set of interrelated interpretations which are ordered in such a way that some are more specific than others and hence capable of being derived from higher-order statements. A less prominent feature of formal theory, which distinguishes it form other types of theory, is the fact that it explicitly rests on empirical referents" (Denzin 1989, 16). Contrasting Goffman with Merton, Denzin argues that

> sociologists should develop middle-range theories of specific problem areas. Merton's formulation is too restrictive. It leads to the endless proliferation of small-scope theories. 'Grand theory' represents the other alternative; it suggests that one very abstract and general theory can be developed to explain all human behaviour. Unfortunately, as it is currently practised, grand theory has few empirical referents. Formal theory, empirically grounded at all points, is preferable to a grand theory with a few empirical referents or to a series of middle-range theories, each of which have their own methods and specific domains (Denzin 1989, 16).

Continuing about formal theory, Denzin states that "[b]asic to formal theory will be universal interactive propositions that are assumed to apply to all instances of the phenomenon studied – at least until a negative case is discovered" (Denzin 1989, 17).

What is more, he also points out that a distinct characteristic of theory is that it is always incomplete and provisional. It has to be reconsidered when returning to the field as a researcher and it is always a means to a goal, i.e. yielding meaningful interpretations. Theories are not to be pursued for their own sake (Denzin 1989, 17).

Multi-Facetted Theory Usage and Triangulation

As the above sections illustrate, empirical findings gained in the field of adult education can be interpreted in different ways, according to a variety of very different theories and theoretical perspectives. Adult education can also be viewed on different levels and the various theoretical approaches applied do not exclude each other but very often complement each other. As such it can be seen as part of a biographical self concept but also as an important part of society.

Jürgen Wittpoth complained in an article on social theories and research that theories are very often chosen to interpret and analyse the findings which fit with the least problems and without causing any frictions. What is more, he points to the fact that very often it can also be observed that the attitude dominates that the one perspective which the researcher adheres to or follows is presented as the one and only and superior to others (Wittpoth 2001, 176/177).

To avoid this, we plead for a multi-facetted theory usage in adult education research and would like to introduce the idea of triangulation. Originating in the methodological discussion, it was Denzin who brought triangulation into the theoretical discourse. In general, triangulation means the usage of different theories and theoretical perspectives to the same objects or findings (Denzin 1989, 237). To give an idea how this process could take place, the following steps have been summarised.

First, a comprehensive overview of all possible interpretations in a given area is constructed. Thus a variety of theories and theoretical perspectives, e.g. interactionism, phenomenology, Marxism, feminist theory, semiotics, cultural studies etc. are referred to the respective phenomena. Then the research is carried out and the empirical material is collected and in a next step the complex theoretical framework developed in the first step is focused on the empirical material. Following those interpretations that do not relate to the material or do not provide a meaningful interpretation are set aside whereas those interpretations that make sense of the phenomena are put together into an interpretative framework that addresses all of the empirical findings. Finally a reformulated interpretative system is developed which bases on all points of the examined and interpreted empirical material (Denzin 1989, 241).

The advantages of such an approach seem rather obvious. Instead of having a limited dimension on the data, a triangulation would give a second and third view on the different hypotheses and also the utility of the applied theories and theoretical approaches could be discovered (Denzin 1989, 239).

On the Selection of Theories Presented in this Book

This volume presents various social science theories and perspectives which are used in or for adult education research. As it is not possible to gather the complete spectrum of approaches used in adult education research in one book, the approaches presented here represent only a cross section of activity in this field. The rationale for selection was determined by three factors.

First, we feel that the theories and theoretical approaches presented in this volume are the ones which were most often used in adult education research in the last decade within the European discourse. Consequently, there are, for example, no articles on system theory which, although of particular importance within the German theoretical discourse, has had little significance in other national theoretical discourses.

Secondly, we also feel that the theories and perspectives presented in this book are the ones offering the most innovative potential for the future of adult education research. Thus we have also decided to neglect theoretical frameworks such as normative educational positions, which certainly have a long tradition in adult education, or approaches focussing on face-to-face communication or group processes, since they seem to no longer provide innovative potential.

Thirdly, we have to concede that our own biases and preferences played a role in making the selection. This means that the chosen theories and perspectives correspond to our own research interests.

Almost all articles presented in this volume, besides the keynote and the epilogue, have a more or less similar underlying structure. They display the most important contours of the theory or perspective in question; they analyse and discuss the relation to adult education research, focussing on examples of other researcher's work and own research; and they give an outlook of what can be expected of the respective paradigm in the future.

The keynote of Piotr Sztompka, a well known Polish sociologist, opens this volume with rather general reflections on social theories typical in teaching sociology. Sztompka points out that the main aim of educating sociologists is to enable them to understand and explain social reality by using sociological imagination, which in turn, is possible to be learned by critical examination of social theories. He categorises theoretical approaches in four groups: explanatory theory, heuristic theory, analytic theory, and exegetic theory. For an adult educationist it is important to be able to approach reality from a critical, reflective, but also theoretical stance. In this way adult education researchers are able to see social institutions and individuals in their social and cultural contexts and, what is more, understand an adult involved in learning both individually, as well as collectively, in different contexts and situations.

We start off the main part of the book with an article by Linden West on the post-modernist perspective and its use in adult education research. Linden West concentrates on both the disadvantages and benefits of this perspective and manages to make clear that the postmodernist paradigm can be fruitful for adult education research.

Michael Schemmann's article on the role of Giddens' social theorising within adult education research can be seen as a counterpart to Linden West's article on postmodernism, since Giddens, as one representative of reflexive modernity, does not see modernity as having come to an end. His theory of reflexive modernity is often referred to in adult education research.

This is followed by an article from Bettina Dausien focussing on the gender perspective. The gender perspective is also often referred to in adult education research. However, it is discussed in an increasingly controversial way and, as Bettina Dausien makes clear in her article, is in flux.

The current significance of constructivism in adult education research is reflected by the fact that there are two articles on this theoretical framework. Constructivism contributed a lot to the shift in approaching learning processes of adults. Horst Siebert, the leading German adult educationist working on constructivism, presents in his article an analysis of the current discourse on the constructivist paradigm in adult education, whereas Etienne Bourgeois from Belgium, stresses the Piaget-inspired strand of constructivism.

Interactionism, or symbolic interactionism also plays a role in our understanding of how adults learn, and what is more, it has some resemblance with constructivism. While there are different ways of approaching learning from that perspective, Agnieszka Bron has chosen to work with G. H. Mead's theory and describes its fruitfulness for understanding adults' learning. She points out that there are still a lot more possibilities to discover Mead's contribution to different social phenomena including adults' learning.

With the aspect of adult's learning we come the closest to what could be considered as adult education theories. This phenomenon remains the main theoretical focus of the two following articles. Jack Mezirow's transformative learning theory is at the centre of the contribution from Lena Wilhelmsson, a Swedish researcher.

Peter Alheit and Bettina Dausien concentrate on biographicity and lifelong learning as two theoretical concepts that, according to them, are useful for research and theorising. Whereas lifelong learning is rarely explored as a theoretical concept, the importance of biographicity in theorising on the learning of adults has increased immensely since the beginning of the 1990s.

The role of informal learning in various environments advanced to be a central issue of adult education research within the last years. The theoretical framework that is referred to when researching about informal learning at the workplace is that of learning organisations. This theory and its usage in adult education research is displayed in the contribution from Jon Olsson from Sweden.

The French researcher Edmée Ollagnier takes up the life history approach which originated in sociology and historical sciences and has recently been frequently used in adult education research.

Barry Hake, from the University of Leiden, The Netherlands, focuses on the historical perspective, probably the oldest one in adult education research. As Barry Hake makes clear in his contribution, it is still fruitful and absolutely valuable for adult education research.

The concluding article by U.S. researcher Barney Glaser takes grounded theory as its starting point and stresses the importance of the ability to analyse and theorise in research. What is more, it explores the conflict between theoretical precondition and unbiased approaches to collected data. Taken together with Piotr Sztompka's article, this epilogue frames the whole volume and again asks for reflection on the use of theory in adult education research.

When reading through the articles, contact points, but also clear distinctions between the various theories and perspectives become clear. This leads to the last point of our introductory contribution. When carrying out adult education research and using theory, the question remains how researchers can deal with the fact that, rather than any kind of all-inclusive theory, there exists a plurality of, often contradictory, theories and perspectives which can be used to explain collected data. It is the hope of the editors of this book that its contents will take us a step closer to the multiple usage of theory in adult education research.

References

Denzin, N. (1989). *The Research Act. A Theoretical Introduction to Sociological Methods*. Englewood Cliffs, N.J.

Föllesdal, D., Walloe, L. (1977). *Argumentasjonsteori og Vitenskapsfilosofi*. Bergen.

Glaser, B., Strauss, A. (1967). *The Discovery of Grounded Theory*. Chicago.

Goffman, E. (1964). *Stigma*. London.

Goffman, E. (1968). *Asylums*. London.

Goffman, E. (1969). *The Presentation of Self in Everyday Life*. London.

Karlsson, G. (1995). *Psychological Qualitative Research from a Phenomenological Perspective*. Stockholm.

Merton, R. (1967). *On Theoretical Sociology*. New York.

Mills, C. Wright (1959). *The Sociological Imagination*. New York.

The Concise Oxford Dictionary of Sociology (1994). Edited by G. Marshall. Oxford.

Strauss, A., Corbin, J. (1998). *Basics of Qualitative Research. Techniques and Procedures for Developing Grounded Theory*. London, 2. Ed.

Tuijnman, A. (1995). The Expansion of Adult Education and Training in Europe: Trends and Issues. In: Raggat, P. (ed.). *The Learning Society. Challenges and Trends*. London.

Wittpoth, J. (2001). Zeitdiagnose: nur im Plural. In: Wittpoth, J. (ed.). *Erwachsenenbildung und Zeitdiagnose. Theoriebeobachtungen*. Bielefeld. pp.155-178.

PART I

KEYNOTE

Piotr Sztompka

SHAPING SOCIOLOGICAL IMAGINATION
THE IMPORTANCE OF THEORY[1]

I had my first taste of sociological theory in Neil J. Smelser's graduate class at Berkeley in 1972/73. Following on the themes already developed in his *Essays in Sociological Explanation* (1968), he discussed the works of the great classical scholars: Marx, Weber, Durkheim, Tocqueville. It struck me immediately that he was not just contemplating, commenting or analytically dissecting them. Instead he was using them, trying to unravel the structure and logic of their theoretical explanation of concrete issues: social inequality in the case of Marx, power in the case of Weber, cultural cohesiveness in the case of Durkheim, functioning of democracy in the case of Tocqueville. It was the ability to explain such crucial social issues that made them great sociologists, because theory, in their view, and clearly in the view of Smelser, was empirically and historically rooted general explanation. It was, as Smelser was defining it "an enterprise of accounting for regularities, variations, and interdependencies among the phenomena identified within the sociological frameworks" (Smelser 1968, 55).

I looked up Smelser's own major theoretical contribution, *Theory of Collective Behavior* (1963) and found the same focus on explanation, but not just any explanation. He put forward a dynamic explanatory model incorporating a temporal dimension in the "value-added sequence": the necessary preconditions for episodes of collective behavior or social movements cumulatively emerge in stages – from structural conducive-

---

[1] An abridged version of an article prepared for a volume "Self, Social Structure and Beliefs. Explorations in Sociology (A *Festschrift* for Neil J. Smelser), edited by J. C. Alexander and G. Marx (to come out at California University Press in 2002).

ness, through structural strain, initiating events, spread of generalised beliefs, attempts at social control to the emergence of the explained social phenomenon. This account, "logical patterning of social determinants, each contributing its 'value' to the explanation of the episode" (Semlser 1968, 99), was obviously the realisation of Smelser's creed that "sociological explanation consists in bringing constructions such as hypotheses, models and theories to bear on factual statements" (Smelser 1968, 58). This was a theory which was causal, empirical, genetic, operational, and which demonstrated forcefully that social facts do not exist statically but are in a state of continual emergence, social becoming, as I later called it (Sztompka 1990). To this day Smelser's model is, for me, an exemplar of what sociological explanation should look like.

Soon after my Berkeley class I had the opportunity to study under two other American theorists who, in spite of basic differences in the orientation and substance of their theories, seemed to share with Smelser the focus on explanation. One was Robert K. Merton with the influential programme of middle-range theory, that he put forward to resolve the dilemma between abstract "grand theory", seen in Talcott Parsons' style, and the narrow-empirical data gathering, which dominated some sub-disciplines of sociology. The other theorist was George Homans, with his critique of Parsonian functionalism in the name of covering-law model of explanation, borrowed from George Hempel's classic logical work. Both Merton and Homans were trying to show what sociological explanation should look like.

I have become more and more convinced that explanatory theory is the most important, illuminating and useful aspect of that vast and multifaceted enterprise that runs today under the label of theory. In my sociological education, and later my own academic work, it was explanatory theory that turned out to be crucial. In this article, I wish to argue why explanatory theory should remain in the forefront of sociological teaching, and not to be put aside by some other trendy modes of theorising.

The Educational Focus: Sociological Imagination

The education of sociologists has four aims: (a) to teach the language of the discipline, a set of concepts with which social reality is understood, (b) to develop a particular vision, a perspective from which social reality is approached, (c) to train in the methods, procedures and techniques of empirical inquiry, (d) to provide information about main facts and data concerning contemporary social life. Let us put the points (a) and (b) – language and perspective – under one label "sociological imagination", borrowed from the classic book by C. Wright Mills (1959). He explains the notion as follows: "The sociological imagination enables us to grasp history and biography and the relation between the two within society" (Mills 1959, 3). Let us elaborate the full meaning of this statement and extend the concept beyond Mills' insight.

I consider sociological imagination to be a complex skill or ability made up of five components: (a) to see all social phenomena as produced by some social agents, individual or collective, and to identify those agents, (b) to understand deep, hidden, structural and cultural resources and constraints which influence social life, including the chances for agential efforts (as Mirra Komarovsky puts it: "It takes patient training of the sociological sight to enable the students to perceive the invisible social structure" (Komarovsky 1951), (c) to recognise the cumulative burden of tradition, the persisting legacies of the past and their continuing influence on the present, (d) to perceive social life in its incessant, dynamic, fluid process of social becoming (Sztompka 1991), (e) to recognise the tremendous variety and diversity of the forms in which social life may appear. As Everett Hughes defines one of the main goals of sociological education: "The emancipation through expansion of one's world by penetration into and comparison with the world of other people and other cultures is not the only aspect of sociological imagination... But it is one great part of it, as it is of human life itself" (Hughes 1970, 16).

To put it another way: sociological imagination is the ability to relate anything that happens in a society to a structural, cultural and historical context and to the individual and collective actions of societal members, recognising the resulting variety and diversity of social arrangements.

C. W. Mills gives us an example:

> One result of reading sociology ought to be to learn how to read a newspaper. To make sense of a newspaper – which is a very complicated thing – one must learn how to connect reported events, how to understand them by relating them to more general conceptions of the societies of which they are tokens, and the trends of which they are a part... My point is sociology is a way of going beyond what we read in the newspaper. It provides a set of conceptions and questions that help us to do this. If it does not, then it has failed as part of liberal education (Mills 1960, 16-17).

Teaching sociology cannot be limited to 'sociology in books', it must go beyond that toward 'sociology in life' allowing deeper interpretation, better understanding of everything that surrounds us. As another classical author, Robert Park, emphasised:

> When there is no attempt to integrate the things learned in the schoolroom with the experience and problems of actual life, learning tends to become mere pedantry – pedantry which exhibits itself in a lack of sound judgement and in a lack of that kind of practical understanding we call common sense (Park 1950, 58).

Mirra Komarovsky makes the same point:

> There is no greater educational danger than this: that the students learn the sociological concepts on a purely formal verbal level without the richness and fullness of meaning; that this body of words remains a sterile segment of mentality, relatively unrelated to the confused stream of life which it sought to interpret (Komarovsky 1944, 195).

I consider the training of sociological imagination and the skill to apply it to concrete problems of social life, as absolutely crucial for the education of sociologists, both those who think about academic careers, and those who go to practice-oriented professions.

Sociological Imagination and Theoretical Resources

To a great extent, training sociological imagination is synonymous with training in sociological theory. However, this is not in the sense of memorising names and schools, definitions and arguments but rather in the sense of using theory, i.e. referring to concrete experience, looking at the current problems in the surrounding society; its dilemmas and opportunities. It also applies to our personal biographies and life-chances. Sociological imagination should provide a map to ensure a better orientation in the chaos of events, change and transformation. It should give us a deeper understanding, a more thorough enlightenment and, in this way, provide more opportunities for informed, rational life and sound practice. In this paper I will review the resources for such indispensable theoretical training that we possess in the sociological tradition as well as in recent social theory.

One huge pool of theoretical ideas is to be found in the history of the discipline, from the early nineteenth century onwards. Teaching history of sociology is not an antiquarian pastime. The tradition of our discipline is still extremely vital. Most of the concepts, models, issues, queries that we study today, have been inherited from the nineteenth century masters. They have put solid foundations under the sociological enterprise, and their work is still very much alive. They should be studied, not in a historical or biographical way but in the context of our time, as their seminal ideas throw light on our present realities. Of course they must be studied critically and selectively, because not all have left an equally relevant heritage. My personal selection includes of course the "big three": Max Weber, Emile Durkheim and Karl Marx – the true undisputed giants of sociology, but also Auguste Comte, Herbert Spencer, Georg Simmel, Ferdinand Tonnies, Vilfredo Pareto, Alexis de Tocqueville, Charles Cooley, William Sumner, and George H. Mead. Reading and rereading them is crucially important to discover new insights and questions and formulate sociological problems by entering into a sort of dialogue with them to assess our own ideas. Perhaps, most importantly, they can show us the best models for intellectual work. As Robert Merton puts it:

Exposure to such penetrating sociological minds as those of Durkheim and Weber helps us to form standards of taste and judgment in identifying a good sociological problem – one that has significant implications for theory – and to learn what constitutes an apt theoretical solution to the problem. The classics are what Salvemini liked to call *'libri fecondatori'* – books that sharpen the faculties of exacting readers who give them their undivided attention (Merton in Sztompka 1996, 31-32).

There is one additional benefit: the student learns that the social world is multidimensional, extremely complex and therefore requires many approaches to understand it. Studying the history of sociological theories is a great lesson in theoretical pluralism, tolerance for variety and diversity of perspectives, and the best medicine against narrow-minded dogmatism and orthodoxy.

But let us leave sociological tradition, as my main focus is the current sociological theory and its relevance for teaching. I will argue that we have four types of theory and theorising in contemporary sociology, and that they are of unequal importance for educational purposes in training the sociological imagination. In order of diminishing importance, I will discuss: (a) explanatory theory, (b) heuristic theory, (c) analytic theory and (d) exegetic theory. This classification partly overlaps with the triple distinction of "theories of", "presuppositional studies", and "hermeneutical theory" as proposed by Jeffrey Alexander (Alexander 1998). But his preferential order is different than mine, and he also does not recognise my third category: analytic theory.

Theoretical Boom

In general, the last decade of the twentieth century was a good time for sociological theory. Only half a century ago, in the middle of the twentieth century there was a lot of talk about the crisis of sociological theory (e.g. Gouldner 1971). Even quite recently a rather pessimistic appraisal was given by Jeffrey Alexander who perceived diminishing influence of sociological theory in the recent period both inside the discipline and without, accompanied by the growing importance of theorietical work in economics, philosophy, and literary studies (Alexander 1998). But now the situation seems to have changed. I would share the opinion of a British sociologist Gerard Delanty: "Social theory is in a position of great strength at the moment" (Delanty 1998, 1).

To support this claim let us first look at some institutional or organisational facts. The Research Committee on Theory (RC 16), which I founded together with Jeffrey Alexander in 1986, has grown to become one of the biggest of more than fifty committees of the International Sociological Association (ISA). In the American Sociological Association (ASA), the theory section is one of the largest groups. During the last decades of the century the circulation of theoretical journals dramatically increased and many new titles appeared: *Theory, Culture & Society*, *European Journal of Social Theory*, *Sociological Theory*, *Theory* (published by ASA), *Theory and Society*. A new publication: *Journal of Classical Sociology* is being launched by Sage under the editorship of Brian Turner. A number of major compendia of theoretical knowledge have come out: *Polity Reader in Social Theory* (1994), The Blackwell companions to: *Social Theory* (1996), *Major Social Theorists* (2000) and *Handbook of Social Theory* at Sage (2000). There are new monographs taking stock of current theory: Patrick Baert's *Social Theory in the XX Century* (1998), John Scott's *Sociological Theory: Contemporary Debates* (1995). Major publishers: Polity Press, Cambridge University Press, Sage, put out rich lists of theoretical work, both classical and recent, including important book series: e.g. *Cambridge Cultural Social Studies* (edited by Alexander and Seidman). All around the world there are theoretical conferences, focusing on theoretical issues, for example, recently: *Reappraising Theories of Social Change* at Montreal 2000, or *New Sources of Critical Theory* at Cambridge 2000.

It is notable that a theory has returned to its cradle, to Europe, after a long detour to North America (Nedelman, Sztompka 1993). Of course, apart from the continuing influence and presence of the 'old guard', such as Robert K. Merton, Neil Smelser, Seymour M. Lipset, Lewis Coser, Peter Blau and others, a number of influential theorists from the younger generation work and publish in the US, like Jeffrey Alexander, Randall Collins, Craig Calhoun, Jonathan Turner, to mention just a few. But it is

Britain, France and Germany that currently provide the most fertile grounds for original theoretical work. As Neil Smelser admits:

> In fact, in the past 50 years, the center of gravity of general theoretical thinking has shifted from the United States to Europe, and this shift is represented in the works of scholars like Alain Tourine, Pierre Bourdieu, Jürgen Habermas, Niklas Luhmann, and Anthony Giddens. Much of current theoretical thinking in the US stems from the influence of these figures on faculty and graduate students (Smelser 1990, 47-48).

From the European side this is echoed by Brian Turner who predicts that "European social theory may once more emerge to evolve to a new form of domination in the world development of social theory" (Turner 1998).

Explanatory Theory

How can the above-mentioned facts and tendencies be interpreted? Sticking to the old, traditional opposition of 'theory *versus* research', or 'theoretical *versus* empirical sociology'[2], could lead one to conclude that the ascent of theory indicates a shift from research toward scholasticism and the realm of pure ideas. In other words, that empirical research is abandoned and real social problems and concrete social facts are ignored. In fact, nothing could be further from the truth, the opposite is actually the case. The impressive reputation of theory is due to the fact that it won its way into all domains of empirical sociology, has found a place in all specialist areas of sociology and has finally become accepted as a valid and necessary component of sociological research. The separation of theory and research is no longer feasible. Instead we witness proliferation of theories dealing with various substantive social problems and issues.

Theorists and researchers now meet halfway. Most theorists no longer

---

[2] As exemplified by Parsons-Merton's debate in 1947 at the annual convention of ASA, see Merton 1948.

pursue purely abstract ideas, but are looking at real problems, such as globalisation, identity, risk, trust, civil society, democracy, new forms of labor, social exclusion, cultural traumas etc. At the same time, empirical researchers no longer confine themselves to fact finding and data gathering but propose models, generalisations of their domains informed by accumulated research: theories of deviance, collective behavior, social movements, ethnicity, mass media, social capital, post-materialist values etc. For example, a just published *Handbook of Sociology* by S. Quah and A. Sales (2000), which sums up the state of the art in various sociological sub-disciplines, in fact includes a considerable amount of theory in each chapter. The book illustrates that theory is coming closer to addressing real 'social problems', as opposed to esoteric 'sociological problems', i.e. the problems experienced by common people as opposed to the professional concerns of sociologists. Theory can provide explanations of pressing social issues by generating, more or less directly testable hypotheses and can thus influence more people in society by providing them with guidelines for thinking and mental maps of specific domains of their social 'life-world'.

This first theoretical approach can be labelled 'Explanatory Theory. It represents, what Bryan Turner calls a "strong program" for theory (Turner 1996, 6). As a start each theory has to answer the three questions of what, for what, and for whom it is made.
Thus, Explanatory Theory consists
- of what?

Of real social problems: why more crime, why new social movements, why poverty, why ethnic revival? For Merton, Smelser, Bourdieu, Turner theory should grow out from research and be directed toward research. "For theoretical contributions to be worthwhile, they need to be question-driven" (Baert 1998). "Social theory thrives and survives best when it is engaged with empirical research and public issues" (Turner 1996, 12).
- It has been developed for what purpose?

For providing explanations, or at least models allowing better organisation of dispersed facts and phenomena, interpretation of multiple and varied events and phenomena.
- For whom can it be useful?

Not only for fellow theorists, but for common people, to provide them with orientation, enlightenment, understanding of their condition. An important role of theories is to "inform democratic public discourse" (Calhoun 1996, 429). This role will become even more pronounced as more societies become democratic, and in a 'knowledge society' of the future, of informed, educated citizens who care about social, public issues where democracy will take a form of "discursive democracy" (Dryzek 1990).

One can formulate a hypothesis in the framework of the 'sociology of knowledge': the driving force behind the developments in explanatory theory are to be found in rapid, radical and overwhelming social change. We are experiencing the next "great transition" (to paraphrase Polanyi). Theories are especially in demand in times of change. There is pressure on sociologists from both the common people as well as politicians to provide explanations of the chaos. Everyone wants to know where we have come from, where we are and where we are going. Facts and data alone cannot answer such questions. An overall view can only be provided by generalised explanatory models. "Nothing presses this theoretical venture on us more firmly than the experience of historical change and cross-cultural diversity" (Calhoun 1996, 431).

Teaching explanatory theories is, in my opinion, the most important goal of sociological education and particularly so in periods of overwhelming social change. These kinds of theories provide the strongest stimulus in developing the sociological imagination, as they link theorising with concrete experience.

Heuristic Theory

Let us move on to a second kind of theoretical approach: theoretical orientation, or what I would call a 'Heuristic Theory' (not directly testable, but useful in generating relevant concepts, images, models). It is closest to social philosophy, and particularly the ontology or metaphysics of the social world, as it attempts to answer three perennial ontological questions about the constitution of social reality: (a) what are the bases of social order?, (b) what is the nature of human action?, (c) what is the mechanism and course of social change? Such questions have been addressed by all classical founders of sociology. Good examples of the classical orientations dominating in the middle of the century, which attempted to deal with such issues, were structural functionalism, symbolic interactionism, exchange theory and Marxism. Since then, several new trends have emerged, which will be discussed later.

What are the characteristics of this kind of theory? Again, let us ask our three questions.
- Theory of what?

Of the foundations of social reality. It poses questions not of 'why' but of 'how': how is social order possible, (how the social wholes exist, how people live together, cooperate, cohabit?), how social action is carried out, how social change proceeds?
- Theory for what?

To provide the conceptual framework for more concrete explanatory theoretical work, to sensitise to specific types of variables, to suggest strong categories, to grasp the varied and dispersed facts.
- Theory for whom?

Mostly for researchers building explanatory models of specific domains of reality, answering concrete problems.

The formidable growth of such heuristic theories by the end of the century cannot be explained by reference to social facts, but rather by intellectual developments. Heuristic theory should be seen in terms of the history of ideas rather than the sociology of knowledge. It seems to be related to new, contingent intellectual developments, that is to say new trends and attractive, innovative, original perspectives. There is the excitement of a "paradigmatic shift" (Kuhn 1970), in fact we have witnessed three parallel paradigmatic shifts in recent theory. The first shift, from "first" to "second" sociology (Dawe 1978), moves from a view of fixed organic systems to fluid fields of social forces. Social order is seen to be a constantly emerging and constructed achievement of agents, produced and reproduced by human action. Examples of such perspectives are to be found in the work of Berger and Luckmann, Elias, Giddens, Bourdieu. The second shift is from evolution or social development to social becoming. There is an emphasis on open-ended historical scenarios, determined by decisions, choices, but also by contingent, random occurrences. Examples of this perspective are found in "historical sociology" – represented by authors like Tilly, Archer, Skockpol, myself (Sztompka 1991, 1993). The third shift is from images of *homo economicus*, the calculating, rational, purposeful actor, (still at the heart of "rational choice theory", e.g. Coleman, Elster), and *homo sociologicus*, the normatively directed role player (still found in "neo-functionalism", e.g. Alexander, Luhmann, Munch), to *homo cogitans*, the knowledgeable and meaningful actor informed and constrained by collective symbolic systems of knowledge and belief. This shift is also seen as an interpretative turn, a cultural turn or a linguistic turn. "Contemporary social theory has done an about-face in analytical terms by giving prominence and priority to cultural phenomena and cultural relations" (Turner 1998). It has many varieties. In one, which somebody has called mentalism, there is a stress on the invariant components of the human mind. Examples would include the structuralism of Levi-Strauss or De Saussure, and the phenomenology of Schütz. The second kind, what some authors call textualism, is represented by poststructuralism, or theory of discourses by Foucault, where social reality appears as a form of text with specific semantic meaning and its own rules of grammar. The third is sometimes also labelled intersubjectivism, to which Habermas made a great contribution in his theory of communicative action. Finally, there is the reaction against the 'overintellectualised image of man'. The emphasis shifts to practical knowledge (Giddens), ethno-methods (Garfinkel), but also seeing body as an instrument of action (Turner), emotions as accompanying actions, things one uses, objects encountered, environment providing context for action. Individuals are seen as the carriers of routine but complex characteristic sets of practices (Bourdieu).

Thus, we presently have a rich and varied menu of heuristic orientations. Teaching should sensitise students to the necessity of using many of these orientations to look at society from various perspectives and different sides, in order to attain a fuller understanding of social life.

Analytic Theory

The third and still different kind of theoretical approach can be called 'Analytic Theory'. It generalises and clarifies concepts, providing typologies and classifications, explications and definitions applicable in explanatory theory. It has an important but subsidiary role to play. However, there is a danger that it can become merely a method to sharpen conceptual tools without ever taking a stand or producing a binding system of concepts. The attempts to construct closed conceptual systems and special languages to cover the whole domain of sociology seem to have ended with Niklas Luhmann's huge effort (earlier only Talcott Parsons had similar ambitions). But, on a more limited level, this variety of theorising is useful and necessary coming close to what Merton labelled "middle range theory" (Sztompka 1996, 41-50): empirically informed conceptual schemes, applicable to concrete empirical problems (e.g. his middle-range theories of roles and role-sets, of reference groups, of stratification, mobility, of anomie, deviance etc.).

What is the nature of such a theory? Again we must ask our three questions:
- Analytic Theory consists of what?

Of rich concepts useful for grasping phenomena.
- It has been developed for what purpose?

For identifying, unravelling, explicating, phenomena, or important dimensions of phenomena.
- For whom can it be useful?

For sociologists providing them with canonical vocabulary, technical language to deal with their subject matter.

Teaching analytic theory is crucial to develop students' ability to think and talk sociologically. It provides students with the basic tools of the trade. The focus in introductory courses of sociology should rest precisely on this kind of theory.

Exegetic Theory

Finally there is the fourth kind of theory which can be called 'Exegetic Theory'. It comes down to analysis, exegesis, systematisation, reconstruction and critique of existing theories. It is, of course, a valid preparation for theoretical work. It should be seen as a stage of a scientific career; a period of apprenticeship. Most major theorists have gone through such a stage: Parsons with *The Structure of Social Action* (1937), Giddens with *Capitalism and Modern Social Theory* (1971), Alexander with his four famous volumes of *Theoretical Logic in Sociology* (1982) and Smelser with *Essays in Sociological Explanation* (1968). With all due proportions, I would also include my *Sociological Dilemmas* (1979) in this category. However, sight of what is truly important can be lost if dissecting and analyzing the work of fashionable authors becomes the main concern, concentrating on what a certain scholar said, did not say, or could have said better; whether he was consistent and transparent. The more esoteric, incomprehensible and muddled a theory, the greater opportunity it provides for exegetic debate. It inspires the frantic search 'in a dark room, for a dark dog, which is not there'. This is the secret of some current theories (e.g. the whole school of 'postmodernism' and 'deconstructionism') and explains their popularity among interpreters. If a theory is straightforward, problem-oriented, precise and clear, there is not much to interpret and criticise.

Our three questions are very revealing in this particular case.
- Theory of what?

Of other theories, certain books, texts, phantoms of sociological imagination, resulting in self-referential exercises.
- Theory for what?

For apologies or destructions of proposed theories, which easily implies factionalism, dogmatism, orthodoxy of schools, sects, fans, and degenerates from the 'free market of ideas' into a vicious 'battlefield of ideas'.
- Theory for whom?

For other theorists who play intellectual games within the sects of the initiated.

In my view, such theories are the least consequential and often futile and irrelevant. They often deteriorate into epigonism. This opinion is shared by several theorists:
- "Social theory is at once the most futile and the most vital of intellectual enterprises. It is futile when it turns inward, closes into itself, degenerates into a desiccated war of concepts or an invidious celebration of the cognitive exploits of this author, that school, my tradition, your orthodoxy" (Wacquant 1998).
- "It is necessary to let fresh air into the often closed compounds of indoor theorizing. Social theory is not only conceptualizations and discourse on other theoretician's concepts" (Therborn 1998).

- "Without commitment to a public role, sociological theory will become an internal leisure pursuit of academics providing merely decorative consequences for academic careers" (Turner 1998).
- "Without these political and public commitments, social theory is in danger of becoming an esoteric, elitist, and eccentric interest of marginal academics" (Turner 1996, 13).
- "Quite a number of scholars seem to assume that theoretical progress depends solely on close scrutiny and recycling of preceding social theories... This strategy is unlikely to provide innovative and penetrating social knowledge" (Baert 1998, 203).

Needless to say, I would not recommend this kind of exegetic theories for sociology students. If at all, their place in the curriculum should be only marginal, perhaps limited to graduate, or post-graduate levels, as a kind of mental exercise in reading and debunking of esoteric texts.

Conclusion

To conclude, it has been argued that the most important, fruitful and promising types of theory, crucial for sociological imagination, are the explanatory and heuristic theories. Analytic theories have a subsidiary role in sharpening conceptual tools and providing the language for sociological thinking. Exegetic theories are only useful in preparing a background for theorising and the development of critical skills, but do not contribute to theory proper and should not replace other forms of theorising.

Explanatory and heuristic theories make up a pluralistic mosaic of theoretical explanations and theoretical orientations. How should we deal with this fragmentation of the theoretical field? The attitude of "disciplined eclecticism" (Merton 1976, 169) is a good way to address explanatory, practical theory, for the people not only the theorists. This should be imparted on sociology students. "Disciplined" – means critical approach, appraising theories on their internal merits, coherence, persuasiveness, and ability to generate hypotheses. "Eclecticism" – means open, inclusive, tolerant attitude, free from one-sided dogmatism. The spirit of Neil Smelser's work is clearly congruent with this strategy. He explicitly suggests "an attitude of permissiveness for a variety of theoretical and empirical activities, combined with an obligation to relate these to the core of sociology" (Smelser 1968, 61). Some recent authors argue in the same, ecumenical direction: "It is generally not possible to ask all the interesting questions about any really significant phenomenon within the same theory or even within a set of commensurable, logically integratable, theories" (Calhoun 1996, 435). "It is possible to gain cumulative knowledge about the world from within different and competing points of view" (Alexander 1988, 79).

Disciplined eclecticism allows to cross inter-theoretical borders, but also inter-disciplinary borders, back toward 'social theory' as practised by the classics, rather than only narrowly defined 'sociological theory'. Already in the 1960s Neil Smelser opted for this kind of true theoretical integration, which is not to be mistaken with creating interdisciplinary institutes: "A major requirement of integration is that some common language be developed so that the elements of the different social sciences can be systematically compared and contrasted with one another" (Semlser 1968, 43). Twenty years later Immanuel Wallerstein argues how by intellectual necessity sociology should link with psychology, economics, anthropology, cognitive sciences, political science, and how important it is to abandon some pernicious interdisciplinary divisions which emerged in the nineteenth century and have proved very resilient (Wallerstein 1988). The same message is forcefully articulated another decade later by Mattei Dogan: "The networks of cross-disciplinary influences are such that they are obliterating the old classification of the social sciences. The trend that we perceive today is from the old formal disciplines to new hybrid social sciences" (Dogan 1997, 442). The persistent emphasis on the same need for integration over several decades proves in itself that the promise is not yet fulfilled. It remains as perhaps the biggest challenge facing sociological theory and sociological education today.

References

Alexander, J. C. (1982). *Theoretical Logic in Sociology*, 4 vols. London.

Alexander, J. C. (1988). New Theoretical Movement. In: Smelser, N. J. (ed.). *The Handbook of Sociology*. Newbury Park, pp.77-102.

Alexander, J. C. (1998). Sociology, Theories of. In: *Routledge Encyclopedia of Philoso-*

phy (ed. by E.Craig). London.

Baert, P. (1998). *Social Theory in the Twentieth Century*. Cambridge.

Calhoun, C. (1996). Social Theory and the Public Sphere. In: Turner, B. S. (ed.). *The Blackwell Companion to Social Theory*. Oxford, pp. 429-470.

Dawe, A. (1978). Theories of Social Action. In: Bottomore, T. B., Nisbet, R. (eds.). *The Histroy of Sociological Analysis*. New York, pp. 362-417.

Delanty, G. (1998). Editorial Introduction. In: *International Journal of Theoretical Sociology*, 1.

Dogan, M. (1997). The New Social Sciences. Cracks in the Disciplinary Walls. In: *International Social Science Journal*, 153, September, pp. 429-443.

Dryzek, J. S. (1990). *Discursive Democracy*. Cambridge.

Giddens, A. (1971). *Capitalism and Modern Social Theory*. Cambridge.

Gouldner, A. (1971). *The Coming Crisis of Western Sociology*. New York.

Hughes, E. C. (1970). Teaching as Fieldwork. In: *The American Sociologist*, 5 (1), pp. 13-18.

Komarovsky, M. (1944). A Note on a New Field Course. In: *American Sociological Review*, 9, pp. 194-196.

Komarovsky, M. (1951). Teaching College Sociology. In: *Social Forces*, 30, December, pp. 252-256.

Kuhn, T. (1970). *The Structure of Scientific Revolution*. Chicago.

Merton, R. K. (1948). The Position of Sociological Theory. In: *American Sociological Review*, 13, pp. 164-168.

Merton, R. K. (1976). *Sociological Ambivalence*. New York.

Mills, C. W. (1960). Introduction. In: *Images of Man. The Classic Tradition in Sociological Thinking*. New York, pp. 16-17.

Mills, C. W. (1959). *Sociological Imagination*. New York.

Nedelmann, B., Sztompka, P. (eds.). (1993): *Sociology in Europe*. Berlin.

Park, R. (1937). A Memorandum on Rote Learning. In: *American Journal of Sociology*, 43, July, pp. 23-36.

Parsons, T. (1937). *The Structure of Social Action*. Glencoe.

Polity Reader in Social Theory (1994). Cambridge, Polity Press.

Quah, S., Sales, A. (eds.) (2000). *International Handbook of Sociology*. London.

Ritzer, G. (ed.) (2000). *The Blackwell Companion to Major Social Theorists*. Oxford.

Scott, J. (1995). *Sociological Theory. Contemporary Debates*. Cheltenham.

Smelser, N. J. (1963). *Theory of Collective Behavior*. New York.

Smelser, N. J. (1990). Sociology's Next Decades. Centrifugality, Conflict, Accommodation. In: *Cahiers de Recherche Sociologique*, 14, printemps, pp. 35-49.

Smelser, N. J. (1968). *Essays in Sociological Explanation*. Englewood Cliffs.

Sztompka, P. (1991). *Society in Action. A Theory of Social Becoming*. Cambridge.

Sztompka, P. (1996). *The Sociology of Social Change*. Oxford.

Sztompka, P. (1996). *Robert K. Merton on Social Structure and Science*. Chicago 1996.

Sztompka, P. (1979). *Sociological Dilemmas. Toward a Dialectic Paradigm*. New York.

Therborn, G. (1998). Comments in "The Tasks of Social Theory" (editorial). In: *European Journal of Social Theory*, 1 (1), pp. 127-135.

Turner, B. S. (1996). Introduction. In: Turner, B. S. (ed.). *Blackwell Companion to Social Theory*, Oxford, pp. 1-19.

Turner, B. S. (ed.) (1996). The Blackwell Companion to Social Theory. Oxford.

Turner, B. S. (1998). Comments in "The Tasks of Social Theory" (editorial). In: *European Journal of Social Theory*, 1 (1), pp. 127-135.

Wacquant, L. (1998). Comments in "The Tasks of Social Theory" (editorial). In: *European Journal of Social Theory*, 1 (1), pp. 127-135.

Wallerstein, I. (1988). Should We Unthink the Nineteenth Century? In: Ramirez, F. O. (ed.). *Rethinking the Nineteenth Century*. Westport, pp. 185-191.

PART II

THEORIES AND PERSPECTIVES

Linden West

POSTMODERNISM AND THE CHANGING 'SUBJECT' OF ADULT LEARNING

> To all those who still wish to talk about man, about his reign or his liberation, to all those who still ask themselves questions about what man is in his essence, to all those who wish to take him as their starting point in their attempts to reach the truth ... to all these warped and twisted forms of reflection we can answer only with a philosophical laugh – which means to a certain extent, a silent one (Foucault 1970, 342-3).

Introduction

In this paper I reflect on the nature of postmodernism and its implications for the 'subject' of adult and lifelong learning. By 'subject' I mean three different but overlapping aspects: first, 'subject' as in the focus of our study, in the sense of the policies, practices, experiences, impacts and meanings of adult learning. This encompasses a complex 'moorland' of diverse activity – in comparison to the clearly delineated 'field' of adult education – located in a range of community, work and more intimate, as well as formal settings, and focused on individuals and groups and the nature and significance of learning to them. The second notion relates to the subject of research, and the assumptions made about researching the terrain, both epistemological as well as methodological. There is, for instance, growing emphasis on more interpretive and reflexive forms of research in studies of adult learning – for instance, in the use of biographical methods – which can be more sensitive to the complexity of people's stories of learning, lifewide as well as lifelong. The third aspect of 'subject' encompasses ontological assumptions about being human, and about subjectivity, which inevitably shape how we conceptualise learning and its purpose. Some assumptions about subjectivity – whether this is defined in terms of the rational unitary self of humanist psychology, or the multiple selves of poststructuralist and radical feminist thought – influence what we consider learning to be and for, and the means by which it is best realised (Clarke, Dirkx 2000).

This paper begins with some reflections on the nature of the conceptual shift from modernism to postmodernism, before considering its impact on the study of adult learning. I then turn to postmodern perspectives on subjectivity, including the challenge to the idea of an essential human nature; and, at an extreme, to the notion of a 'self' on any terms. I explore the recent growth of biographical research – itself a product, at least in part, of postmodern as well as feminist influences – into adult and lifelong learning. This research has shaped some of the ideas at the heart of this paper, including the importance of the power of particular languages to impose themselves on experience and reality, as the truth. Yet biographical research also provides a potential antidote to postmodernism's own more grandiose tendencies. These include the idea that there is little meaning beyond language, or positioning within it. Or there can be no basis to chose between one story, or body of knowledge, and another. There is, I suggest – using two case studies of doctors and their biographical learning – more to the subject of learning and to subjectivity, than positioning in discourse and there are useful and tested psychosocial insights, to enable us to understand all three dimensions of our subject, more fully.

Faith and Modernity

Modernism has, of course, many dimensions but central to its beliefs was the emancipatory potential of particular forms of knowledge. Reason and science were to be applied to human affairs, as well as to the natural world, replacing God as the prime basis for human betterment and social progress. A core aspect of modernist faith was that the world was in principle knowable, and that there were underlying truths and certainties, which could be objectively understood using empirical research methods, free from bias and human subjectivity. The world, and the self within it, was also, in a basic sense, coherent, meaningful and masterful (Usher, Bryant, Johnston 1997). The faith in reason and science, in Lyotard's famous words (Lyotard 1984), constituted one of the grand narratives of modernity, providing, in other words, a higher order of legitimation for the way people, and whole societies, thought and acted. Modernity's gaze, via the high priests of positivism, became ubiquitous and pervasive. There was a world to be objectively known and changed, which included human beings, through the application of empirical methods and the development of scientific i.e. rigorous and objective understanding.

Modernity and the Enlightenment project were at the heart of the adult education movement, in both its liberal progressive as well as radical guises. Adult education, historically, was steeped in modernist faith as to the prerequisites of progress and human emancipation. Liberal adult education – of the kind that emerged in the United Kingdom and Sweden, for example (Bron 2001) – was fuelled by the notion of serious academic study of the external world as a means to a more informed and active citizenship, which would produce a more equitable and democratic civic order. The liberal citizen was rational, individualistic and fired by a belief that progress was inevitable, under the banners of science and the pursuit of truth. Many 'radical' adult educators were also steeped in this tradition, albeit questioning its individualistic and reformist tendencies. Getting to the root of things involved, for them, finding answers in more 'scientific' theories of society and in determining historical laws 'out there', in an observable, controllable but changeable world, if we were determined enough to engage with and transform it.

The faith in the power of reason and empirical science is, nowadays, questioned from many perspectives. The idea that everything can, in principle, be known through mind and empiricism, once the right technologies are in place, has proved illusive as well as reductionist. And the uncritical deification and application of 'objective' science to understanding societies and human behaviour, when arrogantly detached from humane values and psychological insight, has spurned totalising disasters. Such science led to hells on earth like the Gulag and death camps. The German scientists who designed systems of mass slaughter thought they were behaving rationally, like good scientists should (Bauman 1989). Brookbank and

McGill (2000) suggest the deification of reason and science, and objectivity, is rooted in Cartesian philosophy, and the splitting of mind and emotion, for which a price has been paid. The origin of the split lay in the crisis of the established Churches in the sixteenth and seventeenth centuries and the crisis stemmed from a key dilemma: if souls were divine and spiritual yet inhabiting a material body, trapped in the realm of the senses and ruled by mechanical laws, this created a philosophical problem. The problem was resolved by simply denying it, and creating instead a separate mental realm, within each person, known only to that person and to his or her God. The facilities of mind were constructed as higher, even divine, and the lower facilities of senses and emotions were rendered inferior (Brookbank, McGill 2000). This has led to a pervasive neglect of the affective and subjective in the academy, and beyond, to the detriment of learning, not the least about ourselves.

Lost in Language

Postmodernism, in opposition to modernism, insists there is no straightforward passageway to the world, or self, outside text. Even the 'human being' is a construct of human processes, not an essential ground of knowledge and value. Beauty and personhood, like truth or theory, lie in the eye, so to speak, of the discourse. Neither reality nor the observer can stand outside this. In this rendering, scientific knowledge, or the humanist concern for the self, becomes simply another linguistic device, a form of discourse related to the excessively rationalist form of life in the West (Appleby, Hunt, Jacob 1994).

Philosophically, postmodernists deny the fixity of language, or of any convincing correspondence between language and reality; indeed of any 'essential' reality and thus of any proximate truth about it. Richard Edwards (2000) argues that postmodernism represents a conceptual shift, no less than 'tectonic' in its implications. We seek to ground things, he insists, but this is on a moving earth in which there is no longer any confident conceptual mountaintop, such as empirical science, from which to chart what we see, no Archimedean point from which to represent the world, either out there or inside. We cannot occupy, unambiguously, a bounded and confident cultural or epistemological world from which to observe, for instance, other worlds, or even ourselves. Epistemological security has gone, for better as well as worse.

Postmodernism also challenges the privileging of overly intellectualised forms of knowing, (albeit postmodernists often express this in impenetrable and over-intellectualised prose!) and the marginalisation of affective, intuitive and imaginative understanding in human experience. Crucially, for present purposes, postmodernism is deeply implicated in the new politics of identity and representation: in the celebration of diverse and fluid subjectivities, beyond essentialist and fixed notions of personhood. Men and women, for instance, at least in the 'developed' world, have many more opportunities, so the argument proceeds, to break free from the normalising gaze of biologistic, deterministic and even essentialist accounts of 'femininity' and 'masculinity'. Many feminists have enthusiastically embraced postmodern ideas because they underline the contingency, human-madeness and thus the changeability of cultural norms and practices, including those of gender (Appleby, Hunt, Jakob 1994).

But if such ideas may be liberating, they also create problems. These include, ironically, the tendency of postmodernists to play the totalising game, in their own terms, especially in reducing all knowledge to linguistics. We are presented, in effect, with a new grand narrative in which everything becomes relativised, and there is nothing beyond words, surface and performance. We have no criteria to judge one text from another, since we are always and inevitably trapped in some text in seeking to do so. There are no grounds to choose between anything, one truth claim as against another, with philosophical certainty. The trouble is, as a number of commentators have noted, this creates space for either a profound resignation towards the world and its problems – why bother to do anything if there are only words and illusion – and, more frighteningly, for nihilism. Foucault seems to suggest, for instance, that the only motive for the play of language and formation of discourse is the Nietzschean will to power, in which men and women appear stripped of meaningful choices whose reality had once served to distinguish them from animals. "Change comes about through unexpected and unpredictable slips in the fault lines of broad discursive configurations, through lucky breaks in the war of all against all" (Appleby, Hunt, Jacob 1994, 223) rather than any notion of self-determined human action. But then, if all knowledge claims, as the postmodernist insists, are to be treated with incredulity, this must also apply to postmodernism.

These reservations are important. The refusal to accept any values or reality beyond surface brings in its train the demolition of the possibility that something beyond appearance can have meaning. Attempts at understanding history, for instance, whether collective, or private histories of the self, become delusory, as do the disciplinary frames – whether of politics, education, economics, history or psychoanalysis – through which such histories have been made more meaningful. In liberating ourselves from the acceptance of established norms and traditions, and in challenging the pretentiousness of many disciplinary truth claims, we may end up, unnervingly, with nothing better to replace them. On the other hand, certain basic human values, and assumptions about humanity, remain implicit in postmodern writing; in, for instance, Lyotard's opposition to the totalising fantasies of fascism (Frosh 1991). Not all modernity's 'babies' are, it seems, discarded with the postmodern 'bathwater'.

The Paradox of the Postmodern

There are different responses, among adult educators and more widely, to postmodernism, and the extent to which it is seen to present more opportunities for the human subject, either individually or collectively. Some argue that the growth of new communication technologies, and a revitalised capitalism, themselves emblematic of postmodernism, provide access – when set alongside the fracturing of modernity's big stories – to more varied lifestyles, cultural practices and meaning making possibilities (Usher, Bryant, Johnston 1997). Even capitalist consumerism, Usher, Bryant and Johnston (1997) insist, can liberate the play of multiple identities through offering greater lifestyle choice: these are socially communicative acts, markers of difference, providing an opportunity to engage in a much richer range of cultural practices. The manipulative power of consumerism itself, it is claimed, can be subverted, to our own ends, if we chose to do so. Consumerism gives us the means to make our lives, and compose our identities, on more of our own terms. On the other hand, as Richards has noted, successive acts of consumption may provide little basis for an individual's experience to cohere around more stable configurations of feeling and value, and for the "painful, affective interchange with other people upon which development and sustenance of selfhood depends" (Richards 1989, 47). In this reading the very building blocks of personality are destabilised in a world where our deepest needs for meaning and acceptance are the subject of powerful manipulation and where capitalist consumerism offers material redemption yet delivers perpetual discontent.

Other interpretations focus on the dangers of a world bereft of epistemological or ontological foundations. Giddens (1991), for instance, locates people and their struggles in a culture, which, while offering new opportunities for self-definition, also precipitates constant crises of the self. He focuses on what he terms 'late modernity's' inescapable contradictions (late modernity is broadly defined in terms of industrialisation, consumer capitalism as well as by reference to institutions of surveillance and the control of violence). He suggests that as tradition loses hold, as global economic forces deskill entire communities, as male linear biographical certainties – of school, work and retirement – disintegrate, and as the meta narratives of modernity – the belief in progress, science or universalisms of any kind – lose their efficacy or are bitterly contested, individuals must choose, whether they like it or not, between a range of lifestyle options and ethical dilemmas.

Such choice can of course be reflexively liberating but has to be exercised without confident reference to external and or traditional authority, including 'science' and religion. We are existentially and discursively more on our own, which can create a dangerous void. The BSE scandal in the United Kingdom provides a compelling example of 'authority' in crisis, in the form of the scientists arguing among themselves, while many supposed 'objective' observers seemed hopelessly entangled in a web of vested interests, including those of government or research agendas. Incredulity was, in such circumstances, entirely appropriate. But many people, in seeking answers, became confused, bemused and frightened. This can create space for fundamentalist responses, of many kinds. There is, for instance, in many countries evidence of growing nostalgia for order and certainty, on which fascism builds, using the 'threat' of others, otherness as well as uncertainty to build its legions. Fundamentalist religion is similarly a response to uncertainty and fear, providing, however illusory, reassuring answers in a fragile world. Except some of these answers can involve the destruction of others – those individuals and cultures deemed aberrant – witness the appalling slaughter of September 11, 2001. There are other deeply reactionary yearnings in these times, as among elements of the men's movement in the United States, with the desire for lost worlds and certainties, in which men behaved more like men and women returned to their more 'natural' roles. Rampant paranoia and reactionary yearning, as much as learning, characterise the postmodern world (Samuels 1993).

Stephen Frosh has explored these processes from a psychological perspective. He argues that modern states of mind are being forged in cultural instability and insecurity of a potentially 'cataclysmic kind' (Frosh 1991). The fractures of older certainties can, of course, produce fluid and generative creativity, as tradition breaks down, and new opportunities for biographical experiment, and learning of diverse kinds, can emerge between the cracks. But, at the other extreme, there can be pathological defensiveness towards change and uncertainty of whatever kind. Interestingly, Frosh insists that our response to new experience – our capacity to learn from it – depends on some inner subjective strength and cohesion, which in turn is deeply dependent on others and the network of affective relationships in which we are situated. We need to understand more about these intersubjective processes, which may be foundational to human experience, and to the possibility of finding psychological stability, and social agency, in an increasingly unstable and fractured world.

Adult Education, Learning and New Times

Adult education has been affected, like other disciplines, by epistemological uncertainty. Positivistic belief in the primacy of scientific models of research and in the idea of the educator as instrumental problem-solver, drawing on such research as the source of the best and most reliable knowledge is being challenged to the core. In a North American context, the recently published *Handbook of Adult and Continuing Education* (Wilson, Hayes 2000) recalls earlier struggles, in North America, to establish the subject of adult education as a science, in the sense of an empirically verified body of practice, to be applied by instrumentalist problem-solvers using their expert understanding. This would deliver respectable professionalism as well as academic legitimacy. Here was an Enlightenment dream, 'writ small'. As it transpired, in the view of the editors of the volume, this was illusory and dangerously reductionist. The dream of a scientific adult education turned, instead, into an 'iron cage' of technical rationality. The Handbook documents a search for an alternative epistemological rationale for the discipline, in, for instance, ideas of critical reflection as a basis for learning in and about the world. A difficulty is that critical rationality appears to mean many different things to different people, and is hard to distinguish, at times, from technical rationality, while the affective and imaginative in learning, and even the spiritual, remain marginal.

Some adult educators, as noted, take an optimistic view of present uncertainty, and of the possibilities for the human subject, and for learning, in these times. Experience may be uncontrollable, resistant to manageability and mastery but this is to be welcomed, not regretted, if only we can learn to live with it and exploit its possibilities for a constant, never complete and diverse experiment with identity and lifestyle (Usher, Bryant, Johnston 1997). Richard Edwards celebrates the challenge to foundationalism, even to the possibility of foundationalism itself, which can create new, more particular forms of understanding, even if aspirations become more limited, and the process of knowledge creation, more uncertain. The moorland provides diverse settings, practices and identities for learning, and how it can be understood and enhanced. There are many locations and discursive practices in which to engage and through which to generate new texts, and "for inscribing many different meanings into practice, and many different practices into our work with adults" (Edwards 1997, 188).

Other writers welcome Foucault's illumination of the relationship between institutions, knowledge and power, while rejecting some of postmodernism's transcendental tendencies. Foucault has revealed, as Salling Olesen puts it (1999), how educational institutions use knowledge to encourage some kinds of understanding but to block others. The notion of discourse itself carries an important implication that all organised knowledge and communication can privilege certain modes of understanding, while excluding important areas of experience, related for instance, to the practice of adult education and bodily experience. This is, he suggests, how power relations are reproduced. Postmodernist perspectives, in this view, emphasise the situational quality of learning, its location in multiple cultural settings, and the individual subject involved in a perpetually changing acquisition of new life conditions. This in turn encourages interest in biographical understanding and learning in specific psychosocial and historical conditions. But, interestingly, Salling Olesen argues that postmodernism lacks any convincing perspective on the development of subjective life, and he turns to psychoanalysis as a way of explaining some of the processes involved. Subjectivity, as he perceives it, is created in individual life histories, and involves integrating the contradictions of social life, but also developing a capacity for self regulated reconciliation or mediation between desires and reality (Salling Olesen 1999, 2001).

As noted, many feminist writers find postmodernism congenial because it underlines the cultural origins and contingency of gender and subjectivity (Appleby, Hunt, Jacob 1994). Feminist adult educators, such as Carolyn Clarke, while not explicitly 'postmodern', embrace the constructivist approach to subjectivity, as well as the idea of multiple selves and narratives in learning (Clarke, Dirkx 2000). Writing about transformative learning, she uses the case of a student, Ellen, who is confronting a life-threatening illness, to illustrate how notions of multiple selves can enrich our understanding of what it means to learn and be human. Ellen's 'rational self', for instance, carefully assesses her medical options, and the assumptions underlying cultural notions of health and ableness. A self that needs to be in charge reveals a different narrative of resistance and surrender. The spiritual Ellen grapples with the meaning of life and death while the gendered Ellen struggles with her changing understanding of herself as a woman. What is refreshing about Clarke's account is how it challenges the privileging of certainty and unitary voices, which have marginalised the sense of multiplicity, ambiguity and paradox in ourselves and the stories we tell. Mark Tennant (2000) makes a similar point in opting for what he terms a relational self – rather than the rational unitary self – in which a 'multiplicity of self-accounts is invited' but with a 'commitment to none'.

Some postmodern writers, I have suggested, go further still and question the need for a self at all (Frosh 1991). It is, no more and no less than a constraining, modernist fiction of inner unity – denying the idea of selves as multiple and indeterminate – with all the opportunities for self-composure this brings. We are offered a shifting play of subjectivities, using diverse images, consumption choices and lifestyles, which provide escape from the iron cage of fixedness. However, as Tara Fenwick (2000) has pointed out, the poststructuralist dissolution of self can take us dangerously near to the psychotic subject, where there is little or no psychological cohesion, and boundaries between self and others disintegrate. This subject, metaphorically, is split into fragments, and the most unacceptable parts of the ego are projected into otherness; curiosity, learning and relationship become, for the psychotic, sources of terror. Those who most celebrate the dissolution of self may easily forget, or may be unaware of, the subjective cohesion – including a strong enough ego – that makes their postmodern linguistic play more possible. The understanding of learning, and becoming a subject, is reduced to little more than a language game. We need, for sanity's sake, to do better than this.

Making Biographies and Learning in the Postmodern Moment

A key question at the heart of this paper is how people learn to be open to new experience and possibility in uncertain times, and in managing the biographical discontinuities and deep insecurities these bring. Biographical methods have moved centre stage in researching such dynamics, as part of a growing conviction that we require more subtle methodologies than conventional hypothetical-deductive and quasi-experimental approaches to understand more of what learning is, and the conditions for agency, lifewide as well as lifelong. The 'biographical imperative' can be summarised as a subjective as well as narrative turn, giving greater prominence to personal and social meanings, as well as the active role of people as moral agents and participants in creating social processes, including learning (Chamberlain, Bornat, Wengraf 2000). Such a development can be seen, at least in some part, to express postmodernism's predilection for the particular, the diverse, the marginal and the situated, as against a modernist striving for universals, which often turned out to be largely 'his-story'.

Certainly, biographical researchers frequently challenge overly abstract, experience-distant 'modernist' approaches to sociological writing, as, for instance, in discussions of structuration theory or the interplay of structure and agency (Chamberlain, Bornat, Wengraf 2000). As they do the dualism of society as being constructed 'out there', disconnected from inner life and personal experience. Jerome Bruner (1990) has observed how culture and its hegemonic myths, including what it means to learn, or to be a man or woman, penetrates deep into the heart of intimate relationships, shaping, for instance, how people think, feel, act, including the stories they tell. Biographical perspectives emphasise the play of discourses in particular lives and in specific times, of what seems possible and what may be silenced or repressed. Biographies, however, can also serve as sites for resistance and radical opposition to myths which have served their purpose, and for challenging what powerful others might say and wish us to believe. Much of out stock of lived experience, as E. Bruner notes (1986), goes unstoried and is never told or expressed, while some experiences are inchoate and we lack the perfomative and narrative resources or vocabulary to bring them into being. Stories are also shaped by context, by what is easy or not easy to articulate in particular power relationships and sub-cultures (West 1996). Yet the capacity to tell new stories seems central to creating meaning, agency, learning and even psychological health (West 2001, Holmes 1996), and biographical studies suggest we need a range of psychosocial insights into how people learn, and change their stories, rather than ascribing this somewhat amorphously to the 'will' to exploit discursive fractures.

This is not to deny that words are important, rather to insist they are not the whole story, as a number of biographical researchers argue (see for example Gadd 2000, Salling Olesen 1999, 2001, West 2001). David Gadd has written, intriguingly, of what he terms an individual's biographically driven investments in power-conferring positions in a multiplicity of discourses. Anxiety, in this view, using the ideas of Melanie Klein and psychoanalytic object relations theory, is seen to be fundamental to the human condition, and psychic defending may be done by taking up relatively safe positions in discourse – riddled as they are with gendered, classed, raced and other assumptions – as well as by splitting and projecting our vulnerabilities on to others (Gadd 2000, Hollway, Jefferson 2000). Struggles over positions in discourse, and their psychosocial dimensions, were at the heart of stories about learning generated in research among a group of medics working in difficult and demanding inner-city locations in the United Kingdom. There was evidence, in these narratives, of the normalising power of objective and scientific ways of knowing, but also of contestation as particular doctors developed oppositional and more experientially inclusive stories about what learning to be a doctor actually entails, beyond the official myths. Conventional distinctions between formal and informal ways of knowing, between the personal and the professional, identity and role, self and other, disintegrate in this kind of analysis of the subject of, and subjectivity in, learning and professional life (West 2001).

Doctors and the Stories they Tell

The research with the doctors spanned a period of four years involving up to 7 interviews with each of 25 inner-city medics, more precisely General Practitioners (GPs) or family physicians. They worked, as indicated, in difficult areas of the inner city, at a time of challenge to, and crisis in, their role and performance. Their stories illuminated the continuing discursive power of medicine as objective science in which scientific knowledge and method, in research and also the consultation, was brought to bear on the patient's disease. Fiona Ross and Liz Meerabeau (1997) have observed that if there are many and varied mental maps in health care, and disputes about conflicting scientific paradigms, and between theoretical and clinical approaches, as well as between the specialist and generalist, the most powerful and best resourced, the most normatively potent is the modernist medical model based on the power of 'big science'. The most important facts and evidence are, or should be, derived from experimental methods, most particularly the randomised control trial. Diagnostic decision making, however tenuously, follows the procedures of scientific enquiry: the discovery of 'facts' about a person's illness is equivalent to the discovery of scientific truths about the wider universe. Under the imperative of scientific rigour, and best evidence, data must be systematically collected: on the precision and accuracy of clinical assessments, laboratory tests as well as the power of prognostic markers, does professional judgement and clinical effectiveness seem to rest (Greenhalgh 1998). This kind of science involves a whole set of procedures in which precise problems are focused upon and 'extraneous' factors removed. Factors such as the subjective experience of the patient as well as her wider social context, and the nature of the interaction between doctor and patient become marginalised, however unintentionally, in the dominant story the profession tells itself, about essential knowledge, learning and the route to health.

However, the story is under challenge, fuelled by feminism and postmodern ideas. There are various indicators, which include a growing ambivalence towards scientific forms of medicine and of contradictory, paradoxical feelings about its 'technoculture' (Hodgkin 1996). There has been a dramatic growth in the use of alternative therapies and of the 'holistic' health movement. Seidler (1994), drawing on feminist critiques, argues that holistic sensitivity brings people into a fuller relationship with the particularities of their own health. Illness becomes more particularistic and individualistic: less exclusively a matter of breakdown in the body, conceived as a mechanical system to be understood, impersonally and universally. In the medical model symptoms are conceived as 'significations' that are universal, forming, in effect, a language of signs irrespective of the person and context. Scientific medicine, so the argument proceeds, has correspondingly disempowered people from understanding themselves and the totality of their condition.

Some go further in suggesting that the discursive power of medicine rests on a 'modernist' illusion: that there is

> the truth 'out there' which can be known, understood, and controlled by anyone who is rational and competent. The faith that we can accumulate an objective understanding of reality, which is true for all times and all places, underlies our treatments and our clinical trials (Hodgkin 1996, 156).

The 'modernist' view, concludes Hodgkin, is under challenge at its core. "Great swathes of the world increasingly act according to ... a rather different set of assumptions..." (Hodgkin 1996, 156). Yet, despite claims that medicine is, at long last, transcending its modernist roots and encompassing multiple ways of knowing, the objective way – taking us into the real world and out of ourselves – remains dominant in assumptions about learning. However, there are contrary voices, as revealed, for instance, in the biographical work of particular doctors. Getting close to those doctors enabled a fuller understanding to emerge of the intersubjective processes, and resources, that can fuel opposition to powerful myths, and provide greater agency and authenticity across a life.

Two Cases in Point

Drs Daniel Cohen and Aidene Croft both struggled with the power of the medical model, and a need to understand the work of being a doctor, in the inner city, on more of their own terms. For both doctors, knowing the 'science' had to be located within a wider human, relational and discursive frame. New relationships – both professional and personal – provided some of the resources to survive professional and personal crises, and to learn how to exploit the opportunities of uncertain, 'postmodern times'.

Aidene Croft felt divided as a doctor, between learning as prescribed within the medical model, and learning from her identity and experience:

> ... When I started off as a doctor, I think I was just being petrified and stunned... And when I was at medical school they were very separate. That was my person and then I would take the head to medical school. The head: in a motor bike, in leathers, in trousers for my exams and breaking all the images, but still just very much my head and they can take or leave the rest of me. But not really, that wasn't real. It was real in so far as I needed to earn a living, find a role in life. It was real, but they were actually very, looking back, they were very, very separate... I was very much trying to connect the two, but it was that I knew that I couldn't actually tolerate that level of incompatibility.

Aidene was a lesbian and from a non-English background and felt an outsider in medical school. She hated her training, hospital medicine and its scientistic pretensions. Science had a place but was not the whole story. Aidene Croft's learning biography encompassed engaging with the gendered, classed, raced and defended dimensions of her own self. She only learned to be a medic, she said, after she left training. She suffered a 'mental breakdown', underwent psychotherapy and used this, and her own experiences of being silenced, as a lesbian and woman, to connect with many of her marginalised patients. It was her feminist insights, and experiences of being marginalised, which were at the core of her story of becoming a more effective doctor, and person. She learned about mental illness, and its cultural determinants, in response to an 'epidemic' of mental health problems in the marginalised communities she served. Her patients knew, she insisted, that she understood what it meant to be the outsider and its consequences. A learned humanity lay at the heart of good practice, both professionally as well as in personal life.

She had a serious emotional breakdown and considered giving up being a doctor altogether. She felt divided between the science and her own humanity. Psychotherapy helped, as did moving into general practice. She "found more humanity" there than in the hospitals. She forged a strong relationship with a GP trainer. For the first time, she said, she felt seen, valued and 'fed', as she did in her personal life with a new partner. The trainer accepted and respected her as she was, and made her feel that she could be more of herself as a doctor. The secret was being authentic and the experience relieved her, as she put it, "of the burden of the whole hierarchy of medicine. That I could just be the particular doctor that I am, with that particular patient". Aidene was an active lifelong learner, and developed an eclectic style in her work, drawing on a range of therapies. She actively researched mental health issues and talked of being able to understand what it was like to be an outsider, from the inside. Relationships were at the heart of her biographical learning, including challenging and transcending some of the core assumptions of modernist medicine.

Changing relationships were at the heart of Daniel Cohen's story, too. He needed other ways of knowing, and other human resources, to become a more effective medic. He too suffered an emotional crisis and, like Aidene Croft, nearly gave up medicine altogether. His parents were refugees from Nazi Germany, and no suffering could ever rival theirs; no personal traumas possibly compete for attention. Outwardly he was successful and studious but inside he screamed with unhappiness. Daniel, like Aidene, considered science to have a place in his work, but within a relational frame and using his own subjective experience to connect with patients and their stories. We talked about the neglect of the emotions in the medical model. There was, Daniel said, great suspicion of engaging with and learning from our subjectivity within mainstream medicine, which still deified the objective and measurable. Yet emotional insight, including drawing on his multiple identities, as well as an associated cultural literacy, lay at the core of him becoming a better doctor. Daniel insisted that he had become more conscious of these issues, including the importance of being Jewish and different, spurred on by the 'postmodern' politics of identity.

But there was far more to it than this. Daniel, as indicated, placed developing relationships – with his wife, his partners at work, and with patients, as well as in therapy – at the heart of his biographical learning, including learning to be a man and a doctor on more of his own terms. He discovered the 'feminine' in his work and self, the kind of emotional empathy and connectedness, which often lies at the heart of healing. He told me about a Somali woman refugee who came to the surgery one day. She had five children, whose father had been killed in a war. She was an asylum seeker, a 'problem' for the authorities, as she was shunted from one set of shabby accommodation to another. Daniel gave her some of the time and attention she craved, and slowly felt more alongside her in her struggles. One day the patient brought him a gift and he was immensely moved. It was, he felt, a symbol that he was providing 'a secure base' – some support and unconditional regard – which was a product, he now realised, of his own family's experience as refugees:

> I can remember how incredibly important the GP was to us as a secure base. We had a very very intelligent link worker who is a Somali doctor herself, but can't practice here so she works as a link worker. And we ended up having the most extraordinary conversation with the mother about Darwinian evolution in relation to why were her children

getting asthma and eczema here when children didn't get it in Somalia and we talked about the way sort of the immune system might be adapted for one environment but actually then is mal-adapted to another environment because the sort of ancestral immune system as it evolved is not to meet what it meets here. And I found myself having a grown up conversation with this mother of the sort I might have with you and she was transformed from being a sort of exotic stereotype into actually being an intelligent equal. And ... I felt it was part of ... a process of her becoming a person again...

And of Daniel becoming more of a person, too. He hated his profession's antipathy to subjective learning and more diverse ways of knowing and healing. He argued, instead, for a subversive synthesis, taking what was essential from the medical model but locating this within a more psychologically and culturally literate as well as reflective learning paradigm. Changing relationships, and the subjective and cultural insights these brought, were at the heart of learning to challenge some of the discursive power of the medical model and its tendency to silence other ways of knowing.

Back to the Subject

Stories such as these take us into the territory of the 'will', whether to power, to learn, and or relationship, as well as to the nature of the subject we call 'learning' and the 'subject' of the learner. Many educators traditionally embraced the humanist idea of a subject who had the will and inherent potential to be self-motivating and self-directing, unless people and culture got in they way. This was also a subject who was rational and capable of exercising individual and intentional agency (Usher, Edwards 1994). Education's task was to draw out and help individuals realise this potential and drive. Postmodernism and feminism challenged these ideas to the core, as did psychoanalysis. For the postmodernist, as suggested, the idea of the rational, unitary and essential subject, primed to unfold according to a predetermined plan, is merely a linguistic and historical construct; for the feminist, including the feminist psychoanalyst, subjectivity is perceived to be highly contingent and developmental, dependent on others for its realisation, and shaped by cultural practices. Subjectivity is potentially diverse and fluid, rather than essential, offering many and different possibilities for women, as well as men, to be and become on more of their own terms. The humanist ideal of selfhood has been condemned as a constraining fiction, born of a particular time and heavily influenced by male i.e. highly individualistic and overly rationalistic, notions of being.

Yet we are still struggling with the idea of a self, and for a language to fill the void left by the challenge to the humanistic ideal. A language that is sensitive to the constitutive, as well as representational function of language, and to a subjectivity, which is to be produced rather than discovered. Contemporary psychoanalysis, especially feminist object relations theory, takes as its prime focus the changing, multi-faceted and highly contingent subject in the process of becoming, which partly explains its appeal to some educators. In this reading, human beings do not exist in relation to each other as mere physical bodies, positioned according to distance relationships while identities are far more than positioning in text. We exist and develop, rather, in a shared space of affective intercourse in which there is a fundamental overlapping of one and another. The infant, for instance, can be seen to exist in the gestures and meaning of others. Communication and learning cannot be reduced to participants in isolation (Diamond 1998). As with the infant, the adult, especially at times of vulnerability, loss and change, can feel frightened, and easily overwhelmed. If the shared space of affective intercourse in which we are situated – our relationships with others, including those in educational settings – provides some security, a sense of basic acceptance to enable us to acknowledge our vulnerabilities, as well as some challenge, then we can begin to learn, play and tell new stories, in emotionally more open, experientially inclusive, and critically diverse ways.

Psyche, in feminist object relations terms, can usefully be considered as analogous to a cast of characters, of people and interactions in the social world, which become part of inner life. Some people, like the absent or abusive father, may injure and constrain us; others inspire and give us a sense of legitimacy and existential hope. The external drama is internalised, in childhood and throughout a life. But casts of characters can change as new people enter the social stage. Such significant others – 'good objects' in the language of object relations – mirror new biographical learning possibilities for us. The feminist movement provides a case in point as many women have found, in and through the support of others, the psychological resilience to rewrite the story of their lives. New people become part of our inner drama, pushing us, potentially, towards greater agency, and a fuller and critical engagement with our existence. Biographical narratives, like those of the two doctors, are often saturated with material about significant others and the importance of supportive yet challenging relationships in 'life-spacing' and managing biographical discontinuities (West 1996, see also Courtney 1992). Feminist object relations theory provides a language to explain how the intersubjective may be translated into more vibrant, intrasubjective life, providing the energy, and will, to challenge the stories that bind.

Of course, such ideas remain trapped in language, works of fiction rather than the reality itself, and there is no easy escape from the conundrum. Despite psychoanalytic discourse becoming more open to the normalising and constitutive power of language, it can only justify itself with yet more words. There are no objective or transcendental grounds from which to establish its authenticity or claims to truth. But simply because narratives are human creations does not make them all equally fictitious or mythical. Some knowledge is more meaningful, illuminating and truthful than other knowledge, because it has been tried and tested in many and diverse contexts. If there is no 'objective' truth, or confident verification, there is, nonetheless a notion of pragmatic truth: ways of knowing, and stories, that resonate profoundly and meaningfully with lived experience, struggle and sense making. Stories, for instance, about our need for others, especially during times of crisis and transition. Stories about the intersubjectivity and emotionality, which underlie our sense of legitimacy in the world, and fuel the desire to challenge the oppressive. And stories about the complexity of the ontological project of the self – a self always in the process of creation – and needing to play, dream, feel, imagine, as well as think and critically reflect, to succeed in the project.

Here is a subject ontologically driven to make meaning and connectedness, as a precondition of truly being.

Conclusion

I have argued that postmodernism challenges basic assumptions about the nature of knowledge and the subject of learning and of the learner. The postmodernist stresses the power of words and language to shape how we perceive and think, including about ourselves. Importance is also attached to recovering what has often been silenced or repressed in and by dominant stories. Words, some people's words, are especially powerful but can also be challenged and transformed, if the will exists. But biographical research takes us far beyond a bleak and psychologically impoverished Nietzschean will to power. The will to new and different ways of knowing, and to be a subject in history, requires emotional energy and life, grounded in our relationships with significant others. Such relationships provide some of the psychological and emotional robustness and energy we need to challenge and change. Moreover, in making sense of this, we move far beyond highly individualistic and overly cognitive notions of learning, and language, to a focus on whole people in whole contexts, including the intersubjective and emotional foundations of life.

To those postmodernists who might dismiss such ideas as mere words, or celebrate fragmented subjectivity without a human core, my response is one of incredulity, if not silence. They appear to forget, or may be unaware, of the psychological cohesion, boundariness and existential legitimacy that make their postmodernist cultural and linguistic play possible, in the first place. The ability to utter new and interesting sentences, the will to resist totalising tendencies, the capacity to fight back despite the awfulness of what might be experienced rather than staying paralysed, all imply a deeper, developing, distinct and cohesive self beyond as well as within the text (Flax 1990). Postmodernism, as suggested, in overly deifying words and language, is in danger of imposing a new discursive tyranny. John Field (2000) has observed that while postmodernism offers insights into complex and fast moving areas of life, and the role of language, it also presents a potential *cul-de-sac* in a complex society where there is an increasing need to recognise useful and reliable knowledge, albeit in new, more flexible and eclectic ways. Some knowledge, and stories, matter more than others, in the struggle for life and learning, if only because they have been tested in the fire of experience, including our own. Some of the laughter or silence of the postmodernist, however philosophical, needs to be challenged on these grounds. The issues are too serious, for the subject called learning, for a fuller understanding of that subject, and, for each of us, as subjects, struggling to be.

References

Appleby, J., Hunt, L., Jacob, M. (1994). *Telling the Truth about History*. London.

Bauman, Z. (1989). *Modernity and the Holocaust*. Oxford.

Bron, A. (2001). *Civil Society and Biographical Learning*. Paper to the NFPF Congress. Stockholm, March.

Brookbank, A., McGill, I. (1998). *Facilitating Reflective Practice in Learning*. Buckingham.

Bruner, E. (1986). Experience and its Expressions. In: Turner, V., Bruner, E. (eds). *The Anthropology of Experience*. Chicago.

Bruner, J. (1990). *Acts of Meaning*. Cambridge, Mass.

Clarke, C., Dirkx, J. (2000). Moving beyond a Unitary Self. A Reflective Dialogue. In: Wilson, A., Hayes, E. (eds.). *Handbook of Adult and Continuing Education*. San Francisco, pp. 101-116.

Courtney, S. (1992). *Why Adults Learn*. London.

Chamberlain, P., Bornat, J., Wengraf, T. (2000). *The Turn to Biographical Methods in the Social Sciences*. London.

Diamond, N. (1998). On Bowlby's Legacy. In: Marrone, M. *Attachment and Interaction*. London, pp. 193-214.

Edwards, R. (1997). *Changing Places. Flexibility, Learning and a Learning Society*. London.

Edwards, R. (2000). Making Spaces for Lifelong Learning. In: Miller, N., West, L. (eds). *Rising East. The Journal of East London Studies*. 4 (2), pp. 22-37.

Flax, J. (1990). *Thinking Fragments. Psychoanalysis, Feminism and Postmodernism in the Contemporary West*. California.

Frosh, S. (1991). *Identity Crisis. Modernity, Psychoanalysis and the Self*. London.

Fenwick, T. (2000). Putting Meaning into Workplace Learning. In: Wilson, A., Hayes, E. (eds.). *Handbook of Adult and Continuing Education*. San Francisco.

Field, J. (2000). *Lifelong Learning and the new Educational Order*. Stoke-on-Trent.

Foucault, M. (1970). *The Order of Things. An Archaeology of the Human Sciences*.

London.

Gadd, D. (2000). *Just Like their Fathers.* Paper to the Biographical Methods and Professional Practice Conference, London, October.

Giddens, A. (1991). *Modernity and Self Identity. Self and Society in the Late Modern Age.* London.

Greenhalgh, T. (1998). Narrative Based in an Evidence Based World. In: Greenhalgh, T., Hurwitz, B. (eds). *Narrative Based Medicine.* London, pp. 247-265.

Holmes, J. (1996). *John Bowlby and Attachment Theory.* London.

Hollway, W., Jefferson, T. (2000). *Doing Qualitative Research Differently.* London.

Lyotard, J.-F. (1984). *The Postmodern Condition. A Report on Knowledge.* Manchester.

Richards, B. (1989). *Images of Freud.* London.

Ross, F., Meerabeau, L. (1997). Editorial. In: *Journal of Professional Practice,* 11 (1), April.

Samuels, A. (1993). *The Political Psyche.* London.

Salling Olesen, H. (1999). *Lifelong Learning and Collective Experience.* Unpublished Paper, Roskilde University.

Salling Olesen, H. (2001). Professional Identity as Learning Process in Life Histories. In: West, L. et al. (eds). *Travellers' Tales: from Adult Education to Lifelong Learning and beyond.* Proceedings of the 31st Annual Conference of SCUTREA, pp. 342-345.

Tennant, M. (2000). Adult Learning for Self-Development. In: Wilson, A., Hayes, E. (eds.). *Handbook of Adult and Continuing Education.* San Francisco, pp. 87-100.

Usher, R., Edwards, R. (1994). *Postmodernism and Education.* London.

Usher, R., Bryant, I., Johnston, R. (1997). *Adult Education and the Postmodern Challenge.* London.

Wilson, A., Hayes, E. (eds.) (2000). *Handbook of Adult and Continuing Education* San Francisco.

West, L. (1996). *Beyond Fragments, Adults, Motivation and Higher Education. A Biographical Analysis.* London.

West, L. (2001). *Doctors on the Edge. General Practitioners, Health and Learning in the Inner-City.* London.

Michael Schemmann

REFLEXIVE MODERNISATION IN ADULT EDUCATION RESEARCH
THE EXAMPLE OF ANTHONY GIDDENS' THEORETICAL APPROACH

Introduction

In the chapter *Theoretical Thinking in Sociology* of his book *Sociology*, Anthony Giddens states:

> The ideas of the classical thinkers – Marx, Durkheim and Weber – were formed during times of great social and economic change. We are living through a period of change that is probably just as profound – and is much more widely felt across the world. We need to develop new theories to understand the new developments which are transforming our societies today (Giddens 2001, 680).

Indeed, the current period of change is rather productive in developing these kinds of theoretical approaches. Giddens himself introduces as examples Postmodernist theories (which are also dealt with in this volume), but also Ulrich Beck's *Risk Society* (Beck 1986), Manuel Castells' network economy (Castells 1996) and his own approach of social reflexivity (Giddens 1992). This list could easily be prolonged by several other societal analyses, many of which are presented under rather pithy labels such as Transformation Society, Learning Society, Knowledge Society, Service Society, Multicultural Society, and so on. Attempting to compile a list up these interpretations, Klaus-Peter Hufer came up with 54 such labels (Hufer 2001, 76).

Adult Education research has always been a discipline dependent on theoretical impulses from other disciplines. That is why the above theoretical approaches are of particular importance for our discipline, especially since profound social changes also affect our field and we are also asked to simultaneously show and explain the changes adult education is undergoing.

This article takes the theoretical approach of Anthony Giddens as a basis for exploring the difficulties and potentials of applying social theory to adult education research. In a first step the article argues why Giddens' ideas are of particular relevance for adult education research, as well as offering a cursory presentation of his core ideas. The second step concentrates on examples of how Giddens has been used in adult education research thus far and also points out future opportunities for use. Furthermore, some of the problems which come up when using his theory are discussed. Finally, the article concludes with a more general discussion of the problems which can arise when using social theory in adult education research.

Anthony Giddens' Theoretical Perspective for Adult Education Research

As mentioned in the introduction, there is currently a flood of approaches explaining social change. This trend confronts the adult education researcher with the problem of selection. This will be dealt with in detail later in this article as the choice made by the researcher has both a profound influence on the respective research itself, but also on the interpretation of the findings. For now, we will concentrate exclusively on Giddens' theoretical approach because his ideas appear to contain an almost natural proximity to those of adult educationists.[1] In the case of Giddens, we can argue along two lines to make clear why his considerations are of particular importance and why his work is valuable to adult education researchers.

---

[1] However, it has to be pointed out that there are other theorists of reflexive modernisation like Ulrich Beck or Scott Lash (Beck, Giddens, Lash 1996) whose approaches show similarities to Giddens' theoretical approach. For a detailed discussion see Wittpoth (2001a).

A first, and admittedly rather pragmatic, justification has to do with Giddens' standing as a theorist. John Field positions Giddens, as well as Beck, as leading figures in their disciplines: „[E]ven if Beck and Giddens have got it badly wrong, the fact is that they are highly influential figures, not only in their own fields; Giddens and Beck are also leading theorists of the 'Third Way' school of political thought" (Field 2000, 61). The politics of the 'Third Way' is currently very much influencing New Labour's policies and also implies significant changes within the field of adult education and lifelong learning (Giddens 1999). The same holds true, even though to a lesser extent, for the politics of the *'Neue Mitte'* in Germany which also draws links to both Giddens and Beck. Consequently, it makes sense to acknowledge these approaches and to examine them in the context of adult education research.

What is more, the fact that Giddens' theoretical approach puts a particular emphasis on knowledge and reflexivity should attract educationists *per se,* in so far as motivating them to examine the theory in more detail. To illustrate this a little further and to also give an account of Giddens' understanding of reflexive modernity, the following section provides a brief description and analysis of his theory.

Since the early 1990s Anthony Giddens has advanced to become one of the most, if not the most, influential sociologists in Great Britain, as well as within the international context. As quoted above, Giddens assumes that we are undergoing a profound process of social change. As do many other social theorists, he sees an end to modernity and the beginning of a new phase. However, Giddens explicitly disagrees with the belief of postmodernists that we are now entering a completely new era. For them, modernity's basic assumption that history has a shape and that it ultimately leads to progress has come to an end. Consequently, there are no longer any 'grand narratives' providing a comprehensive understanding of both history and society (Lyotard 1985).

Giddens, on the other hand, understands this shift rather as a process of continuation. His concept of "high modernity" is thus more of a continuation of modernity and could not exist without it. In this sense, modernity remains as one of the foundation elements of high modernity, rather than being a conflicting theory.

Similar to Beck, Giddens' high modernity also takes the idea of societal risks as a central cornerstone. He starts off by arguing that modernity brought about a reduction of risk in certain areas compared to former times. However, this reduction was limited to certain areas and modes of life. At the same time, modernity introduced new risks that were completely unknown in previous times (Giddens 1991, 4).

According to Giddens, the deciding factor shaping the transition towards high modernity is globalisation or the globalised character of modernity and its social systems. As a consequence of this, high modernity also creates high-consequence risks such as ecological catastrophes, the collapse of global economy or the rise of totalitarian superstates (Giddens 1991, 4). Furthermore, there is a difference in quality concerning risk factors within both modernity and high-modernity. Giddens points out that human beings always had to face risks which were mostly external, i.e. they originated in nature, while the risks facing people today are manufactured, i.e. they can be traced back to the intervention of human beings in the natural world (Giddens 2001, 65). What is more, there is also a difference regarding the relationship between time and risks. "[The world of high modernity] is one replete with risks and dangers, to which the term 'crisis', is not merely an interruption but a more or less continuous state of affairs..." (Giddens 1991, 12).

These factors taken together clearly establish the connection between modernity and high modernity with the deciding factor being the notion of globalisation: "In high modernity, the influence of distant happenings on proximate events, and on intimacies of the self, becomes more and more commonplace" (Giddens 1991, 4).

What is more, globalisation also leads us to the point that basically no one can withdraw from the processes of transformation. This becomes clear in the following quotation:

> Globalisation means that, in respect of the consequences of at least some *disembedding mechanisms*, no one can 'opt out' of the transformation brought about by modernity – this is so, for example, in respect of the global risks of nuclear war or of ecological catastrophe (Giddens 1991, 22).

As indicated in the quotations above, there are profound consequences for the individual and this leads us to another aspect of Giddens' theoretical perspective. The changes he outlines affect us as individuals, as well as having an effect on our way of life. Again, similar to Beck but less dominant, Giddens focuses on the individualising tendencies of high modernity. The crucial point in this respect is that Giddens talks about disembedding mechanisms.

To start off, Giddens explains the particular dynamics of modernity according to three main aspects. The first aspect is the separation of time and space. Whereas for most people in pre-modern times time and space were connected through the place they were living in, modernity redefined the relationship so that the connection between time and place is no longer defined solely "via the mediation of place" (Giddens 1991, 17).

This is the aspect that, according to Giddens, forms the basis for the second factor of the dynamics of modernity, i.e. disembedding mechanisms. Giddens singles out two of those mechanisms. On the one hand 'symbolic tokens' such as money also embrace time and space. On the other hand 'expert systems' like technical knowledge do the same since it is no longer important where and when the knowledge is being used. What is more, technological knowledge is also accessible to a broader segment of the population and is not confined to the actual experts any more. This fact thus leads to a disembeddeness of social institutions (Giddens 1991, 18).

As a final point, he refers to institutional reflexivity. Unlike reflexivity that is 'normal' for human beings in the sense of monitoring their actions, modernity's reflexivity means being sensitive to social activity and to our relationship with nature, as well as a permanent evaluation and re-evaluation on the background of new information or knowledge (Giddens 1991, 20).

For the individual this has several consequences. As Field points out „... the importance of this account is that it draws attention to the ways in which a whole host of social practices – from the broadest to the most intimate – are always being re-examined in the light of new information" (Field 2000, 60).

However, this of course implies serious challenges which the individual has to face. Individuals must learn to cope with what Giddens calls

"dilemmas of the self" which can be broken down into the following polar opposites:
- Unification versus fragmentation (Giddens 1991, 189)
- Powerlessness versus appropriation (Giddens 1991, 191)
- Authority versus uncertainty (Giddens 1991, 194)
- Personalised versus commodified experience (Giddens 1991, 196).

What is more, tradition plays an important role in the context of new information and knowledge and also illustrates the connection between, and the change from, modernity to high modernity. For Giddens tradition is very close to the notion of rituals. Tradition, in the Giddens' sense implies more than simply being used to something since it also contains both moral and emotional components (Giddens 1996, 124). Thus traditions gave people direction and a certain sense of having guidelines within their social action. In another context, Giddens connects tradition to authority: "Tradition was itself a prime source of authority, not located within any particular institution, but pervading many aspects of social life. Diffuse though it may have been, tradition was in an important sense a single authority" (Giddens 1991, 194). The social change we are witnessing can be seen as the process of getting rid of those traditions through expert knowledge. Thus the individual is liberated from these traditions and now is left with nothing else but choice. "The reflexive project of the self, which consists in the sustaining of coherent, yet continuously revised, biographical narratives, takes place in the context of multiple choice as filtered through abstract systems" (Giddens 1991, 5).

However, Giddens does not end his exploration on high modernity in a pessimistic or even resigned way. On the contrary, following his argument one could even come to understand high modernity as a positive opportunity. As such, democracy is at the heart of his considerations since it is the only form of politics that deals with varying claims and controversial opinions. But this idea of democracy goes beyond a type of rule and beyond the area of 'subpolitics': "Democracy cannot be limited to the public sphere as defined by Habermas. There is a potential, 'democracy of emotions' emerging in everyday life" (Giddens 2001, 680).

Due to the fact that regulation of life through traditions no longer exists and that the individual has to constantly make active choices and decisions in every realm of life, the various choices also have to be argued for and justified. This is certainly a difficult task, but it also means the basis for an authentic form of life. Finally, Giddens sees a far-reaching connection in the symmetric relationship between the democracy of emotions and the potential of democracy on the global level (Giddens 1996, 193).

Examples of Usage in Adult Education Research

As indicated above there are several aspects which are worth considering in adult education research. In the following section, we will concentrate on two main aspects of Giddens' theoretical approach as the basis of a discussion and analysis of how they could be applied in adult education research. As such the rest of the article will focus on Giddens' idea of disembeddedness and his ideas about democracy.

The Idea of Disembeddedness

One way of using Giddens' theoretical approach is to examine his ideas on social reality and to examine these ideas with regard to how far they apply to adult education as a social reality. The effects of this type of examination is twofold. On the one hand, it contributes to understanding social reality and thus verifies, falsifies or modifies our understanding of social reality and helps to "grasp the underlying function and place of lifelong learning in contemporary societies" (Field 2000, 62). On the other hand, such an examination also allows for an understanding of how mechanisms functioning in adult education have changed. Additionally, it helps us to understand in how far adult education is affected by the profound changes in society.

As examples of this kind of research I want to refer to two studies, one carried out by Josef Schrader on the co-operation between full-time and freelance staff in adult education institutions (Schrader 2001), and the other carried out by Marcus Reinecke and myself on the participation in adult education of shop clerks within the trade unions (Schemmann, Reinecke 2001).

In his study, Josef Schrader sets out by stating that the basis for co-operation between teachers in an institution and the institutions themselves is the shared belief in a respective movement. Those engaging in adult education were embedded in the respective milieus, shared the same attitudes and goals, and were equally committed to reproducing them. These traditional relationship structures continue and are still relevant, not only for churches and trade unions, but also for new social movements such as the environmental movement, the women's movement, and the third world movement. Seen in this way, teaching is only one form of engaging within a social movement supported by an individual. However, there were also other ways (Schrader 2001, 145).

Following Giddens or other theorists of reflexive modernity, one of the distinct features of this new phase is that the traditional forms of embeddedness and support lose their power. Tradition as the major principle of social action comes more and more under pressure. Schrader states that this process can also be observed within adult education institutions, one driving force being the further professionalisation of adult educators and the resulting consequence that a different logic or systems of action are involved. Voluntary work and engagement, on the one hand, and professionalism on the other, do not exclude each other, but have contradictory underlying mechanisms. Schrader points out that resulting conflicts have been proved in various studies in different thematic fields of adult education (Schrader 2001, 145).

In his study Schrader examined this phenomenon for different sectors of adult education. As such he focused on institutions which are close to the trade unions, on "public" institutions and also on private institutions.

As concerns the trade unions, most important is the fact that oral agreements were replaced by written contracts and, consequently, instead of an honorarium or equivalents such as participation in the activities of the community or the movement, clearly defined salaries for clearly defined obligations were instituted. The relationship therefore changes from being one between members towards one between employer and employee with a corresponding weakening of shared commitment on both sides. Not only do the people teaching in the trade unions under the new model show less identification with the institution, but also from the institution's side it is no longer requested that the people employed are members of the union – although they still prefer people close to their basic ideas (Schrader 2001, 146-147).

As concerns 'public' adult education, these institutions have always founded their relationship to adult educators on a contract basis. The change that can be observed here is that the status of the adult educators transforms from teaching as a second job to fulltime teaching. The adult educators now see these institutions as agencies of their individual employment interests. As Schrader's study shows, these changes cause problems since the adult educators are more apt to switch jobs, thus leaving already announced courses for better paid positions. No ties towards the institution exists. At most, one finds bonds between individual teachers, i.e. the fully employed adult educator and the freelancer. However, these bonds are not established through didactical co-operation; in this case freelance teachers are on their own. However, the freelancer and the fulltime employee have a clearly established set of mutual goals determined by the rules of the market. As Schrader points out, the marketisation of adult education and the withdrawal of the public funding means that the number of participants counts (Schrader 2001, 148).

Finally, examining the relationship between internal and external educators exemplified in vocational education within companies, and concentrating on the field of human resource development, Schrader shows that another aspect is of importance. The external partners in this field consider themselves professionals and this is a fully accepted condition. Schrader's study in this field shows a completely opposite tendency to the processes observed in 'public' adult education. The external partners are more and more involved in the processes of the company. It is expected that problems are tackled together, based on the external expertise and the internal experiences (Schrader 2001, 149). In terms of recruitment, trust has grown to become the dominant criteria for a successful relationship. Generally, the co-operation is founded on a contract but what is not implied in the co-operation is the notion of bonding since this also would imply responsibilities from both sides with a long term perspective. A long term co-operation is only possible if flexibility is not endangered. As concerns the building up of trust under these conditions it is very much based on mutual experiences. Since building up trust also needs time, the co-operation is also concentrated on very few partners. However, if certain trainers do not justify this trust they face rather harsh consequences. As the interviewees put it, they get "substituted" or "fired" (Schrader 2001, 151). The importance of trust within this co-operation also explains why changes of internal adult educators very often imply changes of the externals as well, a development that is rather unknown in public adult education or in trade unions. In his discussion of the findings, Schrader highlights the fact that the need for trust is especially high in those systems which are the most flexible and modern. This confirms an aspect of Richard Sennett's analysis stating that continuity is of particular importance when flexibility is the basis for contracts (Schrader 2001, 152).

If we come back to the question of how to apply Giddens' theoretical framework it becomes obvious that it could be used for examining the basis of co-operation between institutions of adult education, their representatives and external 'freelance' adult educators. It becomes obvious that different sets of logic are applied in different sectors of adult education.

The second study we will refer to in this context is a qualitative study of the participation of shop clerks in the context of a trade union in North Rhine-Westphalia, Germany. Starting off with Giddens' assumptions concerning the disembedding processes of high modernity and the weakening importance of tradition in the face of technical knowledge, the authors examine possible consequences for participation in adult education. They analyse in how far former important ties to institutions now become fragile and on what background decisions to participate in what courses and what topics are made (Schemmann, Reinecke 2001).

As a further framework of the discussion, it is important to point out that the institutional structure in Germany, as well as in other modern and industrialised countries, changed significantly since the 1980s. The competition between various institutions increased, the idea of the free market dominates. Consequently, established institutions, and as such, also the adult education institutions of the trade unions come under pressure due to the fact that private institutions also offer courses in their realm (Schemmann, Reinecke 2001).

The findings of the study show that the interviewees are aware of the differentiation of the institutions. However, even though there are some who make use of this situation and who make free decisions in the sense of going to other institutions there is still evidence that the ties to the trade union are still of importance when deciding on which institution to attend. Some interviewees expressed this by talking about "feeling at home" at the trade union or by referring to the seminars of the trade union as "something holy". The explanation for this is multi-facetted.

First, it seems that there are certain structures that developed which are not easy to break up. For example, there is a consensus between entrepreneurs and the working councils that further education is mostly carried out by the union. Consequently, to receive permission to participate in further education is easier when seminars with the trade union are applied for.

Secondly, the findings also have to be interpreted within a regional context. The importance of the trade unions within the regional, social culture in North Rhine-Westphalia and the Ruhr area in particular is still very high. Due to a long tradition of heavy industry the Trade Union for Metal Workers has become an important cornerstone of social culture in this area, also having close contacts and relationships to centres of power like the Social Democratic party. Consequently, the ties are still strong, presumably stronger than elsewhere, and it is to be expected that a similar study covering all of Germany would lead to different, maybe even contradictory results.

Finally, it also has to be taken into account that election to the working council is an important change within the biographies and learning biographies of the individuals. But the recognition that goes with this election is mostly awarded by an institution, in this case the trade union. When going to seminars offered by the trade union participants sense this change and it is respected in a positive sense, whereas this aspect is neglected in private institutions. Private institutions do not have the opportunity to convey this emotional feeling (Schemmann, Reinecke 2001).

Coming back to the theoretical framework of Giddens, we can state that the findings of this study do not verify his assumptions in all respects. However, they also do not generally falsify them. John Field pointed out that one major criticism of reflexive modernisation tendencies is: "... their tendency to project the key shifts onto the entire adult population. Yet none of these trends – globalisation, abstract knowledge, institutional reflexivity – impacts equally upon the entire population" (Field 2000, 63). It is exactly in this direction that the findings can be interpreted. Parts of the interviewed group show some signs of disembedding in the sense of choosing other institutions than the trade union, whereas a considerable number of interviewees are still strongly influenced by traditions and existing structure when making their decisions. In conclusion, it can be pointed out that the group is rather heterogeneous and that not everybody seems to be affected by the changes in the same way.

This example of the usage of Giddens' theoretical framework in adult education research shows two things. On the one hand, it makes clear in how far adult education research can also contribute to modifying social theory. On the other hand, it also makes clear how valuable Giddens' approaches are for developing research question within the discipline. The results in this special case are of particular importance for the trade union when considering new strategies of programme development in times of hard competition.

The Aspect of Democracy

Giddens' exploration on democracy and democracy of emotions opens up obvious and interesting research questions for adult educationists. The interest in democracy, active democratic citizenship and adult education has increased since the middle of the 1990s. In a European context these issues have been explored in several conferences within the context of the European Society for Research in the Education of Adults (ESREA)[2], as well as in other publications dedicated to this subject (Bron, Schemmann 2001). Consequently, it is rather logical that adult education research takes notice of Giddens' ideas and makes use of them for their own reflections.

As has been pointed out from several sides, Giddens puts his ideas into the tradition of Enlightenment (Wittpoth 2001c, 171). John Field states:

> Giddens' suggestion is that political behaviour in late mod-

---

[2] So far the following publications were published as documentations of the seminars of the network: Bron Jr, Malewski (eds.) (1995) *Adult Education and Democratic Citizenship*. Bron, Field, Kurantowicz (eds.) (1998) *Adult Education and Democratic Citizenship II*. Bron Jr, Field, (eds.) (2001) *Adult Education and Democratic Citizenship III*. Schemmann, Bron Jr, (eds.) (2001) *Adult Education and Democratic Citizenship IV*. There is also a chapter on Active Democratic Citizenship, compiled by Michał Bron Jr in: Bisovsky et al. (eds.) (1998) *Adult Learning and Social Participation*.

ern societies has not abandoned the emancipatory agenda that followed the Enlightenment. Rather, it is possible to see new forms of politics that express the concerns with identity, choice and reflexivity which characterise other fields of social relations (Field 1995, 38).

Taking this into account, it is rather natural that adult education and research run the risk of resulting in an affirmative appeal and an uncritical continuation of current practice when referring to Giddens. Since democracy and the ideas of the Enlightenment have always been cornerstones of the self-understanding of adult education institutions, conclusions drawn from Giddens' theoretical perspective point to a continuation of current practices, with a critical view appealing for intensification and modification of the endeavour as a whole.

An example of this kind of research is to be found in a separate article published by this author on the topic of environmental rights and education (Schemmann 2001). The article argues that environmental rights became an important issue of citizenship next to social, political and civil rights. It then explores the potential of adult education in establishing this component and concludes as follows: "Adult education and adult educators have an important role in this context – both in providing crucial knowledge, as facilitators in empowering citizens and in helping people to change their attitudes" (Schemmann 2001, 78).

Another way of using Giddens' ideas on democracy is to reflect upon the question of how far democracy is established in adult education institutions and in how far the demand of democracy is realised in adult education practice. One example of employing Giddens' ideas and conclusions in adult education research is Staffan Larsson's analysis of the Swedish study circles which Swedes themselves considered as the archetype of democratic structures in adult education. Even though Larsson does not explicitly derive his research question from Giddens' theoretical perspective, and within the article only marginally refers to Giddens, his research question can still be seen as a conclusion related to high modernity considerations. The question to be asked is if there are democratic structures within the provision of adult education or, in the particular example of Larsson, "[i]s there a contemporary study circle democracy" (Larsson 2001, 144)?

All in all Larsson examines six different aspects related to democracy. As concerns the participation in study circles he concludes that it is rather unequal even though there seems to be a trend that is more egalitarian than in other forms of adult education (Larsson 2001, 145). The relations tend to be more horizontal since there is no power basis to develop vertical relations of dominations (Larsson 2001, 148). What is more, it seems that the dimension of deliberation is rather common in study circles even though there is a lack of evidence on what grounds the standpoints are formed and created (Larsson 2001, 149). In terms of knowledge there is evidence that participation provides people with useful knowledge and that thus it can be assumed that people are strengthened (Larsson 2001, 150-151). Furthermore, study circles also seem to provide a system that supports diversity within society (Larsson 2001, 155). Finally, in terms of democratic decision-making the findings show that there are some study circles which are very much focused on the decision maker, whereas others seem to show genuine co-operative decision making processes (Larsson 2001, 157).

Comparing these two examples of using Giddens' ideas on democracy it becomes apparent that the second example deals more critically with the impulses in so far as they reflect the status and dimension of democracy within adult education, whereas the first example simply connects current adult education practice to Giddens' approach.

However, it seems that the stimulating potential of Giddens' exploration has not yet been fully exploited. What needs to be further explored is, for example, in how far the so-called democracy of emotions connects to democracy in adult education institutions and relationships in adult education in general. How can they connect and how do they influence general practice within institutions? This certainly also implies a profound rethinking of the methodological instruments of research. What is more, it seems that Giddens' work itself is not based on empirical grounds and remains on an either theoretical or speculative level (Field 1995, 45). There is a long list of desiderata which have not been dealt with so far but which emerge as stimulating aspects when dealing with Giddens' theoretical approach.

Conclusion: On the Problem of Using Social Theory in Adult Education Research

As has been shown in this article, the work of Anthony Giddens has a lot of potential when used as a frame of reference in adult education research. The examples that were discussed in this context made clear that his work provides an interesting and fruitful paradigm for evaluating research results and that there remains much more to be explored.

But there remains one final point to be discussed on a more general level when using social diagnoses in adult education research. As was pointed out in the beginning of the article there is a flood of these types of societal analyses. Most of these diagnoses or social theories have to be viewed critically. They very often omit necessary differentiations, sometimes for the benefits of significance within the academic, but also the public, discourse (Wittpoth 2001b, 7). Bearing this in mind those diagnoses automatically result in a rather limited view of society and social life. Taking a particular focus or point of view on social reality restricts the perspective for other social phenomena, makes them less important or even ignores them. Ortfried Schäffter argues that the fact that we have a multioptional society is a distinct feature of our society and our life. Not only is there no clear explanation for our society based on an inner perspective, but it is a characteristic of our time that a lot of options exist which are in direct conflict, which are in competition or which are simply indifferent to the existence of the other. Schäffter concludes that our contemporary society is in itself not definable (Schäffter 2001, 39).

The problems arising from Schäffter's analysis of social reality for adult educationists who use these theories and theoretical perspectives in their own research are rather obvious. They almost automatically run the risk that the respective flaws and shortcomings of the said theoretical approach are reflected in their own research and reflections. The adoption of a restricted view and limited perception of social reality excludes certain research aspects and questions.

This problem has recently been discussed in a publication edited by Jürgen Wittpoth. In his final reflections, Wittpoth hints to the general problems inherent in the use of social theories in adult education research.

To avoid a one-dimensional perspective and accompanying omissions he offers two possible alternatives. On the one hand, the adult educationists could try to develop their own theoretical perspective to diagnose society. However, he admits that this is rather unrealistic. On the other hand, he suggests to approach these theoretical perspectives rather carefully and tentatively but he concedes that this would positively influence the productivity of the research, which is very often shaped by exaggeration or intensification. In conclusion, Wittpoth pleads for a multi-theoretical approach in the sense that when following one theoretical perspective and its innovative potential, reservations about the limited perspective of such a choice must be taken into account. Consequently, this would lead to other results and findings than what can be seen when the attitude of the researcher reflects an acceptance that the applied theoretical perspective is the one and only diagnosis of society (Wittpoth 2001c, 176-177).

Despite their flaws and potentially limited perspectives, it cannot be understated that social theories are an indispensable tool for understanding the changes, trends and developments that take place in contemporary life and which are therefore reflected in research on related structures and relationships in adult education.

References

Beck, U. (1986). *Risikogesellschaft*. Frankfurt/M.

Beck, U., Giddens, A., Lash, S. (eds.) (1996). *Reflexive Modernisierung. Eine Kontroverse*. Frankfurt/M.

Bron Jr, M., Malewski, M. (eds.) (1995). *Adult Education and Democratic Citizenship*. Wroclaw.

Bron, A., Field, J., Kurantowicz, E. (eds.) (1998). *Adult Education and Democratic Citizenship II*. Krakow.

Castells, M. (1996). *The Rise of the Network Society*. Oxford.

Field, J. (1995). Citizenship and Identity. The Significance for Lifelong Learning of Anthony Giddens' Theory of 'Life Politics'. In: Bron Jr, M., Malewski, M. (eds.). *Adult Education and Democratic Citizenship*. Wroclaw, pp. 31-45.

Field, J. (2000). *Lifelong Learning and the New Educational Order*. Stoke on Trent.

Giddens, A. (1991). *Modernity and Self-Identity. Self and Society in Late Modern Age*. Stanford.

Giddens, A. (1992). *Capitalism and Modern Social Theory*. Cambridge.

Giddens, A. (1996). Leben in einer posttraditionalen Gesellschaft. In: Beck, U., Giddens, A., Lash, S. (eds.). *Reflexive Modernisierung. Eine Kontroverse.* Frankfurt/M., pp. 113-194.

Giddens, A. (1999). *Der dritte Weg. Die Erneuerung der sozialen Demokratie.* Frankfurt/M.

Giddens, A. (2001). *Sociology.* 4th fully revised and updated Edition. Oxford.

Hufer, K.-P. (2001). *Für eine emanzipatorische politische Bildung. Konturen einer Theorie für die Praxis.* Schwalbach/Ts.

Larsson, S. (2001). Study Circles as Democratic Utopia. A Swedish Perspective. In: Bron, A., Schemmann, M. (eds.). *Civil Society, Citizenship and Learning.* Bochum Studies in International Adult Education, 2. Münster, Hamburg, pp. 137-167.

Lyotard, J.-F. (1985). *The Postmodern Condition.* Minneapolis.

Schäffter, O. (2001). Transformationsgesellschaft. Temporalisierung der Zukunft und die Positivierung des Unbestimmten im Lernarrangement. In: Wittpoth, J. (ed.). *Erwachsenenbildung und Zeitdiagnose. Theoriebeobachtungen.* Bielefeld, pp. 39-68.

Schemmann, M. (2001). Environmental Rights as a Component of Citizenship Rights. Reflections from an Adult Education Point of View. In: Schemmann, M., Bron Jr, M. (eds.). *Adult Education and Democratic Citizenship IV.* Krakow, pp. 67-79.

Schemmann, M., Reinecke, M. (2001). *Gewerkschaftliche Bildungsarbeit im gesellschaftlichen Wandel. Eine qualitative Untersuchung zum Weiterbildungsverhalten von Funktionsträgern der IG Metall in Nordrhein-Westfalen.* Krakow.

Schrader, J. (2001). Bindung, Vertrag, Vertrauen. Grundlagen der Zusammenarbeit in Weiterbildungseinrichtungen. In: *Hessische Blätter für Volksbildung,* 2, pp. 142-154.

Wittpoth, J. (2001a). Reflexive Moderne. Zum (Anregungs-) Gehalt einer mehrdeutigen Perspektive. In: Wittpoth, J. (ed.). *Erwachsenenbildung und Zeitdiagnose. Theoriebeobachtungen.* Bielefeld, pp.139-154.

Wittpoth, J. (2001b). Vorwort. In: Wittpoth, J. (ed.). *Erwachsenenbildung und Zeitdiagnose. Theoriebeobachtungen.* Bielefeld, pp. 7-8.

Wittpoth, J. (2001c). Zeitdiagnose: nur im Plural. In: Wittpoth, J. (ed.). *Erwachsenenbildung und Zeitdiagnose. Theoriebeobachtungen.* Bielefeld, pp.155-178.

Bettina Dausien

ON THE 'GENDER' PERSPECTIVE IN ADULT EDUCATION
METHODOLOGICAL NOTES

There is a consensus in social sciences and humanities that gender should be viewed as a social and cultural construction. This position implies that gender is not to be treated as a feature or demarcated element of empirical reality, but as a perspective from which structures, processes and features of this reality are interpreted and analysed. 'Gender' is a dimension of the social world that is socially 'produced' as a category for interpreting self and the world, for identification and identity formation, for practical reference and interactive representation. One could also say that gender is 'formed' (or 'learned') in individual and collective processes [1]. In this paper, I examine some aspects of this formation and training process in closer detail, namely those that relate to learning processes in social contexts in the customary educational sense. The guiding question is how education/training/formation processes, particularly those of adults, are inter-related to the 'formation' or 'construction' of gender. The theoretical perspective with which and from within which this inter-relatedness is viewed has been influenced by social-constructivist gender research, on the one hand, and by concepts generated by biographical research (Chamberlayne et al. 2000) that has developed since the 1970s in German social and educational science on the other hand. This research is also gaining in impor-

---

[1] In German, the word *Bildung* has many meanings that come to the fore here: *Bildung* in the sense of formation, production or creation of an internal or external being, form or figure, or *Bildung* in the more specific yet multifarious and differentiated sense of education and training as a complex process of subject formation through learning, skill acquisition and reflection, as discussed in the various pedagogical and social scientific theories.

tance for adult education in Europe (Alheit et al. 1995, Alheit, Dausien 1999, Dominicé 2000).

'Gender' in Adult Education – Preliminary Remarks on the Current State of Debate

In the field of adult education, the gender-related perspective has long since moved from being some marginal or 'special-interest' field – and is increasingly perceived and acknowledged as a fundamental dimension of education and training. The relevance of gender is becoming obvious in the practice of education and training, especially since many adult education institutions have a predominantly female clientele[2]. In many cases, they provide specific courses and programmes for women (and more recently for men as well), there are educational concepts that address the particular learning experience and learning interests of women, and, finally, gender is the actual subject-matter of seminars, conferences, congresses and the like. It is by no means self-evident, or substantiated by 'the nature of things', that the gender-related perspective be discussed first and foremost under the banner of 'women's education' (Gieseke 2001). Rather, it is an expression of a particular constellation of political interests and historical development. Informed by the women's movement and the feminist critique of society, women are and always have been the ones who have addressed the issue of gender in the different areas of adult education, and developed forms of critical educational practice. For a long time, women were excluded from the institutions of, and from theoretical reflection on education and training, or were tacitly subsumed under allegedly general, but factually androcentric concepts. The feminist critique of this state of affairs focused attention not only on the situation of women, but also on gender relations in general, in their historical and societal context.

Concepts for women's and gender-based education and training (Gieseke 1993, Gieseke et al. 1995, Kade 1991, Schiersmann 1993) relate in different ways to that history. Projects of a dedicated 'autonomous women's

---

[2] The courses and programmes offered by the *Volkshochschulen* (adult education centres) in Germany, for example, are attended to about 75% by women (Deutsches Institut für Erwachsenenbildung 1999).

education', on the one hand, and forms of education and training aimed at gender equality, on the other, can be conceived of as two archetypical poles for describing empirically existent types of educational practice that usually involve a mixture of both aspects. For one theoretical perspective, the problem at issue is that of difference and the question raised is how the category 'gender' is conceptualised.

These questions and issues have been central in feminist theory since the 1990s, in which a critical debate has been conducted in terms of 'construction' and 'deconstruction' on women's own epistemological and analytical categories (Butler 1990). Below the abstract level of epistemological or metatheoretical analysis, the question as to 'how genders are made' (Gildemeister, Wetterer 1992) is discussed in different veins among academic experts[3]. Of particular relevance for adult education are the discussions in social and educational sciences. In social sciences, discussions and empirical studies are focused on social constructivist approaches to 'gender', especially the concept of 'doing gender' (West, Zimmerman 1987), and on empirical methods for researching these in different areas, whereas educational sciences are more concerned at present with the critical reception of, and controversial debate on different theoretical ways of 'reading gender', i.e. *"Lesarten des Geschlechts"* (Lemmermöhle et al. 2000).

If we ask ourselves in this broad context what particular significance the (de-)construction debate has for adult education, in particular for women's and gender-based education, there are two points that can be made at first glance: Firstly, the renewed and pointedly expressed acknowledgement that gender, and gender differences by implication, are a social and cultural construction means that the taken-for-granted reference to precisely that difference in women's education as it is practised is called into question in a radical way. This gives rise to a genuine dilemma – the partisan and critical reference to women (in contrast to men), in the sense of defining positions in politics and in the theory of knowledge (Harding 1986, 1991), is necessary, on the one hand, in order to reveal socially con-

---

[3] In the discussion on the research object, I am referring to the German-speaking area. A comparative international discussion would go beyond the framework of this paper.

structed differences and hierarchies, and to develop practical strategies for changing them[4], but on the other hand it harbours the risk of reifying the difference (Gildemeister, Wetterer 1992).

However, reducing the discrepancy between abstract criticism of epistemology and everyday experience in education situations to a 'problem of theory and practice' does not provide any solutions, but at best a starting point for further investigation of the problem. The discrepancy observed is not an external condition for the development of theory, but must be integrated into theory. So the point at issue is not only to develop a convincing gender theory analysis that can then be 'used' in educational practice; the imperative, instead, is that scientific theoreticians must reflect from the very outset on its relationship to gender construction in the everyday world. This brings us to the methodological dimension of the gender perspective.

A second observation relates to the dissatisfying state of theory formation. Not only is there too little theoretical debate on gender within adult education, but the discussion that does occur is also extremely heterogeneous, even eclecticist. At least in the German-speaking context (Gieseke 2001), criticism needs to be levelled at the fact that many theoretical contributions address only singular aspects of the gender debate, in which terms with multiple meanings, such as 'construction' and 'deconstruction', are differently interpreted anyway, and mixed with concepts from other, often incompatible theoretical contexts. Methodological ideas and analysis for linking theory and empirical experience, or regarding the architecture of theory construction, are virtually absent from the debate[5]. This state of discussion may well be a reflection of the uncertainty that has been triggered by the abstract (de-) construction debate for any theoretical understanding of the practice of (women's) education, but amplifies for its part the discrepancy that has been identified.

In view of the situation as outlined so far, it makes sense to discuss some fundamental aspects of the analysis of gender, even if this means

---

[4] How the perspective of change is defined is once again an issue for the theoretical and practical conceptualisation of 'gender'.

[5] One of the few exceptions in the German-speaking debate is the publication prepared by the Tübinger Institute for Women's Social Research (ed.) (1998), which discusses the interrelationship between theory, research and pedagogical praxis.

paying too little attention to 'application centred' issues in adult education. The differentiation of gender perspectives proposed in the following derives from findings in biographical research and is somewhat 'propaedeutic' for adult education. The focus of interest is not on the observation of empirical phenomena, but on the reflection on the theoretical constructions with which those phenomena can be analysed. Reflection is focused first of all on the key concepts of gender, biography and education. The thesis of the social construction of gender is then explained and differentiated with reference to biographical construction. Finally, some aspects of the 'formation/education of gender' in women's biographies are specified with examples.

Gender, Biography and Education. Remarks on the Construction of Concepts

Each of the three terms forming my topical framework refers to a complex subject-matter that can be conceived of in different ways, depending on one's perspective and theoretical tradition. All three categories acquired and modified their meaning in the formation of civil society. In the current historical situation, described as a 'second' or 'reflexive' modernity (Beck, Giddens, Lash 1994), they are particularly pertinent because they are not only significant indicators of social change, but are themselves driving factors of the processes involved – namely the transformation of gender relations, the changing significance of education and training in society (which is increasingly becoming a learning and knowledge society), and the individualisation, institutionalisation and recurrent de-institutionalisation of the life course as modi for the socialisation of the modern work and education society. In this overall context, biography has become a highly significant yet contradictory form of social organisation and orientation for individual action and 'lifelong' learning processes (Alheit, Dausien 1996, 1999).

The key terms mentioned above are not just abstract scientific categories, but also concepts that structure action and thought in the everyday world. In Alfred Schütz' words, the constructs used by the social scientists are, so to speak, constructs of the second-degree, namely constructs of the constructs made by the actors on the social scene, whose behavior the social scientist observes and tries to explain in accordance with the procedural rules of his science (Schütz 1962, 6).

As categories of scientific analysis, they refer to concepts that are used and modified in interactions of the everyday world. Thus, scientific constructions are not dissociated from and independent of everyday thought and action. Schütz' idea of a reconstructivist methodology, which has been included in other approaches using the interpretative paradigm, consists in this interconnection being systematically reflected upon and integrated into scientific theory formation.

The implication for gender research is that scientific analysis should not simply reproduce everyday theories and routine categorisations of gender, but should critically reconstruct them. By applying such strategy, the problem of reification addressed above can be circumvented or at least minimised. In this sense, the purpose of scientific analysis is not to examine the gender differences that are assumed as given in everyday life, but to search for 'female' and 'male' learning strategies or identity patterns. The risk of such a procedure is that research merely confirms and reinforces what has flown as everyday theoretical premises into the experimental design, without being noticed as such[6]. Instead, analysis must focus on the practices, interpretations and other social mechanisms by which differences are generated, and enquire into the contexts in which gender differences are becoming relevant, or made relevant. This methodological perspective is also applied in the present article.

However, this approach, too, is exposed to the risk of focusing excessively on gender as a category. In the pragmatic context of everyday interactions and experiences, the analytically constructed, 'second-order' category does not occur in any 'pure' form. In empirical reality, 'gender' is also blended with other dimensions of social positioning that become situationally and/or biographically relevant: with social class position, attribution to one or more cultural, ethnic, national contexts, to a particular generational and historical position, etc. These interdependencies were long neglected in gender theories (and in gender-based educational practice).

A similar point must be made regarding the categories discussed here. 'Gender', 'education' and 'biography' are accessible to empirical experience in everyday life, and to research, only in very specific combinations – e.g. as educational or learning experience in the biographies of women (or men) of a particular generation, in a specific social, cultural, and historical context.

Like 'gender', the terms 'education' and 'biography' also have certain meanings and functions for societies and the individuals living in them. For the biographical research approach, the very aim and focus of interest is to reconstruct these meanings and societal functions of biographies in the everyday world. The term biographical learning used in the following, attempts to avoid normative definitions *ex ante* and proceeds from the perspective of the subject that is forming itself. By using the term, we now have a broadly conceived educational concept that embraces not only institutionalised learning, but also all forms of informal learning that lead to the formation and transformation of biographical experience. Thus, the category of 'biographical learning' is not aimed at particular contents or 'types' of learning, but at learning as a superordinate process[7] in which individuals process their experience, integrating it and 'constructing'[8] it within the overall meaning and context of their life history. An educational concept that reconstructs this accomplishment by social subjects is advantageous for the combination and interlinking of theory, subject-matter and methods, not only for research[9], but also for educational practice[10].

---

[6] This critique has been formulated above all in studies on 'gender-specific socialisation' (Gildemeister 1992, Gildemeister, Wetterer 1992, Dausien 1999).

[7] In German, we have the term *Bildung*, which embraces the aspect of learning and skilling in the life course with the aspect of identity and personality formation.

[8] Alheit (1995) also speaks of 'biographicity' as the ability or the construction principle with which subjects generate social experience.

[9] Of particular relevance here are qualitative research methods (for biographical research in the context of educational and social sciences, see, for example, Krüger, Marotzki (1995, 1999), Chamberlayne et al. (2000), etc.).

However, before we can discuss the question of how education, biography and gender interact, it is necessary to specify the gender perspective in more detail.

The Social Construction of Gender – Three Process-Centred Analytical Perspectives

Gender is a complex category that can be spelt out on different levels – the social construction of gender can be analysed as a cultural system of difference and duality, or as a social structure of power and dominance, as a symbolic order (e.g. in pictures and language), or as an institutionalised division of labour, as an interaction order (Goffman 1983), or as a form of identity and 'identity work' at the level of individuals. It is important, therefore, to draw distinctions between the perspectives and levels of analysis that are meant in each case, and to name them with greater precision. To explain the idea of an independent biographical dimension in the construction of gender, I focus on just one aspect to illustrate the specificity of this perspective, namely the aspect of time, i.e. the question as to how construction processes can be conceived of in terms of temporality. Borrowing from Giddens (1984, 34ff), we can distinguish between three time levels that are relevant for the analysis of social processes (see also Schuller 1996, 18ff) – the '*longue durée* of institutions' (reversible), the '*durée* of day-to-day experience' (reversible) and the 'lifespan of the individual' (irreversible). As Tom Schuller emphasised, the underlying criterion for this differentiation is not mere duration, but their different 'shapes' (Schuller 1996). The three levels can be interpreted as different 'temporal shapes', each with its own quality, 'perspectivity' and structure. Some examples from the field of gender research should illustrate this idea:

(a) The first level involves protracted historical processes in which gender categories are formed and transformed in specific cultural and societal contexts. This is the time dimension of societies, institutions and cultural systems for the assignment of meanings and interpretations. A

---

[10] Biographically oriented education methods systematically support the process of self-reflection and (re)structuring of experience in life history (Gudjons et al. 1996, Behrens-Cobet, Reichling 1997; for an overview, see Alheit, Dausien 1999).

prominent example is the study by Thomas Laqueur (1990) entitled 'Making sex', which reconstructs historical changes in the notion of physical gender. Other examples are provided by studies on the construction of polar 'gender characters' in civil society and its scientific community (e.g. Honegger 1991) – Hagemann-White (1984) speaks of a cultural system of bi-genderedness – or analyses of gendering processes on the labour market, e.g. on the genesis and transformation of gender-coded occupations (Wetterer 1992, 1995). Research studies on gender differentiation in the education and training system also belong to this level. They show that women were not only excluded from educational concepts and institutions for a long time, but also that cultural models of 'femininity' and 'masculinity' were themselves produced by the education system and its typifications of gender (Kleinau, Opitz 1996). A hundred years ago, it was still not accepted that a woman could or should have an academic education, indeed it was considered 'unwomanly', whereas today it is not only possible but is actually part and parcel of the definition of a 'modern woman'.

Historical analyses at this level usually provide both: arguments for the historical variability of social institutions and cultural concepts in the particular definition of 'female'/'male', as well as arguments for the historical stability of the gender category as a social system of duality, differentiation and hierarchy. The question as to how historical changes are 'made' leads to another level of analysis:

(b) to the prominent concept of doing gender, which examines the micro-perspective of social construction processes, focusing on interactions in the temporal horizon of the situation (West, Zimmerman 1987, Lorber, Farrell 1991). The concept of doing gender pertains to the second perspective, the '*durée* of day-to-day experience'. In the theoretical tradition of symbolic interactionism and ethnomethodology, this approach focuses on the *interaction process* in which individuals produce and reproduce 'gender'. The point of this approach is that gender is conceptualised "as a routine, methodical, and ongoing accomplishment" (West, Fenstermaker 1995, 9). The authors argue that

> doing gender involves a complex of perceptual, interactional, and micropolitical activities that cast particular

pursuits as expressions of manly and womanly 'natures'. Rather than conceiving of gender as an individual characteristic', this perspective conceives ... of it as an emergent property of social situations – both an outcome of and a rationale for various social arrangements and a means of justifying one of the most fundamental divisions of society (West, Fenstmaker 1995, 9).

The strength of this approach consists, beyond a doubt, in analysing gender (or other categories of social order[11]) as a 'fluid' process. The micro-perspective and methods based on it, especially participant observation, provide a view that seems to be very 'close to the ground'. Social reality is analysed 'in actu', in a sense. Examples from educational research are those studies which examine interactions in learning situations and how gender is made relevant in the everyday practice of teachers and learners. In one ethnographic study of schools, Breidenstein and Kelle (1998) investigated, for example, the social order of the peer group and observed situationally changing practices of doing gender. However, they were also able to reconstruct situations and contexts in which social order was not structured according to gender, but according to other criteria. One finding of the study was that a typification based on gender has major pragmatic advantages over other categories in solving problems of everyday interaction, even if these problems have nothing to do with gender. The authors have therefore found a convincing explanation for the pragmatic functionality and stability of gender as an interaction category.

The 'doing gender' perspective is fascinating at first sight because it emphasises the role of social actors in the construction of gender and thereby provides a perspective on action spaces and learning options. If we are all 'doing gender', why should we not have the chance to 'undo' gender (Hirschauer 1994) or to do gender 'differently'? The concept stresses the idea of change and changeability. However, the micro-analytical perspec-

---

[11] West and Fenstermaker extended the original idea of doing gender to the concept of doing difference, including the categories of 'race' and 'class', which are also conceptualised "as ongoing, methodical and situated accomplishments" (West, Fenstermaker 1995, 30).

tive reveals how deeply embroiled we are in a game which rules we follow and which we cannot control as individuals. We might think that we are playing the game, but in reality we are 'played' to a considerable degree by the hidden rules of the situation and by the order it imposes on interaction. So the approach also provides a convincing explanation for the stability, the affirmation and the repetition of gender structures.

It is not possible, in my view, to resolve the paradox of stability and change within this second level of analysis, within the paradigm of interaction and the temporal horizon of the situation. In order to advance any further at this point, we have to consider the interplay of different processual perspectives and integrate a third temporal dimension, namely that of biography.

(c) Whereas the first two perspectives are well established in gender research, the biographical dimension as an independent level of construction has been subjected to little or no theoretical discussion. There are all kinds of empirical studies that investigate the inter-relationship between education and gender using biographical methods, but they mostly assume 'biography' as a first-degree concept without reflecting on the logic of its construction. This can briefly be outlined with reference to the temporality aspect:

Whereas historical time and everyday time are reversible, the lifespan dimension is irreversible (see above). A life can be lived only once. Yet this does not mean that individual learning follows a rigid pattern. A more appropriate notion for explaining learning processes is that of 'diffuse directedness' (Alheit 2001), which can also be applied to biography as *Gesamtgestalt* – structured, yet open in shape and form. There is an aspect of reversibility here, by virtue of the very fact that we live simultaneously in all three temporal dimensions [12].

If reversibility was not possible, there would be no such thing as biography. Experiences are shaped and reshaped, we learn and forget, and at a superordinate level of education and training we form patterns of experi-

---

[12] It becomes clear here that the distinction between three analytical levels is a second-degree construction that is not found in this discrete form in everyday life. The three temporal dimensions distinguished here are necessarily conjoined with each other in real life.

ence, repeat and reinforce them, continue them in variations or transform them to form new patterns. We narrate the little stories of our life and renarrate them anew, but in different ways. In rare situations, often experienced as crisis or incisive changes in our lives, we also have the chance (or are compelled) to reflect on our 'whole life story' and to reorganise it from the bottom up.

Nevertheless, no matter how much flexibility and opportunity there is for change, we cannot simply 'jump out' of our lives. The manner in which we process new events is determined less by the outer characteristics of those events than by the biographical structure of our patterned experience. This is true even or precisely when we enter a 'completely new world' that we are unfamiliar with and in which no-one knows us, in which we do not seem to be fixed in our ways through shared experience and the structures of expectation that ensue from that, e.g. in some cases of migration, religious conversion or a dramatic upward or downward move to a different social milieu. Examples from the field of gender research are provided by studies on trans-sexuality (Hirschauer 1993, Lindemann 1993). Although the classical study on this subject, Garfinkel's 'Agnes' (1967), examines the interactive process of 'passing' and highlights the idea of doing gender, it is also possible to read a biographical perspective between the lines of Garfinkel's text (see Dausien 1998b, 262ff). Continuity is produced even in situations of radical change, and to a certain extent we remain 'ourselves'.

This 'identity' of biographical structuring of experience [13] that crystallises in a kind of process in the field between historically rooted environments (see a) and situated experience (see b) is linked in manifold and flexible ways to the social construction of gender. Gender constructions are inseparably embedded in our life history, in innumerable stories and with innumerable links to single experiences, but also through reference to institutionalised and materialised aspects of the gender order, which, as one of the most stable social orders in existence, structures the

---

[13] The concept of identity addressed here cannot be discussed further within the framework of this paper. From a social constructivist viewpoint based on biography theory, identity is not conceived of as a stable and coherent structure, but as an individual and collective accomplishment of 'production' (construction) and active reconstruction of continuity and coherence through changing biographical situations and in changing social contexts (Somers 1994, Fischer-Rosenthal 1999).

world in which we live as redundant 'information'. Gender is an integral component of our biography and interpenetrates our lives like a finely branching, often invisible web.

The proposed differentiation of analytical levels applies to gender research in general. In the section that follows, specific examples for the third, i.e.biographical perspective, are provided and explained with reference to learning phenomena in education and training. Links are also produced to the other two levels of analysis.

How Education Contributes to the Construction of Gender – Learning Processes in Women's Biographies

The description that follows is intended to provide examples, without claim to any systematic treatment, for the empirical interplay between education, gender and biography in the historical context of German society[14]. The differentiation of three aspects is based, in turn, on the temporal dimension and the 'perspectivity' of education and training processes, and is heuristic in nature[15]:

(1) the formation of gendered life courses through education and training,
(2) education and training as a source and focus of orientation in individual life planning,
(3) 'learning gender' as a biographical process.

Re. (1): Gendered life course patterns. Education, as a societal institution or system of interdependent institutions, forms typical life course structures. This can be clearly illustrated with the archetypical model of the three-phase life course that emerged as a standard biographical pattern in the process of modernisation, but which is meanwhile in a process of dissolution (Kohli 1985). Corresponding to the logic of the labour market, distinctions are made between 'preparatory', 'activity' and

---

[14] At this point the term 'German context' is no more than an indicator for reminding the reader that empirical phenomena are always bound up with specific cultural, historical, national, etc. situations. The following descriptions relate to present-day German society and are not automatically transferable.

[15] The chosen system is developed in greater detail in the paper by Alheit and Dausien in this collection.

'retirement' phases (Kohli 1985)[16], in which education and training plays a differentiated role. In addition to upbringing and socialisation in the family, it is primarily school that structures the biographical phases of childhood and youth as a system through which all members of society must pass. The system of general education schools defines skill levels and profiles, grants certificates of education and defines starting chances and option spaces for people's further careers. Subsequent corrections ('second' and 'third' avenues to education and training) are possible, but they cannot compensate entirely for previous educational pathways (Rabe-Kleberg 1993b). The two key criteria in this control process are milieu of origin (which includes, besides social class and regional origin, one's affiliation to ethnic cultures and one's nationality) and gender.

The formal equality enjoyed by girls in the system of general education schools in Germany has not been in place for a century as yet, but their factual equality with male youths, measured in terms of the quantity and quality of educational accomplishments, is a relatively recent outcome, historically speaking, of the education reforms implemented since the 1960s[17]. (The fact that the reform of education has not eliminated the social inequality between the classes, but that education continues to function as the most important indicator of social positioning, even if there has been a collective raising of the level in the middle classes[18], is something that affects both genders.)

The next biographical phase, that of active adulthood, is determined by employment and is therefore dependent on (vocational) education and training, and on documentary qualifications that structure not only levels, but also careers to a substantial extent – especially in the German occupational system. With the increasing need to engage in continuing vocational training or to retrain for a different occupation, the importance of education

---

[16] The model is based one-sidedly on the ideal-typical male life course. This gender bias has criticised by many (Krüger 1991, Dausien 1996).

[17] For statistics on education-based indicators in Germany, see *Arbeitsgruppe Bildungsbericht* 1994. Co-education as the elimination of historical gender separation in the school system has contributed greatly to this equalisation, but also had some paradox consequences and new inequalities (Faulstich-Wieland 1994).

[18] An initial, sober assessment of the education reform was made by Bourdieu and Passeron as far back as 1971.

and training during this phase is increasing considerably. The 'retirement phase' referred to by Kohli has become a quantitatively and qualitatively significant phase of life, above all due to demographic changes. Not only is its specific design dependent on the material, social and health conditions of previous employment (and hence on education and training, indirectly), but it is also becoming more and more like a separate and autonomous phase of education – courses and programmes for the 'third' phase have long been included in the product range of most education and training institutions, and concepts are ensuing from 'education for aging', which is centred on extensive biographical reflection and development (Kade 1994, Mader 1995).

Although the shaping of life course by education and training applies for both genders, there are some basic, gender-specific differences. After the gendering processes that take place in school (Lemmermöhle 1998), the status passage between school and the employment market and/or vocational training form a subsequent critical point – the constriction of 'career choice' to a narrow range of typical women's occupations, which extends into the academic sphere as well (systematic imbalances in degree course attendance and access to professors), means structurally worse conditions and perspectives for the employment biographies of women compared to the careers of males with the same level of qualification and skill[19]. This discrimination actually increases in the life course, and risks cumulate. Typical 'women's jobs' are 'dead-end' occupations (Rabe-Kleberg 1993a), they reduce and prevent opportunities for continuing vocational skilling, career pathways and promotion opportunities. They are also characterised by lower incomes, less job security, part-time employment contracts and interruptions (not only for family reasons).

The gender difference as described can be explained with the 'double sociation' approach (Becker-Schmidt 1987, Knapp 1990). First, biographical options are influenced by conditions on the labour market and especially by the option spaces and limits embedded in the gender-coded occupational structure. Secondly, the uneven distribution of repro-

---

[19] On the inter-relationships between education and occupation in women's biographies see Krüger (1992), on the construction of gender by the occupational system see Wetterer (1992, 1995).

ductive labour between the genders, with women bearing by far the greater burden, leads to typical interruptions in employment that result, in turn, in reduced skills and usefulness of the original vocational training every time a return is made to the workforce. However, women are structurally disadvantaged not only in these two areas – job and family – but these two systems of disadvantage overlap and reinforce each other in the life course (Krüger 1995).

One aspect that often receives too little attention in this connection is education and training. Precisely because supposedly universalistic criteria apply, education as a socially formalised skilling process is a particularly effective instrument for assigning and prefiguring biographical opportunities, which are differentiated according to gender (but also according to class and ethnic-national-cultural attribution). The education system forms 'typical' life courses of women and men.

Re. (2): education as a focus for orientation in individual life planning. At the same time, education is an individual process for subjects who move within the institutionally shaped framework, work on their experiences, plan their life and shape it through action. From the perspective of the subject, the (gender-) structuring effect of the educational system is only partly and indirectly perceptible. Education and learning are primarily experienced within the biographical horizon. For example, young women who decide to enter vocational training after leaving school are usually unaware that they are not just selecting an occupation on a particular skilling level, but at the same time a 'gendered' biographical trajectory that is institutionally pre-shaped and almost impossible for the individual to influence (Born 2000). In new, gender-critical concepts for occupational orientation in schools, these aspects are addressed, as are the structural problems that arise from the 'double life plan' that most women continue to pursue (Lemmermöhle 2001).

It has already been said that life courses no longer follow the simple three-phase pattern. However, if one takes a detailed empirical look at the temporal sequence of education processes in biographies, one can see that the life courses of women (and to an increasing extent of men) deviate systematically from the linear order of the male, archetypical, educational and vocational career (Krüger 1995). For many women, interruptions, devaluation, and lack of follow-up opportunities due to the double involvement in work and family lead to educational and employment trajectories that are 'disordered' or 'patchworked'.

Generational positioning plays an important role in this context. For example, many women who spent their childhood and youth in 1940s and 1950s Germany[20] acquired skills by completing vocational education and training (Born, Krüger, Lorenz-Meyer 1996), but their educational biographies, at least in the lower and middle social strata, are very clearly geared to the standard, gender-specific expectation that marriage and family determine the greater part of life and that vocational training is only to a limited extent a meaningful and necessary pursuit. When women of an older generation learned an occupation, this was usually based on the economic calculation by which gainful employment is pursued until marriage, or the birth of the first child, or as an insurance policy for the 'emergency' situation that marriage fails to provide the necessary support and care. Statistically, women of a younger generation who received their education in the 1960s and 1970s acquire higher school-leaving qualifications significantly more often, go on to obtain longer and better vocational training, and postpone establishing a family (Tölke 1989). Nevertheless, the calculation of subordinating education and career to marriage and family, at least for certain biographical phases, still remains valid in subtle ways (Geissler, Oechsle 1996, Geissler 1998).

Ever since the relevant education and training schemes were institutionalised in the context of educational reforms, many women of the older generation have caught up on their education, either informally or by acquiring formal qualifications. The option of 'repeating' or continuing education has also gained relevance for younger generations as well. There are more and more biographies in which education and employment phases alternate repeatedly. Education is becoming an ongoing component of biographies, an independent 'activity' that no longer serves as 'preparation' for an externally specified purpose, but can become an end in itself for the subject concerned. Education processes are multivalent and are experienced

---

[20] For female migrants of different generations, the need to 'catch up' on education and training, and the opportunities for life planning associated with the education system are very specific (Apitzsch 1990, 1995).

differently depending on the biographical situation: as compulsion to engage in 'lifelong learning' in the face of changing skilling requirements on the labour market, but also as a medium for structuring one's 'own' lifetime, for developing plans and perspectives for shaping one's life and for generating biographical meaning (Egger 1995, Alheit, Dausien 1996, Dausien 1996, 1998a, Kade, Seitter 1996, Merrill 1999). Women make use of education schemes more frequently as an opportunity for biographical reflection and as preparation and support for restructuring their own lives in the family and career.

Concepts for women's education explicitly address this motivational aspect and provide spaces for reflection in which the participants work individually and together on their contradictory experiences at work and in the family, and can regain biographical perspectives and educational wishes that are often left out of the reckoning on account of a 'typical' life course pattern for women [21]. Thus, deviating from the linear model for educational and employment biography is not a deficiency, but suggests fundamentally new opportunities for arranging educational phases within the life course.

We can summarise by noting the following shift in the life planning of women: the more or less predefined, standard biography of women, prestructured by educationally based (i.e. also stratum-specific) status passages, was increasingly questioned as a norm through the opening of the education system since the 1960s, and factually dissolved. The new opportunities that ensued have led some generations of women to catch up more intensively than before on education they either missed or were historically excluded from obtaining, and to personal as well as political equalisation and emancipation processes. For the younger generations of women, the flexibilisation of education and training, and of one's entire life planning has become a matter of course. Pointedly expressed, 'lifelong

---

[21] The example of 'women's studies', an opportunity for women in various European countries to obtain university education that is relatively independent of existing admission criteria, that addresses the specific life situations of women, shows how narrowly perspectives of returning to one's occupation and of further life planning is linked to 'catching up' on very individual biographical learning processes that go far beyond the curricular content of education and training (Freund 1997, Merrill 1999).

learning' as a necessity and opportunity has changed from being a generational issue to a norm in a 'learning society' that is increasingly binding on both genders.

Re. (3): 'learning gender' as a biographical process. With this third aspect, the perspective shifts even more to the 'internal' organisation of experience and that reflexive dimension of biographies. How these inter-relate with the construction of gender, and how gender is learned 'biographically', will be sketched briefly with reference to the analytical levels presented before.

A major part of the biographical learning processes that we undergo inside and outside the education system takes place informally and follows the logic by which individuals acquire successive layers of biographical experience. Not all the 'biographical knowledge' (Alheit, Hoerning 1989) generated in the process is reflexively available at all times to the subject. The formation of experience is not subject to full intentional control and is not totally transparent – for the simple fact that experience is not a cognitive procedure in an isolated individual, but a context-sensitive, social process. Biographical learning connects or 'networks' individual experience with the structures of the social, cultural and material world, and for that reason with the gender constructions embedded therein as well.

Experience is formed in specific interaction contexts – which means that interactively generated or updated rules of social order penetrate into the biographical experience of the actors involved. In this way, the subject 'learns' aspects of 'doing gender' through practical action, such as referring to the difference between men and women when performing various activities, and ways of making distinctions (see above, analytic perspective b). In innumerable particular situations, actors appropriate certain basic patterns of the dominant gender order. However, this process is not a 'smooth' one. Experiences do not simply add up, and even when dominant gender constructions such as those described by Goffman (1977) for public situations in American society or by Breidenstein and Kelle (1998) for German school children, repeat and consolidate themselves in the temporal sequence of situations, the specific conditions actually vary and exhibit several possibilities. In doing gender, patterns and variations of gender are produced. Depending on the specific contexts of interaction in which they participate in the course of their biography, and the significant interaction partners with whom they have dealings, individuals are always acquiring experience of greater and lesser intensities with deviating, incongruent patterns of interaction that run counter to the dominant culture. The performative scope that is implied in the concept of doing gender, the possibilities of changing gender in action situations, gain a further dimension with the diachronous perspective of biographical experience. Which patterns and variations of the dominant or intractable gender culture are built into the biographical structure of an individual can only be reconstructed on a case-by-case basis. And this reconstruction is by no means a privilege of empirical research, but is also performed (under certain conditions) by subjects in day-to-day life. Pedagogical situations can provide support in this connection, but they can also be obstructive.

In the interpretation and reflection of their experience, subjects rely on symbolic systems and cultural patterns of interpretation, and especially on language (see analytical level a). It holds true for these historically and socially rooted worlds of meaning, too, that they provide a multi-layered and contradictory network of gender constructions. There is a dominant patriarchal culture (Rommelspacher 1995), but the hierarchical construction is multi-layered not only with regard to the meanings assigned to masculinity and femininity, but also with regard to the links with other social classifications (according to origin, skin colour, sexual orientations, etc.). Connell (1995) has elaborated on this aspect with examples and with his concept of 'hegemonial masculinity'. The question as to which interpretations are picked up, applied and reinforced by the members of society, and which are modified, ignored or rejected, is of enormous relevance for any system of adult education that claims to be sensitive to the gender issue. The only meaningful answer, in my view, is one that takes into consideration the individual, biographical structure in which patterns of interpretation are acquired and modified. Taking a reconstructive perspective at this juncture engenders the possibility of reflecting upon and analysing each individual 'life story' with certain interpretations, and placing that story in relation to specific biographical experiences[22]. The ensuing variations and possibilities of interpreting 'gender', the discrepancies and contradictions within available meaning systems and in comparison to one's own experience, are possible starting points for questions, changes of perspective and transformations – in short, for education and training processes.

Finally, learning processes are also shaped and influenced by background societal structures that are more or less 'visible' in particular action contexts or learning environments, but which take effect independently of the latter. Gender is anchored not only in the symbolic order of a society, but also through institutions, social and economic structures and 'material' agencies. As described above, the social division of labour, the system of education and occupations, the family, or indeed life course, are core social institutions in which gender is produced and reproduced as a hierarchical construction of difference (see analytical level a). Even when biographical learning does not follow the logic of institutions, which contradict each other systematically in the biographies of women, anyway (Krüger 1995), the option spaces for experience and educational processes are limited and sanctioned by this logic. In the educational field, too, there are many examples of institutional barriers and procedural rules that, from the historical perspective, have restricted and confined women, especially, (and members of the lower classes) in their learning opportunities and further biographical perspectives. Recognising and acknowledging these 'objective' structures, also in one's own life history, is an essential condition for perceiving, claiming and exploiting one's own scope for action. For this reason, a biographically centred gender formation must not come to a standstill at the 'narcissistic' reflection of one's own story of 'becoming a woman/man', but must include the background social structures and – with

---

[22] The connection, of key importance for education processes, between patterns of interpretation and patterns of experience has been systematically discussed by Alheit (1989). Adult educators know that effective learning processes do not consist in the appropriation of knowledge alone, or in changing social, scientific, moral etc. interpretations, and that effective learning does not come into being until the (critical) connection has been made between such interpretations and one's own experience.

the concept of biography – make the link between the individual and societal levels an object of analysis.

These considerations and observations make clear that individuals appropriate social reality within the horizon of meanings produced by their life history, as well as organise and 'construct' their experience in a unique and special process in the form of their biography. This also holds true for gender-related experience and interpretations. Individuals do not appropriate gender as a prefabricated template ('female/male gender identity') that they then fill with their own version. Gender is not a separated area that is learned in a given phase of life (childhood/youth), nor an isolated category of self-interpretation and self-reflection.

The more appropriate notion, it seems to me, is one of a continuous biographical construction process in which gender (like other categories of social classification and identification) is 'learned', often implicitly and at the same time is brought into interpretations of self and the world, and into practical activities, again and again in new guises. In this reciprocal relationship of 'internalisation' and 'externalisation' (Berger, Luckmann 1967), gender is written into biographies not only as a background social structure, as many socialisation theories assume. It is also actively 'constructed', by forming, reflecting upon and re-forming a superordinate body of experience from a wealth of heterogeneous, often contradictory experiences. The overall biographical form with which an individual constructs his or her identity (Somers 1994) is still usually recognisable as the life story of a man or a woman, for all the differences and multiple meanings in single experiential elements and through all the changes that are undergone.

From the viewpoint of the subject, however, this process is not primarily about the construction of gender – this is a scientific, 'second-order' perspective –, but about one's own life history. Within that history, gender constructions are inseparably entwined. By using the methods of biographical research, it is possible to reconstruct this web of interrelationships empirically for each individual case (Dausien 1996). For (adult) educational research, it would be necessary to intensify systematic theorising on the biographical dimension of learning processes. As far as the practical side of gender-centred educational work is concerned, the preceding thoughts have shown that, at different levels, there are starting points for reflecting upon and changing gender constructions, which can be focused upon as themes within the 'big picture' that is biography.

Final Remarks

The question of the interplay between education and gender needs to be addressed one more time before closing: What role does education play in the construction of gender? At least two key 'hinging points' have been discussed: firstly, all modern societies in which subjects learn and shape their individual educational biographies are structured according to gender in different and differentiated ways. The social and material environments for action and learning are gender-coded in multiple respects and as such are 'built in' to individual experience in an interactive, mostly implicit way. Secondly, subjects link their experience as women or men to a life history. This means they are actively involved in (re)producing and modifying gender typifications anew, again and again. Life plans and lived biographies are also and always documents of women's or men's lives in a certain societal and historical constellation, and particular 'models' for potential biographies.

This means that life histories are 'gendered' in a complex way. They organise experience in a gender-coded world and also (re)construct it in the self-willed form of one's life history as shaped from previous experience. Thus, they create social reality and (re)produce gender as well. 'Biography', according to my thesis is therefore a mode of gender construction that adds to other levels of construction that have been better researched already (Dausien 1998b). The thesis I am propounding requires more precise theoretical elaboration and above all more empirical studies. An analysis of how biographical constructions operate could provide insights into the complex, often contradictory interplay between change and immutability – a dialectic that deeply influences all learning processes, but which is also of enormous relevance for the question of individual and political changes in gender relations. In women's and gender-based education and training, both perspectives meet head-on.

References

Alheit, P. (1989). Erzählform und „soziales Gedächtnis". Beispiel beginnender Traditionsbildung im autobiographischen Erinnerungsprozeß. In: Alheit, P., Hoerning, E. M. (eds.). *Biographisches Wissen. Beiträge zu einer Theorie lebensgeschichtlicher Erfahrung*. Frankfurt/M., New York, pp. 123-147.

Alheit, P. (1995). „Biographizität" als Lernpotential. Konzeptionelle Überlegungen zum biographischen Ansatz in der Erwachsenenbildung. In: Krüger, H.-H., Marotzki, W. (eds.). *Erziehungswissenschaftliche Biographieforschung*. Opladen, pp. 276-307.

Alheit, P. (2001). „Neugier, Beobachtung, Praxis – Forschendes Lernen als Methode erziehungswissenschaftlichen Studierens". Vortrag auf der Fachtagung „Erfahrung mit Methode", 2001-04-27/28, Universität Bielefeld (unpubl. paper).

Alheit, P., Dausien, B. (1996). Bildung als »biographische Konstruktion«? Nichtintendierte Lernprozesse in der organisierten Erwachsenenbildung. In: *Report. Literatur- und Forschungsreport Weiterbildung*, 37, pp. 33-45.

Alheit, P., Dausien, B. (1999). Biographieforschung in der Erwachsenenbildung. In: Krüger, H., Marotzki, W. (eds.). *Handbuch erziehungswissenschaftliche Biographieforschung*. Opladen, pp. 407-432.

Alheit, P., et al. (eds.) (1995). *The Biographical Approach in European Adult Education*. Wien.

Apitzsch, U. (1990). Besser integriert und doch nicht gleich. Bildungsbiographien jugendlicher Migrantinnen als Dokumente widersprüchlicher Bildungsprozesse. In: Rabe-Kleberg, U. (ed.). *Besser gebildet und doch nicht gleich! Frauen und Bildung in der Arbeitsgesellschaft*. Bielefeld, pp. 197-217.

Apitzsch, U. (1995). Frauen in der Migration. In: Gieseke, W. et al. (eds.). *Erwachsenenbildung als Frauenbildung*. Bad Heilbrunn, pp. 104-122.

Arbeitsgruppe Bildungsbericht am Max-Planck-Institut für Bildungsforschung (1994). *Das Bildungswesen in der Bundesrepublik Deutschland. Strukturen und Entwicklungen im Überblick*. Vollständig überarbeitete und erweiterte Neuausgabe. Reinbek.

Beck, U., Giddens, A., Lash, S. (1994). *Reflexive Modernization. Politics, Tradition and Aesthetics in the Modern Social Order*. Cambridge.

Becker-Schmidt, R. (1987). Die doppelte Vergesellschaftung – die doppelte Unterdrückung. Besonderheiten der Frauenforschung in den Sozialwissenschaften. In: Unterkirchner, L., Wagner, I. (eds.). *Die andere Hälfte der Gesellschaft*. Wien, pp. 11-25.

Behrens-Cobet, H., Reichling, N. (1997). *Biographische Kommunikation. Lebensgeschichten im Repertoire der Erwachsenenbildung*. Neuwied.

Berger, P. L., Luckmann, T. (1967). *The Social Construction of Reality. A Treatise in the Sociology of Knowledge*. Garden City, N.Y.

Born, C. (2000): Erstausbildung und weiblicher Lebenslauf. Was (nicht nur) junge Frauen bezüglich der Berufswahl wissen sollten. In: Heinz, W. (ed.). *Übergänge.*

Individualisierung, Flexibilisierung und Institutionalisierung des Lebensverlaufs. 3. Beiheft der ZSE. Zeitschrift für Soziologie der Erziehung und Sozialisation, Weinheim, pp. 50-65.

Born, C., Krüger, H., Lorenz-Meyer, D. (1996). *Der unentdeckte Wandel. Annäherung an das Verhältnis von Struktur und Norm im weiblichen Lebenslauf.* Berlin.

Bourdieu, P., Passeron, J.-C. (1971). *Die Illusion der Chancengleichheit. Untersuchungen zur Soziologie des Bildungswesens am Beispiel Frankreichs.* Stuttgart.

Breidenstein, G., Kelle, H. (1998). *Geschlechteralltag in der Schulklasse. Ethnographische Studien zur Gleichaltrigenkultur.* Weinheim, München.

Butler, J. (1990). *Gender Trouble. Feminism and the Subversion of Identity.* New York, London.

Chamberlayne, P., Bornat, J., Wengraf, T. (eds.) (2000). *The Turn to Biographical Methods in Social Science. Comparative Issues and Examples.* London, New York.

Connell, R. W. (1995). *Masculinities.* Cambridge.

Dausien, B. (1996). *Biographie und Geschlecht. Zur biographischen Konstruktion sozialer Wirklichkeit in Frauenlebensgeschichten.* Bremen.

Dausien, B. (1998a). Education as Biographical Construction? Narration, Gender and Learning – a Case Study. In: Alheit, P, Kammler, E. (eds.). *Lifelong Learning and its Impact on Social and Regional Development: Collected Papers.* Bremen, pp. 507-526.

Dausien, B. (1998b). Die biographische Konstruktion von Geschlecht. In: Schneider, N., et al. (eds.). *Einheit und Vielfalt. Das Verstehen der Kulturen.* Amsterdam, Atlanta, pp. 257-277.

Dausien, B. (1999). „Geschlechtsspezifische Sozialisation" – Konstrukti(vistisch)e Ideen zu Karriere und Kritik eines Konzepts. In: Dausien, Bettina, et al. (eds.). *Erkenntnisprojekt Geschlecht: Feministische Perspektiven verwandeln Wissenschaft.* Opladen, pp. 216-249.

Deutsches Institut für Erwachsenenbildung (1999). Volkshochschulstatistik. 37. Folge, Arbeitsjahr 1998. Frankfurt/M.

Dominicé, P. (2000). *Learning from our Lives. Using Educational Biographies with Adults.* San Francisco.

Egger, R. (1995). *Biographie und Bildungsrelevanz. Eine empirische Studie über Prozeßstrukturen moderner Bildungsbiographien.* München, Wien.

Faulstich-Wieland, H. (1994). Reflexive Koedukation. Zur Entwicklung der Koedukationsdebatte in den Bundesländern. In: Bracht, U., Keiner, D. (eds.). *Geschlechterverhältnisse und die Pädagogik,* Jahrbuch für Pädagogik 1994, Frankfurt/M., pp. 325-342.

Fischer-Rosenthal, W. (1999). Melancholie der Identität und dezentrierte biographische Selbstbeschreibung. Anmerkungen zu einem langen Abschied aus der selbtverschuldeten Zentriertheit des Subjekts. In: *BIOS. Zeitschrift für Biographieforschung und Oral History,* 12 (2), pp. 143-168.

Freund, M. (1997). *"Und was hab' ich dann davon?" Frauenstudien an der Universität*

- *Weiterbildung für Frauen in und nach der Familienphase.* Bielefeld.

Garfinkel, H. (1967). *Studies in Ethnomethodology.* Englewood Cliffs, N.J.

Geissler, B. (1998). Hierarchie und Differenz. Die (Un-)Vereinbarkeit von Familie und Beruf und die soziale Konstruktion von Geschlechterhierarchie im Beruf. In: Oechsle, M., Geissler, B. (eds.). *Die ungleiche Gleichheit. Junge Frauen und der Wandel im Geschlechterverhältnis.* Opladen, pp. 109-129.

Geissler, B., Oechsle, M. (1996). *Lebensplanung junger Frauen. Zur widersprüchlichen Modernisierung weiblicher Lebensläufe.* Weinheim.

Giddens, A. (1988). *Die Konstitution der Gesellschaft.* Frankfurt/M., New York.

Gieseke, W. (ed.) (1993). *Feministische Bildung – Frauenbildung.* Pfaffenweiler.

Gieseke, W. et al. (1995). *Erwachsenenbildung als Frauenbildung.* Bad Heilbrunn.

Gieseke, W. (ed.) (2001). *Handbuch zur Frauenbildung.* Opladen.

Gildemeister, R. (1992). Die soziale Konstruktion von Geschlechtlichkeit. In: Ostner, I., Lichtblau, K. (eds.). *Feministische Vernunftkritik. Ansätze und Traditionen.* Frankfurt/M., New York, pp. 220-239.

Gildemeister, R., Wetterer, A. (1992). Wie Geschlechter gemacht werden. Die soziale Konstruktion der Zweigeschlechtlichkeit und ihre Reifizierung in der Frauenforschung. In: Knapp, G.-A., Wetterer, A. (eds.). *Traditionen Brüche. Entwicklungen feministischer Theorie.* Freiburg i. Breisgau, pp. 201-254.

Goffman, E. (1983). The Interaction Order. American Sociological Association, 1982, Presidential Address. In: *American Sociological Review*, 48, pp. 1-17.

Goffman, E. (1977). The Arrangement between the Sexes. In: *Theory and Society*, 4, pp. 301-331.

Gudjons, H. et al. (1996). *Auf meinen Spuren – Das Entdecken der eigenen Lebensgeschichte. Vorschläge und Übungen für pädagogische Arbeit und Selbsterfahrung.* Hamburg.

Hagemann-White (1984). *Sozialisation: Weiblich – männlich?* Opladen.

Harding, S. (1986). *The Science Question in Feminism.* Ithaca, N.Y.

Harding, S. (1991). *Whose Science? Whose Knowledge? Thinking from Women's Lives.* Milton Keynes.

Hirschauer, S. (1993). *Die soziale Konstruktion der Transsexualität. Über die Medizin und den Geschlechtswechsel.* Frankfurt/M.

Hirschauer, S. (1994). Die soziale Fortpflanzung der Zweigeschlechtlichkeit. In: *Kölner Zeitschrift für Soziologie und Sozialpsychologie*, 46, pp. 668-692.

Honegger, C. (1991). *Die Ordnung der Geschlechter. Die Wissenschaften vom Menschen und das Weib.* Frankfurt/M., New York.

Kade, S. (1991). *Frauenbildung. Eine themenorientierte Dokumentation.* Frankfurt/M.

Kade, S. (1994). *Altersbildung. Lebenssituation und Lernbedarf, Ziele und Konzepte.* Frankfurt/M.

Kade, J., Seitter, W. (1996). *Lebenslanges Lernen. Mögliche Bildungswelten. Erwach-*

senenbildung, Biographie und Alltag. Opladen.

Kleinau, E., Opitz, C. (eds.) (1996). *Geschichte der Mädchen- und Frauenbildung.* Frankfurt/M., New York.

Knapp, G.-A. (1990). Zur widersprüchlichen Vergesellschaftung von Frauen. In: Hoff, E.-H. (ed.). *Die doppelte Sozialisation Erwachsener. Zum Verhältnis von beruflichem und privatem Lebensstrang.* München, pp. 17-52.

Kohli, M. (1985). Die Institutionalisierung des Lebenslaufs. Historische Befunde und theoretische Argumente. In: *Kölner Zeitschrift für Soziologie und Sozialpsychologie*, 37, pp. 1-29.

Krüger, H. (1991). Normalitätsunterstellungen bezüglich des Wandels in der weiblichen Lebensführung zwischen Erwerbsarbeit und Familie. In: Zapf, W. (ed.). *Die Modernisierung moderner Gesellschaften.* Verhandlungen des 25. Deutschen Soziologentages in Frankfurt am Main 1990. Frankfurt/M., New York, pp. 688-703.

Krüger, H. (ed.) (1992). *Frauen und Bildung. Wege der Aneignung und Verwertung von Qualifikationen in weiblichen Erwerbsbiographien.* Bielefeld.

Krüger, H. (1995). Dominanzen im Geschlechterverhältnis. Zur Institutionalisierung von Lebensläufen. In: Becker-Schmidt, R., Knapp, G.-A. (eds.). *Das Geschlechterverhältnis als Gegenstand der Sozialwissenschaften.* Frankfurt/M., New York, pp. 195-219.

Krüger, H.-H., Marotzki, W. (eds.) (1995). *Erziehungswissenschaftliche Biographieforschung.* Opladen.

Krüger, H.-H., Marotzki, W. (eds.) (1999). *Handbuch erziehungswissenschaftliche Biographieforschung.* Opladen.

Laqueur, T. W. (1990). *Making Sex. Body and Gender from the Greeks to Freud.* Cambridge, Mass.

Lemmermöhle, D. (1998) Geschlechter(un)gleichheiten und Schule. In: Oechsle, M., Geissler, B. (eds.). *Die ungleiche Gleichheit. Junge Frauen und der Wandel im Geschlechterverhältnis.* Opladen, pp. 67-86.

Lemmermöhle, D. (2001). Der Blick aufs Ganze fehlt. Geschlecht und Geschlechterverhältnisse in der Arbeitslehre und der berufsorientierenden Bildung. In: Hoppe, H., Kampshoff, M., Nyssen, E. (eds.). *Geschlechterverhältnisse und Fachdidaktik.* Weinheim (in print).

Lemmermöhle, D. et al. (2000). *Lesarten des Geschlechts. Zur De-Konstruktionsdebatte in der erziehungswissenschaftlichen Geschlechterforschung.* Opladen.

Lindemann, G. (1993). *Das paradoxe Geschlecht. Transsexualität im Spannungsfeld von Leib, Körper und Gefühl.* Frankfurt/M.

Lorber, J., Farrell, S. A. (eds.) (1991). *The Social Construction of Gender.* London.

Mader, W. (ed.) (1995). *Altwerden in einer alternden Gesellschaft. Kontinuität und Krisen in biographischen Verläufen.* Opladen.

Merrill, B. (1999). *Gender, Change, and Identity. Mature Women Students in Universities.* Ashgate, Aldershot.

Rabe-Kleberg, U. (1993a). *Verantwortlichkeit und Macht. Ein Beitrag zum Verhältnis von Geschlecht und Beruf angesichts der Krise traditioneller Frauenberufe.* Bielefeld.

Rabe-Kleberg, U. (1993b). Bildungsbiographien – oder: Kann Hans noch lernen, was Hänschen versäumt hat? In: Meier, A., Rabe-Kleberg, U. (eds.). *Weiterbildung, Lebenslauf, sozialer Wandel.* Neuwied, pp. 167-182.

Rommelspacher, B. (1995). *Dominanzkultur.* Berlin.

Schiersmann, C. (1993). *Frauenbildung. Konzepte, Erfahrungen, Perspektiven.* Weinheim, München.

Schütz, A. (1962). On the Methodology of the Social Sciences. In: Schütz, A. *Collected Papers. I: The Problem of Social Reality* (ed. by Maurice Natanson). Den Haag, pp. 1-96.

Schuller, T. (1996). *Modelling the Lifecourse. Age, Time and Education.* Bremen.

Somers, M. R. (1994). The Narrative Constitution of Identity. A Relational and Network Approach. In: *Theory and Society,* 23, pp. 605-649.

Tölke, A. (1989). *Lebensverläufe von Frauen. Familiäre Ereignisse, Ausbildungs- und Erwerbsverhalten.* München.

Tübinger Institut für frauenpolitische Sozialforschung e.V. (ed.) (1998). *Den Wechsel im Blick. Methodologische Ansichten feministischer Sozialforschung.* Pfaffenweiler.

West, C., Fenstermaker, S. (1995). Doing Difference. In: *Gender and Society,* 9 (1), pp. 8-37.

West, C., Zimmerman, D.-H. (1987). Doing Gender. In: *Gender and Society,* 1 (2), pp. 125-151.

Wetterer, A. (ed.) (1992). *Profession und Geschlecht. Über die Marginalität von Frauen in hochqualifizierten Berufen.* Frankfurt/M., New York.

Wetterer, A. (ed.) (1995). *Die Konstruktion von Geschlecht in Professionalisierungsprozessen.* Frankfurt/M., New York.

Horst Siebert

CONSTRUCTIVISM

AN EPISTEMOLOGICAL CHANGE*

Constructivism – a Turning Point in Perception

Constructivism is – first of all – not a social or educational theory, but a meta-theory, describing the possibilities and limitations of the human construction of both scientific and everyday theories. Constructivists are observers of second order, they observe how reality in every day life or in science is observed, and through that constructed.

Theories are, therefore, constructions dependent on observation – literally translated theory means observation. The discerning subject and the object of realisation are inseparably interconnected. What is more, the object of realisation and the problem are being produced by the discerning observer. Humberto Maturana points to this connection: "Everything said has been said by somebody" (Maturana, Varela 1987, 32). "This circularity, this chain of action and experience, this inseparability from a certain way to be and the distinct way the world appears to us, tells us that every act of realisation creates a world" (Maturana, Varela 1987, 31). Thus, constructivism is not an ontology or metaphysics, it does not give any statements about the nature of the world, about 'existence', instead it is a reflexive epistemology making statements about human being's orientation in the world. "In this sense, we have to assess constantly that the phenomenon of realisation cannot be understood as if there were 'facts' and objects out there, which simply have to be grabbed and put into our head" (Maturana, Varela 1987, 31).

---

* This contribution was translated from German into English by Cordula Feld.

Our sense organs, our cognition, our memory do not therefore produce images of an outer reality, instead they construct realities for the purpose of successful actions. "We do not experience the 'space' of the world, we experience our visual spectrum. We do not see the 'colours' of the world, we see our chromatic space" (Maturana, Varela 1987, 28) Strictly spoken, we cannot claim: 'The sky is blue'. At most we can state: 'The sky appears blue to us'.

Constructivists distance themselves from ordinary theories, which understand knowledge as representation, as a portrait or as reflection of the objective world. Francisco Varela states: "In my opinion, the brain serves foremost the constant creation of worlds in the process of the viable history of beings; the brain is an organ, that defines worlds, it does not reflect the world" (Varela 1990, 109).

Although realisation is a biographically dependent and therefore highly individual, unique process, it occurs in social contexts. Viable, i.e. successful is knowledge usually when it is subject of a consensus. In this sense Francisco Varela defines intelligence "as the capacity to enter into a shared world" (Varela 1990, 111). Seen from this perspective cognitive constructivism is always also social constructivism: we construct our reality together with others in our social environments. Varela distinguishes three levels for the creation of life-worlds: the evolutionary-historical development, the individual-biographical development, and the socio-cultural development.

Naturally we do not only construct a world, we also live in a world. The world exists and we cannot ignore it. But the relationship between us and the outer world (the material as well as the social environment) is that of a 'structural joining'. There has to be a minimum of correspondence, of equivalence between our constructions and the environments for our actions to be viable, successful.

Humberto Maturana and Francisco Varela, who can be called the founders of modern constructivism (even though, as far as I know, they do not use the term constructivism) are biologists. Their famous book *Der Baum der Erkenntnis* (The Tree of Knowledge) carries the subtitle *Die biologischen Wurzeln des menschlichen Erkennens* (The Biological Roots of Human Realisation).

A key concept in biology is *autopoiesis*, which literally translated means self-creation. The Chilean researchers define living beings as "autopoietical organisations". "Therefore, in our opinion, the mechanism which turns living beings into autonomous systems is autopoiesis" (Maturana, Varela 1987, 55). "Existence and action of an autopoietical unit are inseparable, and that creates their special type of organisation" (Maturana, Varela 1987, 56).

Thus, also realisation can be understood as an autopoietical process. Perception, thinking, learning occurs – in contact with the environment – as an autopoietical, emergent, self referential process. In a literal sense it means: There is a freedom of thought as they develop a momentum and arise determined by structure rather than by the environment. From the outside thoughts can at best be stimulated, 'perturbed'.

> It seems obvious to us, that the interactions between unit and environment ... create reciprocal perturbations. During these interactions, the structure of the environment only triggers structural changes in the autopioetical units, it neither determines nor instructs them (Maturana, Varela 1987, 85).

The same holds for the relation between teaching and learning. I will focus on this at a later point.

It is possible to prove the autopoiesis of thinking with so called 'image-creating methods'. Our neuronal networks only process a minor part of the inputs from the outside. Instead they operate predominantly self organised and with their own momentum. Our brain communicates with itself, it activates and combines existing contents of our memory and knowledge. To give an example: when the phone rings our brain comes up with several hypotheses, about who would call us at this time with what intention. Even when we are listening to somebody we are carrying on an 'inner monologue', completing unfinished sentences of our conversation partner, connecting one thought to the corresponding areas of association in our brain. Thus, we hear what we hear, which is rarely identical with what the other says. Our brain action is synergetic and emergent and by no means simply receptive.

Erol Basar and Gerhard Roth, two brain researchers from Bremen, state:

> Most of what comes into our cortical networks (over 90%) originate in other cortical networks. From this perspective the cerebral cortex is a structure which basically 'speaks' to with itself. This supports an interpretation of the neo-cortex as an associative (mainly auto-associative) network (Basar, Roth 1996, 269).

Which leads to the thesis "that cognitive activities within the brain are based, at least partially, on the phenomena of resonance between activities of neuron populations" (Basar, Roth 1996, 315).

Chaos theory as well confirms this thesis of self organisation: Hermann Haken developed the "Idea of Self Organisation", "in which each single part of a system, for example the nerve cells of the brain, manage their cooperation all by themselves." Hermann Haken calls this "Doctrine of Cooperation" Synergetics. "Synergetics can be regarded as the most advanced theory of self organisation" (Haken, Haken-Krell 1997, 15).

For a neuro-scientifically 'enlightened' concept of learning this self organisation of the brain reveals that learning is essentially self controlled. Learning is in no way just an 'affirmative' process of assimilation, but it is the tying together of the contents of different neuronal areas. Synergetics can also create new qualities of realisation through the combination of cognitive, affective, and sensory processes. "Synergetics is not simply a theory of self organisation but, in a more general sense, a theory of the emergence of new qualities" (Haken 1996, 179).

One might object that these neuro-biological research results concern our every day realisation but not the scientific-empirical knowledge. It is a fact that our discerning observation of the meso-cosmos differs from the experiential investigation of the micro- and macro-cosmos of natural sciences. That is why the differences between every day lifeworlds and scientific research are not to be underestimated. But research results are dependent on observation and method. With an amusing story about Nils Bohr, who was awarded the Nobel-price for physics, Richard Bandler elucidates that even physics, as a supposedly objective science, only produces models and no timelessly valid truths. Nils Bohr is the 'inventor' of a model of the atom that consists of protons, neutrons and electrones. Based on this model many technological inventions were possible, that of plastic for instance.

> Only recently physicists decided that Bohr's description of the atom was wrong... Truly astonishing is that all the discoveries made possible through the use of this "wrong" model are still existing... Physics is often depicted as a very 'objective' science, but I realise that physics is changing while the world stays the same (Bandler 1987, 31).

Science's constructions of reality often differ from those of 'common sense', but scientists construct their object of research and their formulations of questions as well. Nevertheless, this is not about games of thought, since many of these models work and have changed the world. Helmut Peukert describes the epistemological change of modern natural sciences like this:

> Quantum mechanics, as formulated in the twenties by W. Heisenberg, N. Bohr, E. Schrödinger et al. proves more and more clearly to be the most important break through of natural sciences in the twentieth century... Its basic philosophical significance is due to the fact that the observer of quantum systems gets assigned a role which he does not have in classical physics: Through the choice of measuring devices he decides on reality at the same time... Reality can be determined only in strict correspondence with the action of the measuring person (Peukert 2000, 514).

Scientists do not describe the world as it 'really' is, they confront the world with their formulations of questions and their observations. Scientists see what their research devices 'allow' them to see.
Constructivism uses the concept of truth in a hesitant and relative way.

> Even empirical knowledge is only knowledge of the world as we see it and according to how we phrase this knowledge. The experience that it is possible to inter-subjectify empirical knowledge does not point to an independence of systems and cognitions, but to the degree of cognitive and communicative parallelism" (Schmidt 1998, 44).

Even when the difference of objective versus subjective is given up, scientific statements do neither become arbitrary nor is the necessity of empirical research being questioned.

> Empirical knowledge as the search for the most appropriate problem solutions retains specific qualities of differentiation compared to art, politics or religion. Even if there is no objective measure for the best problem solution at our disposal, science has proven criteria against arbitrariness, starting with the logical consistency of the argumentation, the simplicity of theory up to 'empirical research' (Schmidt 1998, 123).

Scientific knowledge is relative to observation, it is dependent on vantage points and perspectives, on epistemologically leading interests and traditions, on socio-historical and cultural contexts.

Learning as Construction

Learning is the vital process of the active acquisition of reality. Three forms of learning can be differentiated:
- learning as construction, i.e. as the building of action-relevant nets of knowledge,

- learning as reconstruction, i.e. as the acquisition and integration of existing contingents of knowledge (for example specialist knowledge),
- learning as deconstruction, i.e. gradual elimination of conduct patterns and normative orientations which are no longer viable (Reich 1996, 83 ff.).

These three forms of learning are usually interconnected. Learning is a complex process consisting of various activities which are linked circularly. Amongst those are for example
- curiosity, interest
- recollections, experiences, contents of memory
- sensory perception, targeted attentiveness
- declarative and procedural knowledge, nets of knowledge
- emotions, feelings
- physical sensations
- psychomotor actions

The close connection between realisation and action is one of the core theses of biological epistemology. "Each action is realising and each realising is action" (Maturana, Varela 1987, 31).

Needless to say, refraining from acting is part of acting. From a biological perspective learning serves the survival of the individual and the species. Learning facilitates "effective action of living beings in their environment" (Maturana, Varela 1987, 35) The learning of a Rilke poem can also serve life in this sense.

The more complicated, transitory, confused, and fragile our life worlds are the less sufficient is a pragmatic concept of efficiency, and the more necessary are observations of the second order and reflexive learning. Reflexive learning is the required learning quality in a risk society that can be described with Ulrich Beck as "reflexive modernity". Modern societies have reached a stage of endangerment in which the every day observations of the first order are no longer sufficient. What is needed is a meta-cognitive capacity to observe how we observe, how and on the basis of which leading differences we construct reality. The more complex the environment is, the more complex learning processes have to be.

Neuro-scientist Antonio Damasio points to this connection between environment and learning capacity.

When we consider our own species, however, and the far more varied and largely unpredictable environments in which we have thrived, it is apparent that we must rely on highly evolved genetically based biological mechanisms, as well as on suprainstinctual survival strategies that have developed in society, are transmitted by culture, and require, for their application, consciousness, reasoned deliberation, and willpower (Damasio 1994, 123).

In the nineteenth century the "popularisation of science" seemed to suffice for successful orientation, but today – in a time of globalisation, mediatisation, and research on embryos – the possibilities and limits of scientific realisation itself have to be 'learned', which also includes a considered dealing with 'ignorance' and with the dependency of all knowledge on observation.

Such an up-to-date concept of learning can neither be conceived only as a behaviouristic stimulus-reaction-learning nor solely as information processing according to the model of transmitter and receiver. A reflexive process of learning includes elements of the humanistic idea of education but also a rediscovery of common sense, and meta-cognitive competencies. The neuro-physiological patterns of this new quality of learning are yet unknown to a large extend, for example the question about the neuronal basis of meta-cognition. Antonio Damasio writes: "A task that faces neuroscientists today is to consider the neurobiology supporting adaptive supraregulations, by which I mean the study and understanding of the brain structures required to know about these regulations" (Damasio 1994, 124).

From a constructivist perspective the concept of learning can be characterised by the following features:

Emergence: Based on the self-organisation of the nervous system cognitive processes are emergent, which means that insights and ideas grow, ripen, and develop, partly even 'before-conscious'. Colloquial language uses vivid images for that: "It dawns on us" and "sudden insight". "Aha-experiences" are autopoietical achievements which cannot be planned.

Structure-determination: In the course of phylogenesis and ontogenesis cognitive and affective structures develop which constitute the frame for our understanding of the world. These structures – and not environmental stimuli – determine what is possible for human beings. (We have, for example, no sensory perception of ultraviolet radiation or radioactivity.) In other cultures – for example in Buddhism – different structures of the construction of reality have developed. Within our realisation structures "drifting" is possible (Kösel 1993).

Self-referentiality: The references for what is important, meaningful and remarkable for us, are within ourselves – even though meanings have developed in social and cultural contexts. That is why merely information can be 'communicated' in a linear way, meanings cannot be transmitted from one person to another.

Contingency: Learning processes are contingent, that is ambiguous, enigmatic, fleeting. Learning, thinking, and feeling develops a momentum and withdraws partly from conscious control. Nobody is able to 'read thoughts', and often our own thoughts are not clear to us, there is a seething unrest in our head.

Connectability: Learning is most of all making connections. New material is anchored in the familiar. When we read or hear something memories awaken, areas of association become active. Thus, learning is biographical and highly individual. One and the same message will be discerned and encoded differently by each person. The assumption that in a seminar group everyone learns the same thing at the same time is one of the common myths in (adult) education. Learning is – metaphorically spoken – differentiation, supplementation and correction of existing nets of knowledge.

Perception of difference: Even when new contents of learning should be connectable, they have to differ from the already existing knowledge. Adapting everything to existing cognitive systems means being resistant to learning. Perceiving only confirmations and no differences means stagnation. The acceptance and testing of new distinctions and leading differences present a qualitative 'jump' in a learning biography. New leading differences facilitate new perspectives and new crossings of perspectives. In this sense Heinz von Foerster defines learning as the increase of possibilities of thinking and feeling (von Foerster 1993, 78).

Situation relevance: We do not learn abstract rules but learn in a situated way, i.e. through experiences in concrete situations. Learning refers almost always to situations of usage. This holds for mathematics and foreign languages as well as for poetry of the baroque period. The learning activity is situated, too, which means it happens at a certain time, at a certain (learning-) place in social and biographical contexts. "Situated cognition" is a consequence from the science of cognition made of constructivist ideas (Weinert, Mandl 1997, 366).

Viability: Learning goals, contents and methods have to be viable, i.e. they have to be experienced as appropriate, useful, and helpful. Not all subjects and learning challenges are psycho-hygienically reasonable for everyone at any time. Thus, many educators often do with good intentions too much instruction and teaching. Included in viability is the need for homeostasis, i.e. a cognitive equilibrium, coherence of world view, a need for 'tidyness in the head'. Insecurities and perturbations have to be measured in careful doses; motivation psychology speaks of "measured discrepancy".

Circularity: Learning processes do not proceed in a linear or straight forward way, instead they are interdependent, interlinked, with loops and detours. Most of all thinking, feeling and doing can often only be comprehended as circular processes. Hartmut von Hentig spoke of learning as being messy. The circularity of learning cannot be controlled, but it can be allowed and supported.

Emotionality: Learning is not a purely cognitive process, it is emotionally embedded. Learning tasks, but also learning methods and learning contents are affectively tinted, coupled with feelings of pleasure or reluctance. Learning successes 'are fun', learning disorders are annoying. Luc Ciompi draws attention to the "affect-logic" of learning. Emotions are the "motors" of cognitive processes and control our sensory attention. Emotions and moods are "organisers" of our thinking and realisation, emotions influence our memories and the choice of our memory contents, they choose the contents of thinking and thus facilitate a "reduction of complexity" (Ciompi 1999, 95 ff). Also Antonio Damasio emphasises the connection between cognition, emotion and physical being:

The hypothalamus, the brain stem, and the limbic system intervene in body regulation and in all neural processes on which mind phenomena are based, for example, perception, learning, recall, emotion and feeling, and ... reasoning and creativity. Body regulation, survival, and mind are intimately interwoven (Damasio 1994, 123).

Production of knowledge: Constructivism emphasises the constructivity of human knowledge. Our world consists foremost of nets of concepts and knowledge, which, on the one hand, are fed from 'outside' – for example through mass media – but which are, on the other hand, active and constructive achievements of individuals. Knowledge in this sense cannot be compared with information and communication, knowledge is dependent on life phases and life circumstances, on social and cultural contexts, and on offers of the media. Thus, knowledge is relative, provisional and dependent on observation. Even scientific knowledge is not learned receptively, but is being mixed with personal experience, with emotions, with implicit knowledge. In this way distinctive nets of knowledge and patterns of interpretation are built. Learning requirements rise with the complexity of the world and the speed of social and technical change. Lifelong learning is indispensable, learning resistance is, in the long run, life threatening. Permanent learning requests can become an unreasonable and excessive demand. That is why learning capacity includes the setting of priorities and the differentiation between the important and the unimportant. Partial learning refusals can be viable, too.

The Reception of Constructivism in Adult Education

Constructivist thinking has a tradition in German adult education. At the beginning of the twentieth century – in the context of reform pedagogy – a feeling of uneasiness grew towards the dominant idea of popularising science. Most of all, the 'new direction' in adult education of the Weimar Republic, which was influenced by the youth movement, criticised the predominantly schoolish, 'extensive' transmission of knowledge and propagated an 'intensively' life-world oriented acquisition of knowledge. The organisational form of study groups in which theoreticians and practical workers were learning with and from one another, was to replace methods of lecturing and didactic chalk and talk teaching. *Bildung* was no longer defined as knowledge of classical cultural assets, but as a learning process anchored in biography and life-world. Education was less seen as a result than as a 'searching process'.

In 1926 Eduard Weitsch said that the study group should reflect on the difficulties of life in an experience oriented way, so that what is found anchors deeply in the mind (Weitsch 1926, 285).

Alfred Mann, head of an adult education institute in Breslau, developed a didactics of adult education from the 'I-perspective'. Education is not about replacing wrong knowledge of the participants with right, scientific knowledge, but taking the world view and the questions of the learning persons serious. "The duty of the teacher is not the simple transmission, but to deal with the student's view of life... He has to pay attention and respect, yes, observe the students' questions, he has to look with a loving soul right into the depth of the student soul" (Mann 1928/1948, 30).

The interpretative paradigm runs like a red thread through the discussions about the self-understanding of adult education, and makes visible some moderately constructivist positions. For example, Hans Tietgens, nestor of modern adult education, speaks of "life in the modus of interpretation". He says:

> Human beings are able to learn because they can refer to themselves... To assume that the world meets us directly is fictitious... One has to reflect on the societal reality being only existent in the way of human interpretation. The idea that subject and object can be clearly separated, that it can be stated what belongs to the "I" and what to the world, that it is possible to draw a line between the inside and the outside has to be overcome... Learning is a debate between the new offer and the way in which new material has been processed so far (Tietgens 1981, 90-91).

In this way Hans Tietgens points implicitly to the self-referenciality and the structural determination of learning.

To my knowledge, the first adult educationist to explicitly refer to the epistemology of (radical) constructivism was Ortfried Schäffter in 1986. He problematised the "mostly tacidly assumed link between 'Teaching' and 'Learning'" (Schäffter 1986/1997, 28).

Teaching and learning can be conceived as two self referential, at the most structurally joined systems. "A total identity of meanings between living beings is ... basically impossible. 'The Other' remains ... unreachable as regards immediate, externally controlled information" (Schäffter 1986/1997, 30).

> For teaching to be something different than instruction, indoctrination or conditioning can only mean that the teaching person has to limit himself to the fostering and methodological support of an autonomously proceeding cognitive development in the learning person" (Schäffter 1986/1997, 33).

Ortfried Schäffter problematised a naive orientation towards the participant. If the thesis of an operational unity and emergence of cognition is taken seriously, each participant can only learn self oriented. Teaching cannot control these autopoietical processes, it can, at the most, observe, create stimulating environments etc. Ortfried Schäffter's indication to the relevance of constructivism in adult education died away without resonance, at that time.

However, the approach of interpretation patterns made a career for itself (Arnold 1985). Learning in adult education was most of all conceived as reflection and differentiation of experiences and interpretations, thus as constructions of reality (Arnold, Siebert 1997). Interpretations are relative to observation and dependent on a context, they are shaped by biographical experiences and socio-economic circumstances. Interpretations are tied to interests and cannot be replaced by scientific knowledge. Though, in many ways the differentiation of appropriate and inappropriate interpretations, of 'right' and 'wrong consciousness' remained untouched, in which those teaching secretly valued their interpretations higher, so that a pedagogical 'monopoly of interpretation' and the 'gradient of maturity' was maintained.

In the middle of the nineties the leading concept of participant orientation was superseded by the metaphor of self-directed learning.

Self-directed learning is a continuation and radicalisation of participant orientation. The participant is released from a – well meant but paternalistic – teacher-student relationship. At the same time, self-directing refers to a change of perspective. In the middle of the nineties the programme of "lifelong learning for all" was propagated globally, for instance at the UNESCO-World Conference. At the same time, the extension of further education and the exemption of employees for the participation in qualification measures seemed to have reached its limits in terms of financing and business management. Furthermore, empirical proof was piling up that the linear equation "more participation in further education = more competencies = more competitiveness" does not work out. Personal and social competencies can hardly be learned in seminars, instead they are acquired in the social and professional every day settings (Erpenbeck, Heyse 1999). 'Lean education' appeared not only as an economical compromise, but also as modernisation strategy justified by learning theories. Self-directed learning was regarded as an attractive alternative to externally organised and institutionalised further education. As a theoretical justification it was referred to humanistic psychology, epistemology, chaos theory, and biological, but even more, constructivist system theory. Simplified the message read: "From the basic assumptions of constructivist system theory follows a very radical and sceptical evaluation of the controllability of social systems." And: "Plotability, targeted action, and success are, in the light of this theory, no more than myths" (Greif, Kurtz 1996, 56-57).

Balance and Perspectives

Critical doubt, as to whether the world really is the way we perceive it, are not new in European history of philosophy. The constructivist literature refers to Phyrron of Elis, Socrates, Vico, Berkeley, Kant, Schopenhauer, Nietzsche, but also to Piaget, Gadamer, Berger/Luckmann, symbolic interactionism, and the American pragmatism. What is remarkable about the contemporary constructivism is the transdisciplinary discourse, the links between biological, neuro-scientific, psychological, communication theoretical, and social scientific perspectives, so that we can talk about a systemic-constructivist paradigm. Wolf Singer, Hermann Haken, Antonio Damasio, John Searle are also scientists who contribute to the discourse, but without expressively using the concept of constructivism. In Germany it was most of all Siegfried Schmidt who pushed forward constructivist ideas. In 1987 two main publications appeared in German: *Der Baum der Erkenntnis* (The Tree of Knowledge) by Humberto Maturana and Francisco Varela, and *Der Diskurs des radikalen Konstruktivismus* (The Discourse of Radical Constructivism), edited by Siegfried Schmidt. Also, Paul Watzlawick: *Wie wirklich ist die Wirklichkeit?* (How Real is Reality?) in 1976/1987 (fifteenth edition), and later Niklas Luhmann with a.o. *Soziologische Aufklärung* (Social Enlightenment) 1990 (fifth edition) have contributed to the circulation of constructivist ideas.

In the 1990s the profile of constructivism has been sharpened and at the same time a differentiation of the positions is noticeable – for example in a cognitive, social and cultural constructivism, but also in moderate and radical trends.

One of the foremost representatives of radical constructivism is Ernst von Glasersfeld. The core thesis of his cognition theory is: "Radical constructivism is based on the assumption, that all knowledge ... only exists in the heads of the people, and that the thinking subject is only able to construct knowledge on the basis of his personal experience" (Glasersfeld 1997, 22). But the thesis derived from this, that outer reality were totally 'inaccessible' to us in a cognitive way, is even within constructivism rather a minority position. Nevertheless, Glasersfeld's concept of knowledge is pedagogically stimulating: "(a) Knowledge is not passively absorbed by the thinking subject, but actively developed. (b) The function of cognition is adaptive and allows the organisation of realms of experience, not the discovery of an ontological reality" (Glasersfeld 1997, 48). Glasersfeld is the first one to design a frame for constructivist pedagogy.

Most of all it was Siegfried Schmidt who contributed to a reflexive, self-critical discussion within constructivism.[1] When I interviewed Siegfried Schmidt in August 2000 he stated in retrospect: Since 1987

> an intensive analysis of the criticism towards constructivism has taken place, which was justified, from my point of view. I mean the criticism that neuro-biological root positions remained unquestioned and were accepted as objective knowledge. Also the second accusation of a too narrow subject orientation... A third criticism came from the former colleagues from Erlangen, Peter Janich for instance, and was concerned with a lack of action in constructivism. His argument was: Constructivism concerns itself with language, with consciousness, but not with practical action (Schmidt in Siebert 2001, 42).

In this interview Siegfried Schmidt pleads for a stronger connection between constructivism and cultural- and media sciences:

> In how far is the media a structurally semantic instrument of cognition? Does the media achieve a structural link between cognitive and communicative processes? How are the offers of the media lined up with cultural patterns? (Schmidt in Siebert 2001, 42; see also Schmidt/Zurstiege 2000)

The 'career' of the constructivist paradigm has to be interpreted in a socio-historical context. There is, without any doubt, an affinity between constructivist realisation theory and philosophy of the post-modern age (Welsch 1996), but also to the thesis of individualisation, and the concept of reflexive modernity (Beck 1995). In view of the erosion of scientific and religious claims of truth, and looking at the omnipresence of virtual realities and an aestheticising of our life-worlds Paul Watzlawick's question "How Real is Reality?" is more relevant than ever. A new title says very

---

[1] Compare also the controversial discussion with Ernst von Glasersfeld (Glasersfeld 1997, 310 ff).

appropriately *Reality in the Age of Disappearance* (Urban, Engelhardt 2000). The conventional codes true/untrue, real/unreal prove to be increasingly insufficient. Is it 'right' or 'wrong' when young people chain themselves to train tracks in order to oppose transports of radioactive waste containers, when a physician is sentenced because he administered euthanasia, when the Chancellor says that the critics of embryo research wear "ideological blinkers"? Siegfried Schmidt carries out a change of perspective when he states: "There is always as much reality as there is active differentiation in communication" (Schmidt in Siebert 2001, 43).

What is more, in the past years the insight has gained prominence, that complex systems – social as well as psychic systems – can only partially be organised and controlled administratively and socio-technologically. The more complex the system the more momentum and self-organisation have to be admitted. Bureaucratic overcontrolling is rather contra-productive, also in the educational system. Curricular concepts striving to standardise and regulate learning by learning goal operationalism and programming have also in didactics only partly proven their worth.

Thus, self organisation has become a key concept within systemic-constructivist thinking. As regards further education John Erpenbeck and Volker Heyse point out: The "correlation of self organisation, competency development, and biography suggests to now move the theory of self organisation into the centre of consideration" (Erpenbeck, Heyse 1999, 133).

Constructivist epistemology is trendy and *en vogue*. But constructivism is not a supra-theory offering answers to all political, economical, and moral questions. Klaus-Peter Hufer criticises: "Constructivism cannot offer answers to right wing extremism, xenophobia, unemployment, climatic shifts" (Hufer 2001, 5). In fact it does not want to do that. It is interested in the perception of those problems. Klaus-Peter Hufer continues:

> The dissolving of connections, desolidarisation, the elbow mentality, self assertion, self regulation, and self production are considered legitimate on the basis of a convenient epistemology. Thus, constructivism gets under suspicion to

administer ideological aid to societies in which the stronger, faster, and more beautiful push through" (Hufer 2001, 6).

These presumptions call to mind a moralising pedagogy, everything gets mixed up here.

Educational scientists have occupied themselves with constructivism relatively late and rather restrained. Educational constructivists are a small minority even today (Reich 1998, Voß 1996, Kösel 1993). On the other hand, a 'subject orientation' in teaching and criticism towards normative didactics of instruction are widely spread at least in theory.

In his book *Orientierung Erziehungswissenschaft* (Orientation Educational Science) from 1999, Dieter Lenzen deals with the system-theoretical and constructivist conception as one of seven theoretical orientations.

> If what we usually call 'perception' of reality has to be seen rather as a construction of this reality, it would mean that also learning, as being related with perception, has to be viewed as a construction of reality... This has far reaching consequences for education and the classroom" (Lenzen 1999, 155).

This conception parts with the idea that education and classes could be guided by goals, or processes determined by norms, which help to educate or even manipulate people (Lenzen 1999). The assumption that "people could be influenced to the extent that they alter their behaviour cannot be maintained today", says Dieter Lenzen (1999, 157).

Ewald Terhart, educational scientist from Bochum, draws a critical balance from the debate on constructivism. Terhart reconstructs the systemtheoretically constructivist positions carefully. He is

> surprised that virtually nothing really surprises... What is the reason for this normality – after such a 'radical' beginning? One of the reasons is the fact that in didactic contexts constructivism is never represented in its radical, but always in an already moderated form (Terhart 1999, 637).

This "moderation" has good reasons: "Only a moderate position opens systematically as well as practically the possibility and legitimacy of an activity such as teaching" (Terhart 1999, 638). Terhart emphasises the claim of the subject matter, which "is in my mind constitutive and thus irrefutable for organised teaching and learning in schools" (Terhart 1999, 642).

The question is not whether constructivism is good or bad, right or wrong. The decisive factor is whether it stimulates pedagogical action, whether it facilitates new experiences, and opens new didactic possibilities.

It is obvious that constructivism is also momentous for (adult) educational research. Research is also observation, and research results are dependent on observation. "As regards to research concerned with communication in class, the interpretative direction has in general much more asserted itself than the examining one. There is "an increasing attempt to use the full wealth of interpretation of data" (Nolda 2000, 26). One example for the variety in perspectives is the comparison of different versions of a seminar protocol (Arnold et al. 1998).

In principle it has to be remembered: Constructivism is an analytical, descriptive epistemology, and the science of education offers action theories. Pedagogical action has to be examined in regards to how it gets along with constructivist positions; but pedagogical action cannot be derived from an epistemology.

References

Arnold, R. (1985). *Deutungsmuster und pädagogisches Handeln in der Erwachsenenbildung.* Bad Heilbrunn.

Arnold, R. (1993). *Natur als Vorbild.* Frankfurt/M.

Arnold, R. et al. (1998). *Lehren und Lernen im Modus der Auslegung.* Hohengehren.

Arnold, R.; Siebert, H. (1997). *Konstruktivistische Erwachsenenbildung.* Hohengehren.

Bandler, R. (1987). *Veränderung des subjektiven Erlebens.* Paderborn.

Basar, E., Roth, G. (1996). Ordnung aus dem Chaos: Kooperative Gehirnprozesse bei kognitiven Leistungen. In: Küppers, G. (ed.). *Chaos und Ordnung,* Stuttgart, pp. 290-322.

Beck, U. (1995). *Die feindlose Demokratie.* Stuttgart.

Beck, U., Giddens, A., Lash, S. (1996). *Reflexive Modernisierung.* Frankfurt/M.

Ciompi, L. (1997). *Die emotionalen Grundlagen des Denkens.* Göttingen.

Damasio, A. (2000). *Descartes' Irrtum.* München.

Damasio, A. (1994) *Descartes' Error, Emotion, Reason, and the Human Brain.* New York.

Erpenbeck, J., Heyse, V. (1999). *Die Kompetenzbiografie.* Münster.

Foerster, H. von (1993). *KybernEthik.* Berlin.

Gerstenmaier, J., Mandl, H. (1999). *Konstruktivistische Ansätze in der Erwachsenenbildung.* In: Tippelt, R. (ed.). *Handbuch Erwachsenenbildung/Weiterbildung,* Opladen, pp. 184-192.

Glasersfeld, E. von (1997). *Radikaler Konstruktivismus.* Frankfurt/M.

Greif, S., Kurtz, H. J. (eds.) (1996). *Handbuch Selbstorganisiertes Lernen.* Göttingen.

Haken, H. (1996). *Der synergetische Computer.* In: Küppers, G. (ed.). *Chaos und Ordnung,* Stuttgart, pp. 176-199.

Haken, H., Haken-Krell, M. (1997). *Gehirn und Verhalten.* Stuttgart.

Hufer, P. (2001). Konstruktivismus in der Kritik. In: *Erwachsenenbildung* 2(2001), pp. 2-6.

Janich, P. (1996). *Konstruktivismus und Naturerkenntnis.* Frankfurt/M.

Kösel, E. (1993). *Die Modellierung von Lernwelten.* Elztal.

Küppers, G. (ed.) (1996). *Chaos und Ordnung.* Stuttgart.

Lenzen, D. (1999). *Orientierung Erziehungswissenschaft.* Reinbek b. Hamburg.

Luhmann, N. (1990). *Soziologische Aufklärung.* Opladen.

Mann, A. (1928). *Denkendes Volk, volkhaftes Denken.* Frankfurt/M.

Maturana, H., Varela, F. (1987). *Der Baum der Erkenntnis.* München.

Meixner, J. (1997). *Konstruktivismus und die Vermittlung produktiven Wissens.* Neuwied.

Müller, K. (1996). *Konstruktivismus.* Neuwied.

Nolda, S. (2000). *Interaktion in pädagogischen Institutionen.* Opladen.

Peukert, H. (2000). Reflexionen über die Zukunft von Bildung. In: *Zeitschrift für Pädagogik* 4 (2000), pp. 507-524.

Reich, K. (1996). Systemisch-konstruktivistische Didaktik. In: Voß, R. (ed.) *Die Schule neu erfinden,* Neuwied, pp. 70-91.

Reich, K. (1998). *Die Ordnung der Blicke.* Neuwied.

Schäffter, O. (1986). Lehrkompetenz in der Erwachsenenbildung als Sensibilität für Fremdheit. Reprinted in: Schäffter, O. (1997). *Das Eigene und das Fremde.* Berlin, pp. 18-31.

Schmidt, S. (ed.) (1987). *Der Diskurs des Radikalen Konstruktivismus.* Frankfurt/M.

Schmidt, S. (1998). *Die Zähmung des Blicks.* Frankfurt/M.

Schmidt, S., Zurstiege, G. (2000). *Orientierung Kommunikationswissenschaft*. Reinbek b. Hamburg.

Searle, J. (1997). *Die Konstruktion der gesellschaftlichen Wirklichkeit*. Reinbek b. Hamburg.

Siebert, H. (1999). *Pädagogischer Konstruktivismus*. Neuwied.

Siebert, H. (2001). *Selbstgesteuertes Lernen und Lernberatung*. Neuwied.

Terhart, E. (1999). Konstruktivismus und Unterricht. In: *Zeitschrift für Pädagogik*, 5 (1999), pp. 629-647.

Tietgens, H. (1981). *Die Erwachsenenbildung*. München.

Tippelt, R. (ed.) (1999). *Handbuch Erwachsenenbildung/Weiterbildung*. Opladen.

Urban, C., Engelhardt, J. (eds.) (2000). *Wirklichkeit im Zeitalter ihres Verschwindens*. Münster.

Varela, F. (1990). *Kognitionswissenschaft – Kognitionstechnik*. Frankfurt/M.

Voß, R. (ed.) (1996). *Die Schule neu erfinden*. Neuwied.

Watzlawick, P. (1976). *Wie wirklich ist die Wirklichkeit?* München.

Weinert, F., Mandl, H. (eds.) (1997). *Psychologie der Erwachsenenbildung*. Göttingen.

Weitsch, E. (1926). Zur Technik des Volkshochschulunterrichts. Reprinted in: Tietgens, H. (1969). *Erwachsenenbildung zwischen Romantik und Aufklärung*. Göttingen, pp. 199 ff.

Welsch, W. (1996). *Vernunft*. Frankfurt/M.

Etienne Bourgeois

A CONSTRUCTIVIST APPROACH TO ADULT LEARNING

Adult Learning and Learners: A Special Species?

Before discussing the constructivist model of learning and its relevance as a frame of reference to study adult learning, we first need to clarify some epistemological assumptions underlying this theory as used in our research on adult learning. First, this model is a theoretical model, that is, whose primary function is to describe and interpret how the learning process works rather than how it should work. In other words, it is primarily an intelligible model, not a prescriptive model, or a guide for practice. In this sense, in our view there is no such a thing as a 'constructivist' method or practice of (adult) teaching. The constructivist model in itself does not say anything about the best practices to teach adults in a given context. However, understanding how the learning process works is of course essential to develop teaching practice. Whereas it is crucial to be able to articulate the two levels – i.e. intelligibility of the learning process and reflection about practices to promote learning – it is no less important to avoid confusion between them.

Secondly, we are not using the constructivist model with a view to building a theory of adult learning as opposed to child learning, or school learning, or any other learning. Such a perspective would assume that the adult learner is to be approached *a priori* as a specific species (as heavily emphasised by Knowles and the Andragogy movement behind him in the 1970s) of learner, which would be different by essence from other learners. In contrast, we prefer to start with the constructivist model as a general theory of learning, which highlights some key variables and relationships among them that characterise the learning process. Then, in the light of such a theory, we can examine the particular configuration of factors that characterise the learners and the learning setting under study and its consequences for the learning process. From this perspective, we can examine for instance the difference between learning in a particular school situation and learning in a particular adult learning situation with respect to some factors (individual and/or situational) whose role is supposed to be crucial according to the (general) theory. Therefore, in this perspective, it might happen that learning in a given school setting turns out to be more similar to learning in an adult education setting than to learning in another school setting, depending on the variables on focus and the specific characteristics of those learning settings and learners with respect to those variables. In sum, what we are trying to do in our research on adult learning is to examine how some of the factors and processes that are underlined by the constructivist theory of learning operate in particular adult education settings.

The third assumption derives from the second. If the study of adult learning (as learning in any other setting) is to be driven by a general theory of learning, then research on adult learning should be informed not only by adult education research but also by research conducted in other educational areas. For example, research on group learning in adult education settings could be enriched by considering the research outputs on sociocognitive conflicts or cooperative learning originally developed in relation to school settings. This is not to say of course that the hypotheses that have been validated in one setting should *a priori* be taken for granted in another setting, but at least, they should be given serious theoretical and empirical attention to inspire further research. In our view, the same reasoning should also prevail with respect to research methodology. Instead of trying to define a supposedly specific methodology of research on adult learning, it seems to us that research in the field would gain much by combining various methodologies, including those that prevail in research on learning in other settings. In fact, the constructivist theory of learning is grounded on empirical research that appears quite diverse in terms of methodologies.[1]

---

[1] Incidentally, such epistemological assumptions also have very concrete implications in terms of institutional position and professional identity for adult education in the field of social sciences. In particular, they urge us to take the research on adult learning out of the theoretical and methodological ghetto in which it is too often

Piagetian Constructivism and Adult Learning

Piaget's theory of cognitive development (Gruber, Voneche 1977) basically consists of two major components. On the one hand, it provides a fine description of the successive stages of the human cognitive development. It details the various operational schemata that characterise each development stage and the order in which they develop over time. On the other hand, Piaget also provides a theory to explain how one goes up from one stage to another. More specifically, this theory accounts for the process through which a cognitive structure can be transformed into another structure of a higher developmental level. In this sense, Piaget provides not only a theory of intelligence (describing the different stages of the cognitive development and their succession) but also a theory of learning (explaining how the cognitive schemata that are characteristic of a given developmental stage can be transformed into schemata of higher levels). It is therefore mainly this second part of Piaget's work that we are referring to. Although Piaget's theory of learning was originally designed to account for learning of cognitive operational schemata specifically (e.g. conservation of weight or volume, or logical operations) it has since been extended to various types of learning, including the learning of concepts and theories (see e.g. Schnotz, Vosniadou 1999), in different educational contexts, including school[2], on-the-job training (see Pastré 1999) and adult education more broadly (Bourgeois, Nizet 1997).

Constructivism, Cognitivism and Behaviourism

One of the most central assumptions of the constructivist paradigm is its emphasis on the role of the individual's mental activity in her interactions with the environment. With this assumption constructivism opposes behaviourism, which postulates that the individual's behaviour is entirely determined by external influences, without any mental mediation by the

---

confined. They induce us to bridge the gap with other fields of research instead of striving to assert and defend the alleged specificity of adult education against other areas of educational research and complaining about the lack of legitimacy of adult education research.

[2] See the extensive literature on learning and instruction in various disciplines, in particular science education.

individual. Clearly, Piagetian constructivism shares this assumption with contemporary cognitivism and, more generally, with other constructivist approaches in social sciences (e.g. Berger, Luckmann 1991). For them, what matters in order to understand human behaviour is not the influence of the external reality *per se*, but the influence of reality as mentally constructed (or represented) by the individual (or the social group, depending on the level of analysis). From a psychological point of view, the mental activity exerted by the individual upon his or her significant environment in a given situation is structured, organised, guided by internal mental structures (procedural and/or declarative knowledge activated by the individual in that situation). However, as opposed to the cognitivist paradigm (and its ancestor, the *Gestaltpsychologie*), Piagetian constructivism focuses primarily on the history – or to use the Piagetian vocabulary, the genesis – of those cognitive structures. The cognitivist paradigm accounts for the processes through which internal cognitive structures are activated and used by the individual to deal with situations but it does not pay much attention to the origin of those structures in understanding the individual's cognitive activity. Likewise, it also tends to neglect the question of the evolution of the structure as a result of its use in the current situation. In contrast, Piagetian constructivism focuses on the process through which cognitive structures change as a result of their mobilisation by the individual in his or her interactions with the environment. In sum, Piagetian constructivism is constructivist in two ways. First, it emphasises the role of the mental construction of reality by the individual. The individual-environment interactions are mediated by the individual's mental activity and this activity is based on internal cognitive structures activated by the individual to deal with situations. Second, it focuses on the construction (genesis) of the cognitive structures that are mobilised in that mental activity, that is, the process through which an existing structure may be transformed into a new structure as a result of its use by the individual in her interactions with the environment.

Assimilation and Accommodation in the Learning Process

In the Piagetian constructivist view[3], such a transformation is called learning. Basically, it consists of two distinct but closely intertwined subprocesses, namely, assimilation and accommodation and can be roughly described as follows. Let us take an example: Barbara is an adult student attending a course in sociology at the university. The teacher is starting a new chapter focusing on the theories of power. At the beginning of the class session, she provides the students with a case telling the story of a conflict between a group of teachers and the school headmaster. The sociology professor asks students to read the case, to summarise and interpret the problem at issue and to make their own suggestions as to how the problem could be solved.

Activation. Barbara thus starts to read the case. While doing so, she is activating some of the knowledge structures she has stored in her long-term memory as a result of previous learning experiences. In particular, it is very likely that in this situation, she is tackling the text with her own 'theory' of power in mind. In this theory, resulting from past experiences (formal education and life experience), power is seen basically as an attribute possessed to a variable degree by individuals in an organisation. It is a function mainly of the formal position one occupies in the hierarchy and is manifested by a wide variety of specific artefacts and behaviours. Why has this knowledge structure been activated by Barbara in this situation rather than any other structure yet available in her memory? Typically, both situational and individual factors may influence the activation process (Beauvois, Deschamps, 1990). For example, it is very likely that the general context of the task (a sociology course on power) and the teacher's specific instructions (to deal with a case describing the use of power relationships in a given organisation) does play a major role in that 'choice', as well as, for example, the fact that Barbara has recently experienced a similar situation in her life, which left her with a particular vivid memory, and which she had interpreted in that way.

---

[3] The following presentation of the learning process from a Piagetian constructivist view is based on Piaget (1967, 1968, 1975) as well as Gruber and Voneche (1977). The example is adapted from Bourgeois and Nizet (1997).

Assimilation. The conception of power activated by Barbara will now serve as a 'reference guide' in her approach to the case. She is selecting and organising the available information on that basis. For example, her attention is being drawn to all clues informing her about who in the story has the power and who does not have it. She is looking at all the relevant indicators which, according to her prior conception, characterise the amount of power possessed by the actors. She is also establishing relationships among all the selected pieces of information. For example, while going through the story, at some point she is making predictive (and/or causal) inferences about the actors' respective behaviours and their consequences. In short, she is gradually making sense out of the text, she is building a representation of it (Richard 1990), on the basis of (i) the prior knowledge structures activated in the situation, (ii) the information contained in the text and (iii) the information about the task and its context. In Piaget's terms, the individual incorporates the new information she is confronted with into the structure activated to deal with that information (assimilation structure). This is the assimilation process.

Cognitive Conflict. It may happen that all the information attended to by the individual 'fits' the activated assimilation structure into which it has been incorporated. For example, all the inferences made by Barbara are confirmed, or at least, are not refuted in the case study, on the basis of the information attended to. In that case, her prior conception of power remains unchanged. It may even come out reinforced by such a confirmatory application. However, this is not always the case. Sometimes, as the assimilation (sense-making) process goes on, a piece of information may turn out to be discrepant from the activated assimilation structure, for instance, when an inference made at some point in the reading process is contradicted by further information in the text. This phenomenon is referred to as a cognitive conflict by Piaget. For example, on the basis of her conception of power and the available information Barbara had first inferred that (i) the school headmaster is more powerful than the teachers (given their respective formal positions in the formal hierarchy and other relevant individual attributes) and (ii) therefore the headmaster will eventually 'win' the conflict with the teachers. However, below in the text, she is discovering that the teachers, not the headmaster, have won the struggle.

Homeostatic Regulation of Cognitive Conflict. The emergence of a cognitive conflict generates a perturbation, an imbalance of the activated structure. At least for a while, Barbara's prior conception of power is being challenged by the unexpected information she is provided with. Such an uncomfortable situation typically urges the individual to try to restore the equilibrium, the 'fit' between the activated structure and discrepant information. Piaget distinguishes two types of cognitive conflict solving strategy. One is what he calls the homeostatic regulation. By this strategy the individual strives to solve the conflict in a way that leaves the initial assimilation structure unchanged. Barbara could for instance discard the discrepant information, or reinterpret it so as to have it eventually fit the initial structure (e.g. she can rationalise that in fact, beyond the first impression, the headmaster did lose the battle against the teachers, or else that some of the teachers do possess more power attributes than originally envisioned). By doing so, Barbara is solving the conflict (the discrepancy is eventually reduced) while maintaining the initial structure unchanged (her original conception of power as an individual attribute is eventually maintained). In other words, she is restoring the equilibrium by adjusting the information to the initial structure.[4] Thus, no learning has occurred. The initial structure has 'resisted' to change.

Accommodation. However, the cognitive conflict may be solved in another way, that is, by adjusting (or in Piaget's words, accommodating) the initial structure to the discrepant information. In our example, the sociology teacher could emphasise the discrepancy between Barbara's inference based on her initial conception of power and the information and have her think about it. She could for instance have Barbara read a chapter of the textbook on a theory of power which views power not as an individual attribute but as a relationship between at least two actors based on dependence. This reading and the additional information it provides help Barbara to look at the case from a new perspective and eventually to transform her original conception of power into a new one which can (better) account for the once discrepant information. This is what Piaget calls the accommodation process. It is only in this case that learning occurs.

---

[4] See Bourgeois and Nizet (1997) for an extensive discussion of cognitive strategies related to the homeostatic regulation of cognitive conflicts.

Assimilation and Accommodation in Action

In a first set of studies, we examined how these assimilation-accommodation processes actually operate in real adult learning situations. Several case studies were conducted with adult learners attending a sociology class in a university non-traditional programme of social and economic studies (undergraduate level). These studies were longitudinal. Four adult learners were interviewed individually three times: at the beginning of the course, right after it, and six months later. The objective of the interviews was to explore the learner's conceptions (declarative knowledge) in relation to the issues being dealt with in the course and to identify the changes in those conceptions over time.[5] These studies provide very fine descriptions and illustrations of how the activation, assimilation, cognitive conflict and accommodation processes actually operate in real adult learning situations. With respect to the original theory, those studies highlighted quite interesting points (Bourgeois, Nizet 1999).

For example, it was shown that most of the time the accommodation of a given knowledge structure does not result from the learner's confrontation with a single source of new (discrepant) information but rather from the interaction between two main sources of information, namely, current or past life experiences and concepts and theories met in the course of study. In other words, the learner's meeting with a new concept or theory does bring about change in her prior knowledge structures only to the extent that this concept or theory is related by the learner to some life experiences. Conversely, it is the learner's meeting with the concept that made the assimilation (Piagetian sense) of the information provided by those life experiences, and subsequently the accommodation of the initial structure, possible.

Another interesting observation is that the learner's exposure to new (discrepant) information may sometimes lead to accommodation only indirectly. We observed that in some instances the assimilation of a new concept does not result immediately and directly in transformation of the initial assimilation structure. What may happen though is that the assimi-

---

[5] One of these case studies is extensively presented and discussed in Bourgeois and Nizet (1999). Those studies were followed by dozens of similar studies conducted by our students in the last six years.

lation of the concept enable the learner subsequently to take into account and cognitively elaborate past experiences (which would not have been cognitively processed otherwise), which in turn brings about cognitive conflict and ultimately accommodation.

The case studies also highlighted the effects of accommodation in terms of reinforcement of learning as a result of its transfer to life experience. Changes in the learner's perspectives (her way of looking at the others, the world and herself) may have consequences for real life experience that are perceived by the learners as positive both in terms of action (e.g. it leads the learner to consider new strategies for solving significant problems in her life) and in terms of understanding (e.g. it provides the learner with new interpretations of reality that will appear more relevant). These consequences also appear to be often associated with positive emotions.

Another striking observation is the great inertia of the prior knowledge structures activated in the learning process. This is observed in the massive use of homeostatic strategies, which enable the learner to solve a cognitive conflict without changing her assimilation structures. It is also evidenced by the tremendous gap that may sometimes be observed between the concept as originally taught in the course and the same concept as actually assimilated by the learned into her prior structures.[6]

Questions for Adult Learning Research and Practice

One of the key issues for the researcher and the practitioner dealing with adult learning is to identify the factors which are likely to influence (positively or negatively) the learning process in a given context and the mechanisms through which they operate. The constructivist view of learning briefly sketched above provides a framework for pointing out the specific 'entry points' through which both individual and situational factors may affect the learning process. Several questions can be raised at each of these strategic points.

---

[6] This phenomenon was elaborated by Moscovici (1961) in his famous study on the social representations of psychoanalysis in different social groups. It has also been widely evidenced and discussed in the field of science (and other disciplines) education. See Bourgeois and Nizet (1997) for a review.

At the starting point of the learning process, activation implies first of all that the learner engages into the situation and is ready to spend the cognitive and affective efforts to deal with it. Therefore, the first question concerns the factors that explain why the learner chooses to attend to certain situations rather than others, what makes certain situation 'significant' enough to have her engage cognitively and affectively into it?

In the constructivist model, activation requires two additional conditions. First, the learner must actually possess the relevant cognitive structures that are likely to be used to deal with the situation. These structures must be available in her memory. This raises the question of prior learning and prerequisites. Second, provided that the relevant structures are available, under which conditions will they be actually activated in the situation? What are the key factors that influence the activation process?

Learning requires the relevant knowledge structures not only to be activated but also to be actually used as an assimilation structure to process the information the learner is exposed to and make sense of it. It is only through the assimilation process that a cognitive conflict can occur and ultimately lead to accommodation. This raises several questions: What factors are likely to influence the learner's cognitive, affective and behavioural engagement into the assimilation process? What type of cognitive strategies is the learner likely to use in that process and what factors influence her 'choice' of strategies?

Assimilation is a necessary but not sufficient condition for learning to occur. One further necessary condition is the occurrence of a cognitive conflict. Provided that assimilation does not necessarily lead to the emergence of a cognitive conflict, the question can therefore be raised as to the factors that influence the probability of occurrence of a conflict cognitive in the situation.

The emergence of a cognitive conflict does not necessarily lead to learning. The key condition at this point is that the conflict is overcome through accommodation of the initial assimilation structure rather than through homeostatic regulation. This of course raises the question of the factors that determine the choice of a cognitive conflict regulation strategy: under which conditions accommodation will prevail over homeostatic regulation?

Beyond the question of the occurrence of change in the initial structure one can also raise the question of the size (or level) and the direction of the change. Piagetian constructivism is essentially a structuralist theory in that it views knowledge as organised into hierarchical structures. In this view, learning implies not only coordination and regulation between the individual's internal structures and the external world but also between internal structures themselves. Therefore, the question can be raised as to the structural characteristics of the change: At which level of the knowledge structure does the change occur? Is it a change towards more integration or differentiation? Vertical or horizontal? etc. The question also concerns the factors that can affect the structural characteristics of the change. Another set of questions relates to the direction of the change. In educational settings in particular, the question becomes crucial when considering the set of norms and expectations which define the expected learning outcomes. Learners are expected not only to change their prior knowledge structures but also to change them in a specific direction as defined by the learning objectives. In this perspective, the question of the factors affecting the direction of the change becomes crucial.

To examine all the factors that are likely to impact the various aspects of the learning process pointed out above would of course be out of the scope of this paper. However, we can here address some questions and problems concerning the role of some factors in the learning process as we have approached them in our own research in relation to adult education settings. More specifically, we have been concerned primarily with factors that can explain the activation and the plasticity of knowledge structure: why, for a given learner in a given learning situation, are some knowledge structure more likely to be activated than others and why some knowledge structures are more prone to change than others? In response to these questions we have explored the role of the learner's identity in the learning process.

Identity and Motivation to Learn from a Constructivist Perspective

Identity Dynamics, Salience and Plasticity of Prior Knowledge Structures
As mentioned above, one of the striking observations that were made in

the first set of studies we conducted on adult learning from in the constructivist perspective was the great inertia of the learner's prior knowledge structures activated in the learning process. One hypothesis that was explored both theoretically and empirically to explain this phenomenon focuses on the role of the learner's identity (Bourgeois, Nizet 1997, 1999, Bourgeois 1998, 2000, Bourgeois, Frenay, Blondiaux in press). The result of this investigation can be roughly summarised as follows (Bourgeois 2000). First, some knowledge areas at issue in the learning process may be more or less closely related to the learner's identity. This is the case when the learner defines herself as similar to or different from others through conceptions and/or behaviours which happen to be on target in the learning process. The extent to which it is central to the learner's identity is what we called identity sensitiveness of the knowledge structure. For example, an adult educator in the field of literacy may ground his professional identity partly in a certain conception of adult literacy (he asserts his difference or similarity to others in reference to this conception) while philosophy and theory of adult literacy is on focus in the learning setting (e.g. a seminar on literacy in a continuing education programme for literacy teachers). Second, the 'identity sensitiveness' of the knowledge structure has an impact on the salience of this structure in the learner's mind and therefore on the activation process. The more central the structure to the learner's identity the more salient the structure, hence the more likely to be activated in the learning situation. Third, the identity sensitiveness of a knowledge structure may affect its plasticity in quite different ways, depending on the learner's related identity dynamics. If the learner is in the process of identity transformation, then the cognitions and behaviours attached to her transforming identity will be prone to change. Conversely, if the learner is in the process of identity preservation (typically, when the individual's current positive identity is being threatened), the cognitions and behaviours attached to the identity to be preserved will be highly resistant to change.[7] So, more generally, we sug-

---

[7] Other authors have further specified the variety of identity dynamics (or sometimes called strategies): Barbier (1996), Barbier and Galatanu (1998), Kaddouri (1996), Camilleri et al. (1990), Dubar (1992). See Bourgeois (2000) for a review. For the impact of identity dynamics on motivation to learn, see in particular Kaddouri (1996).

gest that the learner's readiness to learning is dependent on the meaning she attributes to learning in relation to her current working identity dynamics. If learning is perceived or expected to be relevant, consistent and instrumental to the ongoing identity transformation or preservation process, then the learner's readiness to have the relevant prior knowledge change is likely to be high. Learner's engagement into the task will be high, so will be the salience and plasticity of the relevant prior knowledge structures. Conversely, if learning is perceived as discrepant from the ongoing identity dynamics (e.g. because it is likely to challenge prior conceptions attached to the positive identity) or irrelevant to it (because the identity sensitiveness of the knowledge structure at issue is low), then readiness to learning is likely to be low. In practice, in the context of adult education, it can be expected that most of the time learners undertake the learning process with mixed feelings. On the one hand, they may fear that learning will lead them to give up their familiar ways of thinking and acting. On the other hand, their decision to enter the learning process, and hence to invest all the time and energy usually required to achieve such an enterprise, implies that they are ready to change, they are willing to take the risk of upsetting their conceptions and behaviours and to accept the consequences of such changes in terms of identity. In sum, identity dynamics is rarely an 'either-or situation'. Most of the time adult learners appear rather torn by tensions between the fear and the desire to change, between identity preservation and identity transformation.

Identity, Goals and Engagement into Learning
More recently, we have tried to reinterpret these findings from a broader motivational perspective relating motivation, goals and self-concept. The aforementioned notion of meaning attributed by the learner to the learning process is not far from the concept of value in the expectancy-value paradigm in motivation theory (Pintrich, Schrunk 1996). In this theoretical perspective, the higher the value attributed by the learner to the learning process, the higher her engagement into the learning task. Eccles, Wigfield, and their colleagues have distinguished four components of the achievement task value: intrinsic interest value, extrinsic utility value, cost and importance (or attainment value) (Wigfield, Eccles 1992, 2000, Eccles 1983). The latter component is defined as the extent to

which the task allows the learner to confirm or disconfirm salient or central aspects of their self-schemata. The perceived importance of the task specifically has been shown to have a positive effect on the learner's engagement into the learning task and her learning, independent from the other value components' performance (Battle 1965, Ford 1992, Brophy 1999).

Other theories also emphasise the motivational impact of self-concept in the individual's relationship to a task. Carver and Scheier (1999) suggest that the perceived importance of a task is a function of the degree of abstraction of the individual's goal to which the task is related. Referring to a hierarchical model of goals (Vallacher, Wegner 1987, Austin, Vancouver 1996, Brett, Vande Walle 1999), they assume that the top of the hierarchy consists of what they call be goals, i.e. goals that are directly related to self-concept (e.g. achieving or confirming a positive self-image). From the top to the bottom goals become more and more concrete, operational, action oriented (do goals). In other words, any operational goal (the goal to do something, like for example to learn something in particular, in a given context) is always related in one way or another to be goals. Furthermore, the authors hypothesise that the higher the goal in the hierarchy, the higher its importance: thus, be goals are perceived as more important than do goals. The latter can also be perceived as important to the extent that they are perceived to directly contribute to the achievement of higher-level goals and/or if they are perceived to contribute to more higher-level goals than to only one. Learning can therefore be perceived as important if viewed as instrumental to goals related to self-concept.

Higgins (1987) also emphasises the motivational role of self-concept. Like the theory of identity dynamics mentioned above, his theory relates motivation to perceived discrepancies in the self-concept and the specific emotions associated with them. Furthermore, he specifies the range of possible self-discrepancies. Like Dubar (1992), Barbier (1996) and Kaddouri (1996), he suggests that discrepancies may arise between different aspects of the self. Among these aspects, he distinguishes between two dimensions. One concerns the standpoint being considered: one's perception of oneself *versus* one's perception of others' perception of oneself[8]. The

---

[8] This dimension is also specified in the theory of identity dynamics mentioned above.

other dimension distinguishes between perceptions of actual self (what one is), ideal self (what one wants to be), and ought self (what one ought to be). For some authors, actual-ideal self discrepancies have more positive motivational effects than actual-ought self discrepancies. For example, Deci and Ryan's (1985) theory of self-determination suggests that motivation will be higher when the goal aimed by the individual in the task is self-determined than when it is externally determined. In the context of learning, the individual tends to engage deeper in learning if she feels that it will enable her to achieve self-determined personal goals and aspiration expectations rather than others' expectations. To put it in Higgins' words, engagement into the task will be higher if it is motivated by the individual's effort to reduce an actual-ideal self discrepancy than if her motivation lies in an actual-ought self discrepancy. A similar idea is suggested by the theory of goal orientation (Pintrich, Schrunk 1996). This suggests that the learner will engage deeper into a learning task if she is motivated primarily by learning goals as opposed to performance goals. In the former case, what counts most for the learner in the achievement of the task is to actualise her own expectations in terms of learning outcomes, whereas in the latter case, what counts most is primarily to show a positive image of herself to significant others, or to avoid to give others a negative image of herself. Again, this is consistent with the idea of more positive motivational effects of actual-ideal self discrepancies as opposed to actual-ought self discrepancies.

Markus and Nurius (1986) followed by others (e.g. Carver, Scheier 1999) have distinguished, among all the selves that the individual thinks she could become (possible selves), between the desired selves, which she strives to approach, and the feared selves, which she strives to avoid. The individual tends to engage preferably into tasks (and related achievement goals) likely to confirm a positive self-image, whereas she tends to avoid those which are likely to confirm a negative self-image. Carver and Scheier (1999) further suggest that the approach orientation (striving for a positive self-image) is motivationally far more powerful than the avoidance orientation (avoiding a negative self-image). This is consistent with the research in social psychology on stereotype threat (Desért 2000), which suggests that the individual tends to withdraw from a task (including learning tasks) when this is perceived as involving an aspect of the individual's identity that is stigmatised by a social stereotype. A similar hypothesis is supported by recent research on goal orientations in learning (see above), which suggests that performance goals have more positive motivational effects, in terms of engagement, if the approach orientation rather than the avoidance orientation prevails (Pintrich 2000, Elliot, McGregor, Gable 1999).

Motivation, Engagement, and Performance

The theories presented above deal with various aspects of the relationship between self-concept (or identity) and motivation to task achievement. In fact, most of them focus on the impact of self-concept upon the individual's engagement into a task. However, the question of the relationship between the individual's engagement and her actual performance on the task must be addressed. A large part of the motivation literature converges to emphasise the positive effect of engagement upon performance. In empirical research, the former variable is most often specified in terms of cognitive, emotional and behavioural engagement whereas the latter is most often defined in terms of academic achievement (grades). However, the question whether engagement is a good predictor of finer qualitative aspects of learning we discussed above remains open. In particular, the question can be raised as to what extent the learner's engagement into the learning task is likely to result in (i) activation of the relevant knowledge structures in the learning situation, (ii) transformation of the activated structures (as opposed to maintenance of status quo) and (iii) transformation in the expected direction. We suggest that engagement is certainly a necessary condition for activation and transformation of the assimilation structures to occur, but not a sufficient one. The learning process is quite costly, both cognitively and emotionally, and it is rather clear that cognitive conflicts could not emerge and ultimately lead to accommodation of the assimilation unless the learner is sufficiently engaged into the learning process. However, we suggest that in some cases the learner's engagement may not lead to accommodation. Furthermore, it could sometimes even be counterproductive and operate against learning. This would be the case when the conceptions or behaviours at stake in the learning process are 'identity sensitive' while the learner is in the dynamics of identity preservation. In such case, it could be hypothesised that the learner could either disengage from the learning process or actively engage into it but only to actively resist change. This type of phenomenon has been observed in recent research on the attribution bias (Nils 1995). It was observed that if the attribution bias is consistent with the individual's activated positive identity, the individual will be highly motivated and engaged into the task – in the sense that she will use deeper information processing strategies – but at the same time, the attribution bias will be very active. In other words, in such a case, the learner is highly engaged into the task and yet actively resisting change in the conceptions that relate to her positive identity. Such a resistance is achieved by the use of cognitive biases such as the attribution bias. Pintrich (2000) raises a similar argument about the role of self-efficacy. In short, he suggests that self efficacy can indeed have a positive effect on engagement (as predicted by the expectancy-value theories of motivation) and yet have a counterproductive effect on conceptual change to the extent that learning aims at prior conceptions that are highly resistant to change from the start. It is clear that further research should be conducted into the relationship between self-concept (especially in terms of perceived discrepancies), engagement into learning and 'qualitative' aspects of learning like those which are highlighted by the constructivist perspective (activation, plasticity and change direction).

Situational *versus* Individual Factors: What Can Teaching Do about Identity-Related Factors?

The discussion so far has focused mainly on individual factors of learning. Self-concept, identity dynamics are typical individual characteristics. They relate to the learner's life history and internal dispositions. Now, in keeping with the constructivist paradigm, learning is to be viewed as involving both situational and individual factors in interaction. This implies that one should consider the role of situational factors likely to mediate the aforementioned effects of identity factors. In particular, the question can legitimately be raised about the mediating role of situational factors such as teaching conditions and practices, which can be affected directly by the teacher or educator. What can be done, for example, about the fact that most adult learners undertake learning with both the fear and the desire to change? The Vygotskian notion of zone of proximal development (ZPD) could be useful to address this question. It could be hypothesised that in some cases (below the ZPD), the individual resistance factors are so powerful that teaching conditions and practices, whatever they are, could hardly make a difference. In other cases (beyond the ZPD), the change factors are so strong that the learners will engage into learning anyway, whatever the teaching conditions and practices. In between (within the ZPD), there are cases in which the teacher and teaching setting will make a real difference in that they will actually help the learner to overcome her resistance to change and gradually engage into learning and change. What are the situational factors that could make such a difference? We addressed this question extensively in Bourgeois and Nizet (1997). In summary, we had suggested the notion of learning setting as a transitional space, that is, a secure space within which the learner can experience new ways of thinking and acting without any immediate risks for her identity, without being urged to immediately and definitely give up her 'old' ways of thinking and acting. The analogy can be made with the idea of a theatre stage on which the actor plays without consequences for her real life (at least immediately), or with the idea of the psychoanalytic cure within which the patient can replay relationships with his parents or any other significant others without affecting (at least immediately) those relationships in reality. We suggested that organising learning as a transitional space is likely to help the learner overcome her resistance to change. We then reviewed some of the conditions that characterise learning as a transitional space. We pointed out three basic sets conditions (Bourgeois, Nizet 1997).

- Facilitating exploration of novel ways of thinking and acting, through (i) teaching methods emphasising discovery learning and transfer, (ii) learning assessment practices emphasising informative feedback rather than control, and giving 'mistakes' a positive meaning, (iii) and teaching practices allowing for social interactions which enhance sociocognitive conflicts and socioaffective support to learning.
- Facilitating thinking reversibility (i.e. the capacity to adopt alternative standpoints on reality) (i) by encouraging the expression of the learner's own point of view, (ii) by organising constructive confronta-

tion of the learner's point of view with others, (iii) and by providing metatheoretical and methodological tools for the learners that enable them to achieve and benefit from the confrontation of alternative points of view in terms of learning.

- Facilitating critical and personal thinking beyond reversibility, through appropriate teaching practices and institutional conditions, including specific places and times in the learning process where learners have the opportunity to reflect upon the cognitive and affective aspects of the ongoing learning process and its personal implications.

Conclusions

The constructivist approach to adult learning proposed here is based on some epistemological assumptions. One is that it is clearly a model for understanding the learning process, rather than a prescriptive model of teaching, although a reflection on teaching practice can be based on a constructivist understanding of the learning process. The second assumption is that our understanding of the adult learning process specifically is derived from a general theory of learning on the basis of which the role of the specific characteristics of the learning setting and the learners can be subsequently identified. Thirdly, research on adult learning is to be informed by research on learning in other educational settings.

From a constructivist perspective, learning is viewed as a process through which the learner's prior knowledge structures are transformed into new structures and this process results from the learner's interactions with her significant environment. More specifically, learning involves three basic processes in interaction: activation, by which prior knowledge structures are selected and activated in the learning situation; assimilation by which the activated structures are used to process the information available in the situation in order to make sense of the situation; and accommodation, by which the activated structure is transformed so as to accommodate to discrepant information and thereby solve cognitive conflicts.

Our empirical research on adult learning from a constructivist perspective points to interesting elements that may enrich the original theory. For example, it shows that accommodation rarely results from exposure to one single source of information but rather from interactions between several sources, typically life experience and teaching. It also points out that accommodation does not always result directly and immediately from assimilation of the concept and theories taught in the classroom. The establishment of relationships between the new concepts and life experience is sometimes required for accommodation to ultimately occur. Our research also highlighted the importance of subsequent reinforcements of learning resulting from its transfer to life experience, as well as the great inertia of the prior learning structures.

The constructivist approach is also quite useful to identify both individual and situational factors that are likely to affect the adult learning process and to identify the specific 'entry points' through which those factors can affect the learning process as a whole. Our own research over the last years has focused on the impact of the learner's self-concept and identity on learning. We showed that the salience and plasticity of prior knowledge structures may be deeply affected by the meaning the learner attributes to the learning process in relation to his or her current working identity dynamics. We also explored other aspects of the relationship between self-concept and motivation to learn in relation to various theories of motivation. All those theories emphasise the motivational consequences of the goals the learner tries to achieve in the learning process in relation to his or her self-concept. They account for the impact of self-concept upon the learner's engagement into the learning task but they can hardly predict the more qualitative aspects of the learning process and outcomes typically identified by the constructivist model of learning. What remains problematic is the relationship between the learner's motivational engagement into the learning task and his or her actual learning performance. In this respect, we suggested some hypotheses that remain to be empirically investigated, for example, as to the conditions under which motivational engagement can be negatively related to performance.

The identity factors discussed in this chapter are clearly individual factors. However, from a constructivist perspective, learning is influenced neither by individual factors only, nor by situational factors only, but rather by interactions of both. We therefore sketched some suggestions as to some of the teaching conditions and practices that are likely to mediate the effects of identity on learning.

In conclusion we would like to address two more points. First, the constructivist model is most often used to account for the transformation of the cognitive structures (concepts, theories, skills, etc.) directly on target in the learning process. Now, most of the factors affecting learning that were examined here are also cognitions – representations of the learning situation and process (e.g. the meaning and value attributed by the learner to learning) and representations of the learner herself (e.g. working self-concept). To that extent, just like the cognitions at issue in the learning process, the constructivist model of cognitive change could also apply to those particular cognitions. This calls for a more integrative view of learning, as a process involving different 'flows' of cognitive change developing in parallel and interacting with each other throughout the learning process. The learner's self-concept and representation of the learning situation interact with each other and with changes in the cognitions at issue in the learning process (e.g. the learner's conceptions related to the concept or theory being taught).

The second concluding remark is about research methodology. As argued above, research on adult learning in a constructivist perspective is to widely benefit from combining and cross-fertilising various research methodological and epistemological traditions. As an illustration, we highlighted above the complementarity of the research on identity dynamics and the research on the role of self-concept in motivational engagement, although grounded in quite different methodological and epistemological paradigms. Whereas the former is grounded in more clinical qualitative research, the latter is based mainly on correlational and experimental research. However, it seems to us that if research is to account for the finer (socio)cognitive and affective processes involved in learning as viewed from a constructivist perspective, very 'fine grain' research instruments are needed. More specifically, as pointed out when we discussed the relationship between engagement and performance, questionnaire surveys (as widely used in the research on motivation) appear to be quite limited. Much finer instruments and methods are requested and in this respect we think that qualitative clinical (monographic) research on the one hand and lab experimental research on the other may be extremely complementary despite the epistemological gap that traditionally keep them far apart. We also want to insist on the need for more longitudinal research in order to account for the dynamics of interaction among the multiple factors involved in the learning process over time.

References

Austin, J. T., Vancouver, J. B. (1996). Goal Construct in Psychology. Structure, Process, and Content. In: *Psychological Bulletin*, 120 (3), pp. 338-375.

Barbier, J.-M. (1996). De l'usage de la notion d'identité en recherche, notamment dans le domaine de la formation. In: *Education Permanente*, 128, pp. 11-26.

Barbier, J.-M., Galatanu, O. (1998). *Action, affects et transformation de soi*. Paris.

Battle, E. (1965). Motivational Determinants of Academic Persistence. In: *Journal of Personality and Social Psychology*, 2, pp. 209-218.

Beauvois, J.-L., Deschamps, J.-C. (1990). Vers la cognition sociale. In: Ghiglione, R., Bonnet, C., Richard, J.-F. (eds.). *Traité de psychologie cognitive 3, cognition, représentation, communication*. Paris, pp. 1-110.

Berger, P., Luckmann, T. (1991). *The Social Construction of Reality*. London.

Bourgeois, E. (1998). Apprentissage, motivation et engagement en formation. In: *Education Permanente*, 136, pp. 101-109.

Bourgeois, E. (2000). Sociocultural Mobility. Language Learning and Identity. In: Bron, A., Schemmann, M. (eds.). *Language-Mobility-Identity*. Contemporary Issues for Adult Education in Europe, Bochum Studies in International Adult Education, 1. Münster, Hamburg, pp. 163-184.

Bourgeois, E., Frenay, M., Blondiaux, M. (in press). *Attainment Value, Identity and Motivation to Learn in Adult Literacy Education. Three Qualitative Case Studies*. Paper presented at the EARLI Conference, Friburg, 2001/08/27 – 2001/09/01.

Bourgeois, E., Nizet, J. (1997). *Apprentissage et formation des adultes*. Paris.

Bourgeois, E., Nizet, J. (1999). *Regards croisés sur l'expérience de formation*. Paris.

Brett, J. F., Vande Walle, D. (1999). Goal Orientation and Goal Content as Predictors of Performance in a Training Program. In: *Journal of Applied Psychology*, 84 (6), pp. 863-873.

Brophy, J. (1999). Toward a Model of the Value Aspects of Motivation in Education. Developing Appreciation for Particular Learning Domains and Activities. In: *Educational Psychologist*, 34 (2), pp. 75-85.

Camilleri, C. et al.(1990). *Stratégies identitaires*. Paris.

Carver, C. S., Scheier, M. F. (1999). Themes and Issues in the Self-Regulation of Behavior. In: Wyer Jr., R. S. (ed.). *Advances in Social Cognition* (Vol. 2), pp. 1-105.

Deci, E. L., Ryan, R. M. (1985). *Intrinsic Motivation and Self Determination in Human Behavior.* New York.

Dubar, C. (1992). *La socialisation. Construction des identités sociales et professionnelles.* Paris.

Désert, M. (2000). *La menace du stéréotype, gardienne des inégalités sociales? Situations, identités et contrôle.* Université Catholique de Louvain: Ph.D. Dissertation. Unpublished.

Eccles, J. (1983). Expectancies, Values and Academic Behaviors. In: Spence, J. T. (ed.), *Achievement and Achievement Motives.* San Francisco, pp. 75-146.

Elliot, A. J., McGregor, H. A., Gable, S. (1999). Achievement Goals, Study Strategies, and Exam Performance. A Mediational Analysis. In: *Journal of Educational Psychology*, 91 (3), pp. 549-563.

Ford, M. E. (1992). *Motivating Humans.* London.

Gruber, H. E., Voneche, J. J. (1977). *The Essential Piaget.* New York.

Higgins, E. T. (1987). Self-Discrepancy. A Theory Relating Self and Affect. In: *Psychological Review*, 93 (3), pp. 319-340.

Kaddouri, M. (1996). Place du projet dans les dynamiques identitaires. In: *Education Permanente*, 128, pp. 135-151.

Markus, H., Nurius, P. (1986). Possible Selves. In: *American Psychologist*, 41 (9), pp. 954-969.

Moscovici, S. (1961). *La psychanalyse, son image et son public.* Paris.

Nils, F. (1995). *Au-delà des limites cognitives et motivationnelles de l'observateur social: approche pragmatique du biais de surattribution dispositionnelle.* Université Catholique de Louvain: Licence thesis. Unpublished.

Pastré, P. (1999). La conceptualisation dans l'action. Bilan et nouvelles perspectives. In: *Education Permanente*, 139, pp. 13-35.

Piaget, J. (1967). *Biologie et connaissance.* Paris.

Piaget, J. (1968). *La naissance de l'intelligence chez l'enfant.* Paris.

Piaget, J. (1975). *L'équilibration des structures cognitives.* Paris.

Pintrich, P. R., Schunk, D. H. (1996). *Motivation in Education.* Englewood Cliffs, NJ.

Pintrich, P. P. (2000). An Achievement Goal Theory Perspective on Issues in Motivation Terminology, Theory, and Research. In: *Contemporary Educational Psychology*, 25, pp. 92-104.

Richard, J.-F. (1990). *Les activités mentales.* Paris.

Schnotz, W., Vosniadou, S., Carreto, M. (1999). *New Perspectives on Conceptual Change*. Amsterdam.

Vallacher, R. R., Wegner, D. M. (1987). What Do People Think They're Doing? Action Identification and Human Behavior. In: *Psychological Review*, 94, pp. 3-15.

Wigfield, A., Eccles, J. (1992). The Development of Achievement Task Value. A Theoretical Analysis. In: *Developmental Review*, 12, pp. 265-310.

Wigfield, A., Eccles, J. S. (2000). Expectancy-Value Theory of Achievement Motivation. In: *Contemporary Educational Psychology*, 25, pp. 68-81.

Agnieszka Bron

SYMBOLIC INTERACTIONSIM AS A THEORETICAL POSITION IN ADULT EDUCATION RESEARCH

Introduction

The assumption that a theoretical and conceptualised thinking is inseparably connected with good research practice seems obvious. In social science we need both theory and empirical research, as research strategies and results without theoretical grounds are empty and cannot help us either in understanding or in explaining social reality.[1] Moreover, without being anchored in theoretical perspectives research methods are not very useful. Norman Denzin (1989b) points to a wide gap in sociology between theory and methodology and calls for a combination of theories, methods and knowledge of the substantive area that is investigated. Yet, this seldom occurs in sociological work, not to mention other disciplines, e.g. adult education. He gives two examples to support his thesis that there is both possibility and necessity for bridging that gap. The first is Herbert Blumer who strongly advocated that theory and method must go hand in hand in a proper methodological study that demands a consistent theoretical perspective.[2] The second is the work of two interactionists, Howard Becker and Harold Garnfinkel, who "have also called for a blending of theory and method" (Denzin 1989b, 2). This is also exactly what Denzin is doing himself in his own research (see Denzin 1986a, 1986b).[3]

---

[1] In this context Kurt Lewin's words that "nothing is as practical as a good theory" should be again emphasised.
[2] He gives as illustration Thomas and Znaniecki's (1918-21) study.
[3] It is quite obvious for him that "[t]heory cannot be judged independently of research activity. Research methods are of little use until they are seen in the light of theoretical perspectives" (Denzin 1989b, 1).

David Silverman, another sociologists (1993, 1) points out that "without a theory, there is nothing to research". Among social science theories he mentions symbolic interactionism which generally speaking focuses on how we attach symbolic meanings to interpersonal relations. Depending what we focus on in our research the choice of the theoretical perspective will help us to understand the research phenomenon.

Thus, the choice of theoretical perspective is clearly important for both the empirical as well as theoretical results in social science, and in this matter also in adult education research. Symbolic interactionism, as one of the interpretative theories in social sciences, is one possible choice. It is a specifically American tradition even if it is possible to find some resemblance in Max Weber's and Georg Simmel's humanistic sociology, as well as in German hermeneutics and phenomenology. However, the influence was very small, even though American pragmatists visited and studied in Germany. Pragmatism was very influential for symbolic interactionism – this very American philosophy – along with the Chicago tradition of sociology, but most important of all were George Herbert Mead's writings and lectures, in which he personified both directions, i.e. pragmatism and symbolic interactionism.

Symbolic interactionism can be regarded as a leading theory in American social psychology, with its main focus on how meanings emerge through interaction. Analysis of the meanings of everyday life was possible through close, deep-rooted observation of accustomed behaviour. From such examinations one could develop an understanding of the underlying patterns of human interaction. Generally, it is possible to distinguish four foci of this theory. The first concerns how human beings in particular can be 'symbol-manipulating animals', as it is through symbols that they are able to produce culture and express their complex history. For interactionists it is always significant how people give meaning to their bodies and their feelings, to their selves and the situations they encounter, to their biographies as well as to the wider social worlds they live in and become, i.e. to their *Lebenswelt*[4] (Marshal 1994).

---

[4] We can see great resemblance between symbolic interactionism and phenomenology. For an interesting comparison between Mead and Merleau-Ponty see Rosenthal and Bourgeois (1991).

The second topic of symbolic interactionism is that of process and emergence. The social world is seen, according to this theory, as a constantly dynamic and dialectical net, the outcome of encounters and situations being continuous and hard to predict as the lives and peoples' biographies are shifting and becoming, thus neither fixed nor unchanged. Symbolic interactionism is concerned with the flow of activity, with their adjustments and outcomes, and never with fixed structures as in many other sociological theories. Ideas and concepts like becoming, encounters, career, role taking, and impression management are pivotal to symbolic interactionism (Marshal 1994).

The third theme points towards the social world as essentially interactive. That means that there are no singular, lone individuals but that they are always connected to 'others', they see and understand themselves through others. Thus, for interactionists the most important concern of analysis is the self, which points precisely to the necessity of people to view themselves as objects by taking the attitude of others through role-taking processes. Both the notion of the "looking-glass self" of Charles Horton Cooley and Mead's more general idea of "the self" clarify this idea in the best way (Marshal 1994). Moreover, intersubjectivity as a core dimension allows interactionists to understand human conduct.

The last dimension, derived from the work of Georg Simmel, is the idea that to determine underlying patterns or forms in social life, we need to look below or underneath the symbols, processes, and interactions people are involved in. Thus interactionists, pursue 'universal social processes', and try to generate and understand common, generic processes by studying the life-experiences of specific groups, such as the dying, drug-abusers, taxi-drivers or medical doctors. Interactionists want to establish a formal theory grounded in the data, and derived from the data. An excellent example of such work is Glaser and Strauss' *Status Passage* (1967) with the interactionist theory of status changes (Marshal 1994).

In this article I will concentrate on presenting this theory from its origin, i.e. by discussing G. H. Mead and by pointing to symbolic interactionism's fruitfulness for research on adult learning as well as showing its consequences for adult education research generally, while also being aware that there might be other ways of presenting, discussing and interpreting it.[5] The rationale for concentrating on Mead in considering symbolic interactionism, derives, partly, from what Strauss (1977) wrote, with continuing relevance: "Mead seems due for increasing reconstruction, rediscovery, reassessment, rephrasing, redeciphering, and no doubt continuing retranslation. Since his thought is so rich, the reworking will doubtless reflect his complexity" (Strauss 1977, xxxi).

The richness in Mead's theory makes it possible to find an interesting point of departure for understanding social phenomena without examining the different ways in which symbolic interactionism subsequently developed.

Symbolic Interactionism – 'A Critical Examination'

George Herbert Mead (1863-1931) was, during most of his active academic life, professor of philosophy at Chicago University. He came there on the recommendation of his close friend and colleague John Dewey. He was inspired strongly by German idealism and by Darwin's evolution theory and was one of the leading American pragmatists, who contributed not only to the development of American social psychology, but also sociology. He was one of the founders of symbolic interactionism, but the term itself was invented, in 1937, by Herbert Blumer, Mead's student and follower.

Mead is important for sociologists as he provides a much needed 'unifying theory of sociology', of both society and the active individual, of subjectivity and objectivity, by pointing towards intersubjectivity as a linking factor. Strauss, in the introduction to Mead's selected papers "On Social Psychology", writes that "almost exclusively, sociologists lit upon Mead's ideas about socialization, notably his concept of 'generalized other' and his rather strikingly socialized 'self'" (Strauss 1977, xi-xii). Sociolo-

---

[5] Mead's symbolic interactionism has developed in different directions. Denzin (1989a) stresses that it can be pragmatic, dramaturgical, negotiating, and political interactionism, as well as feminist, phenomenological, formal and everyday life sociological interactionism. It includes also existential sociology about absurd discourse and structure, theories on role-identities, and everyday constructions. It can be interpretative and connected to contextual interactionism. There are also real or mystical differences between such schools as Iowa or New-Iowa, Chicago, Minnesota or Illinois. The differences are not only theoretical but can also be seen in a range of qualitative methodologies.

gists were interested in these concepts as they found them more than helpful in the argument against biological explanations of behaviour that dominated at that time. Even the notion of self was useful when opposing Freudianism and the individualistic psychologies, and also helpful when conceptualising the socialisation of group members. In this context, is it possible to treat Mead as a real behaviourist and his theory as a behaviouristic theory, as we often hear?

Connections to Behaviourism

Mead is often wrongly accused of being a behaviourist, for two main reasons. First, he often called himself a social behaviourist, but precisely by using the term social he contradicted behaviourism and its reductionism which he opposed strongly. Second, he even employed the behaviourist language in some of his writings, for example by frequent use of such concepts as stimulus and response. The reason for that was again his engagement in active dialog with behavioural psychologists, but such language disturbs contemporary reading, and only if we decide to go beyond this jargon, the understanding becomes much easier and deep (Von Wright, 2000). Mead was an active anti-behaviourist, and criticised behaviourism on several grounds. For example, that it accounted only for what people were doing, and not what they were feeling and thinking.[6] In this way it ignored many aspects of human conduct, which might not be readily observable.

Rosenthal and Bourgeois write that perceiving Mead as a behaviourist is misleading in two ways "it can falsely bring to mind shades of reductionism. And it can just as falsely hide a phenomenological dimension to

---

[6] Mead understands a human as intentional, or having an agency: "the 'I' as creative dimension of the lived body, gives the sense of freedom, of agency..." (Mead 1934, 177). "It is the sense of the 'living act which never gets directly into reflective experience' as an object" (Mead 1934, 203). As Rosenthal and Bourgeois (1991) point out, the development of a selfhood means to get a sense of one's own agency while sensing the temporal present. They describe it in the following way: "...the novelty of the 'I' is the sense of its passing from an old 'me' out of which its novelty has arisen into a new 'me' which accommodates it and renders it continuous with what came before" (Rosenthal, Bourgeois 1991, 158). The sense of novelty is always a temporal sense as it is situated freedom, thus, it involves being between past and future.

Mead's thought, a dimension not usually associated with behavioristic approaches of any type" (Rosenthal, Bourgeois 1991, 6).

By contrasting Mead's social behaviourism with Watsonian behaviourism, we can see how the former views behaviour as explaining mind and consciousness without explaining it away. Mead does not want to reduce mental functions, mind or consciousness to corporal behaviour, instead he looks at these dimensions by focusing on human action, which is objectively observable in other words 'from the outside'. For Mead, social behaviourism is useful as a methodological, not an ontological position. What occurs between the organism and its environment, according to Mead is essentially reciprocal, thus it cannot be termed behavouristic. Thus, to the contrary, his "behaviorism is pervaded by a phenomenological dimension in which the dynamics of experience are grasped from within. ...it is elusive, as he tends to view his examination of behavior from the perspective of psychology" (Rosenthal, Bourgeois 1991, 8)[7].

Von Wright (2000) rightly underlines that Mead was interested not in behaviour but in human conduct or action, as there is a fundamental difference between these two. According to her the first concept i.e. behaviour connotes what people are doing habitually, which is predictable and measurable, while the second i.e. conduct is unique and not foreseeable before hand, but yet anticipated during the process of making. Thus, conduct includes sociality and reflexivity.

Overcoming the Dualism between Body and Mind. Temporality

This view leads us to Mead's other contribution to sociology, which he shares with phenomenologists, and which derived from Hegel, that is his way of overcoming the dualism between mind and body.[8] He strongly be-

---

[7] His psychological language leans "to both hide and house" such a phenomenological approach. For Mead it is important to see the meaningful experience as inseparable from the structure of human behaviour and this he shares with Merleau-Ponty, state Rosenthal and Bourgeois (1991).

[8] It is to the Cartesian dualism between mind and body, object and subject, which Mead opposes. This point of view is characterised by the Descartes philosophy with its culmination in Kant. Mead chooses instead the Hegelian tradition which is typical for phenomenology and feminism, the relational instead of the punctual (individual) position, totality instead of the sum of individuals, in other words intersubjectivity. A human is not completed and cannot be described as a thing, but s/he is in the making, in constant becoming (Von Wright 2000, 70).

lieved that scientific thinking could give opportunities for better solutions and more democratic social forms. He also wanted to overcome the dualism between body and mind in a time, when positivism started to influence psychology and other social sciences. In his writing Mead is dialogical and relational and expresses the shift from the substantial view of ontology to a functional or process oriented: Consciousness, writes Mead, "is spoken of, as a something that appears at a certain point, it is something into which the object of knowledge in some sense enters from without" (Mead 1964, 105).

The most important consequence of this shift, as von Wright points out, is to perceive consciousness as temporal, and not as substantial. Mead solves dualism between soma and psyche, between body and mind, by describing through a range of angles the human aspects that we attribute in everyday life to our spiritual existence and by differentiating between the psychic and the subjective. Mind is temporal and not substantial, and in temporality he finds a way against the dualism of body and mind (Von Wright 2000, 106). Mead's understanding of an individual as communicative and socially responsive directs attention towards the complexity of human being as corporal and sensitive, cognitive and spiritual. In Mead's theory the emergence of meaning and a self are grounded in reflexive communicative processes, where feelings, through their anticipating character, also embrace reflexive thinking (Von Wright 2000, 210).

As Rosenthal and Bourgeois (1991) stress, in Mead's theory it is not possible to reduce mind to behaviour. It is, however, functionally related to it, as it emerges within the context of behaviour. Neither is mind "reducible to brain, nor can it be container for, or confined within, subjective experience" (Rosenthal, Bourgeois 1991, 9). As Mead writes about mind: "Significance belongs to things in their relations to individuals. It does not lie in mental processes which are enclosed within individuals" (Mead 1964, 247). In this way Mead bypasses the dualism-reductionism disagreement and avoids the mechanical distinction of the subject-object in favour of an active, intersubjective organism.

Another major aspect of Mead's work was the theory of the social construction of time, which was closely related to the subject-object dimension. For him lived time was a basic source of all derived senses of time. He objects to the realist view that the time is objective and independent from any structured perspective, as well as the view that it has a subjective structure based on an inner stream that is against a fixed objectivity. Mead thus reaches a position in which temporal experience crosses the subject-object split and supplies the ground for all derived understandings of time. Thus, as Rosenthal and Bourgeois write, the nature of time is deep-seated in the present, but "is not a knife-edged moment, a series of now points, but rather a durational spread which contains in its temporal span both past and future" (Rosenthal, Bourgeois 1991, 53). The temporality we experience in life is characterised by both depth and movement, as well as by pointing to a privileged position of the present that is opened to past and future. This explains the unity between perceiver and perceived as being the definite unity of self and world, which is possible just because of the temporal nature of the self (Rosenthal, Bourgeois 1991, 85).

However, it is still not easy to understand Mead's concept of the self. He treats it as intrinsically temporal, while yet sometimes using atomistic terms when discussing the I-me distinction. The awareness of the self is never of the passing, but always of the 'moment passed'. For him even the most simple way of being another to one's self is temporal and characterised by a strange twists that involves breaks in the continuous flow of events (cf. Rosenthal and Bourgeois 1991, 117). Thus, it is impossible to "be another and yet himself except from the standpoint of a time which is composed of entirely independent elements" write Mead (1934, 367). In the present which is temporal the 'I' is the locus of immediate present that is separated from both the immediate sense of change as well as from the dynamics of sociality. "This relapse allows for an invisible 'I' which catches a past 'me' in reflective activity", as Rosenthal and Bourgeois write (1991, 117). It seems as if Mead ignores the characteristics of temporality which his own analysis has exposed. Perhaps this is his reaction, stress Rosenthal and Bourgeois to bypass any remains of psychical contents, which he opposed so much. According to them:

> Mead, in his discussion of the self, seems more often than not to deal with the self in terms of the abstraction of instants, forgetting that any discussion of the self which draws from this view of time is ultimately an abstraction from the

sense of lived temporal passage (Rosenthal, Bourgeois 1991, 118).

The Theory of Social Act and the Self

Mead's theory of interaction and social conduct includes both the development of the self, and the emergence of meaning. But to understand Mead's way of dealing with 'the self' and 'generalized other' it is best to start with his theory of the social act. The core concept in this theory is a gesture, that he borrows from Wilhelm Wundt, and that he qualified to include initial conduct in communication processes. Another important link in communication processes is the ability to place oneself in the situation of the other. Mead suggests it is essential to be able to imitate someone's behaviour. To take the attitude or perspective of the other, is the concept that Mead attributes as a central aspect of the process of communication or interaction between people, where the role-taking plays an important part, not only because this ability contributes to reflexive thinking, but because it is even a prerequisite of common act or conduct (Von Wright 2000, 80). Mead comes to terms with the idea of imitation as an explanation to how we give meaning to our own and others conducts and instead outlines his own theory on interaction and the social act. There he emphasises the social situation, or more precisely the social conduct, as a central aspect for describing how it happens that we give meanings to our own and others' acts. Additional aspects of meaning, that he stresses, but inseparably connected with the social conduct, are feelings, or emotions (Von Wright 2000, 87).

Generally, Mead's central theme is not to rely on qualities given by nature, but to see the individual as all the time in making, and in becoming. With both William James and John Dewey, Mead shares the view that social conduct is a meaningful conduct in such a respect that meaning to which we respond is possible to be found in the response itself. Mead's concept of meaning includes the view that it can be neither copied nor aroused within ourselves, but it is constructed, reconstructed and modified. Meaning emerges from social conduct in social situations. Social conduct happens between people and is not something that occurs outside the individual's meaning, i.e. the first immediate response to the conduct can be transferred to awareness about meaning in social situations. This exactly expresses, according to Von Wright (2000, 105), a shift from a substantial to an intersubjective understanding of consciousness.

This can be explained in two ways. First, awareness of meaning is constructed and reconstructed through reflexive thinking and problematising. Awareness thus becomes something other than subjective or psychic. Second, there is a shift from understanding human consciousness as an individual entity to understanding it as relation. Consciousness can have different expressions, as social experience, as reflexive intelligence or as subjective experience, and can be found primarily in a triadic relation of emerging of meanings, i.e. in the logical structure of meanings (Von Wright 2000, 106). As Von Wright stresses, the most important consequence of this shift will be to understand consciousness as temporal, and not as substantial. According to Rosenthal and Bourgeois (1991):

> For Mead, the 'triadic relation holds between organism and nature' and this triadic relationship is incorporated within the very structure of meaning. Meaning ... is neither subjective nor psychological. It has an existence which can perhaps best be termed logical, for it arises out of a triadic relational matrix (Rosentha, Bourgeois 1991, 34).[9]

This has consequences for the self. Once it has emerged, it seems to form the foundation to recognise "one's body as ... both sensing and sensed" (Rosenthal, Bourgeois 1991, 18). Moreover, the emergence of the self is possible because of the human ability to take the role of the other and always stands within a social context. This "allows humans to take many different perceptual viewpoints simultaneously and in this way reach a universal grasp of the object" (Rosenthal, Bourgeois 1991, 19) and has profound consequences for understanding how people learn, especially when they are maturing, where similarities with post-formal, post-Piagetan perspectives in learning become visible. Furthermore, Mead draws a differ-

---

[9] Mead writes about it in the following way: "This triadic relationship can be analogous to the interplay of gestures in the social emergence of meanings, a threefold relationship of gestures of first organism, gestures of second organism, and gesture of subsequent phases of a given social act" (Mead 1934, 80).

ence between instrumental and communicative action, but it is only a difference in kind. However, the instrumental is too often incorrectly associated with the technological as it is seen solely as active use of knowledge to change society or the environment. But that was not the sense Mead was using.[10] Essentially, 'instrumental' indicates for Mead "the manner in which one knows the world through the structures of the meanings one has created by one's responses to the environment" (Rosenthal, Bourgeois 1991, 19). Thus, the focus here is not on what one should do with knowledge, but simply on what knowledge is. What occurs between humans and their environment that includes purposively directed transformational factors and is incorporated in the very heart of the internal structure of meaning.

Purposive, instrumental or goal oriented activity, then, is united with the very structure of meanings in general, as well as with its character, which is consolidated within these meanings, that integrates and combines them. Again in this context, the distinction of what is meant by instrumental action is important for adult educators.

The self is seen by Mead as having two dimensions, i.e. the 'I' pole, and the 'me' pole. Both poles are inseparably interrelated, even if they make only a functional distinction. The 'I' is characterised by immediacy of the present, spontaneity and creativity, the subject pole, which includes an individual perspective. The 'me' represents the constraints of the past, of tradition, of culture and institutionalised practices. It is the shaping of the self by the other, as a community perspective, i.e. the object pole. In the process of rejection of traditional notions of psychical immediacy Mead introduces these two dimensions (Rosenthal, Bourgeois 1991).

In Mead's theory 'I' serves as a guarantee for that what is unique and individual. The human being only consisting of 'me' would be a chameleon without any power of self (Von Wright 2000, 135). The I-me poles are in a constant dialogue, as the self is both a knower and a known. Furthermore, the selfhood is a cognitive relation emerging from the 'me' by incorporating the generalised other, and arising before the 'I' aspect can emerge. There is no other 'I' but only "against or in relation to the 'me'. The 'I'

---

[10] This was later taken by Mezirow in his theory of transformation learning, as well as

emerges subsequent to the 'me' pole as its correlates, and the internal conversation between the 'I' and the 'me' as the voice of the other, becomes possible" write Rosenthal and Bourgeois (1991, 104). The I-me distinction, which is always involved in a conversation with each other, links the concrete subject, the lived-body with the cognitive self, that is also situated in the body. This is also shown in Mead's elaboration of subjectivity.

To sum it up, for Mead the 'I' and 'me' are not metaphysical distinctions but functional relations as they represent two ways in which the lived body, the decentered subject, functions. In this way Mead rejects physiological reductionism. As Rosenthal and Bourgeois stress "The 'I' is the elusive pole of the I-me reflective, cognitive, relationship, but subjectivity is the living reality of the concrete or decentered subject in its organic or vital intentional activity" (Rosenthal, Bourgeois 1991, 106). Once a mentality emerges it is not just added to the lived body, but functions as some higher level that transforms the lower level, and in this way returns to subjectivity. This, however, cannot be confused with subjectivism, that Mead strongly rejected, emphasise Rosenthal and Bourgeois. Subjectivism according to him avoids the intentional character of the creativity of the vital body. Mead (1964, 53-54) writes that "It is an immediate and direct experience, the point of immediacy that must exist within a mediate process".

From the moment selfhood has developed, the ability of the dialogical relation of the cognitive I-me is present (Rosenthal, Bourgeois 1991, 123). To have a sense of self is possible, for Mead, only by taking the roles of others and by that incorporating the generalised other within the structure of the lived body. This development of selfhood is possible already by experience while being a child, while going through the stages of playing. The first is the stage of play, when a child takes different roles, being able to go from one role to another. For example a child plays to be a parent, a doctor or a teacher. The self is constituted in this stage by an organisation of specific attitudes of other individuals both towards oneself and one another in social acts. In the second stage, more advanced, "the self reaches its full development by organising the individual attitudes of others into the

---

developed further by Habermas.

organised social or group attitudes" (Rosenthal, Bourgeois 1991, 91). This happens in a game when an individual, a player is able to anticipate or to incorporate another person's moves in the game, e.g. as playing a chess or a football game. In other words "each one of the participants' own acts is set by 'his being everyone else on the team'" (Rosenthal, Bourgeois 1991, 91). The self is cognitive or dialogical, there is no other possibility, and thus, "any nonreflective awareness of self presupposes the cognitive structure involved in taking the role of the other" (Rosenthal, Bourgeois 1991, 91). What is more, this very cognitive structure of the self is always deep-seated in the lived body and its temporal features. At the same time such unity of the 'I-me' that is reflective and cognitive as well as dialogical is always rooted in the "creativity and sedimentation of the lived body... Time consciousness, role taking, and self-awareness are inseparably linked" according to Mead's theory (Rosenthal, Bourgeois 1991, 123f).

Theory of Language

There is however another crucial dimension without which the theory just presented could not be completed. It is the role of the language that itself is inseparable connected with the emergence of the self and meaning. "For Mead, language, thought, and action are inseparably intertwined in the ongoing social act constituted by the 'conversation of gestures'" write Rosenthal and Bourgeois (1991, 136). Language, according to Mead is a purely social process that develops out of gestures and includes awareness of meaning. It is broader than speech, as it starts to grow from the gestures made by little children before they can even articulate any speech. These are significant gestures, but the vocal gestures have the most importance, as it is from them that language develops (Rosenthal, Bourgeois 1991, 138). We can communicate with each other as we share the same meaning of what we want to say within the group to which we belong and address ourselves. It is through taking the attitudes of the others that the special character of human intelligence is formed.

Mead's theories of language and of role taking are closely interrelated to the way that selfhood emerges. He writes about it in such words: "I know of no other form of behavior than the linguistic in which the individual is an object to himself" (Mead 1934, 142). An interesting characteristic is that while mind emerges out of language, language "itself is possible because of 'the triadic relation on which the existence of meaning is based" stress Mead (1934, 145). Here he partly agrees with Watson who claimed that thinking involves using certain words. Speaking will be then to think aloud, and there is actually an internal link between speaking and thinking. Silent thought will be a 'silent speech', that gains its structure because of language. Thus, language is also a part of the social act, and it contributes to it as being creative especially in a new situation, as it emerges from the reconstructive activity of individuals. That is why it is perfectly legitimate to study language as a part of social conduct in which both meaning and the self emerge. It is also possible to get insight into the process of learning by studying a language and its role in identity formation and change.

There are at least two features of language that Mead differentiates. First, it is characterised by temporality, even if we are born into a common language, we use it creatively by developing it. Second, as language reveals thinking, both language and thought are intersubjective or social.

According to Rosenthal and Bourgeois' interpretation of Mead, language creates new situations by creating new meanings, allows new ways of acting and thus leads to new shared experiences. These experiences are at the same time objective, or objectified, and 'universal'. Mead's theory of expression echoes his view of the self because according to him language is intrinsically temporal and internally related to thought. When an individual learns a new language s/he gets a new soul, or a new identity, as s/he takes the attitudes of those who are using this particular language. This observation has pivotal consequences for forming new attitudes and identities for example among newcomers to the culture of a social group. An individual will be unable to converse with those who belong to the community without reading its literature or without taking its peculiar attitudes. In this sense s/he becomes a different individual, thus it is impossible for a human to convey a language as a pure abstraction. Thus, one is also engaged in conveying the life that lies behind the language of a given community. "And this result builds itself into relationship with the organised attitudes of the individual who gets this language and inevitably brings about a readjustment of views" states Mead (1934, 167-68). This has profound consequences for different identity constructions and role-taking in a rapidly changing world, and is therefore important for adult education research concerned with processes of learning and becoming.

Rosenthal and Bourgeois sum up Mead's view about language in the following words:

> Language is expressive of a manner or style of behaving in a significant world. To truly appropriate a language is to understand the language, and that involves, ultimately, to live the life of the language, to live the social process it expresses (Rosenthal, Bourgeois 1991, 142).

Theory of Intersubjectivity
While comparing Mead with Merleau-Ponty, Rosenthal and Bourgeois (1991, 125) point out that "the self is inherently intersubjective" for both alike, in other words it is social, and in its very structure incorporates the role of the other. Von Wright (2000, 50) labels Mead's theory as one of human intersubjectivity. And even if Mead does not use the word intersubjectivity, nevertheless this can capture the core of his theorising. The source to human individuality and a self can be found, according to Mead, in communication between people, in their intersubjectivity. It is understood by him as in changing or changeable, as subjectivity in making. That is why Von Wright emphasises that Mead's theory can be seen as an intersubjective point of departure for becoming human, for subjectivity construction/constituting or forming.

Looking for the origin of reflexive thinking Mead leads us to the social situations that are understood as reciprocal processes of constructing meaning rather than the individual intentions that are coming from a particular mind. Thus, the social interaction inhabits a source of co-ordination conduct from which the reflexive thinking takes form. Mead's intersubjectivity in social situations is characterised by unpredictability, as people's involvement in social conduct and interaction are unique, and human conduct is characterised by constant changes. Thus each situation is unique and creative depending on what different actors contribute to it, and how it develops because of their interaction with each other. New meanings are constructed, or reconstructed and created. To predict what is going to happen is impossible. Mead's contribution to the concept of intersubjectivity thus derives from identifying a shift from the predicted or possible to the unexpected.

The Relevance of Symbolic Interactionism in Social Science Research

Symbolic interactionism is used in sociological research as a theoretical foundation, an ontological point of departure, and an interpretative approach. First it became known to Chicago sociologists and was used extensively by them. Inspired by Robert Eraz Park, Chicagonians started to do field research that resulted in compelling descriptions and analyses of urban society. Thomas and Znaniecki (1918-1921), who developed their own theoretical perspective were influenced by pragmatism and most of all by Mead. Thomas, however, contributed to symbolic interactionism with his concept of "the definition of the situation"[11]. In their empirical research, Thomas and Znaniecki (1918-1921) used personal documents for the first time in sociology.

Participant observation was usually employed by interactionists to get insights into people's meanings and symbols, but they also used life history. An example for the first can be found in Howard S. Becker's *Art Worlds* (1982) or Arlie Hochschild's *The Managed Heart* (1983). The second can be noticed in Clifford Shaw's *The Jack-Roller* (1930), as well as in Thomas and Znaniecki's *The Polish Peasant* (1918-1921), but also in Denzin's *The Alcoholic Self* (1986a), and *The Recovering Alcoholic* (1986b). Most interestingly, symbolic interactionism was used as an ontological basis for dealing with empirical data and generating theory in Glaser and Strauss' *Time for Dying* (1968), and in *Status Passage* (1967).

Writing about research methods in sociology, Denzin (1989b) emphasises that they imply a highly theoretical relevance.

> While I have chosen to employ symbolic interactionism as my theoretical perspective it would have been possible to employ any of a number of others theoretical stances.

---

[11] According to Thomas "when men define situations as real, they are real in their consequences" (Thomas, I. W., Thomas, D. C. 1928, 571-572).

Structural functionalism, social behaviourism, conflict theory, feminist theory, critical theory, cultural studies, or ethnomethodology could have been used. Any of these approaches would lead to significantly different conclusions (Denzin 1989b, 2).

Thus, the choice of the theory as a starting point has decisive consequences for the analysis of qualitative data. Symbolic interactionism is a useful ontological and methodological point of departure in order to understand and analyse as well as problematise human conduct and learning. What is more, it helps to interpret educational processes in practice, i.e. human encounters and interactions, as well as learning both as an individual and collectively, emphasising intersubjectivity and sociality.

In educational research, and especially in sociology of education, symbolic interactionism is a basis or a theoretical perspective in classroom research, where the focus is on negotiation as a social reality, on the meeting between teachers and pupils, as well as interaction among pupils themselves. David Hargreaves' research provides an example. In his book "Interpersonal Relations and Education" (1975) he applies interactionism when studying teacher-pupil relations. His point of departure is that pupils enter into a school, in which teachers have the power to determine and enforce their definition of the situation. Thus, it is wise to first look at the teacher's definition of the situation, and this definition must be congruent with his/her classroom role. Hargreaves finds three general types of self-conception of teachers: 'liontamers', 'entertainers' and 'romantics'. What is interesting, however, is Hargreaves' assumption that all three types are only provisional and based on stereotypes. According to him all teachers are unique in certain ways, thus the typology is an artificial construction. Teachers have also their own self-conception, and within it several sub-roles. Each particular teacher, however, cannot define his role as he wishes: there are constraints and expectations which force him to include disciplining and instructing in his self-conception. There is of course some freedom in this. But the individual's conception of his role is only one part, however an important part, of what has to be considered in understanding the interaction of teacher and pupil. The teacher's self-conception also includes an expectation of the ideal pupil's role. Thus, there are ideal self-conceptions as teachers, an understanding of the ideal pupil, realistic expectations of pupils, and in the end an idea of the actual role (Blackledge, Hunt 1985, 244).

Hargreaves analyses pupils and teachers separately to bring them together in a comparative analysis. Both parties define their definition of the situation. Both, teachers and pupils use different strategies to foster their own definition or modify the other's view. Teachers usually use 'negative techniques' in the form of promises and threats, they appeal to higher authority, they divide and rule; pupils on the other hand used appeals to justice, to higher authority (e.g. my mum says), etc. Hargreaves suggests that the 'pseudo-concord' is the typical situation. The process of negotiation is a continuous one. For him the classroom is a place where conflict, but not open war, is taking place. The parties impose their definitions of the situation upon each other, by using techniques which maximise their own goals.

Von Wright (2000) uses Mead's ideas to understand the educational processes occurring between teachers and pupils in school. In Mead's thoughts she finds excellent and fruitful examples of how educational practice – the interaction between pupils and teachers – can be seen not as substantial or punctual but as a process, in the making, in other words as a relational one that is conceptualised and used in everyday experience. Both teachers and pupils are in the process of making or becoming. She is using an intersubjective turn from Mead's theory that explains "how we can extend and complicate our understanding, by turning it from an individualistic and substantial into a social and action-oriented one" (Von Wright 2000, 221). The meetings or encounters between the actors are social situations, and education is also a social situation which contributes to the democratic way of looking at each other, understand each other, live and work with each other. Those meetings can be used as educational tools, as relational. Von Wright concludes:

> The teacher is understood in relation to the student, and the student in relation to the teacher. Individuality is not a property of the self, but is constituted and changed in social

action. The uniqueness of a person is found within the intersubjective in-between space, the encounter. Therefore a presupposition for the pedagogical encounter is directing attention towards the encounter in which the student may be met as a concrete other, as a *who*, and not as a *what* (Von Wright 2000, 224).

In adult education Mezirow's theory of transformation learning serves as a good example of one inspired by Mead's ideas, especially his theory of the self. In a private communication, Mezirow said he knew Herbert Blumer as a friend and colleague, and read both Mead and Blumer before his theory emerged (October 2001, Stockholm). When Mezirow uses critical reflection and self-critical reflection as categories that help us to understand how transformation learning is possible, either in the stance of instrumental or communicative learning, we can easily see the influence of Mead and symbolic interactionism on Mezirow's way of conceptualising adult learning. I am not going to explore this issue further as there is Lena Wilhelmsson's article on Mezirow's theory in this collection of articles.

Even Peter Alheit's theory of biographicity and his research based on adults' biographies (life stories) can serve as a good example of Mead's influence, especially his concept of the self, and intersubjectivity (Alheit, 1995). What is more, Alheit incorporates in his theory the views of Bourdieu about linking agency with structure, when he describes the interrelation between the individual's intentionality and structure (expectations of others) within their narratives. According to Bourdieu's constructivist approach to sociology the objective and subjective aspects of social life are inescapably connected with each other and this calls for careful examination of the dualism of macro versus micro and of structure versus agency bound. These aspects of Bourdieu's theory are similar to Mead's way of bridging the macro (social) with the micro (individual) issues, as well as to Mead's view of the self which incorporates 'me' as a socially oriented pole of the self with the reference to 'the generalized other', with the 'I' pole that is unique, individual and hard to predict.

Even if she was not directly influenced by Mead Marianne Horsdal (2000, 2001) is using ideas similar to symbolic interactionism in the analysis of narratives she collected with several hundred people in Denmark. Interestingly, Mead's ideas are of general validity as they became a heritage for understanding our identities, and the social and temporal process of becoming, the unity of body and mind as well as the emergence of meaning, the self, the role of language, and other symbols as crucial for these processes. Horsdal sees the narratives as emerging from different configurations that affect how we act in the present with the prospect of the future and looking back to the past.

Also in Linden West's writings (1996, 2001) it is possible to see influences of Mead in looking at the human being as constructor and reconstructor of his/her identity, dealing with complexity issues of our time. And again, there is a greater link to Mead as common social knowledge than in specific references to him.

We can also see how symbolic interactionism has influenced such theoretical perspectives as Berger and Luckmann's social constructivism, or Habermas' critical theory, and especially the latter's communicative and instrumental action, as well as transformative and dialogical interaction. Both perspectives have interesting consequences for understanding how people learn and become, and in this way contribute to adult education research.

Symbolic Interactionism in my Research

My way to biographical research seems more natural from the time perspective, by looking back at my academic career. Coming to Sweden from continental Europe and its traditions, and then settling down to work in Swedish universities was not greatly different for me, either in scientific discourse or research methodology, especially in the beginning. Experiences of scholarship and work at universities in the US and Canada also contributed to an easy or smooth readjustment. There were, however, other experiences that furnished my interest in biographical research as well as changes in my own perception or perspective on what is knowledge, science and human nature. This was the meeting with Swedish culture in general, and with the language and culture of common people (Folk high school teachers' candidates at Linköping University). This made a profound impact on my ontological and epistemological perspective and reconstruction of my identity both as a person and researcher. To be able to understand the processes I was going through in my own biography, while both floating and learning, the writings of Florian Znaniecki, Chicago school tradition and G. H. Mead's symbolic interactionism were more than helpful.

Since 1986 I have been involved in collecting life stories from different groups of people in Sweden (Polish immigrants, PhD students, non-traditional students in higher education) (Bron 1995a, 1995b, 1998, 1999, 2000, Bron and West 2000). Even if this range of people seems very different, nevertheless there are many commonalties they share with each other. Viewed from Mead's perspective we are dealing with constructing and reconstructing or making and remaking identities, through interactions and language learning, as well as adjustment and readjustment to culture, subcultures and their symbols, all in the process of social interaction and within a range of social institutions. The stories people tell are temporal products, which show that the individual life is never ending and always open to new experiences and changes, often unexpected, so are identities and social roles. This makes each life unique and dynamic, and yet within the same culture and language so similar that it enables us to understand each other and to change ourselves and the others. As Denzin (1989) writes:

> All stories and narratives are temporal products. They are either tales or stories of time, or stories about time (Ricoeur) ... all stories deal with temporal order of events, some events being anterior to or simultaneous with other events, while some are posterior, or come after events (Denzin 1989, 185).

According to Mead "the memories of the past self are memories as essentially related to, and emanating from, a present self" (Rosenthal, Bourgeois 1991, 121). Thus, again the temporality of the self and of the biography is emphasised and has profound consequences for analysing and understanding of the story told.

I used life history as a research method and approach that enabled me to know and theorise adults' lives in more depth and with greater theoretical subtlety, including experiences of managing change, risk taking and learning. Here the influence of Mead is more than obvious. The processes that can be looked at from a symbolic interactionist point of view are those including learning, both formal and informal, motivation, career development as well as the construction of social roles, ethnic and gender identities. By collecting life stories we can get insight into the existential, psychological and social well being of adults; their struggles as individuals, and whole groups, to compose identities and biographies in a paradoxical late modern culture characterised by flux, frightening uncertainties and exposed to risks, but also new opportunities for self-definition (Bron, West 2000). This includes the idea of intentionality but also having socially defined roles and expectations. In the meeting points between these two processes, self-identity is developed and change is negotiated.

One of the results of my research that is both grounded in the data, i.e. life stories, but also influenced by symbolic interactionism's analysis is the category that emerged from the stories of both Polish immigrants and PhD students. I called this category 'floating', that involved a basic uncertainty about self, identity, place and belonging. It includes a feeling of being fragmented, of not having a past, and of being afraid to form or plan a future. Ewa Hoffman (1989), who emigrated as a child with her family from Poland to Canada, has captured this experience:

> I can't afford to look back, and I can't figure out how to look forward. In both directions, I may see a Medusa, and I already feel the danger of being turned into stone. Betwixt and between, I am stuck and time is stuck within me. Time used to open out, serene, shimmering with promise. If I wanted to hold a moment still, it was because I wanted to expand it, to get its fill. Now, time has no dimension, no extension backward or forward. I arrest the past, and I hold myself stiffly against the future; I want to stop the flow. As a punishment, I exist in the stasis of a perpetual present, that other side of "living in the present", which is not eternity

but a prison. I can't throw a bridge between the present and the past, and therefore I can't make time move (Hoffman 1989, 116-117).

It can also be said that "the feeling of being fragmented, of not having a past and being afraid to form or plan a future, is a typical situation for individuals who are 'floating'" (Bron, West 2000, 167). Humans need to move on and reconstruct biographically, they need to become more of a self while interacting with others. From the fragments, illusions and disillusions, a new whole is reorganised and created. Missing pieces and a lacking sense of authorship in life do not make us feeling happy (Bron, West 2000). Such situations may be typical for immigrants, but also for newcomers to the academic world, where both culture and language, as well as ways of conduct and meeting people, differ considerably from settings outside. This of course is not the only example: all social institutions create a specific way of being through their members. Informal learning and tacit knowledge are the phenomena that can be investigated through biographies of people involved in social encounters.

Biographies are thus useful or knowledgeable cases that can give insights into how identities are changing and becoming. It is possible to have different identities, or several, at the same time, and cope with them accordingly in different social situations, family, work, by being with friends. Because of changes in life, like in emigration or changing the career, where new culture, new language, and symbols as well as meanings are involved we can enrich and shape our lives again and again. To capture such processes is essential for understanding human conduct and becoming, but most of all, for adult educators, to capture the intersubjectivity of human learning.

Conclusions

Symbolic interactionism, particularly Mead's, can be seen as a potential for guiding research in adult education and adult learning. Especially but not only in cognitive and reflective thinking and acting the view about the world is constructed together with others and the meanings are emerging and given. The strengths for adult education lie in Mead's ontology where human beings are seen as situated in a process of becoming.

There are, however, difficulties in presenting Mead's theory, and not only because it is so complex, but because, firstly, it is based on interpretation of his scanty written publications, consisting of articles.[12] Thus, the emphasis is mostly based on his students' notes during his lectures in Chicago, and than published in book form. Secondly, because all the concepts and arguments Mead uses in his theory interlink with each other, it is difficult to grasp any single one or subset of them adequately without attending to their interrelationships with the others. This is true for his analysis of how meanings and the self emerge, how language contributes to that as well as how identity is formed and how all these processes include temporality, and finally how the unity of body and mind contribute to, but also is influenced by, human intersubjectivity and sociality. Thus, by interpreting Mead's work it is important to refer to the relations between these various concepts, aspects and processes rather than to take any of them as a separate entity.

Mead's ideas are echoed in writings of others, in sociology, social psychology and psychology, thus we can see similarities in dealing with everyday life conduct of human beings that contemporary researchers describe from their data. Mead's thoughts are useful again in today's research especially when dealing with everyday life issues and narratives or biographies of individuals and collectives at the time of uncertainty, risk taking and flux.

References

Alheit, P. (1995). 'Patchworkers'. In: Alheit, P. et al. (eds.). *The Biographical Approach in European Adult Education*. Wien, pp. 151-171.

Becker, H. S. (1982). *Art Worlds*. Barkeley.

Berger, P., Luckmann, T. (1966). *The Social Construction of Reality*. Garden City, NY.

Blackledge, D., Hunt, B. (1985). *Sociological Interpretations of Education*. London.

Bourdieu, P. (1977). *Outline of Theory and Practice*. Cambridge.

---

[12] These are edited as selected writings, but there is also archived material at Chicago University worth studying (see Von Wright 2000).

Bron-Wojciechowska, A. (1995a). *Att forskarutbilda sig vid Uppsala universitet.* Om kvinnliga och manliga doktorander. (Post-Graduate Studies at Uppsala University. About Female and Male Doctoral Students). Pedagogisk forskning i Uppsala (Educational Research in Uppsala) No.120, Uppsala.

Bron-Wojciechowska, A. (1995b). The Use of Life History Approach in Adult Education Research. In: Alheit, P. et al. (eds.). *Biographical Research and Adult Education. A New Approach.* Vienna, pp.107-118.

Bron, A. (1998). Graduate Women and Men Research Careers at Uppsala University. Is there any Difference? In: Wulf, C. et al. (ed.). *Commonalities and Diversities in Europe.* Berlin, pp. 559-574.

Bron, A. (1999). The Price of Immigration. Life Stories of Two Poles in Sweden. In: *International Journal of Contemporary Sociology,* 36 (2), pp. 191-203.

Bron, A. (2000). Floating as an Analytical Category in the Narratives of Polish Immigrants to Sweden. In: Szwejkowska-Olsson, E., Bron Jr. M. (eds.). *Allvarlig debatt och rolig lek.* En festskrift tillägnad Andrzej Nils Uggla. Uppsala, pp.119-132.

Bron, A., West, L. (2000). Time for Stories; the Emergence of Life History Methods in the Social Sciences. In: *International Journal of Contemporary Sociology,* 37 (2), pp. 158-175.

Bron, A. (2001). Civil Society and Biographical Learning. In: Schemmann, M., Bron Jr. M. (eds.). *Adult Education and Democratic Citizenship.* Vol IV. Karkow.

Denzin, N. K. (1986a). *The Alcoholic Self.* Beverly Hills, CA.

Denzin, N. K. (1986b). *The Recovering Alcoholic.* Beverly Hills, CA.

Denzin, N. K. (1989a). *Symbolic Interactionism. Perspective and Method.* Princton-Hall.

Denzin, N. K. (1989b). *The Research Act. A Theoretical Introduction to Sociological Methods.* Englewoods Cliffs, NJ.

Glaser, B., Strauss, A. (1965). *Time for Dying.* Chicago.

Glaser, B., Strauss, A. (1967). *Status Passage. A Formal Theory.* Chicago.

Hagreaves, D. (1975). *Interpersonal Relations and Education.* London.

Hochschild, A. (1983). *The Managed Heart. Commercialization of Human Feelings.* Berkeley.

Hoffman, E. (1989). *Lost in Translation.* London.

Horsdal, M. (2000). *Vilje og vilkår. Identitet, læring och demokrati.* Copenhagen.

Horsdal, M. (2001). Democratic Citizenship and the Making of Cultures. In: Schemmann, M., Bron Jr. M. (eds.). *Adult Education and Democratic Citizenship.* Vol. IV. Karkow.

Marshal, G. (ed.) (1994). *The Concise Oxford Dictionary of Sociology.* Oxford.

Mead, G. H. (1934). *Mind, Self, and Society. From a Standpoint of a Social Behaviourist.* Chicago.

Mead, G. H. (1964). *Selected Writings.* (ed. by Reck, A. J.) Chicago.

Rosenthal, S. B., Bourgeois, P. L. (1991). *Mead and Merleau-Ponty. Toward a Common Vision.* New York.

Shaw, C. R. (1930). *The Jack-Roller. A Delinquent Boy's Own Story.*

Silverman, D. (1993). *Interpretating Qualitative Data.* London.

Strauss, A. (ed.) (1977). *Mead, George Herbert: On Social Psychology.* Selected Papers. Chicago.

Thomas, I. W., Znaniecki, F. (1918-1921). *The Polish Peasant in Europe and America. A Monograph of an Immigrant Group.*

Thomas, I. W., Thomas, D. S. (1928). *The Child in America. Behavior Problems and Programs.* New York.

Von Wright, Moira (2000). *Vad eller vem? En pedagogisk rekonstruktion av G. H. Meads teori om människors intersubjektivitet.* Göteborg.

West, L. (1996). *Beyond Fragments, Adults, Motivation and Higher Education. A Biographical Analysis.* London.

West, L. (2001). *Doctors on the Edge. General Practitioners, Health and Learning in the Inner-City.* London.

Lena Wilhelmson

ON THE THEORY OF TRANSFORMATIVE LEARNING

Introduction

The theory of transformative learning is carried by a passion for emancipatory change.[1] It strives for change in societal power relations and aims at developing knowledgeable voices in every adult person through promoting individual transformation. The theory is highly relevant in today's world of rapid change since its core mission is to make adults reconsider old frames of reference. Perspective transformation is seen as the central learning process in adult development. The theory could, for example, be of relevance for research on human issues of working life transitions. It could also be used to reach a better understanding of what concepts like "the learning organisation" has to offer when all employees are demanded to adapt to and learn new ways of working. But so far the theory has mostly been used in educational settings, maybe because that is where it has its empirical roots.

The transformation theory was first developed by Jack Mezirow (Mezirow & Ass. 1990, Mezirow 1991) out of his research experience as an educationist (Mezirow 1978a). This experience concerned women's re-entry programmes in community colleges[2]. The personal development of

---

[1] I am grateful for the kind comments of Professor Mezirow on this text, any remaining errors are of course my own.
[2] These re-entry programmes were part of the women's liberation movement in the US at the time. They were chosen by Mezirow and his colleagues because of: the large number of such colleges, the high proportion of adult working class students, their community service orientation and their diversity. The aim was to "identify factors that impeded or facilitated the progress of these programs" (Mezirow 1978a, abstract).

these women, liberating themselves from social dependency roles in an educational setting, is the empirical origin of the theory.

The explicit purpose of the transformation theory is to be useful for adult educators whose goal is not only to teach a subject but also to assist the development of their adult students' capacity for living in a complex and dynamic society.

> Adult education may be understood as an organized effort to assist learners who are old enough to be held responsible for their acts to acquire or enhance their understandings, skills, and dispositions...
> Fostering these liberating conditions for making more autonomous and informed choices and developing a sense of self-empowerment is the cardinal goal of adult education (Mezirow 2000, 26).

Adult cognitive development, with affective and conative dimensions[3], is about how to develop a capacity to be a responsible adult in the "late modernity"(Giddens 1991) society, where no traditional truths hold any more. According to transformation theory, this can be reached through critical reflective thinking, deliberately bringing assumptions out in broad daylight.

In this chapter I will first give a brief presentation of the theory, followed by an overview of some empirical usage of the theory including some results from my own research, as the main part of the chapter. Finally some views on the further development of the theory are referred to.

Overview of the Transformation Theory

The following description of transformation theory is mostly based upon Mezirow's own writings from the seventies up to the present time (1978a, 1978b, Mezirow & Ass. 1990, Mezirow 1991, 1996), with an emphasis on

---

[3] In other words, with feelings as well as with one's own free will.

the latest contribution (Mezirow 2000), since the core propositions have evolved over time [4].

Mezirow claims that transformation theory is a general, abstract and idealised model of the learning process, based on the nature of human communication. The theory of transformative learning wants to illuminate general but invisible conditions for human development. It deals with adult learning and views perspective change as the active dynamic of learning. Learning is seen as an interactive process among people, dependent on contextual factors – as the individual transforms his/her way of understanding.

Theoretical Frame of Reference

Transformation theory is inspired by empirical findings and informed by various theories (Mezirow 1991). It aims at being a means of guidance for adult educators who want to trigger personal development in their students. The intention is to create a synthesis that might be helpful in the daily education work. In the long run the aim is to contribute to a democratic and open-minded society.

> This theory is derived from culturally specific conditions associated with democratic societies and with the development of adult education as a vocation in Western Europe and North America, a liberal tradition that depends ultimately on faith in informed, free human choice and social justice (Mezirow 2000, xiv).

One source of inspiration is Freire's (1970) pedagogy for arousing critical consciousness [5] with political and emancipatory purposes in liter-

---

[4] The development of transformation theory has been a process of empirical findings in the seventies, theoretical underpinning in the eighties resulting in the main theoretical work 1991 (Mezirow 1991), and in the nineties an ongoing discussion, in the "Adult Education Quarterly" and other journals, between Mezirow and several critical voices. These discussions have informed the theory's development continuously.

[5] Freire's concept is conscientisation.

acy education for oppressed people in the Third World. Epistemologically, transformation theory leans on Habermas' theory of communicative action (1984), using the concepts of instrumental and communicative learning. Another theory of importance is Dewey's (1938/1951) thinking on learning from experience with its emphasis on reflection and critical reflection, as a way of questioning what is taken for granted. Symbolic interactionism (Blumer 1969, Mead 1934) concerning how consciousness and self is created in the social process of communication is another theoretical source. Sociology of knowledge (Berger, Luckmann 1966) is also of importance, highlighting the process of objectivisation and the creation of normality in society. Activity theory (Wertsch 1979) is another ingredient, in which learning is seen as an activity dependent on social interaction, for example the importance of language for abstract thinking to develop is emphasised. But learning is also seen as prereflective, not always as being a function of language, as in the psychodynamic theories of Jung, interpreted by Boyd and Myers (1988).

Epistemology[6]

A major influence on transformation theory is Habermas' extension of Critical Theory (1984), especially in defining two domains of learning, instrumental learning and communicative learning.

Instrumental learning is the traditional objectivistic epistemology, rooted in the eighteenth century Age of Enlightenment. Here reality has an independent existence, truth is seen as a claim on correct reproduction of reality, knowledge and validity is objective, logic and rationality are emphasised. Instrumental learning aims at obtaining an ability to manipulate and use the environment, including other people, to obtain goals of one's own.

Communicative learning belongs to an interpretative subjectivist epistemology. Research within this realm focuses on language and social interaction. Social reality is defined by power(-relations), notions of reality are

---

[6] The branch of philosophy that deals with the varieties, grounds, and validity of knowledge (The New Shorter Oxford English Dictionary, 1993).

seen as socially constructed, the framework of an individual constitutes his/her experience. Communicative learning aims at understanding the meaning and interpretations of others, getting hold of the lived experience of others, it involves the making of a judgement:

> In communicative learning, we determine the justification of a problematic belief or understanding through rational discourse to arrive at a tentative best judgement. The only alternatives to discourse for justifying a belief are to appeal to tradition, authority, or force (Mezirow 2000, 10).

The third learning domain, according to Habermas, is emancipatory learning[7]. This is the domain that has been further developed by Mezirow (2000), as transformative learning. Both instrumental and communicative knowledge can be used in the transformation process. But to be able to learn transformatively, the learner has to develop an ability to reflect critically. Through both critical reflection, and critical self-reflection, the learner can use the transformative potential in his/her own and others' interpretative frames of reference, as is illustrated in the figure below.

Figure 1: A Model Describing the Three Learning Domains Referred to in Transformation Theory[8]

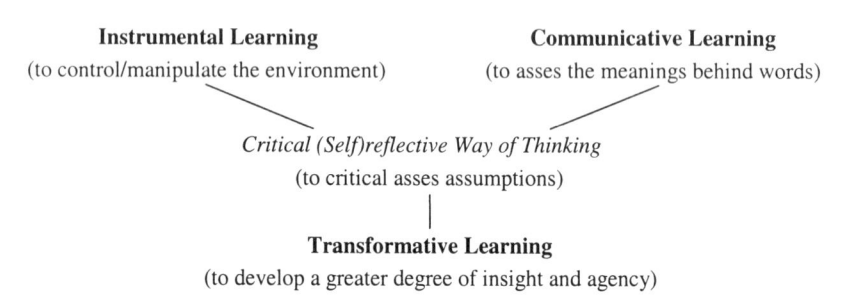

Instrumental Learning   **Communicative Learning**
(to control/manipulate the environment)   (to asses the meanings behind words)

Critical (Self)reflective Way of Thinking
(to critical asses assumptions)

Transformative Learning
(to develop a greater degree of insight and agency)

---

[7] This learning domain is aimed at overcoming relations of domination, conditions of autonomy must be informed by "action-orienting self-understanding" (McCarthy 1984, 99).

Competence for transformative learning is reached through the safe sharing of experiences:

...social linkages are often developed inside classes through the sharing of personal experiences. This is encouraged by staff, who themselves contribute perspectives and insights. When women speak from their experience, they lose anxiety about being "wrong". This has the ancillary effect of building the academic competitive skills of discussion, verbalizing ideas, logical argumentation, and assertive behaviour (Mezirow 1978a, 21).

The need for transition support is one of the main findings in this early empirical work that is not much addressed in the later theoretical thinking [9]. The main road to transformative learning, as several empirical studies point out, is through symmetrical communication [10], and our western culture is one of argument (Tannen 1998). Rational discourse, according to Habermas, (1984) theory of communicative action, is of importance for a democratic society. There is a risk though, in an argument culture, that rational discourse is mistaken for debate. It is important to stress that rational discourse needs the quality of trust, solidarity, security and empathy. Rational argumentation is reliant on feelings of safety in the individual, for free and full participation in interaction with others.

Main Concepts

Important concepts in transformation theory are "frame of reference", "critical reflection", "action", and of course "transformation".

---

[8] The model was developed at the Adult Education Seminar at the Department of Education, Stockholm University.
[9] At least not in Mezirow 1991, in the later writings (Mezirow 2000, 10-16) this is elaborated on.
[10] Symmetrical communication with dialogical qualities, will be further developed in the presentation of my own research below. Dialogue competence seems to consist of ability of integration as well as ability of differentiation.

Frame of Reference

Mezirow's two main concepts are "meaning perspectives" and "meaning schemes" (Mezirow 1991). Or, in other words, "habits of mind" and "points of view" (Mezirow 2000). Taken together, these constitute the selective frame of reference through which our perceptions are filtered. A frame of reference consists both of cultural paradigms and idiosyncrasy from our personal history. The habits of mind and points of view we develop are in tune with the social, historical and cultural currents in society. These currents are created in social discourse, where power relations are unequal. Cultural frames of reference create the borders within which humans can learn while transformative learning means to discover these frames and to be able to exceed them.

Habits of mind are inclusive world-views that constitute habits of interpretation, i.e. habits learned through our socialisation as human beings. Within this socio-cultural learning we construct our belief-systems, our self-perception, our grounded values and our taken for granted assumptions. Habits of mind are expressed in points of view. Points of view are clusters of opinions that often determine how we interpret cause-effect relationships, mostly without being aware of it. Points of view are revealed when individuals experience difference, e.g. through sharing narratives. If we do not make those opinions visible intentionally they tend to form our actions in ways we are not fully aware of. Transformation of these habits of mind and points of view is a painful process, since "our values and sense of self are anchored in our frames of reference. They provide us with a sense of stability, coherence, community, and identity. Consequently they are often emotionally charged and strongly defended" (Mezirow 2000, 18).

Critical Reflection

Learning within existing frames of reference means developing meaning structures since long taken for granted, it is an assimilative process. Critical reflection is needed (see Figure 1) to make us conscious of our distorted assumptions; this is an accommodative process that focuses on instrumental learning. The intent is to improve performance, the reframing is objective. But to free ourselves from personal or cultural limitations in our world-view, we have to develop ability for critical self-reflection on assumptions. This is an accommodative process that focuses on communicative learning. The intent is to look through constraints that have become a part of ourselves, but hinder us on our way to become responsible adults able to contribute to the development of a democratic society.

Action and Transformation
Action is of importance to transformative learning. To have a frame of reference implies having a habit leading us as we act. To act means to try out this frame, acting through the guidance we get from our habits of mind and points of view. When actions fail we get a cause to alter our opinions and ways of understanding. This might offer a possibility to make our assumptions visible. In this way, disorienting dilemmas can offer important learning opportunities.

Adults may become restrained by the frame of reference they use to interpret and understand perceptions and experiences made. The learning individual is forced to revise a former assumption in order to be able to better handle the demands put upon her or him in a given situation. Transformation is necessary to be able to better manage in the surrounding world as reality answers back on our talking and acting. "Transformation refers to a movement through time of reformulating reified structures of meaning by reconstructing dominant narratives" (Mezirow 2000, 19).

Perspective transformation leads to a revised frame of reference, and a willingness to act on the new perspective. A new way of acting is the clearest indication that a transformation has occurred. A transformation may occur sudden and dramatic as well as cumulative over a longer period of time.

Mezirow speaks of ten phases of transformation when meaning becomes clarified in the process of transformative learning:

1. A disorienting dilemma
2. Self-examination with feelings of fear, anger, guilt, or shame
3. A critical assessment of assumptions

4. Recognition that one's discontent and the process of transformation are shared
5. Exploration of options for new roles, relationships, and actions
6. Planning a course of action
7. Acquiring knowledge and skills for implementing one's plans
8. Provisional trying of new roles
9. Building competence and self-confidence in new roles and relationships
10. A reintegration into one's life on the basis of conditions dictated by one's new perspective (Mezirow 2000, 22).

In this way a disorienting dilemma creates a state of disequilibrium which can stir us up and force us out of assumptions earlier taken for granted. This is the trigger of perspective transformation.

Empirical Usage of Transformation Theory in Adult Education Research

Most empirical studies that have been conducted in line with transformation theory are doctoral dissertations at US universities. These studies are mostly unpublished (Taylor 1998, 2000). First I present a rough overview of empirical research from 1982 to 2000, thereafter I present some of my own research results in more detail.

Empirical Studies

This presentation of empirical studies using transformation theory is based on an analysis made by Taylor (1998, 2000), involving more than forty-five unpublished empirical studies (from 1982-1998). A complementary search made in March 2001 by myself resulted in the findings of thirty-four [11] empirical studies from 1999-2000 [12].

---

[11] Twenty-four of those are US dissertations from a range of universities, two dissertations come from Canada, the rest (8) are empirical studies presented in journal articles.

[12] Online: http://dialogweb.com (Searching on: Mezirow, transformative learning, transformation theory).

The analysis of empirical studies made by Taylor[13] focuses on "a series of themes that emerge naturally from the findings and others in response to unresolved and often debated issues about transformative learning" (Taylor 2000, 286). This presentation follows most of the themes as Taylor discusses them, with additions made from the complementary research[14]. The themes give a brief overview of what is presently empirically known and what has been of interest for researchers to study in relation to transformation theory.

Frame of Reference and Perspective Transformation

The theoretical construction of a frame of reference, which is the corner stone in transformation theory, lacks strong empirical foundation, according to Taylor (2000). Meaning perspectives and meaning schemes are conceptual constructions, hard to identify in empirical studies due to their habitual nature. Also, Mezirow's definition of perspective transformation seems to be too narrow and rationally based. The following variety of phenomena has been connected to perspective transformation in empirical studies:

- new concepts of knowledge
- mystical experience
- personal power increase
- redefined perspective
- sustained change over time
- spirituality
- transpersonal realm of development
- compassion for others
- creativity
- shift in discourse
- courage

---

[13] For further references to the studies in Taylor's analysis, I recommend Taylor (1998, 2000).

[14] The thirty-four studies from 99/00 have been thematised by reading only the abstracts. This complementary analyse of empirical studies I call "99/00-studies" in the text that follows. The 99/00-studies focused on the following issues: personal growth (12), society development (3), working life (3), and education (15).

- sense of liberation
- new connectedness with others

According to Mezirow's theory, the transformative process of change is a significant personal event, triggered by a disorienting dilemma, and causing an internal personal crisis. In the studies, transformation is seen as a more complex process, still with a disorienting dilemma, but with the integration of circumstances as an important ingredient. Maybe the theory is not clear enough regarding the collective and contextual aspects of communicative learning (e.g. Mezirow 1991, 75). The concept of communicative learning in itself implies interaction with the environment, including other human beings.

Some studies confirm Mezirow's ten phases of transformation, other studies describe the phases more as recursive, evolving, and spiralling. The journey of transformation is seen as less linear, it is more individualistic and fluid. Also recognition of feelings (surprise and anger) seems to be of importance before critical reflection can take place. The cumulative nature of transformative learning is emphasised; meaning schemes change over time and culminate in perspective transformation. It is an evolutionary process rather than a response to crisis. Transformation seems to involve the development of multiple intelligence, to cultivate critical thinking as well as expressing one's voice. This also involves the training of capabilities that are not part of the traditional gender role. For women this could be successfully confronting authority, and for men it could be attaining a greater awareness of their feelings.

The 1999/2000-studies mostly confirm transformation theory concerning perspective transformation. Perspective transformation seems to be stable over time (Courtenay, Merriam, Reeves 2000); critical reflection and self-examination lead to personal development and perspective transformation (King 1999, 2000). It is the coercion to change, e.g. career growth as a result of job loss (Coleman-Hoeppel 1999), that forces transformation and development. A disorienting, critical life event leads to critical reflection, and a more open flexible worldview that contributes to changed behaviour. But there are also studies that contradict the importance of critically assessing assumptions. It is rather the accumulation of responses over time which gradually create new habits of expectation that result in perspective transformation. This process is mostly driven by non-reflective assimilative learning, such as the impact of cultural differences on Chinese immigrants in the US (Temple 1999).

The 1999/2000-studies also mostly emphasise the transformative experience as a personal development depending on contextual conditions, such as the importance of the learning environment for teachers (Magro 1999), psychological growth for elderly (Shaw 1999), developmental growth for criminals (Bolduc 2000), change and empowerment for adult community college students (Candales 2000), and human qualities in leadership (Lamm 2000). Lamm recommends adding the affective dimension (empathy, humility, tolerance and patience) to future research on transformative learning, and broadening out from a sole focus on rational outcomes.

Affective Learning and Relational Knowing as Means for Critical Reflection

Taylor states that transformation theory does not pay enough attention to the interdependent relationship between critical reflection and affects in the transformative process. Empirical studies reveal that the unwillingness to respond to feelings can be a barrier to learning, and that exploring feelings in depth lead to self awareness and changes in meaning structures.

It seems that transformative learning is more than rationally based according to results from various studies: critical reflection can only begin after emotions have been worked through. Empathetic viewing of other perspectives is of importance as well as the trusting of intuition. Feelings are a trigger for reflection and more complex learning will happen if affective change occurs. Transformative learning and critical self-reflection involve intensive emotional experience. Affective learning plays a primary role in the fostering of critical reflection.

There is also a lack of attention to relations in Mezirow's original model, Taylor says. The importance of relationships is the most common finding in all the studies. Rational discourse (where critical reflection is played out) is dependent on relational ways of knowing, such as:

- trust
- friendship

- support
- modelling
- interpersonal support
- social support
- family connections
- networking
- learning-in-relationships
- intuition
- empathy
- faith

Relationships with like-minded persons who share the new perspective support reinforcement. Trusting relationships facilitate management of the threatening experience of transformation, offering an outer stability when the inner sense of stability is shaky.

Several of the 1999/2000-studies focus on critical reflection. For example, social movements can build and strengthen knowledge through critical reflection and action, with the purpose of social and political change (Golding Rosenberg, 1999). Kauffman (1999) describes the collaborative learning process as a "dance between the cognitive and affective domains of adult learning", as it evolves in a three step process of critical self-reflection, small group sharing, and large-group discussion.

Only a few of the 1999/2000-studies have focused on relational knowing. Cox (1999) for example found seven key elements that fostered transformative learning in a computer mediated education programme. Cox states that personal story telling and virtual group discourse extended the individual and encompassed relatedness to others, the natural world, or the cosmos.

Context

Taylor divides studies on contextual factors of perspective transformation into personal and socio-cultural categories. Examples of personal contextual factors described in the empirical studies include: readiness for change, role of experience, prior stressful life events, and predisposition towards transformation experience. Socio-cultural contextual factors can be perspectives of difference, historical or geographical influences, traditions, and national trends in response to larger or more complex historical events.

The importance of context for transformative learning is addressed in several of the 1999/2000-studies. One example is Roosta (1999), who states that individual and social transformations are simultaneous processes. Social intentions should be integrated in the curriculum for adult education, since adult learning and community development are interdependent. Sherlock (2000), in a study of learning experiences of non-profit association CEOs [15], concludes that the context is so politically intense that the CEOs cannot learn through dialogue. Feelings of vulnerability and isolation make them self-absorbed, and not likely to develop transformative learning.

Educational Settings

The fostering of transformative learning in educational settings has been studied empirically in several ways, according to Taylor. A variety of theoretical perspectives and settings are used focusing on how to facilitate personal change and achieve a sense of safety, openness, and trust.

There are studies on instructional methods, how to achieve qualities such as autonomy, participation, collaboration, and exploration of alternative personal perspectives in educational settings. Several studies look into how to establish a democratic, open and, rational learning situation. The need for participants to situate themselves historically, politically, and culturally, within a group context is emphasised. Embracing conflict is seen as a means for transformative learning, to explore differences creates learning opportunities. Some studies focus on how to be a good teacher, emphasising personal qualities such as:

- trustworthiness
- empathy
- care
- authenticity
- sincerity

---

[15] Chief Executive Officer

- high integrity
- involvement – giving confidence in the learner
- personal self-disclosure
- ability to work through emotions before critical reflection
- ask for feedback for self-assessment
- create hands-on learning activities
- solitude for self-dialogue

Most of the 1999/2000-studies concern educational matters in some form, and generally confirm transformation theory, using it as an analytical tool, often together with other related theories. Many models and learning programmes have been developed for transformative purposes in educational settings (e.g. King 2000, Kroth, Boverie 2000, Kauffman 1999, Hadaway 1999, Cox 1999, Karlen 1999, Robbins 1999, Barlas 2000, and Pineiro 2000). A wide range of issues are addressed, such as: information technology supporting transformative learning (Cox 1999), the use of a transformative model for transference of biblical ideals (Hadaway 1999), the empowerment of students to experience personal transformation (Karlen 1999), critical/feminist pedagogy in the context of a cultural diversity course (Robbins 1999), and the creation of educational opportunities in corporations as a vehicle for organisational capability migration (Treichler 2000).

To conclude, transformation theory has been used both as a guidance for pedagogical method development and as an analytical tool for interpreting empirical results. Many methods have been developed for transformative learning purposes in educational settings, all with the intention of triggering perspective change and development in the life of adults. What has not been done in the empirical studies, according to Taylor (1998, 2000), is an accumulation of empirical results, the studies do not relate to each other. All the same, some results seem to lead in the same direction; the transformation process is complex and involves feelings, context and relations are of importance, as well as time. An issue that arises is to what degree transformative learning is a process within awareness (a deliberate effort to change perspective, characterised by critical reflection) – and to what degree it is a cumulative process outside of awareness. This is a question brought to the fore by the empirical studies that might need to be developed further in the theory. Moreover further elaboration of the emotional side of the transformation process seems to be needed, since cognitive and affective learning coincide.

Learning in Dialogue Meetings

The connection to transformation theory in my own research is the focus on perspective change in adult experiential learning through communication, as a way to foster knowledgeable adults capable of contributing to the forming of a democratic society.

Through my former experience as an adult educator[16], working with groups of women in working life, I became interested in dialogue as a pedagogical tool for perspective change. The theory of transformative learning integrated most of the thoughts, concepts and ideas I had become interested in and was useful for analysing the empirical findings (Wilhelmson 1998).

Field Experiment
Conversations, it is assumed, are means for us to better understand a complex world and to be able to agree on important issues. Organised group communication emphasising a dialogical quality has been of importance in a number of current models of organisational development (Toulmin, Gustavsen 1996, Isaacs 1993, and Senge, 1990, among others). This implies a growing need to investigate the phenomenon labelled dialogue in order to understand better what it is and what it can be used for as a pedagogical tool in a communicative context. Is the idea of such types of conversation merely an illusion or is it a real possibility? In my research I wanted to investigate the prospects of learning by talking in small groups. I wanted to understand more about the conditions for dialogue. Group talk deliberately arranged for perspective change was the means for my empirical work, a kind of field experiment. Perspective change is seen as the

---

[16] Like several other adult educationists I was inspired by Freire's (1970) pedagogy of conscientisation.

working ingredient for learning. In my research I used this assumption to create opportunities for learning.

The field experiment was conducted through arranging dialogue meetings in co-operation with the childcare authority in one municipality in the Stockholm area. Different interested parties such as parents, politicians, staff, administrators and managers were invited to participate in small group communication concerning the field of child-care. Apparently basic questions [17] were used as topics of discussion, topics that might lead to talk about dilemmas and complex issues [18]. The participants were grouped with the aim to diminish mutual interdependencies and create opportunities for free and open communication. Interviews were made before and after group talk sessions and group talk were taped. The data was analysed in different ways; discourse threads were followed, the amounts of words were counted, interaction analysis on micro-power was made, learning possibilities were interpreted.

Learning and Dialogue

Learning and dialogue are thus two vital concepts in the study. Dialogue is understood as a normative ideal, comparable to Habermas' concept of "the ideal speech situation" (McCarthy 1984, 306) and to the concept of "discourse" in transformation theory: "Discourse, in the context of Transformation Theory, is that specialized use of dialogue devoted to searching for a common understanding and assessment of the justification of an interpretation or belief" (Mezirow 2000, 10).

In the analysis of the empirical data, however, it became difficult to use dialogue or discourse as a description of the object under study because of its normative connotation. Instead the more neutral concept "group conversation" is used.

Perspective change is seen as a central process in adult learning. It is the individuals who learn by changing their assumptions. In group com-

---

[17] Questions that were bringing up issues that could be labelled as "essentially contested concepts" as described by Gallie (1956). Questions such as e.g. "What is good child-caring according to your experience?".
[18] Issues with the character of "ill structured problems" as described by Kitchener and King (1990).

munication this learning takes place in social interaction where the participants together may create new knowledge by going beyond the individual perspective of each person. This definition is close to what Mezirow means is central to the adult learning process: "Formulating more dependable beliefs about our experience, assessing their contexts, seeking informed agreement on their meaning and justification, and making decisions on the resulting insights are central to the adult learning process" (Mezirow 2000, 4).

Results

The results of the study deal with participant perspectives, dialogue competence, discursive power, gender conversational styles, perspective change and collective learning.

Perspectives of Participants
The term perspective is used to understand how a change of assumptions may come about in group conversation. All the participants in the conversation groups were requested to express their own personal experiences and opinions.

An individual's social role(s) with regard to a certain (municipal) undertaking is decisive for the kind of experience the individual will have of such an activity. The social role is crucial for the development of which perspective [19] to adopt. From this perspective the individual constructs his or her knowledge and values in interaction with others. The social roles of the participants present them with different approaches to the child care system.

I have used the following classification with regard to these various approaches:

---

[19] I found it hard to differentiate between meaning perspectives and meaning schemes in the empirical analysis, and thus used only the concept of "perspective". This included both aspects.

Figure 2: The Participants' Social Roles, Decisive for their Various Points of View.

	A Superior Perspective	A Subordinate Perspective
An Outsider Perspective	Politicians	Parents
An Insider Perspective	Managers	Child care personnel

Figure 2 could be seen as a 'statue of the child care system' once it is filled with different intentional voices. In the group conversation such a virtual statue (as an image of the child care system) is created when different voices are raised in the interaction. The statue emerges when it is collectively created out of different perspectives, different viewpoints (see figure 3).

Figure 3: Voices in the Child Care Statue

	A Superior Perspective	A Subordinate Perspective
An Outsider Perspective	Wants to carry through political visions by contributing in the management of the work	Wants more resources Wants less restrictions
An Insider Perspective	Wants to manage the work independently	Wants to influence working conditions Wants more information

Depending on the participants' dialogical competence, the statue will be more or less well developed, more or less "inclusive, differentiating, permeable (open to other viewpoints), critically reflective of assumptions, emotionally capable of change, and integrative of experience", as Mezirow (2000, 19) describes the characteristics of an individual frame of reference that permits learning through transformative change. This characterisation can also be used to describe the dialogical quality of interaction in group conversation.

The interaction quality is dependent on the dialogical competence of each participant. The statue looks different depending on the capacity of individual participants to establish a communicative context for each other in the interactive process (the speech context). Walking around the statue together means giving each other pictures of reality; "this aspect is seen from my perspective". Discovering other aspects of reality, might create a distance from one's own perspective, seeing it as a construction and not as the truth. Together participants might discover dilemmas: if your world looks like that and mine looks like this, then how do we solve problems? Problems arise as a dilemma when seen from multiple perspectives.

Dialogue Competence

As to the capacity to contribute to dialogical group talk, I have found the competence to speak and listen important as well as the ability for critical reflection and critical self-reflection, as is illustrated in figure 4 below.

Figure 4: Dialogue Competence

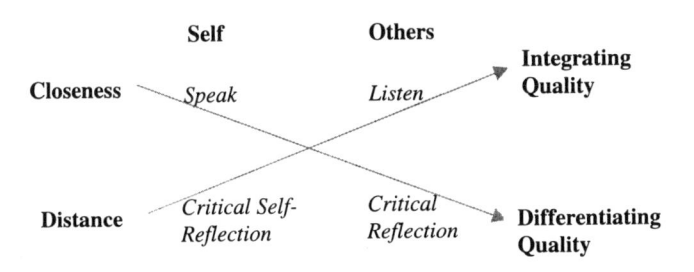

	Self	Others	
Closeness	Speak	Listen	**Integrating Quality**
Distance	Critical Self-Reflection	Critical Reflection	**Differentiating Quality**

This means that a participant needs to use all four competencies in group conversation to be able to contribute to the dialogical quality. Closeness to the own perspective means to contribute to the knowledge formation by speaking in a voice of one's own, to assert reflected experiences relevant for the topic under discussion. Closeness to the perspectives of others means listening carefully and seriously trying to understand what is meant: being curious of other people's ways of seeing. Distance from your own perspective means being prepared to think of your truths as prejudices, it even means to critically reflect on your self-perceptions. Distance from the perspectives of others means to critically reflect, with integrity, on assertions made by others from your own experience and knowledge.

Taken together, these abilities create an integrating as well as a differentiating quality in group conversation. The integrating quality is made up by distance from the self and closeness to others, the participant is able to connect his/her way of thinking to those of others in an open-minded way. The differentiating quality is made up by closeness to self and distance to others, the participant is able to separate between perspectives and to analyse and penetrate problems in more depth. Dialogue competence is difficult to achieve: most of us are trapped in communicative habits of power-relations and gender conversational styles.

Discursive Power

Asymmetrical conversations (one-sided dominance) recreate the social positions of superiority and subordination among the participants. Symmetrical interaction (balanced with regard to dominance) does not recreate superiority and subordination, regardless of the participant's hierarchical positions.

Dominance is established when both superiors and subordinates rally to the perspective of the superiors and dissociate themselves from the perspective of the subordinates. I call this a "communicative vice". Each locks the other in asymmetric communicative patterns. Superiors are close to their own perspective and distance themselves from the notions of others; they strive to have their own way. Subordinates demonstrate their closeness to superiors and refrain from asserting their own experiences. In this way, superiors might experience superstitious learning ("I am right!") and subordinates might experience negative learning ("I am wrong and I can not contribute in group conversation!").

In symmetrical groups a "communicative weaving" takes place instead, which is quite the opposite of the vice. Both superiors and subordinates focus first on the subordinates' perspectives. The superiors make an effort to come close to the perspectives of the others and encourage them to speak out. To some extent the superiors also refrain from asserting their own perspective. The subordinates thus get the space to formulate a voice of their own and courage to question what others say. The "discourse weaving" encompasses many voices and creates a dynamic interaction.

Having a superior or a subordinate position may involve various difficulties for individuals who try to go beyond their own perspective. The superior, according to my study, needs to develop the capacity for critical self-reflection and listening, the subordinate needs to develop the capacity for critical reflection and assertive talking. This involves a demanding and transformative learning process, becoming aware of how the communicative interaction is collectively built and in what ways the self is contributing.

Gender Conversational Styles
Men and women seem to have developed different skills that are of importance for dialogue competence. Women's conversational style seems to contribute to integration while men's conversational style seems to contribute to differentiation.[20]

According to my study, in female group conversation differences in experiences and opinions are rather vague and disagreements remain hidden. Female groups are co-operatively relation-oriented, both regarding the discussion as such and the choice of topics. In male group conversation, differences in experiences and opinions are openly displayed. Men's way of speaking in groups has the character of a monologue, being more individualistic and competitive. These differences I see mostly as a result of gender, being socially constructed. It is not surprising that women's conversational style is subordinate and men's superior in character, since such is the traditional gender-power relation in our society (Hirdman 1987).

Perspective Change
The notions of reality that are constructed in group conversation become more one-sided and simplistic if only one perspective dominates, and more varied and complex the more perspectives are unfolded. Perspective change is a condition if the group members are to create a new transcending perspective within which new ways of understanding can be developed. I have found three modes in which perspectives were changed

---

[20] This is also found in sociolinguistic studies (Edelsky 1981, Coates 1996, 1997, Tannen 1998).

in group conversation: the broadening, shifting and transcending of perspectives.

Broadening within a perspective means that no change of perspective occurred, participants confirmed each other's statements or just ignored deviant statements. This can be seen as an assimilative process.

Shifting between perspectives means that a discussion occurred where different opinions met. This created a state of disequilibrium, which might open up for perspective change or alternatively might get stuck in debate.

The **transcending** of perspectives creates a mutual and qualitatively new understanding. A collectively built new knowledge on social dilemmas emerges that no one could have developed on his/her own. This can be seen as an accommodative process. No one can keep to his or her old assumptions, everyone is adapting to the assessing of reasons as they collectively build a new understanding. The transcending of perspectives might lead to collective transformative learning.

The Learning of the Participants
First, whether communication is symmetric or asymmetric in character is decisive for learning quality. As has been seen earlier, symmetric communication contributes to positive 'developmental learning', more or less for all participants. Asymmetric communication may lead to 'false learning' for those who dominate, and 'negative learning' for those who are dominated.

Second, whether communication is characterised by competitiveness or co-operation also influences the possibilities for participants to learn. Moreover these different ways of talking seem to be gender related. A women's group conversation was either symmetrically or asymmetrically co-operative, while a men's group conversation was symmetrically or asymmetrically competitive.

The combination of symmetric / asymmetric and co-operative / competitive discourses provide us with the following four discourse types (Linell 1996) which, according to my analysis, provide prospects for learning in the following ways:

- The symmetric/co-operative discourse type implies that all participants learn from each other's different perspectives. Subordinates learn that they are able to speak freely in group communication and they learn to be self confident in the prospect of future group meetings. Superiors learn to be competent in dialogical talk when they critically reflect on their own (powerful) role in group communication.
- The symmetric/competitive discourse type implies that each participant learns to argue his or her own opinion. The participants practice the ability to hold on to their own assumptions in communicative situations and to differentiate themselves from other group members. They learn to distance themselves, to unfold an opinion of their own and to be clear about what they think. They also learn to keep a distance to those they disagree with.
- The asymmetric/co-operative discourse type implies that all participants learn the perspective of the most dominant person(s). The dominating person is further supported in his/her knowledge and experience and learns to be dominant. Those who adjust themselves learn to comply with authority and to practice subordination.
- The asymmetric/competitive discourse type implies that the participants learn to hold on to their own assumptions. The superior learns to actively dominate others in communicative situations. The subordinate learns that his or her ability to argue is insufficient and may instead develop silent opposition in communicative situations.

Single individuals may, through their own reflections, in as well as on their experiences of group conversation [21], develop a personal transformative learning. One condition is, however, that the group communication is experienced as positive and corresponds to a felt need.

If a group is to be able to develop collective transformative learning, the group members have to go beyond the participants' different perspectives and develop a new mutual approach. To get there, the participants need to interact in a dialogical way, that is, to both integrate and differentiate various perspectives, as stated above. They need to generalise their

---

[21] The concepts "reflection-in-action" and "reflection-on-action" are from Donald Schön (1982).

experiences into a matter of societal importance. Collective learning in this respect is an active and explicit transformation, which comprises and digests several different perspectives into a new alloy of knowledge. The collective skill needed is to reflect together in communicative action. This is the process of "reflective discourse" (Mezirow 2000, 10).

Conclusion

The ability to create new mutual learning in collaboration with other people seems to demand of the participants in group conversation the difficult skill of being at the same time close to and distanced from themselves and others. It also appears to demand a difficult balancing act of the discussion process, in that it has to be symmetric, co-operative and competitive in nature, at the same time. In Belenky's and Stanton's (2000) words, separate and connected knowing have to be used at the same time. This is open and mutual reflection based upon giving voice to different perspectives, and the search together with others for new ways of understanding, which provide the prospects for a genuinely new knowledge construction. The driving force behind all this is the existence of problems, seen by the participants as meaningful and vital to better understand and perhaps to solve dilemma. For such a communicative process to be successful, the situation needs to be characterised by both safety and disequilibrium at the same time, what is taken for granted needs to be questioned.

In this study, I aim to add to the knowledge of discourse intending to increase participation in societal matters. Such understanding involves an awareness of the difficulties embedded in any interaction, and in this I include both micro- and macro-power. Macro-power (hierarchical organisational structures) displays itself in attitudes of superiority and subordination as well as conversational styles among the participants in the micro-context. To use group communication as a pedagogical tool in adult education we need to be aware of what actually happens in the communicative context.

A next research step could for example be to study the dynamics of the micro context of group communication in established groups. What is problematic in creating the ideal speech situation or reflective discourse in teams or other groups in working life where power relations and mutual interdependencies are part of the interaction? It would also be interesting to further investigate similarities and differences in interaction in groups made up by gender homogenous and heterogeneous groups in working life. How do gender conversational styles affect the possibilities for dialogue and reflective discourse in various branches of working life?

Further Development of Transformation Theory

Transformation theory has been criticised from various angles and has thus been developed since it was first formulated. Here I connect to ideas for further development of transformation theory as they are presented in a recent book on the issue (Mezirow & Ass. 2000), and also contribute with some reflections from my own study.

Taylor (2000) points to the importance of theoretical comparisons to obtain insights in the complexity of transformative learning. For empirical work he recommends indepth component analysis and the use of alternative method designs, such as following participants as they experience transformative learning, and also conducting longitudinal studies. The future research needs, according to Taylor (2000), are manifold. Some of these are:

- influence of context: cultural/contextual variations, how groups respond to and make meaning of significant experiences;
- relation critical reflection – affective learning: to focus feelings and how they inform the reflective process;
- relational nature of rational discourse: how to initiate safety in the transformation process;
- broadening of definitional outcomes of perspective transformation: to understand more of the transformative process for phenomena such as learning strategies, internal conditions, external conditions, timing, regression, and acting differently;
- transformative learning in the classroom: how to deal with emotionally laden issues in classrooms? Is it ethical to put students in emotionally challenging experiences? Whose interest does transformative learning serve?

- frame of reference: to observe the change in behaviour in response to a perspective transformation.

Kegan (2000), from a constructive-developmental theory perspective, focuses upon the epistemological issue of transformational learning. Only epistemological change means a change of form, other changes allow us to stay within the same epistemological worldview. Kegan speaks about "the form that transforms" (Kegan 2000, 52), form being the frame of reference (habit of mind and point of view) that is a way of knowing, this makes the transformation an epistemological endeavour. "What is "object" in our knowing describes the thoughts and feelings we say we have; what is "subject" describes the thinking and feeling that has us. We "have" object; we "are" subject" (Kegan 2000, 53).

Developing a transformative way of learning means developing an "internal authority" (Kegan 2000, 59) so we can more deliberately make our own choices and not be the puppet on a string – victims of our socialisation. So, the concept of transformative learning should be saved for the specificity of epistemological change in this self-authoring direction, and not just any change that might occur.

Belenky and Stanton (2000) state that the goal of transformative learning is to "achieve consensus about the best judgement the discourse community is capable of reaching with the information currently available" (Belenky, Stanton 2000, 87). This goal is seen as part of "separate knowing", since it is the capacity for critical reflection on basic assumptions that is emphasised in transformation theory. The authors state that other ways of knowing, such as "connected knowing", are equally vital but not described enough in the theory. Connected knowers "look for strengths, not weaknesses, in another's argument" (Belenky, Stanton 2000, 87). They try to understand from the other's point of view, from the other's perspective, seeing things holistically, not analytically. But, the authors conclude, both ways of knowing are essential for the potential of transforming communities as well as people.

Daloz (2000) points to the importance of relativistic ways of thinking for emancipatory learning to occur. If we depart from the notion that "we human beings are radically socially constituted from the earliest moments of our lives" (Daloz 2000, 120), it will be easier to retain from an either-or thinking of self versus other. The conclusion is that this way of thinking helps us (as teachers and citizens) to "foster critical reflection on the meaning of differences", and "create mentoring communities" (Daloz 2000, 121). The acknowledgement of difference is the road to societal perspective transformation, one could say.

Finally, in the light of my own study, I will make some reflections on the possibility of adult education through communicative activities such as those of the dialogue meetings in my research. In a society that strives for democracy, it might be important to highlight the difference between parliamentary democracy and what could be called 'knowledge constructing democracy'. This knowledge construction could concern activities such as those in the (local) public sector. Adult education, which strives to be emancipatory and leading to a less narrow outlook, may be utopian. After all, people live under different circumstances, each in their own sociocultural context with different access to various kinds of resources. Yet, I believe that the study proves that it is possible to create opportunities for 'learning through talking' within, as in this case, the context of a municipality. Group conversations could contribute to a more integrated knowledge construction, if they are designed for perspective change and have a dialogical quality. In this way the micro-context of a group is part of the macro-context of society. Transformation theory, as it is developing its own framework, is useful as a guide for the practical work of connecting the micro world to the macro, fostering adults capable of building a democratic society.

References

The New Shorter Oxford English Dictionary (1993). Oxford.

Barlas, C. (2000). *Towards a Changing Paradigm. Transformative Learning and Social Change Action*. California Institute of Integral Studies.* [22]

Belenky, M., Stanton, A. (2000). Inequality, Development, and Connected Knowing. In: Mezirow, J. & Ass. (eds.). *Learning as Transformation. Critical Perspectives on a*

---

[22] References marked with * are theses from 1999-2000, found online at: http://dialogweb.com

Theory in Progress. San Francisco, pp. 71-102.

Berger, P., Luckmann, T. (1966). *The Social Construction of Reality. A Treatise in the Sociology of Knowledge.* New York.

Blumer, H. (1969). *Symbolic Interactionism. Perspective and Method.* Berkely.

Bolduc, A. (2000) *Transformative Learning in a Drug Court Program.* Columbia University Teachers College.*

Boyd, R., Myers, J. (1988). Transformative Education. In: *International Journal of Lifelong Education,* 7 (4), pp. 261-284.

Candales, B. (2000). *Nuestras Historias ("Our Stories"). Transformative Learning Process and Female Puerto Rican Community College Graduates.* The University of Connecticut.*

Coates, J. (1996). *Women Talk. Conversation Between Women Friends.* Oxford.

Coates, J. (1997). One-at-a-time. The Organization of Men's Talk. In: Meinhof, H., Johnson, S. (eds.). *Language and Masculinity.* Cambridge, Mass, pp. 107-129.

Coleman-Hoeppel, P. (1999). *Meaning Construction through Job Loss. The Transformative Effect of Organizational Change.* Northern Illinois University.*

Courtenay, B., Merriam, S., Reeves, P. (2000). Perspective Transformation Over Time. A 2-year Follow-up Study of HIV-positive Adults. In: *Adult Education Quarterly,* 50 (2), pp. 102-119.

Cox, R. (1999). *Web of Wisdom. A Field Study of a Virtual Learning Community.* Institute of Transpersonal Psychology.*

Daloz, L. (2000). Transformative Learning for the Common Good. In: Mezirow, J. & Ass. (eds.). *Learning as Transformation. Critical Perspectives on a Theory in Progress.* San Francisco, pp. 103-123.

Dewey, J. (1938/1951). *Experience and Education.* New York.

Edelsky, C. (1981). Who's Got the Floor? In: *Language in Society,* 10, pp. 383-421.

Freire, P. (1970). *Pedagogy of the Oppressed.* New York.

Gallie, W. (1956). Essentially Contested Concepts. In: *Proceedings of the Aristotelian Society.* London, pp. 167-198.

Giddens, A. (1991). *Modernity and Self-identity. Self and Society in the Late Modern Age.* Cambridge.

Golding Rosenberg, D. (1999). *Action for Prevention: Feminist Practices in Transformative Learning in Women's Health and the Environment* (with a focus on breast cancer). A Case Study of a Participatory Research Circle. University of Toronto.*

Habermas, J. (1984). *The Theory of Communicative Action.* Vol. 1: Reason and the Rationalization of Society. Boston.

Hadaway, T. (1999). *Perspective Transformation as a Theoretical Model for Curriculum Development and the Teaching of Adults in Sunday School.* The Southern Baptist Theological Seminary.*

Hirdman, Y. (1987). Makt och kön. In: Petersson, O. (ed.). *Maktbegreppet*. Stockholm, pp. 188-206.

Karlen, F. (1999). *Education for Transformation. Understanding Adolescents' Most Meaningful Experiences in a Learning to Learn Course*. The Fielding Institute.*

Kauffman, W. (1999). *Spiritual Development within Adult Learning Programs. How Stories Trigger Identification of Our Shared Humanity through Reflection, Group Sharing and Storytelling Processes*? National-Louis University.*

Kegan, R. (2000). What "Form" Transforms? A Constructive-Developmental Approach to Transformative Learning. In: Mezirow, J. & Ass. (eds.). *Learning as Transformation. Critical Perspectives on a Theory in Progress*. San Francisco, pp. 35-69.

King, K. (1999). Unleashing Technology in the Classroom: What Adult Basic Education Teachers and Organizations Need to Know. In: *Adult Basic Education*, 9 (3), pp. 162-175.

King, K. (2000). The Adult ESL Experience. Facilitating Perspective Transformation in the Classroom. In: *Adult Basic Education*, 10 (2), pp. 69-89.

Kitchener, K., King, P. (1990). The Reflective Judgement Model: Transforming Assumptions about Knowing. In: Mezirow, J. (ed.). *Fostering Critical Reflection in Adulthood*. San Fransisco, pp. 159-176.

Kroth, M., Boverie, P. (2000). Life Mission and Adult Learning. In: *Adult Education Quarterly*, 50 (2), pp. 134-149.

Lamm, S. (2000). *The Connection between Action Reflection Learning (TM) and Transformative Learning. An Awakening of Human Qualities in Leadership*. Columbia University Teachers College.*

Linell, P. (1996). *Approaching Dialogue. Talk and Interaction in Dialogical Perspectives*. Linköping University, No. 1996:7.

Magro, K. (1999). *Exploring English Teachers' Conceptions of Teaching and Learning in Adult Education Contexts*. University of Toronto.*

McCarthy, T. (1984). *The Critical Theory of Jürgen Habermas*. Cambridge.

Mead, G. H. (1934). *Mind, Self and Society. From the Standpoint of a Social Behaviorist*. Chicago.

Mezirow, J. (1978a). *Education for Perspective Transformation. Women's Re-entry Programs in Community Colleges*. Columbia.

Mezirow, J. (1978b). Perspective Transformation. In: *Adult Education Quarterly*, 28 (2), pp. 100-110.

Mezirow, J. (1991). *Transformative Dimensions of Adult Learning*. San Fransisco.

Mezirow, J. (1996). Toward a Learning Theory of Adult Literacy. In: *Adult Basic Education*, 6 (3), pp. 115-126.

Mezirow, J. (2000). Learning to Think Like an Adult. Core Concepts of Transformation Theory. In: Mezirow, J. & Ass. (eds.). *Learning as Transformation. Critical Perspectives on a Theory in Progress*. San Francisco, pp. 3-33.

Mezirow, J. & Ass. (eds.) (1990). *Fostering Critical Reflection in Adulthood*. San Fransisco.

Mezirow, J. & Ass. (eds.) (2000). *Learning as Transformation. Critical Perspectives on a Theory in Progress*. San Francisco.

Pineiro, C. (2000). *Analysis of Professional Reflections by Nontraditional Novice ESL Teachers*. Boston University.*

Robbins, C. (1999). *An Examination of Critical Feminist Pedagogy in Practice*. Columbia University Teachers College.*

Roosta, M. (1999). *Adult Learning and Community Development*. A Case Study of the FUNDAEC's University Center for Rural Well-being in Risaralda, Colombia. Northern Illinois University.*

Shaw, M. (1999). *A Model for Transformative Learning. The Promotion of Successful Aging*. The University of British Columbia.*

Sherlock, J. (2000). *Learning in a Professional Context. An Exploration of Nonprofit Association CEO's Learning Experiences*. The George Washington University.*

Schön, D. (1982). *The Reflective Practitioner*. New York.

Tannen, D. (1998). *The Argument Culture*. New York.

Taylor, E. W. (1998). *The Theory and Practice of Transformative Learning. A Critical Review*. Columbus, Ohio.

Taylor, E. W. (2000). Analyzing Research on Transformative Learning Theory. In: Mezirow, J. & Ass. (eds.). *Learning as Transformation. Critical Perspectives on a Theory in Progress*. San Francisco, pp. 285-328.

Temple, W. (1999). *Perspective Transformation among Mainland Chinese Intellectuals Reporting Christian Conversion while in the States*. Trinity Evangelical Divinity School.*

Toulmin, S., Gustavsen, B. (eds). (1996). *Beyond Theory. Changing Organizations through Participation*. Amsterdam.

Treichler, D. (2000). *A Comparison of Corporate and Non-corporate Adult Education as a Vehicle for Organizational Capability Migration*. State University of New York at Binghamton.*

Wertsch, J. (ed) (1979). *The Concept of Activity in Soviet Psychology*. Armonk, NY.

Wilhelmson, L. (1998). *Learning Dialogue. Discourse Patterns, Perspective Change and Learning in Small Group Conversation*. Doctoral thesis (in Swedish with English summary). Arbete och Hälsa 1998:16, Solna, National Institute for Working Life, pp. 260-268.

Peter Alheit / Bettina Dausien

LIFELONG LEARNING AND 'BIOGRAPHICITY'
TWO THEORETICAL VIEWS ON CURRENT EDUCATIONAL CHANGES

Introduction

'Lifelong learning' continues to be a somewhat diffuse term. It is obvious that we learn our whole lives long. From our first attempts at walking and talking, to familiarising ourselves with the old people's home, we experience new things, acquire new knowledge and new skills. Like breathing, this kind of learning occurs without our being aware of it. We also learn in schools, enterprises, universities and continuing training, of course. But even there, the most important things we learn often have little to do with the official curriculum. We learn facts, acquire skills, learn to handle our feelings – in the most effective 'school' there is – the "university of life" (Field 2000, vii). We learn through conversations with friends; we learn by trying out new things; we learn from watching television and reading books, by leafing through catalogues and while surfing on the Internet. We learn while we reflect and plan. Whatever the type of learning, be it trivial or meaningful, we cannot act differently – we are lifelong learners.

In the educational debate of the past 30 years – and especially during the most recent decade – the concept of lifelong learning has been sharpened strategically and functionally. In a certain sense, it stands for a new way of specifying the educational tasks in the societies of late Modernity. In its recent and highly influential document on educational policy, the *Memorandum on Lifelong Learning*, which was adopted in March 2000 in Lisbon by the European Commission, it is stated that "Lifelong learning is no longer just one aspect of education and training; it must become the guiding principle for provision and participation across the full continuum of learning contexts" (Commission of the European Communities 2000, 3). Two decisive reasons are given for this assessment:

- Europe has moved towards a knowledge-based society and economy. More than ever before, access to up-to-date information and knowledge, together with the motivation and skills to use these resources intelligently on behalf of oneself and the community as a whole, are becoming the key to strengthening Europe's competitiveness and improving the employability and adaptability of the workforce;
- today's Europeans live in a complex social and political world. More than ever before, individuals want to plan their own lives, are expected to contribute actively to society, and must learn to live positively with cultural, ethnic and linguistic diversity. Education, in its broadest sense, is the key to learning and understanding how to meet these challenges (Commission of the European Communities 2000, 5).

This double rationale has narrowed the scope of the concept in a functionalistic manner, on the one hand, but on the other hand it also adds precision to its definition. The *Memorandum* explicitly states that lifelong learning relates to all meaningful learning activities:

- to the *formal* learning processes that take place in the classical education and training institutions and which usually lead to recognised diplomas and qualifications;
- to the *non-formal* learning processes that usually take place alongside the mainstream systems of education and training – at the workplace, in clubs and associations, in civil society initiatives and activities, in the pursuit of sports or musical interests, and
- to *informal* learning processes that are not necessarily intentional and which are a natural accompaniment to

everyday life (Commission of the European Communities 2000, 8).

The point or purpose behind this new understanding of the term 'learning' is the option of networking these different forms of learning in a synergistic way – learning should not only be systematically extended to cover the entire life span, but should also take place 'lifewide', i.e. learning environments should be engendered in which the various types of learning can complement each other organically. "The 'lifewide' dimension brings the complementarity of formal, non-formal and informal learning into sharper focus" (Commission of the European Communities 2000, 9).

Lifelong, 'networked' learning thus seems to become an economic and social imperative of the first degree. And in this sharply focused sense it does not relate to classical educational elites alone, but to all members of society. A key point in the *White Paper on Lifelong Learning* published by the British Department for Education and Employment in 1998 is that,

> To cope with rapid change and the challenge of the information and communication age, we must ensure that people can return to learning throughout their lives. We cannot rely on a small elite, no matter how highly educated or highly paid. Instead, we need the creativity, enterprise and scholarship of all our people (Department for Education and Employment 1998, 7).

The 'new concept' of lifelong learning betrays an ambition that John Field, the British education researcher, has termed "the new educational order" (Field 2000, 133ff). Learning acquires a new meaning – for society as a whole, for education and training institutions, and for individuals. The shift in connotations exposes an inner contradiction, however, in that this new learning is initially 'framed' by political and economic precepts. The goals are competitiveness, employment and adaptive competence on the part of the 'workforce'. The intention is also, however, to strengthen freedom of biographical planning and the social involvement of individuals. Lifelong learning 'instrumentalises' and 'emancipates' at one and the same time, quite obviously.

So there appear to be different perspectives from which to view lifelong learning: (a) a concern, driven by educational policy, with changed conditions in the labour and education society, with consequences for the social organisation of individual and collective learning (Longworth, Davies 1996, Dohmen 1996, Brödel 1998, Alheit, Kammler 1998, Williamson 1998, Gerlach 2000, Field 2000, Achtenhagen, Lempert 2000); and (b) a more educationalist perspective of the conditions and opportunities for biographical learning among the members of society (Dominicé 1990, 2000, Kade, Seitter 1996, Alheit 1999, Alheit, Dausien 1996, 2000b, Delory-Momberger 2000).

Since the 1960s, the first perspective has formed the basis for an international policy of 'lifelong learning' – or 'lifelong education' – (for a summary, see Dohmen 1996, Gerlach 2000, Field 2000), in which the central concern has been to explore and develop new concepts for education and training with the aim of tapping the economic and cultural resources of western societies, in particular. The background to this approach is the diagnosis that a faster pace of social change, structural changes and transformations involving a greater role for civil society require competencies and flexibility on the part of society's actors that can no longer be acquired at the speed and in institutionalised forms of 'traditional' education and training. Institutional and curricular frameworks for education and training must be changed, and new social networks and learning environments created (buzzword: 'the learning society') (for detailed treatment, see Alheit 1999, Field 2000, 69ff). Policy-centred thinking in this context is still largely confined – even at the end of the twentieth century – to the level of 'guidelines' (Dohmen 1996) and Memoranda (Field 2000). Scientific concepts and findings that could prove relevant in the context of educational research are discussed in greater detail below (Section 1).

The second perspective focuses – in the sense of a subject-centred science of education – on the learning processes of individual social actors. Here, the lifelong learning perspective has heightened attention for nonformal, informal, non-institutionalised and self-organised learning. The buzzwords 'everyday learning', 'learning through experience', 'appropriational learning', 'lifeworld-related' or 'self-managed learning' (Dohmen

1996, 1998, Kade, Seitter 1996, Konzertierte Aktion Weiterbildung 1998) denote new themes, issues and research fields. In the following, we will bring together various aspects of this debate, which is conducted from a heterogeneity of theoretical approaches, under a single biographical theory perspective (Section 2) and point out the implications for educational research (Section 3).

The following analysis will focus on the curious tensions between these two perspectives. Section 1 looks at the social framework for lifelong learning – Perspective I. In Part 2, we put forward our own theoretical view on 'education in the life span', namely the concept of biographical learning, and extrapolate the idea of the 'biographicity' of social learning processes – a Perspective II, if you so wish. Finally, in Section 3, we briefly suggest the main perspectives and desiderata for research. In the thoughts that follow, we deliberately adopt a perspective that addresses the international discourse on these topics. Lifelong learning is obviously linked to 'globalisation imperatives' in education policy that are taken into consideration in our line of argument.

Perspective I: 'Lifelong Learning' as Reorganisation of the Education System

To begin with, however, we must explain the astonishing fact that, at the end of the twentieth century, a global political consensus was generated on the concept of lifelong learning (Field 2000, 3ff). The debates of the 1970s – especially the report by the UNESCO Commission headed by Edgar Faure, the former French prime minister and education minister (*Learning to Be*, Faure 1972), and a series of key publications by the Organisation for Economic Cooperation and Development (e.g. OECD, CERI 1973) – triggered some modest educational initiatives at national government level, at best, (for details, see Gerlach 2000), a single statement of the 1990s, namely the *White Paper on Competitiveness and Economic Growth* authorised by Jacques Delors (Commission of the European Communities 1994), and especially the follow-up Delors Report produced by the UNESCO Commission (*Learning: The Treasure Within*, Delors 1996) led to veritable inflation in lifelong learning initiatives worldwide.

Since the European Commission's call to make 1996 the *European Year of Lifelong Learning*, Great Britain has seen the appointment of a Minister for Lifelong Learning; Green and White Papers on these new objectives for the education system have appeared in Wales, Scotland and England, with the Netherlands, Norway, Finland and Ireland following suit soon after. The German Ministry of Education, Science, Research and Technology is supporting several reports and symposia on the subject (Dohmen 1996, 1998). The European Commission has itself been active, issuing a *White Paper on Education and Training* (Commission of the European Communities 1995); UNESCO (Delors 1996), OECD (1996) and a group of eight industrialised nations (Group of Eight 1999) have also become engaged.

The factors triggering this astonishing paradigm shift at international scale in programmes for education and training are four trends in the post-industrial societies of the western hemisphere, trends that mutually overlap and which led – in the words of John Field (2000, 35ff) – to a "silent explosion" at the close of the twentieth century: (a) the changing meaning of 'work', (b) the new and totally transformed function of 'knowledge', (c) the experience of increasing dysfunctionality on the part of mainstream education and training institutions and (d) challenges facing the social actors themselves that are characterised only roughly with labels such as 'individualisation' and 'reflexive modernisation' (Beck 1986, Giddens 1990, 1991, Beck, Giddens, Lash 1996).

The Changing Nature of 'Work' in the Societies of Late Modernity

The twentieth century has drastically modified the meaning and significance of employment. Most people spend much less of their lifetime in work than their great-grandparents ever did. As recently as 1906, an average working year comprised approx. 2,900 hours, in 1946 the figure had fallen to 2,440 and in 1988 to a mere 1,800 hours (see Hall 1999, 427). Changes have also occurred to the 'inner structure' of work. The large-scale shift of jobs from the industrial to the services sector is merely a superficial symptom of the changes taking place. The more crucial aspect is that the notion of a consistent 'working life' is finally a thing of the past, even granting that women were traditionally excluded anyway. Average employment no longer means practising one and the same occupation over a substantial span of one's life, but now involves alternating phases of work and further training, voluntary and involuntary discontinuities of occupation, innovative career switching strategies, and even self-chosen alternation between employment and family-centred phases (Arthur, Inkson, Pringle 1999).

This trend has not only irritated people's expectations regarding the classical life course regime (Kohli 1985, 1989) and made individual life planning a much riskier enterprise (Heinz 2000b), but also poses new problems for the institutions involved, in their capacity as "structuring agents of the life course" (Heinz 2000a, 5) – namely the agencies of the employment system and the labour market, the social and pension insurance institutions, but above all the institutions of the education system. It is they who must compensate for the consequences of deregulation and flexibilisation in the labour market, to provide support for unanticipated and risk-laden status passages and transitions to 'modernised' life courses, and strike a new balance between the options held by individual actors, on the one hand, and the functional imperatives of the institutional 'meso-level' (Heinz 2000a). As an innovative instrument for managing essential 'life politics', 'lifelong learning' is the obvious answer.

The New Function of 'Knowledge'

This idea of managing life politics seems all the more necessary, the more diffuse its subject-matter starts to become. The trivial, overriding consensus that, in the wake of the technological innovations engendered by the post-industrial 'information society', k n o w l e d g e has become the key resource of the future, conceals the perplexity over the actual function and character of this 'knowledge' (Rahmstorf 1999). The core issue, quite obviously, is not simply to disseminate and distribute a definable stock of knowledge as efficiently as possible, nor is it the fact that all areas of life are subjected to increasing scientification (Wingens 1998, Stehr 2000), but rather a phenomenon that expands successively by virtue of the specific uses to which it is put, and which devalues itself again to a certain degree. 'Knowledge' is no longer that 'cultural capital' that, according to Bourdieu, determines social structures and which guarantees its astonishing persistence through ever-recurring reproduction (Bourdieu 1987). 'Knowledge' is a kind of "grey capital" (Field 2000, 1) that generates new, virtual economies. The stock market crash of the New Economy in the year 2000 is merely one dark side of the almost intangible quality of 'new knowledge'.

The communication and interaction networks of the IT age, which has long since permeated, extended and modified the realms of conventional industrial production and the character of classical services and administrations, remain dependent – more so than traditional forms of knowledge in the past – on the individual user. The latter's personal options in respect of the new, virtual markets, his contacts, productive inputs and his consumer habits in the Internet are what create the future forms of knowledge. The 'knowledge' of the information society is doing knowledge, a kind of 'lifestyle' that determines the structures of society far beyond the purely occupational domain and lends them a dynamic of ever-shorter cycles.

This very quality of 'new knowledge' now necessitates flexible feedback procedures, complex self-management checks and permanent quality management (Rahmstorf 1999). In the process, the nature of 'education' and 'learning' is dramatically changed (Nolda 1996). They no longer entail the communication and dissemination of fixed bodies of knowledge, values or skills, but rather a kind of 'knowledge osmosis' for ensuring what must now be a permanent and continuous exchange between individual knowledge production and organised knowledge management. The idea of 'lifelong learning', and especially 'self-managed learning', seems highly predestined for this process – as a framework concept at least.

The Dysfunctionality of the Established Educational Institutions

The conditions thus generated by a 'knowledge society' in the making render classical teaching-learning settings problematic, and above all the idea that accompanied the 'first career' of the lifelong learning label in the early 1970s – the human capital theory. The latter concept 'measures', as it were, the capital invested in education and training according to the length of full-time schooling, and assumes that extending its duration will have positive impacts on willingness to engage in lifelong learning (for a critique, see Schuller 1998, Field 2000, 135). A number of recent empirical studies, particularly in Great Britain (e.g. Tavistock Institute 1999, Merrill

1999, Schuller, Field 1999), provide evidence that the very opposite is the case – simply extending primary 'schooling', without drastic changes to the conditional framework and the quality of the learning process, led in the majority of those affected to a loss of motivation and to an instrumental attitude to learning that is in no way conducive to continued, self-managed learning in later phases of life, but which tends rather to suppress such learning (Schuller, Field 1999).

Lifelong learning as it is now conceived requires a kind of paradigm shift in the organisation of learning – not in adulthood, but in the very first forms of schooling. The goals for orientation are no longer the efficiency of learning, effective didactic strategies and the consistency of formal curricula, but rather the situation and the prerequisites on the part of learners (Bentley 1998). This also means addressing non-formal and informal options for learning. The key educational question is no longer how certain material can be taught as successfully as possible, but which learning environments can best stimulate self-determined learning, in other words how learning itself can be 'learned' (Simons 1992, Smith 1992).

Of course, this perspective must also include the conveying of basic qualifications such as reading, writing, arithmetic, or computer literacy, but even these basic skills must be linked to practical experience; the owners of cognitively acquired skills must be able to combine these with social and emotional competencies (see Giddens 1998, 125). Enabling such options demands a high degree of institutional 'self-reflexivity' on the part of education and training institutions in their classical form. They must accept that they, too, must become 'learning organisations'. The necessity of preparing their clientele for lifelong, self-determined learning implies a concept of lifewide learning, or 'holistic learning'.

Schools must network with the community to which they relate, with companies, associations, churches and organisations that are active in that district, and with the families of the schoolchildren in their care. They have to discover new locations for learning and invent other learning environments. Recent school development concepts, particularly those in which the separate institutions are granted substantial autonomy, are certainly providing for greater scope. What is valid for schools is equally valid, of course, for universities, adult education facilities and public administration academies. As John Field correctly points out, lifelong learning necessitates a "new educational order" (Field 2000, 133ff) – a 'silent revolution' in education.

'Individualisation' and 'Reflexive Modernisation'

This demand is neither absurd nor utopian when one looks at the situation faced by a growing group of society's members. The demands levelled at individuals in the second half of the twentieth century have changed considerably. Economic factors are by no means the only ones responsible – social and cultural changes also play a critical role. Despite the continuation of social inequalities, the bonds to social milieus and classical mentalities have become looser (Beck 1983, 1986, Vester et al. 1993, Alheit 1994). Patterns of orientation have become more 'localised' and tend to relate more now to generational or gender-based experience, to the perception of one's own ethnicity, or even to preferences for certain lifestyles (Alheit 1999). Inflationary increases in the range of information and consumer products on offer has dramatically increased the number of options open to the members of society (Giddens 1990, Schulze 1992). Life courses are therefore much less predictable than in the past. What is more – the compulsion to make decisions on a continual basis and to perform incessant changes of orientation is being devolved to the individuals themselves to an increasingly clear extent.

> Individuals are highly dependent on institutions and resources over which others dispose; nevertheless, they are compelled as actors to produce their own lifeworld themselves through their own praxis ... (They) must learn, or pay the penalty of personal collapse or permanent social disadvantage, to link up different fields of experience and activity of their own accord... Indeed, (they) must spontaneously establish a balance between seemingly incompatible demands and requirements levelled at them by institutionally differentiated subsystems, areas of life and fields of learning, if they are to tolerate them on an everyday basis in the first place. This is increasingly the case in respect of so-

cial integration as well – Individuals, not primary social groups as before, are becoming the centres of cooperation and coordination of activities and aims in life... They actively generate sociality, or otherwise face the threat of social isolation and loneliness (Körber 1989, 139).

This visible trend to 'individualisation' of the life course regime, and the concomitant pressure to engage in continuous 'reflexivity' on one's own actions has led – as expressed in the prominent theses of Ulrich Beck or Anthony Giddens – to a different, "reflexive Modernity" (Beck, Giddens, Lash 1996). Yet to be able to handle this different Modernity (Beck 1986), individuals need completely new and flexible structures of competence that can only be established and developed within lifelong learning processes (see Field 2000, 58ff). And it demands fundamental changes in the entire educational system.

Contours of a New 'Educational Economy'?
The astonishing consensus that appears to reign on these doubtlessly plausible and complementary analyses of the age we live in extends from representatives of the traditional business community, to protagonists of the New Economy, to education experts in the modernised left-wing parties. What makes that consensus problematic is its indifference to the social consequences that would be unleashed if such educational policies were implemented without a measure of distance. The delusion of a lifelong learning society does nothing whatsoever to eradicate the selection and exclusion mechanisms of the 'old' educational system. Indeed, it may conceal and exacerbate those mechanisms instead (see Field 2000, 103ff).

It can already be shown with present empirical evidence that labour market segments requiring low skill levels are in chronic decline (OECD 1997a). In other words, the expectations of the 'knowledge society' are raising the pressure on individuals to meet certain standards of skilling and knowledge before they can be employed. The risks of exclusion for those who fail to meet those standards are more draconian than was ever the case in bygone industrial societies. Of course, the logic of exclusion is by no means new – 'class' and 'gender' remain the decisive indicators (Field

2000, 115f). As would be expected, age plays an increasingly significant role (Tuckett, Sargant 1999). Anyone who never had the chance to learn how to learn will not make any effort to acquire new skills late in the life course.

The crude mechanisms of economic valuation prompt a sceptical view of any future scenario for the 'learning society' – a small majority of 'winners', but with a 'life sentence' to learn, may close its borders to a growing minority of 'losers' who never had a chance, or who voluntarily liberated themselves from the straitjacket of having to perpetually acquire and market new knowledge. The OECD forecast, in any case, comes close enough to the scenario just painted:

> For those who have successful experience of education, and who see themselves as capable learners, continuing learning is an enriching experience, which increases their sense of control over their own lives and their society. For those who are excluded from this process, however, or who choose not to participate, the generalisation of lifelong learning may only have the effect of increasing their isolation from the world of the 'knowledge-rich'. The consequences are economic, in under-used human capacity and increased welfare expenditure, and social, in terms of alienation and decaying social infrastructure (OECD 1997b, 1).

Alternatives are therefore needed.

A reasonable consequence would be to realise that lifelong learning cannot be reduced to investment in short-lived, exploitable economic capital, but that it must also be an investment – of equal value – in 'social capital', in the way we treat those next to us, the family, the neighbour, the co-worker, the other club members, the people we meet in citizen's action groups or at the bar counter (see Field 2000, 145ff). In this field of life we are all lifelong learners. Nobody is excluded from the outset. Everyone is an expert. Shrinkage of this type of capital, declining 'confidence', the moratorium on 'solidarity' that Robert D. Putnam identified years ago in US society (Putnam 2001), is also economically counter-productive in the medium term. A balance between these two intractable types of 'capital', on the other hand, could lead to a new kind of 'educational economy', or, more correctly perhaps, to a social ecology of learning in modern, modernised societies (for detailed treatment see Alheit, Kreitz 2000). However, the precondition for such balance is that learning individuals be taken more seriously – which would also involve a shift in analytic perspective.

Perspective II: On the 'Biographicity' of Educational Processes – Aspects of a Phenomenology of Lifelong Learning

The following lines of thought are concerned with the individual side of lifelong learning. Interest centres here not on situative learning acts by isolated individuals, but on learning as the (trans-)formation of experience, knowledge and action structures in the context of people's life histories and lifeworlds (i.e. in a 'lifewide' context (see above)). We therefore speak of 'biographical learning', by which we mean not so much a sharply and empirically delineated entity – such as learning processes that are bound up with specific forms, locations or times – but rather a theoretical perspective on education and training that takes as its starting point the life history perspective of the actual learner (Krüger, Marotzki 1995, 1999), in the sense of a phenomenological concept of learning (Schulze 1993a, b).

At the level of biographical experience, analytical distinctions such as those between formal, non-formal and informal learning are not necessarily sharp. On the contrary, one of the peculiar features of biography is that, through the accumulation and structuring of experience in one's life history, institutionally and socially specialised fields of experience become integrated, congealing to form a new and particular construct of meanings. This accomplishment on the part of living subjects can be circumscribed with the term 'biographicity' (Alheit 1993, Alheit, Dausien 2000b), which embraces the notion of 'self-willed', subjective appropriation of learning schemes (Kade 1994, Kade, Seitter 1996), while going beyond that aspect to accentuate the opportunity to generate new structures of cultural and social experience. Policies and pedagogical concepts of lifelong learning take the potential for education and training implicit in the biographical, constructional logic of experience and action as their cue – in an affirmative, rather than analytically reflected way.

Nevertheless, the distinction between formal, non-formal and informal learning also makes sense from the perspective of biography theory, as long as it is not interpreted as a typology of learning processes, but is related instead to the structures and frames of the respective learning contexts. Learning processes take place in educational institutions and formalised learning settings (see above) to a lesser extent only, but structured institutions for education and training nevertheless structure the 'option spaces' for biographical learning processes (Kade, Seitter 1996); they also shape the historical and cultural notions of 'biography', within which frame subjects interpret their experience and generate biographical meaning. Biographical learning is embedded within societal structures and cultural contexts of interpretation. For that reason, it is also essential when analysing educational and learning processes at the individual, biographical level to be clear about the 'external' structures that frame the life course. The following conceptualisation begins with this aspect and goes on to differentiate between some empirical phenomena of life-wide learning.

The Social Structuring of the Life Course by Educational Institutions

The life course is an institution that crystallised with the onset of Modernity (Kohli 1985) and provides a formal 'framework' for the biographical education and training processes that individuals undergo. This framework exists regardless of the specific way in which individuals orient themselves to it (e.g. in a more affirmative manner, striving for preset goals, or rubbing up against it, breaking with it, modifying it, etc.). There is a societal 'curriculum' for the individual's life from birth to death that is more or less defined in norms and expectations, constantly renegotiated and subject to historical change.

One part of the education and training processes that we pass through or actively shape during our life is based relatively closely on this 'curriculum' and regulated by formal learning objectives and qualifications. To emphasise this aspect, Schulze (1993a) speaks of 'curricular learning'. 'Learning in the life history context', in contrast, obeys other (biographical) rules, but cannot dissociate itself entirely from the aforementioned framework. There are tensions and frictions between these two dimensions, which are mutually dependent on each other (Schulze 1993a, Kade, Seitter 1996).

In order to understand biographical learning processes, it is therefore essential to reflect on the respective life course models that operate within a given society. These are not 'external variables' that are always pre-existent, but are shaped and formed in decisive ways by institutionalised education, for example. This was shown by Kohli (1985) for the classical subdivision of the life course in modern western societies into 'preparatory, activity and retirement phases'. In the latter life course model, times and spaces of formalised learning are defined by institutional classification (school, vocational training system) and by the temporal localisation of socialisation and skilling in childhood and youth, and all members of society are obliged to pass through these predefined phases. However, the role of education and training in the life course is not confined to the 'preparatory' phase, but structures, in the form of a chain of options and branching points, the entire biographical 'curriculum'. This holds true for the model, described by Kohli, for the standard biography in modern societies – the school system for general education, and the skilling levels and profiles defined by it, specifies certain starting opportunities and establishes the direction that the individual's life subsequently takes, as well as the social positioning of the individual; these steps are almost impossible to achieve with subsequent qualifications (Rabe-Kleberg 1993b). The school is simultaneously a key location for practising formal learning. By internalising the specific content of learning, individuals also learn the various forms of learning.

Qualifications and experience gained in school structure the subsequent status passages of biography to an enormous extent – vocational training and/or the transition to employment – and together with initial vocational training they establish the framework for the entire employment biography. Although continuing vocational education or retraining can create new options, these are always dependent on the initial level achieved and on prestructured career patterns that differ considerably not only from one occupation to the next, but also according to social positioning criteria (class, gender, ethnicity, nationality), and are largely absent in the typical women's occupations, for example (Rabe-Kleberg 1993a, Born 2000). The last major phase of biography, retirement, is also defined in crucial ways in terms of its basic conditional framework – not only one's economic, cultural and social capital, but also one's health, physical and (life)time resources – by one's previous employment biography, and to that extent is dependent at least indirectly on the person's education and training history.

Although the three-phase life course regime has lost some of its validity (see above) with changes in the nature of employment, the new, individualised and 'pluralised' life course patterns are still shaped, in increasing measure, by educational institutions that for their part must adapt to the new 'lifelong learning biographies' (Faulstich-Wieland 1997, Nuissl 1997). However, the type of structuring has changed – education and training are not necessarily linear any longer, in the sense of continuous skilling and social positioning ('career'), but are 'patchworked' or cyclically repeated in the sense of a 'timeless, sectoral life form' (see Kade, Seitter 1996, 143ff).

Independently of this differentiation of the biographical forms taken by education and training, which are only starting to be researched, it remains a fact that education and training, as a social institution or as a system of interwoven institutions, shapes typical life course structures and exerts a major influence on subjective life plans and experience. A historical and sociostructural comparison reveals that this shaping process occurs along the social axes of differentiation – class, gender and 'ethnicity' – and that life courses distribute opportunities unevenly and typify them according to social position. From the lifeworld perspective of individuals, they represent 'models for a possible life'.

The Temporal Organisation of Education and Learning in the Life Course

In addition to one's positioning in the social space, education and training generates above all a temporal order for learning processes along the axis of an individual's biography. At present, we have to assume a mixture comprised of persistent norms dating from the three-phase, 'standard' (i.e. male) career, and a more contradictory model for the 'standard female biography' (for a critique, see Dausien 1996), on the one hand, and more recent models involving flexible 'lifelong learning', on the other. Ever since the educational reforms of the 1960s, especially, new skilling pathways have been created by education policymakers that enable formal education and training in adulthood as well. These second and third routes to formal education and training (especially on the part of women) have been accepted and have not only led to higher educational mobility (for women's mobility, see Schlüter 1993, 1999), but have also generated new life course patterns in which 'work', 'family' and 'education' may frequently alternate and be combined with each other in different constellations. Although space prohibits a review of specific, empirically identified patterns, we should distinguish here between three aspects of the temporal ordering of education and training within the life course that do not follow linear trajectories or curricula, but which are typical for biographical experience within the context of increasingly individualised conduct of life:

(a) Educational qualifications and alternative routes to training and education for adults: these are schemes providing adults with a second (third, fourth, ...) 'chance' to make up for missed opportunities or to correct a previous educational status by means of various adult learning pathways within the education and career system. However, the possibilities for making up lost ground are limited, simply by virtue of the fact that lifetime cannot be repeated, and by the lack of opportunities for follow-up and further advancement within previous education and training. This is clearly evident, for example, in typical women's occupations (Rabe-Kleberg 1993a), which are also referred to as 'dead-end occupations'. The subjective enrichment that adult learning usually provides is offset by social structures that until now have predominantly imposed negative sanctions on any deviations from the standard (male) model of an ongoing career, despite the newly propagated flexibility in education and training (Rabe-Kleberg 1993b). In Germany, neither the education and training system nor the occupational system are systematically geared to recognising and integrating 'deviating' skills and competencies acquired during the individual biographical process, especially when these were acquired through non-formal biographical learning or – in the case of migrant biographies – in other societal and national contexts (cf. the 'Assessment of Prior Experiential Learning' tradition in England, Alheit, Piening 1999). The problems of 'fit' that arise must be handled by the individuals concerned and in certain circumstances may lead to unforeseeable conflicts, to discontinuities and 'distortions' of educational schemes offered by institutions. The freedoms gained from the opening of the education and training system also conceal new biographical risks (Kade 1997).

(b) Continuing training and skilling as an ongoing task: The experienced necessity and/or subjective interest in continuing vocational and occupation-related training has increased enormously in recent years (see Field 2000, 69ff). The causes are generally seen to lie in the faster pace of technological change and the ever-shorter 'half-life' of job-related knowledge. Education and skilling are no longer restricted to 'preparation' for working life, but are becoming a permanent support factor within individual careers. Two other social changes contribute to the greater relevance of ongoing continuing education and training: the social transformation of the old-age phase, in combination with the changed biographical significance of old age (Kade, S. 1994a, b, Mader 1995), which is progressively becoming a separate learning phase (Kade, S. 1964a). Women, too, are expressing greater interest in a continuing (occupational) education and training. As Schiersmann (1987, 1993) has shown, however, this area of education and training is part of a genderised structure. Systematic disadvantages and barriers for women in the vocational training system extend the reach of gender-specific channelling and hierarchisation within that system. The gender-critical perspective on continuing (vocational) education and training also highlights some new aspects, however. For women, continuing training is not a 'neutral' instrument of career planning, but is embedded within a form of life planning that is closely tied to opportunities and perspectives in the familial domain. This experience of biographical networking between different areas of life is increasingly a general feature of continuing training (also for men).

(c) Education and training in 'one's own time': Achieving formal schooling qualifications as an adult, as well as ongoing vocational training also have a personal, biographical significance alongside the strategic value aspect. People's concerns are not restricted to what is often an uncertain outcome when exploiting their acquired skills on the labour market – in many cases this is not even their prime concern – but are also focused on compensating for biographically experienced deficits in education and training, and unfulfilled educational wishes. Such biographically based motivation leads similarly to the ordering of life-time by decisions, transitions and learning processes. The inherent temporal structure of education and training may be based on and utilise institutional structures during specific phases, but it can also subvert them or even have 'contrary' effects. Temporal patterns that are biographically organised follow an individual logic in which past, present and future are linked, often across large intervals of time and areas of life that are institutionally separated. Within the individual, biographical perspective from which individuals draw meaning, there is a temporally structured need for education, training and personal development that influences learning processes reflexively in terms of an 'implicit' biographical structure. There are recurrent phases or situations in which the need for reflexivity and reconstruction, for synchronisation and to redesign one's 'own life' is uppermost. These phases or situations are often provoked or occasioned by conflicts with socially structured (educational) timetables. As empirical studies using the methods of biographical research have shown, adults often use continuing training schemes not merely in an instrumental way in order to follow pre-structured learning pathways, but also to gain spaces of time for their 'own' learning processes and reflection (e.g. in adult education courses, see Alheit, Dausien 1996; or in distance learning courses, see Kade, Seitter 1996).

Education as a Biographical Process
This pointer to the individual, biographical time structure of learning processes leads us to the fundamental question as to how education and training can be conceived of as a biographical process that is relatively autonomous in relation to life courses and curricula. Education and training do not only take place in organised and institutionalised forms. They also include the shaping of everyday, life-historical experiences, transitions and crises. Thus, lifewide learning is also tied at all times to the context of a specific biography. On the other hand, it is also the precondition or the medium in which biographical constructions can be created and modified at all

as reflexive forms of experience. Without biography there can be no learning, without learning, no biography.

(a) Implicit learning, reflection and pre-reflexive knowledge: many learning processes occur 'implicitly' and congeal to form patterns of experience and dispositions without these being explicitly reflected upon in every case. Concepts such as implicit, tacit learning emphasise this aspect, but say nothing about the complexity of this phenomenon in the dialectics of appropriating the world and forming one's self. Through implicit learning processes that operate from the beginning of one's life, both inside and outside institutions, we not only appropriate single experiential elements as components of the social world, but we develop the 'appropriation system' itself. What this process involves, therefore, is the formation of supra-ordinated, generative structures of action and knowledge that can be interpreted, depending on one's theoretical leanings, as the acquisition and expansion of biographical 'learning dispositions' (Field 2000), cognitive structures in Piaget's sense, 'emotional orientation systems' (Mader 1997), habitus formation (Bourdieu 1987) or the construction of self- and world-references (Marotzki 1990).

All these experiential processes form a person's biographical stock of knowledge (Alheit 1993, Alheit, Hoerning 1989) consisting, like a landscape, of different layers and regions, some near, some far, and which changes in the course of time (through learning). In everyday action (and also in explicit learning situations; Dewe 1999) we focus explicitly on a particular 'problem' – a mere excerpt from our stock of knowledge, experience and actions – and make recourse at the same time to large portions of our knowledge (and non-knowledge) in a taken-for-granted way, without querying what we do. In a certain sense, we 'move' within our biographically acquired landscape of knowledge, without consciously reflecting on every step we take, every twist in the path and every signpost along the way. In many cases, we do not turn to such elements in our biographical 'background knowledge' until we find ourselves stumbling, or at a crossroads, or we feel as if the ground is slipping away from beneath our feet. Theoretically at least, we are able to retrieve large parts of this pre-reflexive knowledge into the present, to process it explicitly and perhaps even to change structures of the entire landscape in which we find ourselves. Such reflexive processes can be interpreted as moments of self-education (Alheit 1993). They are the basis of each person's organising of learning and justify speaking about the biographicity of all educational processes.

(b) Sociality of biographical learning: Reflexive learning processes do not take place exclusively 'inside' the individual, but depend on communication and interaction with others and relations to a social context. Biographical learning is embedded in lifeworlds that can be analysed under certain conditions as 'learning environments' or 'learning milieus'. Experience-based, lifeworld learning or learning in contexts are terms that take this aspect of lifelong learning into consideration, as is also reflected in the greater interest now shown in integrating and shaping learning environments (Dohmen 1998). However, there are two tendencies that can be observed here and which need to be critically assessed using the biographical analysis of education processes: an 'anti-institutional interpretation of lifelong learning, whether welcomed or feared (Gieseke 1997, Nuissl 1997), that overlooks the fact that biography (biographical learning) and institutions are inter-related (see, for example the study by Seitter 1999); and the technological idea of the trivial 'feasibility' of learning environments. This latter idea overlooks the fact that 'learning worlds' are embedded within historically rooted, interactive and biographically 'produced' lifeworlds that are integrated and shaped in education processes, but which cannot be artificially generated or managed (Lave, Wenger 1991).

(c) Individuality and the 'self-willed' nature of biographical learning: Learning within and through one's life history is therefore interactive and socially structured, on the one hand, but it also follows its own 'individual logic' that is generated by the specific, biographically layered structure of experience. The biographical structure does not determine the learning process, because it is an open structure that has to integrate the new experience it gains through interacting with the world, with others and with itself. On the other hand, however, it significantly affects the way in which new experience is formed and 'built into' a biographical learning process (Alheit, Dausien 2000a). There is a necessity here, as well, to subject some current concepts such as self-organised, self-determined, self-managed or self-directed learning (Straka 1997, Dohmen 1998, Konzertierte

Aktion Weiterbildung 1998) to critical debate (Report 39, Hoffmann, von Rein 1998). All too often, they presume an autonomous learner who has a reflexive and strategic 'grip' on his own education and training. This model overlooks the multi-layeredness of biographical reflexivity. Biographical education and training processes operate in self-willed ways, they permit unexpected experiences and surprising transformations that in many cases are not foreseen by the 'learner' himself, or are not 'understood' until after the event, but which still pursue their own 'direction'. Terms such as 'seeking movement' or 'diffuse directedness' are more appropriate here than cybernetic models involving some well-targeted 'self-management' that for its part is oriented to institutionalised pre-givens (e.g. the acquisition of knowledge). A biographical understanding of 'self-determination' would have to be developed with reference to the 'formation' concept (*'Bildung'*), rather than the notion of learning as 'training'. If the biographical organisation of learning processes is to be given practical educational (and institutional) support, then spaces for reflection and communication, as well as interaction with 'spaces of opportunity' are at least as important as developing 'instruments for individual self-management'.

Education as the 'Formation' (= 'Structuration') of Social Structures

If lifelong learning is researched using an approach based on biography theory, the various aspects of that approach we have discussed above would provide ways of relating back to Perspective I, which was also discussed in the foregoing. Biographical education and training processes must be understood not only as appropriational and constructional accomplishments, given the individual and reflexive organisation of experience, knowledge and ability. They also include the biographical formation of social networks and processes, of collective knowledge and collective praxis, which can be also understood theoretically – as in Berger and Luckmann (1969) – as 'institutionalisation', as the formation of social networks and 'social capital' (see above) or as the crystallisation of cultural practices (empirical examples include the formation of cultural and social centres, associations, local community initiatives, etc.; Seitter 1999, Field 2000, Alheit, Dausien 2000b). It holds true for these collective formation processes, too, that they are explicitly negotiated and reflexively planned only to a partial extent. Social formations, such as new models and experiential contexts for possible educational routes, for potential women's and men's biographies, for gender relations, for learning processes and forms of interaction between cultures and generations can ensue even from the uncoordinated, biographical praxis of individuals in educational matters.

The biographicity of social experience lends itself here, too, as a useful theoretical concept for explaining such phenomena. If we conceive of biographical learning as a self-willed, 'autopoietic' accomplishment on the part of active subjects, in which they reflexively 'organise' their experience in such a way that they also generate personal coherence, identity, a meaning to their life history and a communicable, socially viable lifeworld perspective for guiding their actions (Alheit 1993, Alheit, Dausien 2000a), it becomes possible to comprehend education and learning both as individual identity work and as the 'formation' of collective processes and social relations.

The analysis of biographical learning has shown clearly that, within this analytical perspective, there is not only a focus on individual processes, but also that different levels converge within it and may generate discrepancies that must be dealt with biographically and coped with in a pragmatic way by the subjects themselves: one aspect is that the programmatics of 'lifelong learning' evoke new patterns of expectation and interpretation that may be experienced subjectively as burdensome pressures, but also as a biographical opportunity. Secondly, biographical learning processes and life plans depend on institutional structures and lifeworld contexts that may foster or obstruct education and training processes that are 'self-determined' by individuals and collectives. Finally, from the perspective of subjects, there is not only a contradiction here between 'wish' and 'reality' – both levels are biographically 'real', must be processed by the individual and re-integrated into his own educational history again and again in a genuinely lifelong process of biographical construction and reconstruction. Yet, if we are to grasp and explain these processes with greater theoretical precision, to analyse them greater empirical differentiation, and on this basis to design methods and approaches for possible educational practices, then further empirical research studies are urgently necessary. The complexity of the problem certainly demands a substantiated, well-grounded framework concept – such as the biographical approach outlined here – that is able to fill the lifelong learning programme with theoretical and empirical substance.

Research Desiderata in the Context of Lifelong Learning

It seems, indeed, that any serious, analytical involvement with the complex phenomenon of 'lifelong learning' will be contingent on a paradigm shift among educationalists:
- at the social macro-level, in respect of a new policy for education and training that aims at striking a different balance between economic, cultural and social capital (Alheit; Kreitz 2000);
- at the institutional meso-level, also in respect of a new 'self-reflexivity' of organisations that should conceive of themselves as 'environments' and 'agencies' of complex learning and knowledge resources, and no longer as the administrators and conveyors of codified, dominant knowledge (Field 2000);
- at the individual micro-level, with regard to the increasingly complicated linkages and processing accomplished by the specific actors in the face of the social and media-related challenges of late Modernity, which call for a new quality in the individual and collective construction of meanings (Alheit 1999).

We still know too little, in fact, about the systemic balances between economic and social capital. We hardly know anything yet about that 'grey capital' of new knowledge (Field 2000, 1) and its impacts on long-term learning processes. Of course, the comparison of different types of post-industrial society – e.g. the distinct differences between Danish or British of German strategies for arriving at a 'learning society' – makes it worthwhile to carry out systematic international comparisons of educational economics.

Yet we have only scraps of information about the institutional prerequisites for the paradigm shift required.

> What pressures to change are operating on education and training institutions? What responses and solutions are there, what scope do changes have (e.g. partial reorganisation, total redefinition of educational responsibilities, etc.)? What steps are needed to safeguard scope for action, stability and innovative capacity? What concepts and measures are applied and accepted as best practice in the fields of quality management, organisational development and personnel development? What theoretical and empirical conditions justify speaking of educational establishments as 'learning organisations'? What frameworks and structures foster their (further) development (*Forschungsmemorandum für die Erwachsenen- und Weiterbildung* 2000, 13)?

We are discovering more and more new, more complex and riskier status passages and transitions in modern life courses (Heinz 2000b). We observe astonishing and creative (re-)constructions in individual biographies (Alheit 1994, Dausien 1996, Kade, Seitter 1996). However, we are still missing a systematically elaborated theory of biographical learning.

> In which learning cultures and dependencies of supra-individual patterns, mentalities and milieus does individual learning develop? What implicit learning potentials and learning processes are shown in social milieus and groups (e.g. within families and between generations)? ... What interdependencies can be identified, e.g. between supra-individual and political problems and solutions, on the one hand, and learning by individuals in groups, organisations, and institutions, on the other (*Forschungsmemorandum für die Erwachsenen- und Weiterbildung* 2000, 5)?

These open research questions are raised by the 'new' concept of lifelong learning. They include the idea that social learning is obviously – more than ever before in history – an achievement of the subjects concerned. The 'biographicity' of learning affects institutional and even societal macro structures. It would be extremely welcome if the answers to those questions were to be sought not only in academic discourse, but also among practitioners of continuing education and training, and through international dialogue.

References

Achtenhagen, F., Lempert, W. (eds.) (2000). *Lebenslanges Lernen im Beruf – seine Grundlegung im Kindes- und Jugendalter.* Opladen.

Alheit, P. (^{2}1993). Transitorische Bildungsprozesse: Das „biographische Paradigma" in der Weiterbildung. In: Mader, W. (ed.). *Weiterbildung und Gesellschaft. Grundlagen wissenschaftlicher und beruflicher Praxis in der Bundesrepublik Deutschland.* Bremen, pp. 343-418.

Alheit, P. (1994). *Zivile Kultur. Verlust und Wiederaneignung der Moderne.* Frankfurt/M., New York.

Alheit, P. (1999). On a Contradictory Way to the 'Learning Society'. A Critical Approach. In: *Studies in the Education of Adults*, 31 (1), pp. 66-82.

Alheit, P. Dausien, B. (1996). Bildung als „biographische Konstruktion"? Nichtintendierte Lernprozesse in der organisierten Erwachsenenbildung. In: *Report. Literatur- und Forschungsreport Weiterbildung*, 37, pp. 33-45.

Alheit, P., Dausien, B. (2000a). Die biographische Konstruktion der Wirklichkeit. Überlegungen zur Biographizität des Sozialen. In: Hoerning, E. M. (ed.) (2000) *Biographische Sozialisation.* Stuttgart, pp. 257-283.

Alheit, P., Dausien, B. (2000b). 'Biographicity' as a Basic Resource of Lifelong Learning. In: Alheit, P. et al. (eds.). *Lifelong Learning Inside and Outside Schools.* Vol. 2, Roskilde, pp. 400-422.

Alheit, P., Hoerning, E. M. (eds.) (1989). *Biographisches Wissen. Beiträge zu einer Theorie lebensgeschichtlicher Erfahrung.* Frankfurt/M.

Alheit, P., Kammler, E. (eds.) (1998). *Lifelong Learning and its Impact on Social and Regional Development.* Bremen.

Alheit, P., Kreitz, R. (2000). 'Social Capital', 'Education' and the 'Wider Benefits of Learning'. Review of 'Models' and Qualitative Research Outcomes. Göttingen, London (unpublished manuscript).

Alheit, P., Piening, D. (1999). *Assessment of Prior Experiential Learning as a Key to Lifelong Learning.* Evaluating European Practices. Bremen.

Arthur, M. B., Inkson, K., Pringle, J. K. (1999). *The New Careers. Individual Action and Economic Change.* London.

Beck, U. (1983). Jenseits von Stand und Klasse? Soziale Ungleichheiten, gesellschaftliche Individualisierungsprozesse und die Entstehung neuer sozialer Funktionen und Identitäten. In: Kreckel, R. (ed..) (1983). *Soziale Ungleichheiten. Soziale Welt.* Göttingen, pp. 35-74.

Beck, U. (1986). *Risikogesellschaft. Auf dem Weg in eine andere Moderne.* Frankfurt/M.

Beck, U., Giddens, A., Lash, S. (1996). *Reflexive Modernisierung. Eine Kontroverse.* Frankfurt/M.

Bentley, T. (1998). *Learning Beyond the Classroom. Education for a Changing World.* London.

Berger, P., Luckmann, T. (1969). *Die gesellschaftliche Konstruktion der Wirklichkeit. Eine Theorie der Wissenssoziologie.* Frankfurt/M.

Born, C. (2000). Erstausbildung und weiblicher Lebenslauf. Was (nicht nur) junge Frauen bezüglich der Berufswahl wissen sollten. In: Heinz, W. (ed.). *Übergänge. Individualisierung, Flexibilisierung und Institutionalisierung des Lebenslaufs.* 3. Beiheft 2000 der Zeitschrift für Soziologie der Erziehung und Sozialisation, Weinheim, pp. 50-65.

Bourdieu, P. (1987). *Die feinen Unterschiede. Kritik der gesellschaftlichen Urteilskraft.* Frankfurt/M.

Brödel, R. (ed.) (1998). *Lebenslanges Lernen – lebensbegleitende Bildung.* Neuwied.

Commission of the European Communities (1994). *Competitiveness, Employment, Growth.* Luxembourg.

Commission of the European Communities (1995). *Teaching and Learning. Towards the Learning Society.* Luxembourg.

Commission of the European Communities (2000). *A Memorandum on Lifelong Learning.* Lissabon.

Dausien, B. (1996). *Biographie und Geschlecht. Zur biographischen Konstruktion sozialer Wirklichkeit in Frauenlebensgeschichten.* Bremen.

Dausien, B. (2001). Lebensbegleitendes Lernen in den Biographien von Frauen. Ein biographietheoretisches Bildungskonzept. In: Gieseke, W. (ed..). *Handbuch zur Frauenbildung.* Opladen, pp. 101-114.

Delors, J. (1996). *Learning. The Treasure Within.* Report to UNESCO of the International Commission on Education for the Twenty-first Century. Paris.

Delory-Momberger, C. (2000). *Les histoires de vie. De l'linvention de soi au projet de formation.* Paris.

Department for Education and Employment (1998). *The Learning Age. A Renaissance for a New Britain.* Sheffield.

Dewe, B. (1999). *Lernen zwischen Vergewisserung und Ungewißheit. Reflexives Handeln in der Erwachsenenbildung.* Opladen.

Dohmen, G. (1996). *Das lebenslange Lernen. Leitlinien einer modernen Bildungspolitik.* Bonn.

Dohmen, G. (1998). *Zur Zukunft der Weiterbildung in Europa. Lebenslanges Lernen für alle in veränderten Lernumwelten.* Bonn.

Dominicé, P. (1990). *L'histoire de vie comme processus de formation*. Paris.

Dominicé, P. (2000). *Learning from Our Lives. Using Educational Biographies with Adults*. San Francisco.

Faulstich-Wieland, H. (1997). Zukunft der Bildung – Schule der Zukunft. In: *Report. Literatur- und Forschungsreport Weiterbildung*, 39, pp. 59-68.

Faure, E. (1972). *Learning to Be. The World of Education Today and Tomorrow*. Paris.

Field, J. (2000). *Lifelong Learning and the New Educational Order*. Stoke on Trent.

Forschungsmemorandum für die Erwachsenen- und Weiterbildung (2000). Im Auftrag der Sektion Erwachsenenbildung der DGfE verf. v. Arnold, R. et al. (www.die-frankfurt.de/oear/forschungsmemorandum/forschungsmemorandum.htm).

Gerlach, C. (2000). *Lebenslanges Lernen. Konzepte und Entwicklungen 1972 bis 1997*. Köln.

Giddens, A. (1990). *Consequences of Modernity*. Cambridge.

Giddens, A. (1991). *Modernity and Self-Identity. Self and Society in the Late Modern Age*. Cambridge.

Giddens, A. (1998). *The Third Way. The Renewal of Social Democracy*. Cambridge.

Gieseke, W. (1997). Lebenslanges Lernen aus der Perspektive der Geschlechterdifferenz. In: *Report. Literatur- und Forschungsreport Weiterbildung*, 39, pp. 79-87.

Group of Eight (1999). *Köln Charter. Aims and Ambitions for Lifelong Learning*, 18 June 1999. Köln.

Hall, P. (1999). Social Capital in Britain. In: *British Journal of Political Science*, 29 (3), pp. 417-461.

Heinz, W. (2000a). Editorial: Strukturbezogene Biographie- und Lebenslaufforschung. der Sfb 186 „Statuspassagen und Risikolagen im Lebensverlauf". In: Heinz, W. (ed.) (2000). *Übergänge. Individualisierung, Flexibilisierung und Institutionalisierung des Lebenslaufs*. 3. Beiheft der ZSE. Zeitschrift für Soziologie der Erziehung und Sozialisation. Weinheim, pp. 4-8.

Heinz, W. (ed.) (2000b). *Übergänge. Individualisierung, Flexibilisierung und Institutionalisierung des Lebenslaufs*. 3. Beiheft 2000 der ZSE. Zeitschrift für Soziologie der Erziehung und Sozialisation. Weinheim.

Hoffmann, N., von Rein, A. (ed.) (1998). *Selbstorganisiertes Lernen in (berufs-) biographischer Reflexion*. Frankfurt/M.

Kade, J. (1994). Erziehungswissenschaftliche Theoriebildung im Blick auf die Vielfalt einer sich entgrenzenden pädagogischen Welt. In: Uhle, R., Hoffmann, D. (ed.) (1994). *Pluralitätsverarbeitung in der Pädagogik*. Weinheim, pp. 149-161.

Kade, J. (1997). Riskante Biographien und die Risiken lebenslangen Lernens. In: *Report. Literatur- und Forschungsreport Weiterbildung*, 39, pp. 112-124.

Kade, J., Seitter, W. (1996). *Lebenslanges Lernen. Mögliche Bildungswelten. Erwachsenenbildung, Biographie und Alltag*. Opladen.

Kade, S. (1994a). *Altersbildung. Lebenssituation und Lernbedarf, Ziele und Konzepte*. Frankfurt/M.

Kade, S. (ed.) (1994b). *Individualisierung und Älterwerden.* Bad Heilbrunn.

Körber, K. (1989). Zur Antinomie von politisch-kultureller und arbeitsbezogener Bildung in der Erwachsenenbildung. In: *Bildung in der Arbeitsgesellschaft. Zum Spannungsverhältnis von Arbeit und Bildung heute.* Dokumentation des 10. Bremer Wissenschaftsforums vom 11. bis 13. Oktober 1988. Bremen, pp. 126-151.

Kohli, M. (1985). Die Institutionalisierung des Lebenslaufs. Historische Befunde und theoretische Argumente. In: *Kölner Zeitschrift für Soziologie und Sozialpsychologie,* 37, pp. 1-29.

Kohli, M. (1989). Institutionalisierung und Individualisierung der Erwerbsbiographie. Aktuelle Veränderungstendenzen und ihre Folgen. In: Brock, D. et al. (ed.). *Subjektivität im gesellschaftlichen Wandel. Umbrüche im beruflichen Sozialisationsprozeß.* München, pp. 249-278.

Konzertierte Aktion Weiterbildung (1998). *Selbstgesteuertes Lernen. Möglichkeiten, Beispiele, Lösungsansätze, Probleme.* Bonn.

Krüger, H.-H., Marotzki, W. (ed.) (1995). *Erziehungswissenschaftliche Biographieforschung.* Opladen.

Krüger, H.-H., Marotzki, W. (ed.) (1999). *Handbuch erziehungswissenschaftliche Biographieforschung.* Opladen.

Longworth, N., Davies, W. K. (1996). *Lifelong Learning. New Vision, New Implications, New Roles for People, Organizations, Nations and Communities in the 21st Century.* London.

Mader, W. (ed.) (1995). *Altwerden in einer alternden Gesellschaft. Kontinuität und Krisen in biographischen Verläufen.* Opladen.

Mader, W. (1997). Lebenslanges Lernen oder die lebenslange Wirksamkeit von emotionalen Orientierungssystemen. In: *Report. Literatur- und Forschungsreport Weiterbildung,* 39, pp. 88-100.

Marotzki, W. (1990). *Entwurf einer strukturalen Bildungstheorie. Biographietheoretische Auslegung von Bildungsprozessen in hochkomplexen Gesellschaften.* Weinheim.

Merrill, B. (1999). *Gender, Change and Identity. Mature Women Students in Universities.* Aldershot.

Nassehi, A. (1994). Die Form der Biographie. Theoretische Überlegungen zur Biographieforschung in methodologischer Absicht. In: *BIOS. Zeitschrift für Biographieforschung und Oral History,* 7 (1), pp. 46-63.

Nolda, S. (ed.) (1996). *Erwachsenenbildung in der Wissensgesellschaft.* Bad Heilbrunn.

Nuissl, E. (1997). Institutionen im lebenslangen Lernen. In: *Report. Literatur- und Forschungsreport Weiterbildung,* 39, pp. 41-49.

OECD (1996). *Lifelong Learning for All.* Meeting of the Education Committee at Ministerial level, 16/17 January 1996. Paris.

OECD (1997a). *Literacy Skills for the Knowledge Society.* Further Results of the International Adult Literacy Survey. Paris.

OECD (1997b). *What Works in Innovation in Education. Combatting Exclusion through Adult Learning.* Paris.

OECD, CERI (1973). *Recurrent Education – A Strategy for Lifelong Learning.* A Clarifying Report. Paris.

Putnam, R. D. (2001). *Gesellschaft und Gemeinsinn. Sozialkapital im internationalen Vergleich.* Gütersloh.

Rabe-Kleberg, U. (1993a). *Verantwortlichkeit und Macht. Ein Beitrag zum Verhältnis von Geschlecht und Beruf angesichts der Krise traditioneller Frauenberufe.* Bielefeld.

Rabe-Kleberg, U. (1993b). Bildungsbiographien – oder: Kann Hans noch lernen, was Hänschen versäumt hat? In: Meier, A., Rabe-Kleberg, U. (ed.). *Weiterbildung, Lebenslauf, sozialer Wandel.* Neuwied, pp. 167-182.

Rahmstorf, G. (1999). *Wissensgesellschaft.* Nachricht Nr. 00079 im Archiv der Mailingliste wiss-org, (http://index.bonn.iz-soz.de/~sigel/ISKO/wiss-org-archive/msg00079.html).

Report 39 (1997). Report. Literatur- und Forschungsreport Weiterbildung, 39.

Schlüter, A. (1993). *Bildungsmobilität. Studien zur Individualisierung von Arbeitertöchtern in der Moderne.* Weinheim.

Schlüter, A. (1999). *Bildungserfolge. Eine Analyse der Wahrnehmungs- und Deutungsmuster und der Mechanismen für Mobilität in Bildungsbiographien.* Opladen.

Schuller, T. (1997). *Modelling the Lifecourse. Age, Time and Education.* Bremen.

Schuller, T. (1998). Human and Social Capital. Variations within a Learning Society. In: Alheit, P., Kammler, E. (eds.). *Lifelong Learning and its Impact on Social and Regional Development.* Bremen, pp. 113-136.

Schuller, T., Field, J. (1999). Is there Divergence between Initial and Continuing Education in Scotland and Nothern Ireland? In: *Scottish Journal of Adult Continuing Education*, 5 (2), pp. 61-76.

Schulze, G. (1992). *Die Erlebnisgesellschaft. Kultursoziologie der Gegenwart.* Frankfurt/M., New York.

Schulze, T. (1993a). Lebenslauf und Lebensgeschichte. In: Baacke, D., Schulze, T. (ed.). *Aus Geschichten lernen. Zur Einübung pädagogischen Verstehens.* Weinheim, pp. 174-226.

Schulze, T. (1993b). Zum ersten Mal und immer wieder neu. Skizzen zu einem phänomenologischen Lernbegriff. In: Bauersfeld, H., Bromme, R. (ed.). *Bildung und Aufklärung.* Münster, pp. 241-269.

Seitter, W. (1999). *Riskante Übergänge in der Moderne. Vereinskulturen, Bildungsbiographien, Migranten.* Opladen.

Simons, P. R. J. (1992). Theories and Principles of Learning to Learn. In: Tujinman, A., van der Kamp, M. (eds.) (1992). *Learning Across the Lifespan. Theories, Research, Policies.* Oxford, pp. 173-188.

Smith, R. M. (1992). Implementing the learning to learn concept. In: Tujinman, A., van der Kamp, M. (eds.). *Learning Across the Lifespan. Theories, Research, Policies.* Oxford, pp. 173-188.

Stehr, N. (2000). *Erwerbsarbeit in der Wissensgesellschaft oder Informationstechnologien, Wissen und der Arbeitsmarkt.* Vancouver.

Straka, G. A. (1997). Selbstgesteuertes lernen in der Arbeitswelt. In: *Report. Literatur- und Forschungsreport Weiterbildung*, 39, pp. 146-154.

Tavistock Institute (1999). *A Review of Thirty New Deal Partnerships.* Research and Development Report ESR 32, Employment Service. Sheffield.

Tuckett, A., Sargant, N. (1999). *Making Time.* The NIACE Survey on Adult Participation in Learning 1999. Leicester.

Vester, M. et al. (1993). *Soziale Milieus im gesellschaftlichen Strukturwandel. Zwischen Integration und Ausgrenzung.* Köln.

Williamson, B. (1998). *Lifeworlds and Learning. Essays in the Theory, Philosophy and Practice of Lifelong Learning.* Leicester.

Wingens, M. (1998). *Wissensgesellschaft und Industrialisierung der Wissenschaft.* Wiesbaden.

Jon Ohlsson

LEARNING ORGANISATION IN THEORY AND PRACTICE
ONGOING ORGANISING AND COLLECTIVE LEARNING IN TEACHER TEAMS

The Learning Organisation – Some Problematic Issues

Today adult learning appears to be the key to all kinds of problems in people's everyday life, in working life and in society as a whole. Learning is not only an issue of formal education any more, but people are expected to be 'everyday learners' and 'lifelong learners', which in turn raises demands on societal institutions and working life to give people opportunities to learn and to handle challenging tasks. In contemporary society adult's learning is to a high degree regarded as a work-related issue and organisational challenge, and as a chance to enhance competencies. Many researchers and practitioners think of learning processes as 'two-sided' affairs, good for both the organisation and the people who work there. Thus, the formation of environment as a learning context is regarded as an important way to let adults learn, and therefore, an important tool in the ongoing competition on the market. In this respect the widespread interest in theory and practice of "learning organisation" is quite understandable (Senge 1990, Pedler et al. 1991, Dixon 1994).

Although researchers show somewhat different views on definitions of the concept learning organisation, the orientation toward individual and collective learning processes and interactive and communicative activities is commonly shared. To be a learning organisation is to exceed the individual competence of members of the organisation, and this requires conditions that will enable people to learn from each other, and together. A significant aspect of the learning organisation is the belief in teams. Team organisations appear as the answer on today's organisational problems.

Senge (1990) describes team as one of the central "disciplines" in the learning organisation, and a lot of other researchers emphasise the importance of team work (Engeström 1996, Neck, Manz 1994). Attempts to implement organisational changes in a way that promotes learning and competence enhancement often encounter practical problems and difficulties. Such a problem is the emergence of a gap between the intention to develop the organisation and real life practice in everyday work. Actually, critics mean that the learning organisation discourse leads to separation between a visionary but quite abstract 'world' within the organisation and practice where everyday work is carried out (Hultman, Klasson 1998, Coopey 1996). Practice often remains the same, independent of the attempts to implement new organisational or team-oriented learning models.

With problems like that, the responsible leader sighs, saying: "We are not a learning organisation. Where is the handbook where I can find the ultimate model and the tools needed to implement it successfully?"

However, the issues of learning organisation and implementation are certainly more complex than that. Argyris (1999) identifies two central problems regarding learning organisations and the implementation of it. One is the "theoretical" problem, usually pointed to by academics, which occur when we think about an organisation's ability to learn. Who is it who really learns anything, an individual or a collective? If we think and talk about collective learning, how can we understand this phenomenon? With a point of departure in action theory, using concepts such as experience, action and reflection, it seems problematic to speak of collective learning. As Argyris puts it, it concerns questions of "levels of aggregation" (Argyris 1999, 19).

The other problem concerns the utilisation of theories in practice and the question of implementation. Practitioners are often suspicious regarding the practical importance of theoretical models. Concepts like learning organisation do not make sense to them. The often vague and highly abstract models do not reflect the complexity of practice and the conflicting perspectives of practitioners. Descriptive theories might be interesting on the leaders desk or in the consultant's visions for sale, but using learning organisation just as a metaphor will not have an intended impact on the conditions for learning in practice. If the theories on organisational and team learning processes do not fit real life problems in such a way that they explain or make understandable what factors enable and constrain learning processes, the gap between theory and practice will remain. Therefore, Argyris (1999) points to the necessity of a theoretical elaboration beyond the ideal models in management literature.

These theoretical and practical problems are together a fundamental challenge for the researchers in this field. In order to meet this challenge, this article deals with the issue of learning organisation as a pedagogic problem[1]. This means a perspective on organising as an ongoing contextual process of collective sensemaking and learning. The problems Argyris (1999) discusses are basically pedagogical issues, containing aspects of pedagogy as a scientific enterprise and practical intervention. Scientifically and theoretically, an important issue concerns elaboration of concepts in order to explain and understand the relation between individual and organisational learning. If the latter is described as collective learning, then that concept needs to be explained. What really is collective learning? The practical aspect concerns the question of how to implement the visions of a learning organisation in a concrete organisational context. Pedagogically, implementation is not an application of a ready-made model. It seems reasonable to see implementation as an intervention in ongoing sense making processes and learning. Accordingly, it is appropriate to attend to processes of organising and learning in a specific context, in our attempts to understand the contextual features where the intervention will take place. The organisation and the team, are social contexts where individual members are involved in constant sense making processes (Weick 1995). Therefore, the focus is not on organisation as an object, but rather on organising as processes (Broekstra 1998, Woodilla 1998).

Aiming to clarify and discuss the above mentioned theoretical and practical pedagogical issues this article deals with a central theme in research on learning organisations, namely the organising of team-work and

---

[1] In this article the term "pedagogic" is used in a broad sense and not only as an issue of formal education or a teacher's/instructor's didactical relation to a "learner". Instead it is a focus on how people learn, how they use context as conditions for learning and how they participate in organising and formation of these conditions. Other researchers have used the not so well known term "andragogy" in attempts to clarify these themes (Kornbluh, Greene 1989).

collaboration in teams, and the implications for collective learning. Empirical examples from research on teacher teams in local school organisations contribute to a discussion of some problematic pedagogic aspects. The first part in the article provides a brief theoretical overview regarding theoretical and conceptual attempts to deal with the phenomenon "learning organisation". In the second part I present some empirical results showing that teachers continuously organise their work and their collaboration in two types of processes. The article concludes in a discussion concerning the existence of two parallel organising activities among teachers within the team. A communicative integration of these organising activities appears to be a fruitful pedagogical intervention to enable collective learning processes in the team.

Organisational Theory and the Learning Organisation

During the last decade theories on learning organisations have appeared as enormous outgrowth on the big 'tree' of contemporary organisational theory. The concept of organisational development (OD) gradually has been replaced by the concepts of organisational learning and learning organisation. A characteristic feature of traditional OD-approaches is the emphasis on the rationality of co-ordination of resources, distinct division of tasks and critical evaluative discussions (French, Bell 1990, Schein 1988). Despite structural aspects this rational perspective usually includes an integrated part of humanisation and a normative orientation towards democratisation of organisations. As a discourse of 'modernity', OD-projects attempt to make the organisational goals and tasks more distinct and clear, to improve decision making processes and to specify and divide responsibilities and positions at the individual level. Within this perspective the keys in the rationalisation of the organisation appear to be the enhancement of individual competencies and problem solving abilities of each member of the organisation. Other important aspects are the formation of organisational structures that support co-ordination of resources, and the elucidation of the division of tasks and responsibilities. When Senge (1990) wrote his famous book "The Fifth Discipline" it was a contribution to an ongoing development of organisational theory, related to earlier works by Argyris and

Schön (1978) and Schein (1988). It was also a starting point of a far-reaching expansion of practice oriented research, thereby attending to a more business- and management oriented normative aspect of organisational theory. The earlier emphasis on democratic issues, sensitivity training and workers' well being does not belong to the mainstream of today's research in the field of organisational development and learning. Instead contemporary research is concerned with phenomena and concepts like collective learning processes (Swieringa, Wierdsma 1992, Schein 1993), collective mind (Weick, Roberts 1993), dialogue and thinking together (Isaacs 1993, Schein 1993).[2] By focusing on these, some would say, more 'postmodern' themes opportunities were offered to understand processes of change in a less static way than was the case in many efforts within the OD-tradition.

A learning organisation is "an organisation that facilitates the learning of all its members and continuously transforms itself" (Pedler et al. 1991, 1). Another definition is: "The 'Learning Organisation' is a metaphor, with its roots in the vision of and the search for a strategy to promote individual self-development within a continuously self-transforming organisation" (Starkey 1996, 2). A closely related concept is organisational learning, dealt with by Argyris and Schön (1978) and defined by Dixon as "the intentional use of learning processes at the individual, group and system level to continuously transform the organisation in a direction that is increasingly satisfying to its stakeholders" (Dixon 1994, 5). These definitions contain two main parts, which express two different aspects of importance in research and literature on learning organisations. One of these aspects comes to the fore in the perspective on organisation as an organism, where learning is studied at an organisational level. This aspect relates to the second part in the quotations from Pedler and Starkey, and the "system-level" in Dixon's definition. The other aspect expressed in the quotations concerns organisation as an arena, which means a deeper research orientation towards the learning processes, interactions, communication, and in some

---

[2] Research and development projects have been carried out frequently during the last decade at research institutes like the MIT (Massachusetts Institute of Technology) in the US and Learning Company in UK.

respects conflicting or contradictory interests of individuals.[3]

Referring to the first aspect, learning means transformation of the organisation under pressure from the surroundings and the organisations' inner life. Theoretically this kind of perspective has roots in Durkheim's classic sociological theory of collective consciousness. An organisation can be described as a learning organisation if it transforms itself as a response to events in the outside world or as results from earlier actions. Argyris and Schön (1978) describe organisational learning in terms of single- and double loop learning.[4] Single-loop learning means that an organisation, via correction of errors, changes its way to carry out things in order to achieve the current objectives. Consequences of the collective action indicate whether the action is appropriate or not, and if not, learning how to do things differently is necessary. By single loop learning the organisation corrects itself and starts to act properly. Double loop learning, which is a more complex process, involves change in notions and norms of what to do in the organisation. When building up a new structure adapted to the demands in the surroundings, leading to new insights on what to do, and consequently to new ways of doing, double loop learning takes place. In an attempt to further elaborate this theory Swieringa and Wierdsma (1992) identify a triple loop in the organisational learning, which can be described as existentialistic change in the organisation, as a consequence of reflection on why some actions ought to be done. In this 'organismic' sense of learn-

---

[3] In some respects these directions mirror what Burrell and Morgan (1994) describe as a dimension of on one hand "regulation" and on the other hand "radical change" in organisation studies. The former includes approaches that mainly concern social order, status quo and consensus in society and organisations. The latter includes approaches of radical change, structural conflicts and structures of dominance. With regard to the two mentioned aspects in research on learning organisation it is important to stress that critical studies are rare and it seems inappropriate to talk about a tradition of conflict-related perspectives in this field of research. The dominating theme in studies of learning organisation as an arena, is the dialogue and a management-influenced harmonious relation between the actors in the organisation.

[4] The idea to assign the loop-theory to the "organism"-directed research does not implicate that Argyris and Schön's work ignores the issue of individual learning and the sometimes conflicting perspectives between actors. In their widely spread book on "Organisational Learning" (1978) they reason to a great deal on these subjects, but the central point here is that the loop-theory mainly is an attempt to describe and explain learning at an organisational level.

ing organisation, collective learning is possible to understand as a phenomenon that is not the same as individual learning. Instead it is a change process on a higher level of aggregation. For practitioners such reasoning may be too far removed from practice, and therefore it might be difficult to see the practical value of these theories.

With the other focus mentioned above, the organisation is regarded as an arena for interaction and communication. Learning organisation, in this respect, has two different meanings. A learning organisation is either a metaphor or a concept of coordinated actions between people. In either case a main research focus is the thoughts, actions and interactions of and among members of the organisation. With emphasis on actions and sense making some important theoretical roots will be found in sociological action theory by Weber and further elaborated by Habermas (1984) and in the organisational action frame of reference by Silverman (1970). By focusing on the actor's thoughts and actions in everyday work the strength of this direction lies in the relation between practice and individual learning processes. It is obvious that several researchers regard learning organisation mainly as a metaphor (Kolb 1996, Pedler et al. 1991, Starkey 1996), and therefore do not attend to the conceptual complexity of collective learning. Accordingly, they suggest a main focus on individual action, reflection and learning in different organisational settings. In this respect, an important task for researchers is to discover and explain how the organisation affords learning conditions and enabling as well as constraining factors.

For some researchers the concept of learning organisation means something more than a metaphor. Learning at an organisational level is labelled as a collective learning process, which in turn is a real process of interaction and communication between people. In attempts to understand how interaction and communication influence learning organisations researchers pay attention to the importance of dialogue (Dixon 1994, Isaacs 1993, Schein 1993). The existence of dialogue provides opportunities for people to think together and to learn from each other's experiences. Dialogue appears as the key to triple-loop learning (Schein 1993), and Dixon (1994) shows that a lot of important learning processes, both at a collective and individual level, occur when people talk together in hallways at the work place. Senge (1990) puts dialogue in relation to the organisation of team work, and he describes dialogue and debate as two forms of conversation which need to balance in the development of team learning.[5] In this respect, team-learning is a key to learning organisation. Through dialogue people exchange experiences and think together, which appears as a cornerstone in collective learning.

Collective Learning through Ongoing Communicative Actions and Joint Sense Making

As Argyris (1999) argues, an important challenge for researchers and theoreticians in the field of learning organisation is to develop conceptual frameworks concerning the relation between individual learning and organisational learning. The orientation toward dialogue and team work addresses some opportunities to deal with collective learning in a conceptually meaningful way that goes beyond the metaphor of learning organisation. In this respect sense making in organisations, and peoples' participation in collective sense making processes, are of particular interest (Weick 1995)[6]. Weick argues that sense making is the process by which the organisation structures itself. There will be no organisational activities without continuous sense-making processes. By focusing people's communicative actions within teams and organisations, we attend to learning as an issue of joint sense making and reflective processes. With a starting point in constructivistic theories on learning and cognitive development, and in theories on social construction of reality and affordances, learning is an ongoing, contextually bound process, linked to our daily activities (Löfberg 1996, Ohlsson 1996). The learning process includes a continuous transformation of experiences, through reflection, sense making and concrete actions. To make sense is not conceptually the same process as learning,

---

[5] Senge (1990), as well as Isaacs (1993), links the reasoning on dialogue to the work of Bohm (1990). Bohm makes a distinction between dialogue and debate. The former concerns peoples' freedom to talk and make their thoughts and visions public available. Debate is labeled as a conversation where people are trying to win the argumentation, or defend their own points of view. In an organisational context the researchers argue that both kind of conversation are important.

[6] Weick argues strongly that sense making is not a metaphor: "Sensemaking is what it says it is, namely, making something sensible. Sensemaking is to be understood literally, not metaphorically" (Weick 1995, 16).

but can be described as an inseparable part of the learning process (Argyris 1999, Kolb 1984, Weick 1995).

When people deal with everyday problems and situations they are continually in an action-oriented relation to their environment within a social context. Through learning they build up competence, which is a potential ability to handle tasks and problems appropriately. The meaning and content of competence are socially constituted in the specific context. Therefore, in order to enable learning and competence enhancement pedagogic analyses and interventions need to consider the specific contextual features as important conditions. The "contextual didactic"– perspective is elaborated for this purpose (Löfberg 1996, Ohlsson, Döös 1999). This perspective addresses the questions of how people apprehend, make sense of and use their physical and social environment as conditions for learning, as well as how they participate in the social formation of these conditions.

According to Löfberg's (1989) argumentation, individual and collective learning are not separate entities or processes, but 'two sides of the same coin'. Learning, just like sense making, is an intrinsically social process (Berger, Luckmann 1966). Therefore, it seems inappropriate to talk about a relation between individual and collective learning. But here I will argue for the necessity to make a conceptual distinction. First, to state that learning is a social process is nothing more than trivial. If we agree in the statement that man is a social creature, it is self-evident that what we learn and participate in is also socially formed (Berger, Luckmann 1966, Giddens 1984). The point here is that we still can distinguish between individual and collective learning in a teamwork context or organisational context. When a person deals with her work task, or handles some kind of problem, and learns from her own concrete experiences, it seems appropriate to describe this process as individual learning. But in a situation where several members work together with joint tasks, in a work team for example, and exchange and transform experiences through joint reflection we can understand and describe this as a collective learning process. Through interactive and communicative activities individuals learn together and build up other qualities in thought and action than they would have done on their own. Another way to describe it is to say that when people learn together in such a way, they participate in producing 'synergy' regarding learning qualities

(Ohlsson 1996, Granberg 1996). Therefore, it seems plausible to make a conceptual distinction between individual learning and, what we call, collective learning. It is actually not the same phenomenon, even though the different kind of learning processes are interrelated.

Ohlsson (1996) discusses the relation between individual and collective learning with a starting point in empirical research results from a study on teams of child care workers. The team members were engaged in ongoing everyday communicative activities, which provide both enabling and constraining aspects regarding collective learning. Although team members said that they were using their own "personal style", or "personality", when working with the children, observations showed that they influenced each other's thoughts and actions. Their conversations had a narrative form whereby team members told a story about a concrete experience of an incident or event. In this narrative form the individual expressed his or her understanding of an event, and thereby made thoughts available to the other team members. Another aspect of the conversations was joint reflection. This means that the team members reflected together on the story or the statements that one of them had expressed. They raised and discussed questions: Was it really like that? Why didn't you handle it that way? In this kind of conversation they showed contradictory experiences and were trying to understand together. The third kind of conversation was oriented towards the future, and had the form of joint intention. Through formation of joint intentions, team members built up joint strategies in their work, for example a kind of preparedness regarding how to handle difficult situations or how to treat a specific child. Thereby the team members utilised their conversation as a formation of collective action. They also avoided conversation and joint reflection. This was the case when one team-member's questions and curiosity were shut off with reference to earlier experiences or to common sense. The conversation was thereby stopped, disrupted by some of the team members. A pattern of subgroups occurred within the team, where two or three of the team members talked more together and co-operated more intensively.

Altogether the identified communicative qualities within the team appear as steps in an ongoing collective learning process. Through the ongoing communication team members make sense of tasks and build up competence to handle them. This is a contextually bound collective learning process where team members continuously generalise from their specific experiences, where they make their private thoughts and images public, building up a jointly shared understanding through communicative actions. These activities manifest three structural dimensions in the collective learning process whereby team members construct collective competence (Ohlsson 1996). The collective experience based competence is not an object 'out there' somewhere. Rather it can be described as mutually shared understanding, and joint preparedness for concrete actions, manifested in ongoing processes of construction and reconstruction in a specific and communicative context. In this respect, joint reflection appears as a critical activity, expressed in argumentative conversations, with a potential to let team members co-ordinate their actions (Habermas 1984, Mezirow 1991). In a similar way Weick and Roberts (1993) discuss "collective mind" in organisations, as a phenomenon constituted by people's interrelated heedful actions, enactment and collective sense making.

Organising in Practice

Several researchers describe learning processes ideally, but to get knowledge of learning potential in practice it seems reasonable to consider how organisational practice really works and how interventions will be realised. Many normative attempts neglect or at least underestimate the difficulties and conflicting interests involved in every organisational change (Senge 1990, Pedler et al. 1991). It is easy to see why many practitioners are doubtful attempts are made to implement a model called learning organisation. Everyday work goes on in practice independently of the organisations rhetorical ballast.

Coopey (1996) tries to analyse learning organisation critically, using concepts like power, politics and ideology. He concludes that a lot of research in this field expresses a confusion concerning concepts as control and power, and that critical analysis of how power will be distributed does not exist within the learning organisation discourse. Critical approaches and discourse analysis, show a 'picture' of a more pluralistic organisation where different voices and perspectives exist together in a complex pattern of organisational sense and non-sense (Wallemacq, Sims 1998). Paying attention to the complexity of practice, the research perspective advocated here considers contextual collective sense making, learning and organising processes. In this respect the concept of dialogue as communicative action is of particular interest, and it is also important to underline the ongoing character of organising activities in practice.

Collaboration and Team Work among Teachers in School

To illustrate how the theory of organisational and collaborative learning can be used in adult education research, I want to refer to collaboration and teamwork of teachers in school.

Today collaboration and team work is described as a fruitful way of school development, and it is obvious that researchers in this field show a growing interest in issues on learning organisations (Mulford 1998, Fullan 1993). Mulford (1998) regards the emphasis on collaboration and teamwork as promising "developmental pathways", but the specific context of school and teachers' work also contains important limitations. He points to the risk that the learning organisation discourse confuses concepts of change and learning, implying that a school is only learning if it is undergoing change. He argues for a balance between improvement and the maintenance of a safe base within the organisation. "How to achieve stability for change, how to move ahead without losing our roots, is the challenge" (Mulford 1998, 633).

The complexity of task and the specific culture of teachers work are connected to what Powell (1991) and Weick (1995) call "loosely coupled" organisations, where goals and tasks are vague and a great variety of alternative methods are possible in order to solve the tasks. Relations between intentions and actions are far from clear and unambiguous, and, as a consequence, evaluation and critical reflections on strategies and actions are difficult to accomplish (Fischler 1994). The teacher's practice appears as extremely context-bound and emotional in character, which in some respects restrains possibilities of collaboration and team work (Hargreaves 1998). Empirical findings confirm these difficulties of collaboration, and some researchers pointed out organisational structural and cultural factors as explanations. The teachers' different subject matters and working hours and the school's schedules and schemes make it hard to develop new ways of working together (Hargreaves, Fullan 1998). Some researchers also have a focus on power relations between principals and teachers, and argue that difficulties to promote collective learning are results of different interests of the involved actors (Mulford 1998, Ståhl 1998). The teachers' resistance to leave their own well proved way of teaching and treating pupils in favor for a new direction together with colleagues is accordingly understood as a reaction against unequal power conditions and a lack of opportunities to participate in the formation of collaboration and dialogue. Fullan (1993) emphasises the importance of norms of collaboration in the local school, where teachers are committed to their joint goals and tasks and where they see their work as a collective matter.

Some empirical studies of teacher teams show that teachers work and learn together and that the social support from colleagues was seen as one of the most important aspects of their work (Ahlstrand 1995, Engeström 1994, Nias 1998). Characteristically, teachers' collaboration and dialogue concern social aspects of work, pupil's well-being or social relationships between teachers at the work place. Ahlstrand (1995) found that teachers worked together in informal collaborative relationships. Team meetings in the formal teacher team were not utilised as a forum of collaboration and dialogue regarding pedagogical issues or didactical aspects of work. The meetings usually contain information from team leaders or school leaders, discussions about pupils' well being, and work environment issues.

The Empirical Study

The studies we have conducted were carried out during the period 1998-2001 and include interviews and group interviews with about fifty teachers at different levels in the school system. Each interview was about an hour and was taped. Furthermore, the empirical material includes observations of 21 team meetings in five teacher teams. The observations, about 2 hours each, were taped as well. The data collection was carried out during a period of about two years in three of the five teams. In order to reduce costs we made a shorter data collection period in the other two teams. Three of the teams worked at the compulsory school level with pupils aged 6-11 (one team) and pupils aged 12-15 (two teams). Two of the teams worked at the upper secondary school level with pupils, 16-19 years of age.

The central research questions in the actual study are: How do the teachers organise their team-work in practice? Do the teachers learn from each other in the teams, how do they use the team as a condition for learning? With regard to the well-known difficulties associated with implementation of team work for teachers, this study mainly takes the teachers' perspective into consideration. This means that the interviews and analyses were oriented toward the teachers' ways of thinking, feeling, talking and working in the everyday work and in staff meetings.

Although interesting and expected differences were found between the teams, this article only focuses on some aspects of team work that are characteristic for all of them.[7] The point is to illuminate aspects of teacher's everyday work appearing as resistance against team work embedded in the organisation of practice. The results show a tension between explicit and implicit organising activities manifested in difficulties to practice a collectivisation of teacher's work. These difficulties were, in some respects, expressed in all teams, at team meetings and in everyday work. The results have implications for our understanding of teachers' collaboration, team work and collective learning in practice, as well as on how pedagogic interventions ought to be made in such a context.

Tensions in the Organising of Team Work

In all the schools of the sample the terms "work team" or "teacher team"[8] were used, and all the teachers were obliged to take part in a team and participate in team meetings. The teams were rather dissimilar concerning the organisation of work. In one of them the team consisted of four teachers,

---

[7] Differences are of course expected, at least in some respects. The teams worked under different conditions, with pupils at different age levels etc. The strategy guiding the sampling and data collection in the study, was to study teams that were supposed to show differences concerning qualities in collaboration and collective learning. A comparative study with focus on differences, and similarities, between the teams will be reported 2001-2002.

[8] The Swedish terms are "arbetslag" or "lärarlag".

who closely worked together with a thematic oriented course for pupils in an upper secondary school program. The teachers represented different subject matters and they worked together in order to integrate their competencies. In another team fifteen teachers were involved relatively loosely, and the team was more like an organisational work-unit than a team in a collaborative meaning. The two teams mentioned represent extreme positions in our sample. The other three teams were organised in ways that place them somewhere between the two extremes, with regard to collaborative activities. All the teams had meetings 1-2 times a week (about 2-4 hours) where the team members discussed different subjects. The team leaders were responsible for the agenda at the meetings and the five teams mainly discussed: "information from the leader" (the school principal), "their own work conditions", "didactic issues in their work", and "pupils well-being and social situation".

Joint Planning and Practical Here-and-Now

Depending on how the team was organised, and how many teachers were involved, they were to varying degrees engaged in the joint planning of tasks. The smallest thematically oriented team was naturally more occupied with joint planning of concrete didactic tasks, than the bigger, loosely coupled team. But some kind of planning of joint activities was accomplished in all the teams. Teachers expressed ambitions to work together in the team, and they said that team meetings and joint planning of activities were very important. At the same time they were obviously restrained in their attempts, which manifest an underlying tension between joint planning of tasks and practice. The activities of joint planning often resulted in a taken for granted division of tasks and responsibilities. Team members avoided deeper conversation about what, how and why. On a surface level they talked about tasks or appropriate ways to treat some students, but a deeper discussion relating to real practice did not usually occur. Many of them complained that available time was too short for joint planning, discussions and collaboration. In interviews the most frequently expressed suggestion, concerning difficulties to talk together and develop collaboration further, was that the non-appearance of conversation depends on the organisational structure and lack of time. There were also expressions of resistance against ambitions to develop collective initiatives. Some of the teachers mentioned that the problem had to do with lack of commitment concerning the team's collective work. In one of the teams this statement was exemplified by a teacher who saw an intended collaborative project, where the teachers should be mentors instead of traditional class teachers, as an "extreme" top-down movement, "orders from the boss" and as a "burdensome extra task". She was not committed to the idea of a collective task for the team, and she was not engaged in the team's collaborative efforts.

The mentioned explanations have in common that they were reasonable, and they were easy to agree with. But they do not shed light on the observed tension between the individual "here-and-now" and the joint planning as expressions of collective ambitions. This construction of the individual "here-and-now" came to the fore even in the smallest subject oriented team as difficulties in practice when performing the intended activities. The collective pedagogical intention among teachers 'disappeared' in the specific situation. As one teacher said:

> One thing is what you've said, or what was written on a paper ... another is what's coming out in real life as a lesson. I've thought something that ends up as something else. ... it's of course much more complex to be four teachers making these decisions (to change plans during the lesson as a response to pupils thoughts and wishes), often intuitively so to speak.

The teacher holds her pedagogical intention in an ongoing sense making process during the encounter with the pupils. She makes sense of her initial plan and assigns to it new meaning and form in the "here-and-now" situation. Teacher's opportunities to handle the specific situation demand preparedness, based in earlier experiences, and openness for the "new" and "unique", necessary to meet pupils appropriately. In the specific situation the teacher "stands alone". One teacher said:

> It makes it difficult to follow rules that we have decided in the team ... I think it's very difficult. We have decided together to not accept noise and loudness in our classroom, we ought to intervene against it ... and we have made some plans together for how to handle such situations. But often I think I'm a person who tolerates more than others, I see and I feel the circumstances and I can see why my pupils behave like they do. And I think I have to adjust and adapt my actions to these circumstances, it's about a personal and emotional accounting. My colleagues think I'm too weak... [laughter].

The teacher describes concrete aspects of daily experiences, and she emphasises the "emotional" and "personal" character of teachers' work which makes it difficult to follow rules and to plan collectively in a more detailed way. Team work, and joint planning, were regarded as "slow" processes, sometimes "time-wasting" and "circumstantial". Although two of the teams, and most of the involved teachers, expressed elaborated intentions to work together, some of them said that the character of the teaching work is, to a high degree, an individual task in practice.

Dialogue and the Avoidance of Mutual Critique

Another aspect of tension between ambitions to collaborate in teacher teams and the construction of work as an individual task was the attempt to talk and the simultaneous avoidance to talk about how to treat pupils. Conversations about pupils were frequent in all the teams in the study. At meetings the teams usually used about two third of the time concerning pupils' well being, and reported to each other experiences of encounters with different children or youths. The conversations were organised differently in the teams, but usually team members talked about some problems or problematic pupils, and allowed everyone to contribute as well. Social or learning problems were discussed, and they also discussed what kind of solutions were needed. With regard to this kind of conversation the team members obviously participate in, and contribute to, a discursive organising of collective activities, where they together construct 'pictures' of pupils and situations around them. They express the intention to use each other's experiences and together they try to grasp what is going on. Often their conversations start with an expression of feelings: "Ooh, he is awful ... really terrible ... I don't feel well when he is in my classroom..." Or: "I really love this little girl ... she is so natural, intelligent...". The conversation's character of turn-taking and listening to each other show a movement of systematically organised communicative activities.

Simultaneously the conversation also manifested a systematically organised avoidance of mutual critique and evaluating talk about why some treatment is preferable. The following sequence is from a team meeting conversation, team members talk about a pupil, a boy 13 years of age:

> **Karen**: He is a notorious liar...
> **Fanny** (the team leader): Yeah, he is...
> **Karen**: Unbelievable ... you just look at him and then he shouts that you treat him unfair ... he's got a strange view of reality...
> **Anne**: I've started to ... tell him straight, I saw what you did...
> **Fanny**: I think we all do ... everyone of us...
> **Anne**: It's his style ... you can hear it...

They talked about a pupil and they exchanged experiences through the conversation, but they did not illuminate their own actions or treatments. Anne tries to pay attention to her own actions when she mentioned that she has "started to tell him straight" what he has done and what the problem is. But the others in the team did not respond to her efforts. The conversation continued:

> **Fanny**: But his daddy doesn't see any problem, it has never been a problem with his little boy. Not before he came here... But I said to him that now x (the boy) is at the age of puberty. Well, I've heard from other teachers that this lovely little boy has always been the same...

Karen: I asked him if he used to get angry in athletics, when loosing a game..., but he said: "No, I never get angry". He's got no self-reflection at all! It's strange...
Fanny: Yeah, it's strange...
Betty: This lack of self-reflection is also shown in the theoretical subject matters...
Fanny: Exactly...
Betty: ...he always works so fast, and he never analyses..., but he doesn't understand why he's not succeeding...
Fanny: He never makes it well...
Anne: But how to go further with this...?
Betty: I don't know, it's difficult...
Fanny: Yes, I think it will be hard work ... this talk (utvecklingssamtal, in Swedish) with the parents...
Carl: Do you think I should leave it?
Fanny: No, I think you should..., we can give you a flower [laughter]...no, but seriously...
Betty: We got to write it down, everybody...
Fanny: Very clear...
Carl: Very clear and honest...

After that they went on to talk about what other pupils had told them about x. They talked more about what kind of problems x got, and the teachers delivered experiences and stories regarding the boy's behaviour. And they blamed the boy's parents for being too 'pushy' and 'demanding'. The referred sequences show a mutual avoidance of critical reflections on their own actions. In the latter sequence Anne once again pointed to possible actions when she said "how to go further". This time the others conclude that they ought to write down their observations so Carl can get it before his talk with the parents. Not in this sequence, and not in the rest of the conversation, they directed their "team talk" toward critical reflections on their own actions, strategies or heuristic ways of handling problems or helping the boy. Despite Anne's efforts the main focus is on the boy's situation, his social problems and learning difficulties, and the role of his parents. Team members stop the conversation before they enter an evaluation of their own actions.

Interviews with teachers confirm what the analysis of the conversation shows. Teachers expressed that they did not use to criticise each other. Some of them said that they usually avoided to evaluate a colleague's way of handling problems or treat pupils, even if they saw that the colleagues were acting 'strange' or unsuccessfully in handling the situation. One of the teachers said:

> I think many of us would be unpleasantly affected by such critical comments on what you've done. In this kind of work, you work with your own personality…, and your own values. It's almost impossible to criticise others' actions, and try to separate them from the person…

Partly, the conversations in the team show a strong emotional aspect of teacher's work (Hargreaves 1998). Partly it also shows the problem to mutually criticise actions. Together they were talking and at the same time avoiding it. The team members withdraw from the conversation through attempts to pull back what they have said. Thereby they stop themselves from participating and they also stop a further joint reflection on the actual subject. They do not make their thoughts and reflections accessible. Carefully they avoid drawing attention to each other's actions and thoughts on how to handle the problem. Instead of focusing on questions like "what is a good treatment?" "what is bad?" or "why?", they choose some of the pupils as the subject of conversation. The ongoing interaction in the teams show as a tension between the intention to organise team work together and the simultaneous underlying organising of escape from a reflective team conversation.

Team Work and Selective Collaboration

The emotional aspect of a teacher's work is obvious also in their choice of the collaboration partners. Formally all the teams in the study were trying to organise team-work. Ambitions in this direction were manifested in attempts to plan and carry out joint themes where teachers in several subject matters represented different perspectives on the theme. Together the teachers planned and organised the work formally with regular meetings where they formulate strategies and efforts of evaluation. They were also trying to work together with pupil's well-being by discussing the situation in the classroom, or individual pupil's home situation. The analyses of the collaboration strategies within the team show ambitions and intentions in two different directions. Formally, the teachers were trying to organise team work but at the same time they avoided and refrained collaboration. One teacher said:

> Many teachers think it's their rights to just withdraw from collaboration. They don't say anything, just take it for granted that anyone can work as they always had, and avoid to participate in team work...

The individual teacher thereby confronts the idea of collaboration, but the confrontation seems to be "tacit" or implicit. Invitations or directives regarding collaboration are neglected through a mutual and non-reflected avoidance whereby the teachers maintain their work as individual tasks. Other findings indicate that collaborative efforts were selective and depending on personal relationships within the team. The teachers choose some of the colleagues for a closer dialogue and a more intensive collaboration. This led to an emergence of subgroups within the team, which had consequences for the possibilities to learn together. Contacts between subgroups were rare, and attempts to work together did not occur. One teacher explained:

> You look for persons you like for some reason..., or at least persons with whom you feel you share values and pedagogic assumptions. I can say that I ... I'll confess that I avoid x (a colleague) because we never share attitudes or thoughts ... we never agree with each other ... concerning pupils ... or how you learn, you know ... what knowledge is. We can't work together.

The teacher's avoidance of unwanted or obliged collaboration is well known from earlier studies (Hargreaves 1995, Ahlstrand 1995). Teachers prefer to collaborate in informal ways, and they prefer to work together with one or two colleagues in occasional smaller projects. Teachers express that they see personal qualities as crucial for the opportunity to work together. But in this research example they did not discuss these qualities or the avoidance of collaboration with each other. The rather selective collaboration was surrounded by a mutual and silent agreement that you cannot work together with anyone. According to some teachers, the important ingredient in a collaborative relationship was an emotional starting-point and "mutual feelings". The individual teacher thereby reserves for herself the opportunity to work individually, and it was obvious that the teachers also tacitly resisted invitations to collaboration. This means that team members avoid an explicit organisation of their team work. This avoidance covers potential conflicts between team members, concerning attitudes to collective work, ambitions and intentions.

Other findings show that the presence of a joint concrete task, and a commitment to collective initiatives, in some respects helped the teachers to overcome barriers regarding collaboration. In the smallest team the teachers worked tightly together, and their organised continuous collaboration enabled them to handle difficulties and conflicts through joint reflection and joint concrete actions. They sometimes worked together in the classroom, and they talked with pupils together. This relation to concrete actions, and the opportunities to see each other in action, repeatedly started reflections on what they were doing in everyday work and why they were doing it. The involved teachers said that they never before had reflected critically as much as they did now in the team. Their basic idea to collaborate with a joint theme, and the continuity in the way they carry it out concretely brought them together in an ongoing process, even when they sometimes expressed conflicting ideas, view points, and opinions. This example shows the importance of commitment and concrete collaboration with a joint task in the organising of team work.

The Pedagogical Issue of Organising – Concluding Remarks

Argyris (1999) deals with pedagogical issues when he underlines that organisational researchers have an additional important task besides describing and explaining empirical results They should also be deal with the normative, the possible and potential, regarding organisational learning.[9] Theories of learning organisation often indicate that a prerequisite for practical change is a model of joint planning and shared visions which has to be implemented in the organisation. Strategies behind attempts to develop a team organisation are often grounded in more or less reflected notions on dialogue and "team talk" as ideal models for construction of consensus and shared thoughts and beliefs. This implies that the wanted change would be an issue of implementation of such a model, and that the present situation show a lack of something, or a common need that ought to be satisfied. In some respects these theories show both ignorance regarding the complexity of practice, and sometimes the imagination that complexity expresses a lack of competence needs to be managed.

Viewing learning organisation, and especially team learning, pedagogically is to heed the complex processes whereby individuals work together, make sense together, and act as their own constructors of conditions for learning as well as competence. The observed tensions in the teacher teams are examples of the complexity in the ongoing everyday work, which show that team-work, collaboration and collective learning in practice are much more comprehensive matters than the main part of actual theories explain or deal with. It seems reasonable to think about the observed tensions as rooted in a continuous pedagogical practice of organising activities. To organise collective work, to arrange collaboration between teachers and to form teacher teams is to engage in ongoing interaction with no clear-cut beginning or end. The empirical findings show that teachers are engaged in parallel organising activities whereby they explicitly organise and build up a collective practice and, simultaneously, implicitly organise their work as an individual matter regarding intentions and competence. The tensions

---

[9] This normative aspect, and the problems connected with interventions and implementations, are complex matters and involve aspects of power, domination and manipulation etc. (Ohlsson, Döös 1999).

between explicit attempts to organise team work formally and the implicit organising can be understood as an underlying non-reflected resistance against collectivisation of work. But, as Weick (1995, 33-34) puts it, resistance is a moment in an ongoing process of sense making and would preferably be labelled "confronting ideas and interests". Pinpointing the ongoing character of sense making, Weick emphasises that resistance is not a static condition, but rather an inseparable part of a continuous movement of social interaction and construction, where opinions, ideas and emotions are constantly in flux. The tensions in the teacher teams contain such a movement. In some respects team members socially construct collective work tasks and they also make sense of these tasks together. But the social construction process also includes a tacit, taken-for-granted, construction of individuality concerning work tasks and competence. To put it another way, the team members construct a mutual heedfulness concerning their collective practice, but also a "heedlessness" (Weick, Roberts 1993). Through the ongoing organising activities team members not only make sense collectively. They also make 'non-sense' together, for example, through the avoidance of mutual criticism. Through these activities they are constructing both enabling and constraining aspects concerning team work, collaboration and competence enhancement.

The two parallel collective organising activities are expressions of two different rationality contexts, formed by different principles. A formal and explicit principle lies behind the discursive organising of team work and collective work tasks. The team is formally organised and its legitimacy emanates from political and authorial discourses and decisions, operationally transformed by school leaders in the local school organisation. Team work and collaboration are therefore discursively formed ideas and obligations, which constitute the meaning of teacher's 'competence' and 'rational' actions. In this respect rational team work includes joint planning and decision-making, exchange of experiences, criticism and joint evaluation. At the same time, the individual teacher's emotional engagement and tacit non-reflected action in practice make it difficult to participate in a joint elaboration of team work (Hargreaves 1998). Practical demands and teachers apprehended need of personal qualities to handle specific situations in practice, tacitly bring forward a principle of rationality that includes emotional heedfulness, value-oriented care-taking and "here-and-now"-related preparedness. They construct an individual, personal sense of competence. Although they express emotions jointly, and talk together about pupils, they avoid mutual critique, joint evaluation and collaboration. If these implicit, practice-related organising activities would not be transformed discursively in the team, and if team members took them for granted and constantly kept them non-reflected, the two rationality contexts would remain separated. Accordingly, the teachers will not reflect together on the idea of team work and they will not make their practice available to each other. The parallel relation between the two organising activities, and their related rationality contexts, implies a separation between a "private space" of competence in practice and a "public space" of collective, discursively formed, competence (Ohlsson 1996). This separation strongly restrains the potential of collective learning in the team.

It appears as an essential pedagogic challenge to find a key to this dilemma in teacher teams. In order to intervene pedagogically, and to enable collective learning, it is obviously not enough to establish a team organisation and to talk about the importance of collaboration and dialogue. It is not even enough to let people really talk to each other about it within the team. Concrete actions are also needed. Far from being an issue of implementation of a ready-made 'team-learning'-model, which solves every problem once and for all, a pedagogic intervention needs to consider that everyday practice is ongoing. This means that team member's always and constantly agree and disagree with each other, there are always confronting ideas and values, and ongoing attempts to make sense collectively, as well as attempts to avoid it. The empirical findings, presented in this article, indicate that the most fruitful pedagogic intervention would be to facilitate team members' awareness of the ongoing explicit and implicit organising activities, and their possibilities to integrate these activities through communicative as well as concrete actions. The complex relation between talk and action demands a pedagogical intervention designed as an inescapable invitation to an ongoing joint exploration of enabling and constraining organising activities, as well as an invitation to processes of communicative transformation of apprehended resistance and difficulties into new moments of opportunities. This effort includes joint reflection whereby team members question and criticise development ideas, concrete actions in everyday work, and abstract visions. With reference to the specific context of teacher's work, and to Mulford (1998), it's worth emphasising that learning is not the same as continuous change. An important part of the potential of collective learning is the argumentative conversation through which team members build up competence to solve tasks and handle problems, and mutually shared understanding of what they are doing in everyday work, and why they are doing it. Although changeable and in flux, this mutually shared understanding within the learning team provides relative stability necessary for the teachers to feel safe and to grasp what it means to be a competent learner as well as a teacher in practice.

References

Ahlstrand, E. (1995). *Lärares samarbete – en verksamhet på två arenor*. Linköping Studies in Education and Psychology, No 43 (doctoral thesis).

Argyris, C. (1999). *On Organisational Learning*. Oxford.

Argyris, C., D. (1978). *Organisational Learning. A Theory of Action Perspective*. Reading, Massachusetts: Addison-Wesley Publishing Company.

Berger, P., Luckmann, T. (1966). *The Social Construction of Reality*. New York.

Bohm, D. (1990). *On Dialogue*. Cambridge.

Broekstra, G. (1998). An Organisation is a Conversation. In: Grant, D., Keenoy, T., Oswick, C. (eds). *Discourse + Organisation*. London, pp. 152-176.

Burrell, G., Morgan, G. (1994). *Sociological Paradigms and Organisational Analysis*. Aldershot.

Coopey, J. (1996). Crucial Gaps in "the Learning Organisation". Power, Politics and Ideology. In: Starkey, K. (ed). *How Organisations Learn?* London, pp. 348-367.

Dixon, N. (1994). *The Organisational Learning Cycle. How We Can Learn Collectively?* London.

Engeström, Y. (1994). Teachers as Collaborative Thinkers. Activity-Theoretical Study of an Innovative Teacher Team. In: Carlgren, I., Handal, G., Vaage, S. (eds). *Teachers Minds and Actions. Research on Teachers Thinking and Practice*. London, pp. 43-61.

Engeström, Y. (1996). Developmental Work Research as Educational Research. In: *Nordisk Pedagogik*, No 3, 1996, pp. 131-143.

Fischler, H. (1994). Concerning the Difference between Intention and Action. In: Carlgren, I., Handal, G., Vaage, S. (eds). *Teachers Minds and Actions. Research on Teachers Thinking and Practice*. London, pp. 165-180.

French, W. L., Bell, C. H. (1990). *Organisation Development*. 4th edition. Englewood

Cliffs, N.J.

Fullan, M. (1993). *Change Forces.* London.

Giddens, A. (1984). *The Constitution of Society.* Cambridge.

Granberg, O. (1996). *Lärande i organisationer.* Stockholm University: Department of Education (doctoral thesis).

Habermas, J. (1984). *The Theory of Communicative Action.* London.

Hargreaves, A. (1995). *Changing Teachers, Changing Times. Teachers Work and Culture in the Postmodern Age.* London.

Hargreaves, A. (1998). The Emotions of Teaching and Educational Change. In: Hargreaves, A., et al. (eds). International Handbook of Educational Change. London, pp. 558-570.

Hargreaves, A., Fullan, M. (1998). *What's Worth Fighting for Out There?* Buckingham.

Hultman, G., Klasson, A. (1998). Paradoxes, Mini-Worlds and Learning Processes. The Dynamics of Change in Small Companies. In: *Studies in Continuing Education,* 20 (1), pp. 51-69.

Isaacs, W. (1993). Dialogue, Collective Thinking, and Organisational Learning. In: *Organisational Dynamics,* 22 (2), pp. 24-39.

Kolb, D. (1984). *Experiential Learning.* Englewood Cliffs, N.J.

Kolb, D. (1996). Management and the Learning Process. In: Starkey, K. (ed). *How Organisations Learn?* London, pp. 270-287.

Kornbluh, H., Greene, R. T. (1989). Learning, Empowerment and Participative Work Processes. The Educative Work Environment. In: Leymann, H., Kornbluh, H. (eds). *Socialization and Learning at Work.* Aldershot, pp. 256-274.

Löfberg, A. (1989). Learning and Educational Intervention from a Constructivist Point of View. The Case of Workplace Learning. In: Leymann, H., Kornbluh, H. (eds). *Socialization and Learning at Work.* Aldershot, pp. 137-158.

Löfberg, A. (1996). *Nonformal Education and the Design of Workplaces as Learning Contexts.* International Conference on Learning and Research in Working Life, July 1-4, 1996. Steyr, Austria.

Mezirow, J. (1991). *Transformative Dimensions of Adult Learning.* San Fransisco.

Mulford, W. (1998). Organisational Learning and Educational Change. In: Hargreaves, A., et al. (eds). *International Handbook of Educational Change.* London, pp. 616-641.

Neck, C. P., Manz, C. C. (1994). From Groupthink to Teamthink. Toward the Creation of Constructive Thought Patterns in Self-Managing Work Teams. In: *Human Relations,* 47 (8), pp. 929-952.

Nias, J. (1998). Why Teachers Need their Colleagues. A Developmental Perspective. In: Hargreaves, A., et al. (eds). *International Handbook of Educational Change.* London, pp. 1257-1271.

Ohlsson, J. (1996). *Kollektivt lärande. Lärande i arbetsgrupper inom barnomsorgen.* Stockholm University (doctoral thesis).

Ohlsson, J., Döös, M. (eds) (1999). *Pedagogic Interventions as Conditions for Learning*. Stockholm.

Pedler, M., Burgoyne, J., Boydell, T. (1991). *The Learning Company*. London.

Powell, W. W. (1991). Expanding the Scope of Institutional Analysis. In: Powell, W. W., DiMaggio, P. J. (eds). *The New Institutionalism in Organisational Analysis*. Chicago, pp. 183-203.

Schein, E. (1988). *Organisational Psychology*. Englewood Cliffs, N.J.

Schein, E. (1993). On Dialogue, Culture and Organisational Learning. In: *Organisational Dynamics*, 22 (2), pp. 40-51.

Senge, P. (1990). *The Fifth Discipline. The Art & Practice of the Learning Organisation*. New York.

Silverman, D. (1970). *The Theory of Organisations. A Sociological Framework*. London.

Starkey, K. (1996). Introduction. In: Starkey, K. (ed). *How Organisations Learn*? London, pp. 1-3.

Ståhl, Z. (1998). *Den goda viljans paradoxer*. Lund University (doctoral thesis).

Swieringa, J., Wierdsma, A. (1992). *Becoming a Learning Organisation. Beyond the Learning Curve*. Reading: Addison-Wesley Publishers.

Wallemacq, A., Sims, D. (1998). The Struggle with Sense. In: Grant, D., Keenoy, T., Oswick, C. (eds). *Discourse + Organisation*. London, pp. 119-133.

Weick, K. E. (1995). *Sensemaking in Organisations*. London.

Weick, K. E., Roberts, K. (1993). Collective Mind in Organisations. Heedful Interrelating on Flight Decks. In: *Administrative Science Quarterly*, 38, pp. 357-381.

Woodilla, J. (1998). Workplace Conversations. The Text of Organizing. In: Grant, D., Keenoy, T., Oswick, C. (eds). *Discourse + Organisation*. London, pp. 31-50.

Edmée Ollagnier

LIFE HISTORY APPROACH IN ADULT EDUCATION RESEARCH

Origins and Development

The origin of life history can be traced back to two traditions, one which comes from German philosophy, the other from the field of American sociology. The theoretical framework chosen by most researchers for their work on life history refers generally speaking to one of these two schools of thought.

German Philosophy

Wilhelm Dilthey, at the beginning of the twentieth century, based his theory of "understanding", in opposition to Hegel, on the primary experience of life. In his view, life is the field of reality from which knowledge can evolve and this reality contains the principles of that knowledge. "One's autobiography is the foremost, the most instructive whole through which an understanding of the meaning of one's existence becomes manifest" (Delory-Momberger 2000, 160). The life of an individual unfolds in a realm common to all life, where all individual existences interrelate. The ability to analyse and understand oneself, i.e. to understand the meaning of one's own life, enables us to move beyond our own particularity and to begin to understand others.

This leads us into the hermeneutical approach of Habermas which he bases on both Dilthey's principle of interaction as well as on the tradition established by the Frankfurt School. The question he raises is how individuals develop their sense of autonomy and responsibility. Recounting one's autobiography can have an emancipating effect, especially when retracing one's development in order to understand and to free oneself. That leads to new insight, which some call: 'consciousness grasp' (Finger 1984). This can even be considered the first stage in the transition from the particular to the general, while the second stage opens up when researchers and subjects interact, thus leading to the development of a common discourse, i.e. of Critical Theory.

American Sociology
The New World was shaped at the start of the twentieth century by the heterogeneity of the immigrants, the diversity of their cultures, languages, racial origin and religions. The Chicago School from the very outset presented itself as a group of university sociologists who proposed to base the social sciences squarely on field research and the direct observation of that urban, multi-cultural and sometimes deviant world. The best-known study and the one that is regularly referred to in connection with life history research is one on Polish immigrants published in 1920 by William Thomas and Florian Znaniecki. It is based on the individual life story (autobiography) of an immigrant as well as on other personal documents of immigrants in order to gain an understanding of the cultural disruption engendered by migration and it's consequence for their lives in the United States.

The researchers of the Chicago School drew on personal documents, letters, and life histories. The life history material reflects attitudes and values connected with belonging to a given social class or to specific socio-professional categories. This opens the way to symbolic interactionism on the one hand, which considers social reality to be the product of individual interactions, and, on the other, to the "ethno-mineralogy" of Garfinkel, who considers the practical achievements of the social players as most important. Thus, the life narrative is simultaneously an individual's subjective statement of a unique life experience and a rational construct which can be imparted in transmissible and identifiable terms. This then offers the sociologist the possibility to derive typologies and categorisations for social, cultural or professional groups.

French Sociology: From D. Bertaux to C. Dubar
Some implicit derivations from the theories developed by the Chicago School and the Frankfurt School as well as the events of May 1968 have led French sociologists to stress the importance of "allowing the social

actors to speak out". In the 1970s, Daniel Bertaux utilised life history collections in order to categorise occupational careers from a critical sociological perspective. He is the first who said that the biographical approach is a central element in an ethno-sociological inquiry, and he occupies a place where the historic approach and the social structures meet.

Following the popularity of many studies which were based on narrative practice and made it possible to analyse socio-professional categories, another work (Demazière, Dubar 1997) presented a structural method for analysing the narrative. The authors consider that "it is through the social categorisation introduced in a biographical narration that the individual makes sense of his «social world», makes it emerge, thus enabling himself to appropriate it and the researcher to interpret it methodologically " (Demazière, Dubar 1997, 37). This work, carried out with young people who were social and academic drop-outs, made it possible to analyse life-stories and ultimately to find a common biographical pattern as well as to identify certain elements which contribute to a theoretical understanding of the dynamics of identity, which Dubar has been working on for many years.

Between Sociology and Psychoanalysis: "The Family Novel"

At the present time in French-speaking countries, there is a trend in life history research headed by Vincent de Gaulejac, which he named, "the family novel and social trajectories", in his training workshops (de Gaulejac 1987). In his opinion, it is of crucial importance to refer to history since every person is "a product of history", an "actor on the stage of history" and also "a producer of stories". History is an active ferment and it conditions both the behaviour of the members of a family and their personality. It is necessary to look into the societal origin of psychological conflicts. Mentioning the limitations of Freudian analysis (emphasising the psychic component exclusively) and those of Bourdieu's sociology (every individual being a participant in the scheme of social reproduction), he suggests that the family novel can be used in order to take both of these foundations into account.

The *Involvement and Research Workshops* he organises are intended "to enable participants seeking to become the active subjects of their own story, to see themselves as the products of that story, by exploring the different factors which contributed to shaping their personality" (de Gaulejac 1987, 266). Analysis work covers genealogy (the inheritance), the parental plan (the parents' expectations), the family novel (writing stage: transition from the story as it was endured as an historical attitude to the ability to own one's story), and also focuses on the choices and difficult turning points in one's life. De Gaulejac sees this work as being half-way between research and therapy. The group work enables the participants to develop the capacity to think and to analyse, in other words they acquire the theoretical and methodological tools required to make sense of their own (his)-story. This researcher's approach has given the world a new vision of what clinical sociology could be.

Life History in Adult Education
There is consensus in research circles regarding the fact that the specific merit of life histories for adult education lies in their educational and structuring aspect. However, there are numerous disagreements concerning terminology and above all concerning the nature of life history itself, which some consider to be a methodological approach, others a legitimate subject for research in its own right, and others yet, both of these. We will mainly describe here the work done by researchers in the French-speaking world, without neglecting international aspects.

Linguistic Complexities or Epistemological Quarrels
A range of terms like life history, life story, biography, biographical approach, autobiography, and "biographicity" is in use. The views we refer to below basically share the common aim of achieving greater precision in defining the subject-matter. It seems that everyone agrees, when referring to the sociological approach with D. Bertaux's distinction between life story and life history, that a life history is the result of a life story accompanied by its analysis. The expression "educational biography", that of Pierre Dominicé, adds an essential element since "it implies that a biography used as an educational tool may produce effects of training" (Dominicé 1990, 72). The term autobiography, one of Gaston Pineau's favourites, even though it leads into the field of self-directed learning, does not make directly explicit the reference to its educational dimension. Finally, "bio-

graphicity", the term coined by Peter Alheit, leads to a dynamic concept of action, as determined by history.

Life Histories as a Learning Process

The social practice and procedure of life histories in adult education and training need a contractual basis and time to mature. The process involves a number of participants: the educator-researcher, possibly a group, and above all the person who presents the narrative, oral as well as written. Revisiting one's life and the sense we give it is a learning experience: it means finding out things about oneself and one's relationship to the world, but it also means that one has a grasp on one's story and can go on to project-building.

Some researchers consider that life histories are a kind of pedagogy of project-forming. Christine Josso believes that it's objective is two-fold, theoretical and functional:

> the relationship between life history and life project can be made clear by presenting them as two, mutually fertilising processes: the pursuit of the theoretical project, i.e. gaining an understanding of the learning process on the one hand ... and the utilisation of biographical methods for the realisation of life plans (self-expression, vocational, re-entry in gainful employment, training, altering habitual practices, life project) (Josso 2000, 73).

In this case, life history must indeed be seen as a project for access to knowledge.

A Dynamic Trio

Pierre Dominicé (Switzerland), Gaston Pineau (from Quebec, living in France), and Guy de Villers (Belgium), are a trio who, through their dialogue, respective life trajectories, and fields of interest created and lent solidity to a body of thought which has become a reference in the matter of life history in adult education, especially in French speaking countries. Stimulated by various perspectives in philosophy, psychology and sociology, they also share a common concern for the democratic aspects in continuing adult education.

Gaston Pineau, who defended "andragogy", devoted numerous works to life history as related to self-directed learning. He has recently become interested in the life histories of homeless people as well as in the question of temporality. Guy de Villers has often been asked as psychoanalyst to untangle the never-ending arguments about the boundaries between life history and therapy. A book on this subject is due to come out in 2002. Pierre Dominicé, with whom I have been in collaboration for many years, came to life history through the subject of evaluation. In his view, the adult person learns through and from his/her experiences, his/her life transition crises, and from his dreams. For him, as for his two colleagues, life history has an obvious educational function but remains, itself, a study tool which helps to analyse and to better understand the adult learner.

Developing Networks

In the French-speaking community of scholars, the mutually enriching exchange of views concerning life history carried on between the 'trio' and other researchers in the area of adult education resulted, firstly, in bringing this entire topic to the fore in RIFREP, the International Network for Research and Training in Continuing Education, organised in 1983. Then, seminars, symposia, and various publications brought it to the attention of an ever-growing number of concerned individuals. The Charter of ASIHVIF, the International Association for Life History in Education and Training, set up in 1990, states:

> The purpose of the Association is to promote life history as a social approach in the area of continuing education. The members aim to develop it through their activities in research, education and training, and through publications. Research is meant to clarify the practice of life history in the field of education and training... Education and training activities shall be based on the results of research (draft institutional paper).

From the conceptual point of view, consensus about life history among the members of the Association rests on their recognition of its three basic characteristics: hermeneutics (making sense of one's life), emancipation (ability to position oneself amongst others), and action-orientation (action planning). At the present time, thematic groups are at work delving into issues such as collective life history, life history and mixed cultural background, life history and the concept of subject. One of the topics that keeps coming up in the discussions of these groups is the articulation between societal needs and intellectual interests. Most of the members are academics, but not all; this network thus provides an opportunity to consider conflicts of interest between professionals (educators in adult education) who use the method of life history in their professional activity, and those who want to develop the epistemological basis for the sciences of education.

At the European level, ESREA, the European Society for Research on Education of Adult, from its creation in 1991, has been functioning as a network of thematic groups; one of them is called *Life History and Biographical Research*. This network of academics channels the contacts and exchange of views of researchers from various European countries, thus establishing connections between theoretical concepts arising in specific cultures with a view to improve the conceptual understanding of life histories as used in adult education.

Life Histories in Research

Approaches and Practices

Life history lies at the point of intersection between research and training. They fully come into their own only through practical application in real situations and through the relationship between the educator-researcher and the adult learner.

Some examples will illustrate the kind of studies that are carried out in adult education and the methodological principles on which they are based. Life histories used as a methodological approach require a strict framework in order to guarantee the quality of a practice which is, at the same time, an awareness process, a learning experience, a pedagogic relationship, and an opening up to future possibilities.

First of all, there is a need for a contract between participants and educator. Alex Lainé (1998) devoted a whole chapter in his book to the contract. In his view, the contract is meaningful only if it has been negotiated and if it can vary depending on the specific situation, but yet it must include the following constants or fundamental rules:
- the ultimate purpose: a definition of goals and general objectives pursued through the life history approach,
- the autonomy of the participants: in terms of being volunteers, and also as managing their own degree of involvement,
- confidentiality: every individual owns his/her product,
- respect for the work of others, definition of the role of the group during each participant's narration,
- clarity of instructions, rules, and organisation of the work.

While these terms of contract have been conceived primarily in connection with the educational process, they re-echo the different ethical principles of life history research. These concern also the utilisation of the data (in connection with the confidentiality principle).

Second, there are some visible stages in life history approach as a research process. Whatever the social context in which this approach is used, and despite certain variations, we can identify particular stages which have become set over time. Pierre Dominicé already referred to them in his book (Dominicé 1990, 71-85) when defining the principles of educational biography as practised in Geneva. In a university context, the students are led through the following stages:
- formulation of their own research topic (reflection on the educational process from the vantage point of their own specific interest),
- oral development of the narrative (followed by group discussion),
- writing down the biographical material (maturation phase, reflection),
- interpretation of the stories, in which the group participates.

In this case the narrator is considered to be a full-fledged participant in the research. In other situations, the formulation of the research topic and the interpretation will remain at the discretion of the researcher.

Christine Josso (2001, 79-96), while basing her experiences on students seminars as well as on a number of research-training sessions organised

with professionals, mentioned three stages in this process of training-research which help to identify:
- the training process (explaining what one is learning),
- the knowledge process (identifying an itinerary and the knowledge referents in one's life),
- the learning process (the resources that need to be mobilised for learning to take place, the learning attitude, stages in learning).

The life history approach can be an integral part (optional) of a university curriculum, like that which the founders of ASHIVIF set up in their respective universities, or it can be the subject of specific adult education seminars in different socio-educational settings. However, life histories like those we find in adult education and training settings have also been used in studies which consider biographical narratives as a "field for experimentation and as an educational exploratory tool" (Pineau 2000, 219).

From Apprenticeship Training to Professional Status

In Europe, and referring more especially to colleagues within ESREA, we notice a lively interest in life-histories for their educational potential as helping individuals and groups to gain a better understanding of where they stand in the face of socio-economic realities and challenges. This is the case in Germany, where Peter Alheit took an interest in leaders of the workers' movement and trade unionists, in Denmark, where Henning Salling Olesen stated that "this research strategy has been applied in connection with a number of labour-market related educational activities with a view to improving the position of the unemployed on the labour market" (Olesen 1996, 68). And finally from Linden West in England, who analyses in his recently published book (West 2001) the situation of general practitioners working in the inner city, facing cultural and political changes which have consequences for their professional life. These are but a few illustrations chosen from among many other studies that have been published in national or international publications.

In French-speaking countries, we find a similar tendency, with research focusing on the challenges facing society. We shall mention only a few examples chosen from those selected for *Education Permanente* (2000), on the subject of life history: M. Molinié leads an analysis of student mobility in foreign countries; C. Balestrat looks into the problem of literacy; J. Berton focuses on the world of social work; C. Niewiadomski discusses the problem of alcoholism; G. Francequin and A. Blanché introduce us to the issue of vocational counselling for youngsters with problems; E. Pépin and P. Garel share with us a life history of a group of working people. To end this enumeration, we can add D. Bachelard who used life histories for a study dealing with the vocational training possibilities open to shepherd and the changes occurring in this occupation.

Research in Geneva

Aside from the work done with students in the workshop *Life History – Educational Biography*, Pierre Dominicé's team carried out various studies on life history under the control of the National Swiss Found for Scientific Research. In 1998, the copy of *Cahiers* published by the Section of Educational Sciences under the heading *The Biographical Origin of the Capacity to Learn* reports on studies carried out in three different contexts. The first deals with adults returning to higher education and the impact which their school- and experiential-learning exerts on their attitude to university studies and on the dynamics of competence-building. The second setting is an adult training course for medical nurses, which included work on school memories and experiential competencies. Finally, the third setting involved adults in qualification-oriented vocational training courses in a Geneva adult education institution.

At the present time, Pierre Dominicé is leading a research project on the life experiences of qualified professionals who were involved in different continuing education certificate programmes at university level: in gerontology, management of humanitarian activities, financial management and human resources management. And finally, the Geneva researchers' interest in life history of educators and adult educators in connection with their working activities should be mentioned. "If adult educators have an opportunity to work on their own life histories and their formal and informal learning experiences, they will be more aware of the factors present in the process of adult learning" (Dominicé 2000, 216).

In fact, research on life histories in adult education has collected a wealth of information thanks to the multiplicity of contexts involved. In some cases, training settings offer the necessary operational basis, in others, social groups become witness and actors in a thinking process investigating their past, present, and future learning.

Gender and Life History in Adult Education

There is an obvious connection between gender and life history issues. I am responsible for an academic course, *Women-Training-Work*, at the University of Geneva where I lead studies and research on this issue, using the two approaches in a natural way. In this course we start of with an analysis of sexist theoretical constructs in education, impediments to learning, the standard-bearing ideas from a feminist point of view and the consequences thereof for adult education processes.

In the fields of social sciences and educational sciences, colleagues are more and more convinced of the legitimacy of the gender perspective in the domain of life history. The best evidence of this is ESREA's Life History network seminar at Roskilde (Denmark) in the year 2000. It was entitled *Gender and Life History* and was attended by more than 40 men and women researchers from various European countries [1]. At the beginning of the 1980s, some thinkers had already referred to gender characteristics in life history, like D. Bertaux: "Many older women today, who spent their entire life as housewives and mothers, find it impossible to say «I»" (quoted by A. Lainé 1998, 52). Life history is the road opening up the access to this hidden, invisible, socially not recognised "I".

According to Pierre Dominicé, their "emancipation in their relation to knowledge, in the face of the sway held by masculine knowledge, is thus one of the horizons opened up by the women's liberation movement" (Dominicé 1990, 122). He recognises gender typical aspects in biographical narratives: "If the men are able to keep the different aspects of their lives separate, the women are mostly thinking of themselves as unified persons... They need to share their doubts about themselves as students, and about their ability to think by themselves" (Dominicé 2000, 99). Peter Alheit believes that we internalise genderscripts, or gender worlds (*Geschlechtswelten*). In concluding this rapid overview, here is the position of

---

[1] But already in 1997, a meeting on "Life History, Gender and Experience" had been organised by the University of Roskilde (Weber 1998).

two other European colleagues:

> Biography, under the impact of feminism, has switched analytic attention to the small-scale and intimate in contrast to the modernist concern with the macro level grand sweep of history, which turned out, at least to an extent, to represent «his-story», in which the personal was separated from history, the social from psychological (Bron, West 2000, 160).

Looking at what took place at the two meetings of the ESREA's network *Gender and Adult Education* (Bochum 1999 and Geneva 2001), which had not been publicised as focusing on life histories, we note that about half of the papers that were presented did in fact mention life histories (to be published in 2002).

Life Histories Back Up the Thesis of Gendered Knowledge
As indicated above, the educational biographies carried out with adult students at the University of Geneva make for a most propitious setting for highlighting gender aspects in the relationship to knowledge. Barbara Merrill, in her research carried out at the University of Warwick (1999) states, on the one hand, that "gender differences in interview responses (biographical method) may relate to gender socialisation" (Merrill 1999, 51), and, on the other, that "for the women, learning at university ... was empowering in terms of the acquisition of knowledge which enables them to view the world in a different and critical way" (Merrill 1999, 207). Certain studies carried out on teachers or nursing personnel confirm this finding, all the more so as these professions are considered to be gender-stereotyped. From a feminist perspective, Sue Middleton (1993) demonstrates how gendered life-trajectories and thinking can result in gendered knowledge being transmitted by women teachers.

Women Sharing Life Histories
Narrating life histories presents a special occasion for self-expression, for speaking and sharing on an intimate level. In the section "Strengths and Risks" we shall examine some of the risks connected with placing too

much emphasis on this aspect in certain practices. Still, the technique of life history fosters trusting communication. In their book, *Le récit de vie: transmettre de femmes en femmes*, Danielle Coles and Benédicte Goussault (1995) conclude by saying that thanks to this method, the "I" melted away but re-emerged in the common identity shared with other women, who have the same questions and who are trying to find a balance between their family life, their professional life, and their social life.

Another way of conceiving this shared identity finds its way into biographical work performed with homogeneous cohorts; as is the case with unemployed women. Together with them, this author tries to better define the concept of qualification in connection with educational activities. A similar shared identity is presented by our Geneva colleague Malika Belkaïd (1998) through the narration of former University teacher-training students in Algeria, who grew up as girls in a country in war. Through these women's histories, this work reconstructs a section of the nation's history, of its culture and education. The same objective – to use the shared life stories of individual women in order to present a new version of history – was pursued by the research study presented below.

Life History of the MLF *(Mouvement de Libération des Femmes)*

To quote Franco Ferrarotti, biographies make it possible to "write history from the bottom up instead of writing it from above" (quoted by Lainé 1998, 91). Maryelle Budry, a psychologist employed in the State Office for Youth Orientation and an active feminist since 1975 in Geneva attended the life history seminar in our Adult Education department. Her two daughters were constantly asking her to tell them about the history of the feminist movement, "what did you do, how did you fight for women's rights, why were you protesting...?".

In the autumn of 1996, Maryelle proposed that we set up a life history group with the feminists who had been involved in the movement in the 1970s, with two goals in mind: to write the "history" of the Geneva women's liberation movement, which had never been done, and to explore the reasons for, and the nature of, the involvement of those women in order to pass this on to the younger generation. I saw the idea as an opportunity for me to understand and to explain how women went through a specific learning process and succeeded in constructing and strengthening their feminine identity, by becoming involved in the feminist movement in the 1970s. We undertook to do joint biographical work with women who had been active in the *Mouvement de Libération des Femmes* (MLF) in Geneva in the 1970s.

To begin with, Maryelle and I sent out invitations to about forty women who were involved in the MLF at that time. We received six positive answers from women who were ready to work with us through two weekends, plus some evening meetings. Following the first meeting, which was devoted to clarifying the 'contract', we spent a residential weekend together. Each of the six women presented her life history orally (it was recorded), then, after each narrative, time was allowed for discussion and questions. This was an occasion to build up a spirit of joint commitment again, sharing memories of specific events, actions, and old friendships. During our breaks, members of the group poured over old documents, photographs, political leaflets and other material of that period. During the second residential weekend, Maryelle and I suggested that we explore some very specific topics which had been found relevant as we analysed the first series of narratives. We proposed four pivotal topics: the role models in their life, how they constructed their individual and social identity, their relationship to men, and the effect of their involvement on their present vision of feminism and on their life choices.

In the summer of 1997, the six participants wrote their narratives. There followed the long job of reading the material and sharing comments, both in the group as such and on a two-by-two basis. The final result was published in the autumn of 1999 (Budry, Ollagnier 1999). One chapter relates the chronological events of the movement from 1971 to 1983. The narratives are divided into two chapters, *From Beginnings to the Movement*, and *The Movement and After*. A final chapter is entitled: *Feminists ... and then*. We respected each person's writing style and individual story construction, in accordance with the women's wishes, as well as anonymity, on the basis of the decision taken at the outset.

Biographical Work as a Learning Step

For the six women, the considerable amount of time they devoted to the project was a radical act which resulted in the recording of important feminist events that had been forgotten with the passage of time. They all were, and are, proud of what they have accomplished together. Spontaneously, a new feminist collective enthusiasm was sparked. Some of the women had remained in touch through their activities, others had lost contact with each other or did not see each other for long periods of time. We noticed that each had great respect for the others and the group felt enriched when old memories were recounted; each one respected the others' background and responded sympathetically to their moments of pain and moments of joy.

These women were committed not only to relating facts, they wanted to share and make public through a publication their intimacy, the highlights of their lives – as children, as adolescents and as adult women. The formulation of this material first orally and then in writing constituted a real learning process. The stage of writing was of particular importance to them. All of them held a degree in higher education; even though their educational background was, in our view, a guarantee of their writing ability, all of them reported that this stage presented difficulties and an attendant emotional component. No strict instructions had been given: each woman remained in charge of her own life story and of the manner in which she was to present it. "Writing was a therapeutic event", "I got sick when I wrote because it was a powerful experience", "I literally plunged into the things I wanted to say", "I gave my writing to my mother to read, I had to". The challenge presented by this work of writing was to report not only the events of their life but also to share their current awareness of what had really happened, to them and in their innermost self, and to explain their involvement in feminism.

The Feminist Commitment as an Apprenticeship

The biographical work in itself constituted a learning experience. But the learning dimension also occurred for these women in exploring their involvement in feminism. All the individual stories led both to the question of their own identity as women, and also to that of a collective identity as feminists. When asked what they had learned during their feminist participation, the immediate response of the women was: "to express my ideas, to speak in public, to write slogans, leaflets, and proclamations". They also consulted feminist literature and read a great deal. The motivation to learn, to acquire "constructed knowledge", as Belenky et al. (1986) called it, was obvious. The collective and intense stimulation led each of them to acquire new knowledge and to take a position, arguing, speaking, and writing. Another direct effect of their involvement was the optimisation of their skills through concrete action. They learned to make glue, to print leaflets and posters, and to choose good spots in the street for pasting them up. They also learned how to organise demonstrations: how to advertise them, how to negotiate with public authorities, how to delegate various responsibilities and tasks. They learned how to do things on a shoestring, how to manage a budget, how to obtain funds and to share responsibilities.

They mentioned with some pride that they learned all these skills naturally, without planning to, they just found out how to do things as needed, in different situations. They all say that the women's community was a truly self-managed group, and an efficient network. Participation in feminism must here be recognised as an efficient collective experiential learning process and environment. The six women all say today that the feminist movement played an important role in what they later became. "MLF changed my life", "The MLF drove me to make choices I wouldn't ever have considered before".

This work on biography and the publication of the book was a way to transmit feminism to younger women. The biographical approach improved the chances of transmitting an integrated product to the younger generation. Some of the women who were involved in the feminist movement years ago consider this book to be an intermediary between themselves and their daughters. "My daughter had previously refused to hear me out, she couldn't accept the person I was. But reading the stories of other women impelled her to ask me questions, instead of turning a deaf ear to what I was explaining". During our work, we had a lengthy debate about the objective to be achieved by this 'transmission'. Several of the women involved in the process were convinced that it was not our role or responsibility to influence the younger generation with regard to ideals, values and thinking: "We don't want to transmit this in order to teach, we just want to make this material available – it's up to them do with it what they see fit". In the University, our work brings us in contact mostly with educators, with students, with professionals such as social workers and nurses; the work on biography with feminists opened new perspectives, through a gender approach, on the way to see life history in education for other specific groups of adults and with a learning objective which goes beyond the scope of a formal educational project.

Strengths and Risks

Before ending, we would like to show what it is that makes life history such a precious contribution to adult education. Can it be considered to be an effective methodology for making adult learning easier, and at the same time a coherent subject of research?

Life History as a Social Practice
Looking at the use made of biography narratives from a historical perspective, we see that from the very outset they were a tool for trying to understand as accurately as possible the life-course of individuals and of specific social groups. At the present time, the socio-economic pressures are such that practically no adult can still claim to be following a simple, uncomplicated, linear life-course.

Life-Courses Increasingly Complicated
Countless contemporary individual existences present points of crisis, radical changes, a zig-zag progression in the family, in professional life or even geographically speaking. Only a few decades ago, the life of a village in European countries revolved around birth, marriage and death. Most of the time, people went into the trades of their fathers or inherited their businesses, women did not work outside the home and the choice of schooling for children was rather limited. In this type of 'stable' situation the motivation for a biographical narrative would be to present the history of a profession, the story of a family, of a village or of a social grouping – in other words, it would be the work of sociology.

Since those days, many villages have seen the arrival of strangers in their midst, new types of occupations have emerged while other trades and occupations have disappeared, new buildings have gone up. Means of communication and information have proliferated, numerous new teaching establishments and a diversity of leisure activities have appeared, and relational problems beset many families. This succinct presentation of the mutations in village life is one way among others to highlight the upheavals which affect groups and individuals over time.

In order to find their rightful place in space and time, adults can no longer hang on to the illusion of stability, neither for themselves nor as far as others are concerned. Where did I come from? What did I learn from my life's experiences, from the people I have met, from the know-how I have acquired? These questions can be dealt with more easily through the life history approach in the education process which enables many adults facing new socio-economic demands to find their place more easily.

A New Tool to Manage Competencies?
In French-speaking countries, the life history approach used in education has progressively been incorporated in a series of practical measures assisting adults in vocational orientation, training, or re-entry into active employment. The Quebec portfolio is a good example, as it incorporates the autobiographical narrative into a phase of the 'historic retrospect' which helps to identify what a person has acquired (Robin 1992). Originally conceived with a generous intention, this tool is sometimes taken over and transformed, even manipulated, and used for purposes that are not always praiseworthy. The guidance and evaluation centres that have proliferated these past ten years, and out-placement organisations, use and sometimes misuse biographical narratives. Certain principles, such as that of confidentiality, are institutionalised but the true contract is not always transparent. Some adults are not spontaneously willing to work on the learning they acquired during their life but they submit to this approach, as it is the only choice offered to them in exchange for counselling towards an apprenticeship or a new job, or even for a diploma by validating their prior experiential learning. Thus, in the area of adult counselling, the utilisation of life-histories appears to hold definite dangers, all the more so if one investigates the level of the training of some of the people who practice this approach.

In addition, the importance of knowledge has taken on a new and entirely different dimension in professional circles and in enterprises. Here too, although Schön and Argyris have made us discover the principles of organisational learning and of knowledge management in a positive and stimulating manner, the way these are used by enterprise managers is quite questionable. Professional careers (and personal lives in some cases) are discussed, analysed and evaluated – for the sole purpose of assigning a 'proper place' to an employee in a production structure which must, in a globalised economy, prove its efficiency especially because it finds itself in a permanent process of adjusting to novelty. This topic – implicating the adult person with his/her unique personal history and his/her relationship to knowledge – is not the subject of this paper but deserves mention nevertheless. In these cases, personal life histories are indeed linked to learning but only with a view towards economic productivity.

Life History as Research

What has been described above opens up the prospect for a vast research effort in order to perform a critical analysis of life history practice from the standpoint of educational and professional advantages for adults. However, we return to the academic world.

Research or Training?

This question has not really been answered, even though in Geneva we have found a compromise through the concept of '*recherché-formation*' in which the research role is attributed not only to the research person but also to the narrator. True, to look back over one's life by telling it orally to a person or to a group, or by writing it down, undoubtedly carries a learning function which no researcher has ever denied: to put one's past into words, to name it, means that one has to sift through events, interpret situations, and position oneself as a social being. However, the full learning dimension of life history is really truly guaranteed only when it is made part of a learning objective in a learning setting. In that case, learning is no longer an implicit result, it becomes the very purpose of the process of reflecting on one's past. Thus, in adult education, life histories really do have a status of their own.

For adult educators this clarification is probably sufficient, it really does not help the academic person who derives his professional identity from the double function as educator and as researcher. With some 'records' it will be easy to choose one of the two functions; but the life history approach inevitably requires a combination of the two. In the research work done with a public of students and of professional people registered in continuing education courses, it is the work as educator in a practical setting which offers the person functioning as researcher a deeper perspective on the overall subject of life history. In this case, life history is primarily a learning process which then becomes a subject-matter for research.

In the type of research which we shall call external because it is not tied to an institutionalised training setting and which mostly uses the narrative approach in an individual, direct relationship with the researcher, the research objective is essential and it is stated as such in the contract with the narrator. Nevertheless, and this happened with the research we did with the feminists, the narrator is offered the benefit of a real learning approach while working on the life history. In that situation, the research work generates ideas about its relationship to knowledge, and thus generates learning.

A Tool or a Subject for Research?
What has been said above leaves no doubt about life history being a research tool. Educational biographies, or life history in adult education, have been designed and practised in accordance with well-defined methodological principles and discussed over time in Adult Education scientific circles. In spite of certain distinctions which are made in relation to this approach – individual versus collective, oral versus written – it constitutes a high-quality research tool in its own right in the domain of Adult Education. And, as a matter of fact, this tool or methodological approach is beginning to find its way into university modules devoted to research methodologies.

The life history method opens the access to verbalised thinking, making it possible to analyse and to understand individual life courses and identity-formation, as well as to identify those elements in a biography which led to learning. The method has relevance both for the professional researcher and for the narrator, giving the latter the chance to become a researcher into his own history; thus, it is a participative method. In addition, this method provides a great diversity of research results for clearly stated research objectives, such as the attitude of adults to knowledge, motivations for studying, the characteristics of social groups in relation to acquired learning, and also attitudes to work.

But on the other hand, there are numerous controversies around the idea of considering life history as an object for research. Some colleagues consider that life histories are solely a means, a tool, for gaining scientific understanding about adult learning mechanisms. Others consider that life history constitute an approach which should be explored from the epistemological standpoint, in order to master its meaning. For at the present time, mainly because of the ethical provision of confidentiality, numerous narratives have not been fully explored. Yet a more systematic and critical exchange of views among social scientists might contribute to progress in categorising the analysis and interpretation of a particular, localised story. Research into the material produced, research into the mechanisms and foundation of the approach, research into the effects of a narration: all these are projects that have not been sufficiently explored so far.

In fact, has the life history approach contributed anything new to education and training theories? We will leave the answer to this final question to the pioneers who spoke "looking back at fifteen years of practice" at a round-table discussion published by *Education Permanente* (2000, 217-239). For Pierre Dominicé, his "research subject is adult education ... the component elements of adult learning, as the dynamics, the processes, the mechanisms..., must be taken as entire fields of this subject of research ... in this perspective, the biography is a key to the understanding of idea-production." (Dominicé 2000, 238) For Gaston Pineau, life history represents

> the foundation practices on which to build the continuing education sciences. The use of life history can be turned into an art for achieving subjection and alienation just as it can be turned into an art in promoting autonomy, as an advanced life-promoting learning experience; and between

these two poles: communication methods and knowledge. That's the ambivalence we find ourselves in (Gaston 2000, 239).

References

Belenky, M., et al. (1986). *Women's Ways of Knowing: the Development of Self, Voice and Mind.* New York.

Belkaïd, M. (1998). *Normaliennes en Algérie.* Paris.

Bron, A., West, L. (2000). Time for Stories: The Emergence of Life History Methods in the Social Sciences. In: *International Journal of Contemporary Sociology,* 37 (2), pp. 158-175.

Budry, M., Ollagnier, E. (eds.) (1999). *Mais qu'est-ce qu'elles voulaient? Histoires de vie du MLF à Genève.* Lausanne.

Coles, D., Goussault, B. (1995), Le récit de vie. Transmettre de femmes en femmes. Lyon.

Delory-Momberger, C. (2000). *Les histoires de vie. De l'invention de soi au projet de formation.* Paris.

Demazière, D., Dubar, C. (1997). Analyser les entretiens biographiques: l'exemple de récits d'insertio. Paris.

Dominicé, P. (1990). *L'histoire de vie comme processus de formation.* Paris.

Dominicé, P. (2000). *Learning from our Lives.* San Francisco.

de Gaulejac, V. (1987). *La névrose de classe.* Paris.

Education Permanente (2000). Les histoires de vie. Théories et pratiques, No. 142.

Finger, M. (1984). *Biographie et herméneutique.* Montréal.

Gluck, S. B., Patai, D. (1991). *Women's Words: The Feminist Practice of Oral History.* New York.

Josso, C. (2001). *Cheminer vers soi: un processus-projet de connaissance de son existentialité.* In: Cahiers de la Section des Sciences de l'Education, Université de Genève, No. 95.

Lainé, A. (1998). *Faire de sa vie une histoire. Théories et pratiques de l'histoire de vie en formation.* Paris.

Les origines biographiques de la compétence d'apprendre (1998). Cahiers de la Section des Sciences de l'Education, Université de Genève, No. 87 (P. Dominicé, C. Josso, R. Muller and coll.).

Luke, C., Gore, J. (1992). *Feminisms and Critical Pedagogy.* New York.

Merrill, B. (1999). *Gender, Change and Identity. Mature Women Students in Universities.* Aldershot.

Middleton, S. (1993). *Educating Feminists, Life Histories and Pedagogy.* New York.

Olesen, H. S., Rasmussen, P. (eds.) (1996). *Theoretical Issues in Adult Education.* Roskilde.

Pineau G. (2000). What Exploitation of Life-Stories? In: *Education Permanente.* Les histoires de vie. Théories et pratiques, No. 142.

Regards pluriels sur l'approche biographique: entre discipline et indiscipline (2001). Cahiers de la Section des Sciences de l'Education, Université de Genève, No. 95.

Robin, G. (1992). *Guide de reconnaissance des acquis.* Boucherville, Quebec.

Thomas, W. I., Znaniecki, F. (1920). *The Polish Peasant in Europe and America. Monograph of an Immigrant Group.* Boston.

Weber, K. (ed.) (1998). *Life History, Gender and Experience.* Roskilde.

West, L. (2001). *Doctors on the Edge. General Practitioners, Health and Learning in the Inner-City.* London.

Barry J. Hake

RECOVERING A CRITICAL HISTORY OF ADULT EDUCATION
THE ROLE OF INTELLECTUALS IN SOCIAL AND CULTURAL FORMATIONS

> The materialist doctrine concerning the changing of circumstances and education forgets that circumstances are changed by men and that the educator must himself be educated... The coincidence of the changing of circumstances and of human activity or self-changing can only be grasped and rationally understood as revolutionary practice (Karl Marx 1846).

Introduction: The Assertion of Tradition in Adult Education

An important aspect of the historical study of the development of adult education in any particular country is the reconstruction of a lineage for the growth of particular forms of adult education. The story is often one of institutional success and the survival of particular institutions, or, in Johnson's terms 'a thin unilinear narrative of the development of some set of institutions or practices' (Johnson 1979). There are three main varieties of such unilinear narratives. Firstly, the narrative may be organised around significant individuals who are seen as the great innovators and reformers in adult education. Secondly, the narrative may trace the emergence and development of institutions and practices in the form of institutional histories at the national and local levels. Thirdly, the narrative may be constructed around the development of philanthropic endeavours, public policy-making, legislation and subsidies for the provision of adult education. Such sets of institutions and practices are often regarded as those forms of adult education which constitute the specific 'national' tradition of adult educational forms in different countries. For example, the 'accepted history' of Danish adult education in the nineteenth century, is the history of the folk high school, and is very often a celebration of Grundtvig and his contribution to the building of Danish 'national character' (Borish 1991).

For the early comparative educators, from Sadler onwards (Titmus 1991), through Mallison, Hans, and Kandel to Urich, their understanding of such distinct national traditions often took the form of explaining them in terms of national psychology (Kazamias, Massialas 1976). Tradition was located in a search for national character which suggested patterns of characteristic 'national' behaviour, or in the words of Mallison 'forces of cultural continuity which determine the behaviour of a nation as a whole'. As Marriott and Coles (1991) have pointed out most cogently, however, while it is quite legitimate to analyse the understandings of different national characteristics as these were formulated by contemporary historical actors themselves, these historically specific formulations of 'national character' have themselves to be explained by the historian rather than being considered as providing meaningful explanations.

More recent contributions to the comparative education literature have rejected the spurious notion of national character as holding any explanatory value for the historical development of adult education. The major problem with such an approach is that it ignores what Williams refers to as the 'selective tradition' in the construction of received histories of adult education traditions. In other words, the accumulative approach, or to use another idiom 'the natural history' of national educational traditions, is often manipulative of the historical record. Whether consciously or otherwise, it was used to exclude the repressed, the preferably unremembered, the inconvenient and the plainly embarrassing. Historically speaking, however, the process of innovation, the building of new ideas, new institutions and practices in adult education can no longer be respectably construed as the unmediated product of 'national character'.

The limitations of this search for the grand narrative of national traditions contributes to and reinforces the insularity, indeed parochialism, which is all too evident in much research on the history of adult education. This is reinforced by the fact that the history of adult education often serves a celebratory purpose for the adult education movement. History is part of the legitimation exercise and is implicitly ideological in its purpose. Historical writing on adult education in most countries does not draw on the 'great elsewhere'; it is inward looking and serves domestic, often particularistic, problematics. Ideological legitimation plays a stronger role here than historical evidence.

Reinserting the History of Adult Education into Society

There is an acute need to move towards an approach to historical research which challenges these unilinear and accumulative descriptions of the received selective tradition of asserting the 'successful' in adult education. This is to propose a return to more theoretically informed approaches toward historical analysis. In the past three decades there have been a number of attempts to put the record straight, to bring back into the historical record the contribution of the 'unsuccessful' innovations. These were all too often associated with radical and even social groups that sought to subvert the social order. Interestingly enough, as Johnson (1979) points out, these 'missing links' have remained hidden for long periods, and have usually been rediscovered in recovering the rich educational tradition of political and social movements. Critical rewriting of the history of adult education has questioned the case for explanation in terms of historical continuity and it has made the forgotten sites of struggle for adult learning, which do not fit neatly into received tradition, the major focus for research.

Men and women live in a society not of their own making. But they need to develop strategies of survival often in difficult circumstances, and from time to time they turn to radical change in order to reshape the social order sometimes radically. People live surrounded by a vast accumulation of social institutions and practices, they choose selectively from these, and they adapt them to their own purposes in order to meet the objectives they wish to achieve. Adult education is but one specific historical manifestation of these institutions and practices. The human agency involved in the social processes of the 'making' of adult education can be best understood in terms of organised efforts to come to terms with the experience of social conditions and "... the ways in which these experiences are handled in cultural terms: embodied in traditions, value-systems, ideas and institutional forms" (Thompson 1963, 9). These processes need to be understood within the specific characteristics of the social formation in any particular historical period, and thus have to be interpreted in terms of the active relationships between the social classes.

This must surely lead away from institutional histories into broader social and cultural history. Historical research must indeed devote considerable attention to the detailed study of the personalities, their aspirations indeed hopes, and the activities social groups and movements involved in the wide range of adult educational endeavours in the past. But any reliable account of the development of adult education necessarily leads out to the general history of the period under investigation. The historical development of adult education as socially organised activities can only be meaningfully comprehended in terms of their historical articulations with economic, social, political and cultural forces (Hake 1987). The historical development of adult educational institutions and practices cannot be studied in isolation from the social relations within a particular society. This understanding has informed those studies which examine the history of adult education in terms of the social class relations constitutive of the social formation. Such studies suggest that the historical development of adult education has been determined by the realities of the social, political, economic and cultural dominance or dependence in the relationships between social classes and class factions.

Critical studies of the social relations of adult educational institutions and practices have led, furthermore, to the recognition that the history of success and failure is a highly selective and socially structured process within societies. Institutional innovation is sometimes undertaken by a dominant or emergent, even residual social group, while it may be also carried out by alternative or oppositional, indeed revolutionary, social movements or groups. This suggests the need to examine the historical specificity of the connections between these modes in terms of the social relations of dominance and dependence within society (Williams 1981). The attempt to understand changes in adult education institutions and practices in relation to broader patterns of social change should not be taken as an argument for understanding adult education as an epiphenomenon which can be reduced to its economic base. Adult education is a set of active practices and not merely a part of the cultural superstructure that is a reflection of a determining economic base. Adult education not only reflects society but helps to shape it, and its constituting institutions and practices enjoy an historically variable autonomy. The structures of the social formation constitute the raw materials for cultural processes but do not determine them. This allows us to introduce the notion of the relative autonomy of cultural institutions and practices. Relative autonomy is not merely an abstract theoretical category but is a social and historical variable. The actual relative autonomy of cultural institutions and practices can only be established through empirical research into the degree to which social, economic and political forces exert pressures upon and set limits upon their development.

These observations direct attention to the analysis of the social relations of cultural practices in terms of the social organisation of the social and cultural practices constituting the historical forms of adult education. Such a theoretical perspective is to a great extent based upon Williams' work on the sociology of culture (1977, 1981). This involves a conceptualisation of adult education as structured cultural practices that involve communication and learning. Williams' approach suggests that adults are actively involved in the communication and acquisition of knowledge, skills, attitudes and sensitivities. Historical analysis and description of these cultural practices is focused on the social organisation of communication and learning. The term 'social organisation' is used here to refer to the complex relationships between social institutions, movements and groups and the development of cultural practices, which may be involved in historically specific processes of organising communication and learning. Historical work thus focuses on the ways in which adults have been organised by others or have organised themselves for the purposes of communication and acquiring knowledge, skills, attitudes and sensitivities. This brings to the fore the analysis of social relationships in cultural institutions and practices a the variable patterns of control over and access to cultural meanings.

Analysis of the social organisation of efforts to communicate and acquire cultural messages also demands efforts to identify those who played a role as the educators of diverse publics. This directs attention to the specific social class positions of cultural disseminators and their social relationships with the publics whom they sought to address. Such communicators, understood as 'intellectuals' in the terms of Gramsci and as 'cultural intermediaries' according to Vovelle – played a significant role in mediating the access of specific publics to the knowledge, skills, attitudes and sensitivities in. The relationships between such intellectuals or cultural intermediaries are an important dimension of any historical analysis of the cultural practices associated with communication and learning. The contribution of intellectuals and opinion-makers within social movements has to be understood in terms of specific historical manifestations of the social practices associated with cultural production and dissemination. Williams argues, however, that the role of intellectuals and opinion makers as cultural producers within social movements cannot be reduced to an analysis of their specialised roles within the specific institutions identified with the historical manifestations of communication and learning in the form of 'movement education'.

Williams suggests that it is important to analyse intellectuals in terms of their variable social relations to both social institutions – with an emphasis upon specialised cultural practices – and the broader cultural formations which manifest more general tendencies in cultural production and dissemination. Williams argues that this gives rise to the need for an historical analysis of the relationships between residual, dominant and emergent cultural formations, together with an understanding of the specialised, alternative and oppositional relationships of intellectuals to these formations (Williams 1977). Vovelle has formulated the notion of 'cultural intermediaries' in terms of both objects and people which establish relationships between different cultures, are located between cultures, or take responsibility for communication between cultures (Vovelle 1982). In Williams' terminology, this suggests a distinction between cultural intermediaries as 'material' and 'non-material' resources in (cross-) cultural mediation (Williams 1977). Vovelle's analysis is specifically applied to cultural intermediaries in the "...dialogue between élite culture and popular culture" (Vouvelle 1982, 126). Within one society – perhaps suggesting the term "inter-cultural" communication – his ideas, together with those of Williams, can be applied to an understanding of intellectuals as cultural intermediaries in cross-cultural mediation.

Hake and Marriott formulate the distinction between non-material and material cultural resources as involving a variable focus

> on carriers of influence which were primarily symbolic and documents the kind of cross-cultural learning that came from reading the printed word. More pervasive (and of course overlapping with the symbolic word) was what one might call mediated influence, impact through the advocacy of individuals and groups who adopted exotic ideas and made them accessible to their followers (Hake, Marriott 1992, 2).

This understanding of the cultural intermediary focuses less on the medium of communication, but stresses mediation as a cultural activity, indeed an active relationship which constitutes the mediating process as a social practice. In Williams terms this is to stress the intermediary as part of the social process of active selection, the constitution of meanings, and the social organisation of signification and communication (Williams 1977). This suggests that the mediating activities of the intellectual have to be understood in terms of the social organisation of cultural production as an organised social practice.

It is important to note that both Vovelle and Williams understand intellectuals as cultural intermediaries in terms of their relationships to the dynamics of social movements, institutions and their respective social positions in the social formation. In the first place this involves rejecting the excluding notion of 'intellectuals' as referring only to certain kinds of writers, philosophers and social thinkers, which is no more than a very specific and limiting historical formation more generally recognised as the 'intelligentsia'. As Williams points out, excluded from consideration in such an understanding is a range of cultural producers and particularly "...those many kinds of 'intellectual workers' who are directly instituted in the major political, economic, religious and social institutions – civil servants ... priests, lawyers, doctors as cultural producers and reproducers" (Williams 1981, 97). With reference to the subsequent analysis here, a limiting definition also leaves an important group of modern professionals, such as teachers, adult educators and social workers, out of the analysis. This comes close to Gramsci's understanding of intellectuals as "traditional" and "organic" intellectuals which moved the analysis of intellectuals into these areas of exclusion (Hoare, Nowell 1971). The identification of intellectuals thus involves analysis of the identity of "traditional" and "organic" intellectuals whether they be: "peers, poets, propagandists, priests, peddlers, politicians, performers, publishers, pamphleteers, playwrights, publicans, and practitioners of the plastic arts" (Carlson 1980, 178).

Traditional intellectuals are here understood as deriving from a residual cultural formation in the past which has often diverse and indirect social relations in the modernising social formation. Organic intellectuals are understood as allied to and serving a dominant and more particularly an emergent social class. Furthermore, as Williams analysis suggests, the notion of the intellectual as a cultural producer also opens up the analysis to a broader range of groups and individuals – for example the self-educated artisan – who are also effectively cultural producers.

This suggests that the core concern of an analysis of intellectuals as cultural intermediaries is not limited to a static descriptive treatment of the 'typical' cultural intermediaries in specific societal types such as 'rural', 'urban' or 'industrial' societies. Of much greater significance is the dynamic analysis of changes in social formations which are associated with the process of modernisation in European societies from the pre-industrial to the industrial social formation. Within the modernising social formation, we can then proceed to an analysis of cultural intermediaries in terms of cultural formations and the social organisation of their cultural practices. This involves important questions with regard to their specific relationships with dominant and subordinate social groups, and the degree in which their cultural practices become associated with specific social institutions.

Only some of these institutions, movements and groups will be recognised directly as 'adult education', while others will be primarily embedded in the economic, political or cultural dimensions of social life. This means that no account of the development of adult educational institutions and practices can be provided without extending description and analysis into the general historical development of the social within societies (Williams 1961).

Towards a Theory of Intellectuals in Adult Education Movements

When attention is devoted to the specific contribution of social movements and cultural formations to historical development of adult education in a particular country, there are at least five major questions involved in studies of historically specific development of adult educational institutions and practices.

In the first place, it is necessary to identify the specific social and cultural movements that were actively involved in the practices of adult education. These can be educational reform movements which are concerned with the provision of adult education for the general improvement of society or some specific section of the adult population. But they may also be economic, political or religious movements which seek some measure of social reform and which organise educational activities to these ends. Furthermore, they may be radical, even revolutionary, movements which regard the organisation of adult education as an essential element in the struggles of social groups for economic, political, social, and religious emancipation. It is obviously easier to offer description of relatively established movements in the field of adult education, the University Extension movement for example. It is also necessary, however, to direct attention to the relatively informal cultural movements and associations, often small in numbers and sometimes of relatively short duration, which were characterised by the rapidity of their formation and dissolution, together with the complexity of their internal links and relationships with other institutions and social groups in society.

Secondly, we must also undertake analysis of the relationships between the specific movements and groups involved in the development of adult educational institutions and practices with the diverse range of social institutions, movements and groups in society at large. The movements and groups associated with innovations in the organisation of adult education have often enjoyed historically specific relations to more general programmes of social and political change. These have not always been brought to the surface in the general histories of adult education. Adult education 'movements' have historically formed around more general social, political and cultural programmes of reform, even radical change through revolution. These external relations concern "the proposed or actual relations of a cultural formation to other organisations in the same field and to society more generally" (Williams 1981, 87).

One way of analysing these relationships offered by the distinction made by Williams between three types of cultural formations in society. He refers, firstly, to 'specialised' movements which were concerned with the development of a particular form of adult education or the dissemination of a specific body of knowledge, which we might recognise in those forms of University Extension which sought, for example, to popularise scientific knowledge. Secondly, he identifies the alternative cultural formations which seek to provide alternative forms of adult education for particular social groups when it is believed that existing institutions exclude or tend to exclude them. University Extension directed at women, in the absence of university education for them, might be seen as such an alternative movement. Thirdly, Williams refers to oppositional movements in which alternatives may be developed in active opposition to established institutions. The development by Gramsci of the workers' university in Turin, in direct conflict with University Extension and popular universities provided for them, might be seen a classic case of this oppositional form (Steele 1992). More generally and throughout Europe, however, similar criticisms of the provision of adult education for the working-class, whether by radical liberals, reforming philanthropists or the churches, constituted an important part of the organised working-class critique of University Extension. Further research needs to examine this critique by the organised working-class movement and to contribute to the deconstruction of the celebration of University Extension.

Thirdly, attention must be paid to the complex range of influences, interests and positions prevalent among those involved in social movements. This can provide a basis for the identification of those who play a prominent role in the national and local leadership of social movements and innovative activities. It also becomes possible to locate those groups and individuals who made a specific contribution to the dissemination and adoption of ideas and practices. At the same time we can use this analysis as a basis for the identification of those who played a prominent role in the national and local leadership of cultural formations. It enables us to locate those individuals and groups of 'intellectuals' or 'opinion-leaders' who made a specific contribution to the dissemination, popularisation and adoption of ideas and practices. This exercise in identification must be linked to an analysis of the social class basis of 'organic' and 'inorganic' intellectuals.

In this, it must be remembered that no social class is culturally monolithic, and the development of alternative and oppositional movements may be based on factions within a social class which are not characteristic of the class as a whole. Social class analysis within one class alone is not enough, analysis must also necessarily extend to the variations in the changing relations between a particular social class and its factions, for example middle-class providers of adult education for the workers, and other classes and their own factions. In this case the organised working class itself is an interesting case with its own self-constructed distinctions between movement intellectuals, activists, the labour aristocracy of skilled artisans, and the mass membership.

The location of 'intellectuals' is of importance, fourthly, in terms of exploring the historical specificity of the processes of cultural borrowing by means of identifying their sources of innovative ideas. This is a reference particularly to importance place of 'key texts' to the dissemination of educational ideas, institutions and practices. One of the major problems involved in the reconstruction of cultural mediation in textual forms is that the actual historical processes can be all too easily influenced by the distorted perception of the historian within a received and selective reading of the history of reception. Throughout the period between 1890 and 1939, for example, one can note recurring contemporary references to seminal works which are not necessarily taken into account by historians of adult education. In addition to the cultural formations among reformist intellectuals, both of the wings of the working-class movement recognised their own 'key texts' which influenced and shaped opinion at the time. These have to provide the historical textual materials for the historical researcher. Of particular importance in the work of historical reconstruction is the recognition that many key texts were not necessarily consulted in their original languages, but that they were more usually translated, and indeed re-translated, into different languages as part of the mediating process. This makes it particularly important to identify those cultural intermediaries who were responsible for the actual practice of translation.

The social organisation, and indeed the economics, of the translation, publication, distribution of texts and access to them are also vital aspects of research on cultural mediation. This can be useful in analysing the different processes involved in organised attempts to export and to selectively import particular ideas, institutions and practices. Also of some interest here is the question of selective translation, censorship and the banning of specific texts, which may itself give rise to the organisation of illegal and underground mechanisms for distributing texts. While the overwhelming emphasis upon the translation of texts is obviously of some importance, it is also necessary to examine in particular the role played in mediating processes by double translations. One has to recognise, for example, that the reception of British institutions and practices in much of Central, Eastern Europe, and Scandinavia was very largely mediated by way of German-language publications and translations – sometimes even mediated through Vienna – until the early 1930s. As in an earlier phase in this particular period – when there was some confusion, among Dutch and Spanish supporters of university extension, about the differences between extension and university settlement – research into the practice of translation and mis-translation as the sources of selective representations by cross-cultural intermediaries has to be addressed. This also raises one final but not unimportant aspect of the role of translation in cross-cultural mediation. It is necessary to reconstruct, on the one hand, the changing historical relationships through time in the intensity of translation activity, and, on the other hand, any indications of patterns of preferential translation from major languages such as English, French, German and Spanish.

The identification of 'intellectuals' or 'opinion-leaders' leads, fifthly, to the analysis of the social relations of the means of communication between the propagators of new ideas and practices and their respective publics. These relationships can be seen as "the variable patterns of control over and access to the spoken and the written word as cultural resources" (Williams 1977, 108-114). With regard to the internal organisation of cultural formations, Williams (1981) refers to cultural formations based upon "formal membership", "collective public manifestation", or "conscious association or group identification". It is of great importance to examine to the processes involved in the forming of the 'publics' which were addressed by innovations in institutions and practices. As was suggested above, formative periods in the development of adult education were characterised by the spatial-temporal extension of participation to new social groups – in current terminology known as target groups, users or consumers. This leads to the analysis of the specific positions of 'cultural disseminators' or 'intellectuals' as cultural intermediaries in the social organisation of deliberate, systematic and sustained efforts to disseminate and acquire cultural meanings, and their social relations with those they addressed. It is of vital importance, therefore, to examine the social identity of the participants addressed by those seeking to introduce specific innovations who should be more correctly recognised as 'publics' for organised educational activities. This directs attention, to specific institutions and practices in terms of the degree to which adults have organised themselves, or have been organised by others, for the purpose of learning.

This is not merely an analysis of mediated formulations of target groups by innovators, but an analysis of the public as a collective subject in the field of education. As Steele (1991) points out with regard to the University Extension summer school in the United Kingdom, this is a question of whether participants in educational practices are the object of interventions by others, or consciously constitute the emergence of a active force in the field of education and who help shape educational institutions and practices. As De Sanctis (1984, 265) argues "the aim would be to see if, and how, and with what differences and variations of emphasis ... the problems of the newly forming public emerged". This introduces the historical study of the structural dynamics of the formation of the 'public' in terms of empirical indicators of the connection between the production, distribution and consumption of socially organised learning. This introduces us to the fascinating notion that the emergence of the working-class movement opened up new possibilities for the reconstitution of the 'proletarian public' as a potential consumer of education, and that the all-too-often celebrated institutional forms of adult education have to be considered as bourgeois responses to the possibility that the working-class could organise itself as a producer rather than as a consumer of adult education. From this point of view, most of the celebrations of national tradition can be more appropriately considered as a terrain of social intervention which encouraged no more than a modification of institutionalised bourgeois forms of learning to incorporate a proletarian public. Is the current addiction of the European Union to lifelong learning any different?

This directs attention to the specific modes of communication by means of books, journals, newspapers, pamphlets, correspondence and meetings. The roles of translators, writers, journalists and lecturers require detailed study.

Conclusions

In this paper, the argument has emphasised the need to recognise the complexity of the levels of analysis and interpretation which must enter our narratives about the historical development of adult education. If the history of adult education is about pioneers and their reputations, it is also about the forgotten and the defeated, even the uncomfortable and inconvenient reminders. If it is about social reformers and provision for others, it is also about often radical and indeed revolutionary social, political and cultural movements that organise communication and learning against the established social order. If it is about the latter, it is also about ideologies and struggle between social classes and their factions. If it is about ideologies and struggle, it is also about popular expectations and responses. If it is about the latter, it is also about experience and biography. All these aspects have to be provided with a theoretical perspective to achieve greater understanding and construct our explanations

The argument above has been that our historical explanations of the development of the institutions and practices in the area of the education of adults have to be more firmly rooted in social scientific theories and concepts. Challenging historical work is increasingly informed by the conscious use of theories and concepts from the social sciences and cultural studies. For the history of adult education, we can benefit greatly from the still ongoing debate among neo-Marxist, structuralist and postmodernist theories about the relations between historically specific social structures and the behaviour of social actors in the processes of social production and social reproduction. This should not be construed in any manner as a post-modernist argumentation for the deconstruction and consequent marginalisation of the reform discourses often used to construct the dominant narratives in adult education history. It is intended, however, as a critique of the strong element of 'celebration', the search for genealogies and the construction of lineages in historical narratives on adult educational institutions and practices. There are dangers, however, in looking to the social sciences as sources of inspiration for our interpretative and analytical frameworks. History is no longer history when it becomes no more than disembodied theoretical frameworks in which texts constitute history rather than the praxis of their authors as historical actors. On the other hand, history is not history when it provides us with no more than the unreflected, and hence common sense unilinear collections of the antiquities of the past world of adult education.

This provides a background to the formulation of a final question. To what extent is it possible, or indeed useful, to write the history of adult education across frontiers in Europe? What future is there for a 'comparative social history of adult education'? My own position in this regard is that a cross-cultural perspective may help to relieve the parochialism of much of the historical work on adult education in any single country. My critique here was directed at the narrow range of theoretical and conceptual machinery employed in historical writing and the dominant tendency to fall back upon celebratory narratives of national traditions. The strongest argument for cross-cultural historical studies at the present time in Europe is a political one. I would argue that one of the major prerequisites of cross-cultural historical studies is that it must be an exceptionally self-conscious historiography which confronts us not only with a contested past but also with a contested present. In an age of global neo-liberalism and massive social exclusion resulting from the rapacious accumulation of economic capital, a Marxist analysis is a meaningful way of recovering the real structures of dominance and repression in the so-called knowledge society. This is to argue that there is still a place in intellectual life for critical theory and ideology critique. The current recovery of Walter Benjamin as a critic of the *technischen Reproduzierbarkeit* of social relations and the application of his thinking to a critical theory of the digital age is of major significance. Re-reading the collected works of Benjamin might be regarded as compulsory reading for all would-be historians of adult education.

References

Borish, S. (1991). *The Land of the Living. The Danish Folk High School and Denmark's Non-Violent Path to Modernization*. Grass Valley.

Carlson, R. A. (1980). The Foundation of Adult Education. Analysing the Boyd-Apps Model. In: Boyd, R. D., Apps, J. W. (eds.). *Redefining the Discipline of Adult Education*. San Francisco.

Gramsci, A. (1971). *Selections from the Prison Notebooks*. London.

Hake, B. J. (1987). Patriots, Democrats and Social Enlightenment. A Study of Political Movements and the Development of Adult Education in the Netherlands, 1780-1813. Hull: unpublished Ph.D dissertation.

Hake, B. J., Marriott, S. (1992). Introduction. In: Hake, B. J., Marriott, S. (eds.). *Adult Education between Cultures. Encounters and Identities in European Adult Education since 1890*. Leeds, pp. 1-10.

Kazamias, A., Massialis, B. (1978). *Tradition and Change in Education. A Comparative Study*. Englewood Cliffs, N.J.

Marriott, S., Coles, J. (1991). Necessary Myths. 'National Character' and Adult Educators before 1914. In: Friedenthal-Haase, M. Hake, B. J., Marriott, S. (eds.). *British-Dutch-German Relationships in Adult Education 1880-1930. Studies in the Theory and History of Cross-Cultural Communication in Adult Education*. Leeds, pp. 101-142.

Johnson, R. (1979). Culture and Historians. In: Clarke, J. et al. (eds.). *Working Class Culture. Studies in History and Theory*. London, pp. 41-71.

De Sanctis, F. M. (1984). Problems of Defining the Public in the Context of Lifelong Education. In: *International Journal of Lifelong Education*, 3 (4), pp. 265-278.

Steele, T. (1991). Metropolitan Extensions. Comparison of Two Moments in the Export of British University Adult Education, Europe 1890-1910 and Africa 1945-1955. In: Friedenthal-Haase, M., Hake, B. J., Marriott, S. (eds.). *British-Dutch-German Relationships in Adult Education 1880-1930. Studies in the Theory and History of Cross-Cultural Communication in Adult Education*. Leeds, pp. 73-100.

Steele, T. (1992). A Science of Democracy. An Outline of the Development of University Extension in Europe, 1890-1920. In: Hake, B. J., Marriott, S. (eds.). *Adult Edu-*

cation between Cultures. Encounters and Identities in European Adult Education since 1890. Leeds, pp. 61-85.

Thompson, E. P. (1963). *The Making of the English Working-Class.* London.

Titmus, C. (1991). Reflections on Cultural Borrowing and Cultural Imposition in Continuing Education. In: Friedenthal-Haase, M., Hake, B. J., Marriott, S. (eds.). *British-Dutch-German Relationships in Adult Education 1880-1930. Studies in the Theory and History of Cross-Cultural Communication in Adult Education.* Leeds, pp. 13-32.

Vovelle, M. (1982). 'Les intermédiaires culturels'. In: Vovelle, M. *Idéologies et mentalités.* Paris, pp. 119-132.

Williams, R. (1961). *The Long Revolution.* London.

Williams, R. (1977). *Marxism and Literature.* London.

Williams, R. (1981). *Culture.* Glasgow.

Part III

Epilogue

Barney G. Glaser

Conceptualisation
On Theory and Theorising Using Grounded Theory

Conceptualisation is the core category of Grounded Theory (GT). We all know or have an idea what conceptualisation is in general. In this paper I will detail those properties of conceptualisation which are essential for generating GT.

I discussed at length in *Doing Grounded Theory* (Glaser 1998) the conceptual license that GT offers. The researcher can use his/her own concepts generated from the data instead of using, probably forcing the received concepts of others, especially those concepts of unduly respected theoretical capitalists. Actually generating a concept is very exciting and it is where many an effort at GT stops. This stopping is far short of doing GT through all steps to the end product. The GT perspective in this paper will hopefully move more researchers further toward doing a complete GT.

In *Doing Grounded Theory* (1998) I endeavoured to emphasise the complexity of the world and therefore the freedom, autonomy and license required to write generated theory that explains what is going on in this world, starting with substantive areas.

All that GT is, is the generation of emergent conceptualisations into integrated patterns, which are denoted by categories and their properties. This is accomplished by the many rigorous steps of GT woven together by the constant comparison process, which is designed to generate concepts from all data, but most frequently qualitative incidents.

Through conceptualisation, GT is a general method that cuts across research methods (experiment, survey, content analysis, and all qualitative methods) and uses all data resulting therefrom. Because of conceptualisation, GT transcends all descriptive methods and their associated problems, especially what is an accurate fact and what is an interpretation. It transcends by its conceptual level and its third and fourth level perceptions.

By transcending, I do not say implicitly that description is 'bad', 'wrong' of 'unfavourable'. Description is just different with different properties than conceptualisation, yet these different properties are confused in the qualitative research literature. Actually descriptions run the world, however vague or precise and mostly the former. Precious little conceptualisation affects the way the world is run. We have many immensely funded description producing agencies such as newspapers, police, FBI and so forth as well as an immense multi-QDA (Qualitative Data Analysis) research movement.

It is sociologists, psychologists, social psychologists and other social researchers who are mandated to conceptualise in the social sciences. GT provides a systematic way to conceptualise carefully and its audience, though small, is growing. Yet at this point in time, 34 years after *The Discovery of Grounded Theory* (Glaser, Strauss 1967) was written, many social-psychological researchers still have little or no awareness of conceptualisation, conceptual levels and, therefore, the integration of conceptual hypotheses.

The two most important properties of conceptualisation for GT are that concepts are abstract of time, place and people and that concepts have enduring grab, which appeal can literally go on forever as an applied way of seeing events. In this paper I start by explicating what a concept is for GT, then explain its abstraction from time, place and people, followed by detailed discussions of conceptual ability required, conceptual levels, conceptual grab, conceptual description, conceptual conjecture, conceptual foppery and vagary and conceptual power. Much of this discussion overlaps and cumulates.

Pattern Naming

For GT a concept is the naming of an emergent social pattern grounded in research data. For GT a concept (category) denotes a pattern which is carefully discovered by constant comparing of theoretically sampled data until conceptual saturation of interchangeable indices. It is discovered by comparing many incidents, and incidents to generated concept, which shows the pattern named by the category and the subpatterns which are the properties of the category. A GT concept is not achieved by impressioning out over one incident, nor by preconceived forcing of a received concept on a pattern of incidents. GT is a form of latent structure analysis, which reveals the fundamental patterns in a substantive area or a formal area.

The pattern is named by constantly trying to fit words to it to best capture its imageric meaning. This constant fitting leads to a best fit name of a pattern, to wit a category or a property of a category. Validity is achieved, that is after much fitting of words, the chosen one best represents the pattern. It is as valid as it is grounded.

In *Theoretical Sensitivity* (Glaser 1978) I said that many concepts are '*in vivo*' concepts, that is, they are from the words of the participants in the substantive area. Let me be clear, standard QDA emphasises getting the 'voice' of the participants. *In vivo* concepts are not such 'voice', in the sense that what phenomenon they attribute meaning to with a concept is only taken as a GT concept, not taken as a description. The participants usually just give impressionary concepts based on one incident or even a groundless idea. They do not carefully generate their concepts from data with the GT methodology and try to fit many names to an established pattern. They are not establishing a parsimonious theory. They may have many concepts that do not fit or work. GT discovers which *in vivo* concepts do fit, work and are relevant.

Inviting participants to review the theory for whether or not it is their voice is wrong as a check or 'test' on validity. They may or may not understand, or even like the theory. Many do not understand the summary benefit of concepts which go beyond description to a transcending big picture. GT is generated from much data that many participants may be empirically unaware of. GT is applicable to the participants as an explanation of the preponderance of their behaviour which is how they are resolving their main concern, which they may not be aware of conceptually, if at all. It is just what they do! GT is not their voice: it is a generated abstraction from their doings and its meaning which are taken as data for the conceptual generation.

GT in naming concepts does not try to take a 'concern to understand the world of the research participants as they construct it'. GT is not 'an enquiry that makes sense of and is true to the understanding of ordinary actors in the everyday world', as one QDA writer would have it. GT uncovers many patterns the participant does not understand or is not aware of, especially the social fictions that may be involved.

Time, Place, People

The most important property of conceptualisation for GT is that it is abstract of time, place and people. This transcendence also, by consequence, makes GT abstract of any one substantive field, routine perceptions or perceptions of others, since there is always a perception of a perception, and an abstraction from any type of data whether qualitative or quantitative. Hence GT is a general method.

Thus GT conceptualisation transcends. Conceptualisation solves and resolves many QDA difficulties which are not abstract of time and place. QDA focuses on description of time, place and people, so is confronted with the problem of accuracy, context, interpretation and so forth in trying to produce what 'is'. GT generates conceptual hypotheses which get applied to any relevant time, place and people with emergent fit and then is modified by constant comparison with new data as it explains what behaviour obtains in a substantive area.

Most writers on methodology do not have a theoretical clue of what it means to be abstract of time, place and people. The result is that GT is down-abstracted to just another QDA with some concepts. Strauss and Corbin do this in the following:

> Grounded Theory procedures force us to ask, for example: What power is in this situation and under specified conditions? How is it manifested, by whom, when, where, how, with what consequences (and for whom or what)? Not to remain open to such a range of questions is to obstruct the discovery of important features of power in situ and to preclude developing further conceptualization. Knowledge is after all linked loosely with time and place. We carefully and specifically build conditions into our theories.

Thus, Strauss and Corbin force descriptions, irrespective of emergence, on the theory to locate its conditions, to contextualise it and to make appear accurately pinned down, thereby losing its true abstraction hence generalisability.

Personal distance for accuracyt is supposed to be an 'attitude' of the QDA researcher. The GT researcher, in contrast, does not need this attitude to get a description accurate, which is not his goal. The GT method automatically puts him/her on a conceptual level, which transcends the data.

In fact, it is hard to give up time, place and people for many researchers as it is most natural, taught in QDA method classes and requires an ability they may not have fully developed if they have at all.

GT in abstracting allows the researcher to develop a theory on a core variable, such as cutting back, supernormalising, credentialising, cultivating, pluralistic dialoging, atmosphering, toning, abusing and so forth which can be applied to any relevant time or place. This delimiting by conceptualisation stands in stark contrast to QDA lengthy descriptions which try to cognitively map an area in a nontranscending way. There are no QDA rules for delimiting but arbitrary cut off points in the face of data volume and lengthy descriptive complexity. The QDA researcher's need to be different, hence appear original, is subverted by an inability to assimilate and extend a method devoted to description. GT, of course, simply generates original concepts and hypotheses as a result of the method.

Relational: Conceptualisation is the medium of grounded theory for a simple reason: without the abstraction from time, place and people, there can be no multivariate, integrated theory based on conceptual, hypothetical relationships. Concepts can be related to concepts as hypotheses. Descriptions cannot be related to each other as hypotheses since there is no conceptual handle. Concepts can relate to a description, but that single hypothesis is as far as it can go. While concepts are 'everything' in GT, many researchers find it hard to stay on that level to relate them to each other. They relate the concept to a description and go on and on with description as QDA would have it.

Because GT operates on a conceptual level, relating concept to concept, it can tap the latent structure which is always there and drives and organises behaviour and its social psychological aspects, all of which are abstract of objective fact. For example, we have theories now of cautionary control, supernormalising, default remodelling, desisting residual selves, atmosphering, competitive knowing and many more, none of which could have been generated without conceptual abstraction.

Place: While a GT may have been generated from a unit, or many units if adequate theoretical sampling was used, it does not describe the unit, as I have said many times. The GT gets applied to the unit to explain behaviour or any other unit in which the process has emergent fit. Thus, GT does not generalise from a researched unit to a larger unit or a similar unit, as a description might. GT generalises to a transcending process or other form of core variable, and in the bargain may relate seemingly disparate units to each other by an underlying process. For example a four year medical school may be seen as the same as a six week contractor's course, from the point of view of credentialising, one property of which is to insure quality work. I have written at length on this in *Theoretical Sensitivity* (Glaser 1978, 109-113).

The delimiting aspect of abstraction is clear. A GT need not describe the whole unit, just a core process within it. Yet many a researcher doing GT finds it hard to give up unit wholeness or full, accurate description no matter how good they are at generating abstraction. Thus they throw in many unit variables, e.g. face sheet data (sex, age, marital status, etc.) and context, that have not proven themselves as emergently needed in the generated theory, but are treated as if necessary to understand the GT. But they are not necessary unless earned into it by making a conceptual difference. Some authors even generate a good theory, such as host tolerance, but keep going on since, although it resolves the main concern, it does not fully describe the unit. Conceptual abstraction limits this 'overdue'.

Researchers not clear on the distinction between conceptual and description get easily confused on whether the theory describes a unit or conceptualises a process within it. Listen to this confusion in the writings of a well known QDA researcher, Janice Morse:

> Conversely, qualitative researchers develop theory that as accurately as possible represents the empirical world. Data analysis consists of organizing reality with inferences that

are subsequently systematically confirmed in the process of inquiry. Qualitative data theory, as a product, is abstract but consists on minimal conjecture. These theories are rich in description, and the theoretical boundaries have been derived from the context and not from the researcher's arbitrary goals for delimiting the scope (Morse 1997).

Morse continues elsewhere:

Recall that theory is theory, not fact, but as a theory is confirmed, it is moved into the realm of fact and is no longer theory. Because of the abstract nature of qualitative data theory, and because of the conceptual nature of knowledge, QDA, by and large, remains at the level of theory, not fact. Theory is not reality, but our perception or organization of reality, perhaps closely resembling reality, but not reality per se. It remains a representation of reality, malleable and modifiable (Morse 1997).

In Morse's work (1997), as the reader can see, there is no end to the confusion and mix between abstraction and concrete phenomenon or between conceptualisation and description.

People: It is hard for many GT researcher to only relate concepts and not to relate concepts to people. People become labelled or actioned by a concept like it is their whole being. In GT behaviour is a pattern that a person engages in, it is not the person. For example, he is a cultivator of people for profit; this is not GT. In GT a person engages in cultivating behaviour and cultivating is a basic social process. Labelling, a well known sociological theory, has no descriptive place in GT. People are not categorised, behaviour is. Or labelling as a basic social process occurs: people are labelled by laymen and processed accordingly. But the GT theorist only describes the labelling pattern as a social control event.

Time: Perhaps the most important aspect of conceptualisation is that concepts last forever, descriptions are stale dated. Concepts are timeless in their applicability. For example, awareness context theory can still be applied 35 years later, (see Glaser, Strauss 1965). The authors (King, Keohane, Verba 1994) make the point that concepts even last longer than any of the hypotheses in which they were originally generated.

> Max Weber has suggested that the essence of social theory is in the 'creation of clear concepts'. Indeed, concepts such as 'charisma' or 'division of labor' or 'reference groups' have been longer lasting than any valid claims about the causal effects of these concepts. Many such concepts guide our thinking and theorizing today (King, Keohane, Verba 1994)!

Since GT concepts are rigorously generated and since they can make a continuing mark on us compared to soon outdated QDA descriptions, the GT researcher has been set up to become enduringly famous or achieve renown for his/her best concept. The longevity and history of the concept is continually associated with his/her name. GT does offer fame to its researcher as opposed to QDA. It offers, also, freedom from received concepts and theoretical capitalism, because, however enduring received concepts may be, often these concepts are pure conjecture of little relevance.

Just think, the GT researcher can generate a theory, such as pluralistic dialoguing, that can be applied over and over for a 100 years or more. What significance for his GT research!

Conceptual Ability

GT is an advanced graduate level methodology used for MA and PHD theses. This statement assumes that there has been an educational institutional sifting that brings people who have conceptual talent to this level. This institutional sifting of ability puts by the wayside those who have too much difficulty in conceptualising.

But at this level ability still varies between the few who got through and have no ability to conceptualise, those who conceptualise sufficiently well, and those who are very capable. The former drift into QDA and use a few received, preconceived concepts for a forcing framework the yields lots of description. The QDA approach is just waiting to be used by those unable, or with little ability, to conceptualise.

At this level, many who can, may still have some skill difficulty in conceptualising clearly with its meaning. GT provides the method (constant comparisons) which develops skill to generate the researcher's own concepts and at the same time gives him/her the legitimacy to not jump to using the received concepts that would force the data. So, though some researchers cannot conceptualise, many more researchers can, than have heretofore generate their own categories for a study. In the beginning they no doubt will exhibit their unskilled, untrained but strong ability to conceptualise using GT techniques. But ability grows as these techniques are developmental.

Some people have a natural ability to conceptualise based on data. One external examiner of a PhD dissertation wrote me of her candidate:

> Her grasp and skill in the use of grounded theory methodology is high for her career level. What ever problems she may have can and should be solved in her next study. Her generation of substantive categories and their properties achieve parsimony and scope and fit and worked well. Her theoretical coding was very weak, but no one at her level is strong on this.

I have known many other candidates who are similar in conceptual skill. They all show that GT taps methodologically what many people do normally: conceptualise what is going on in their everyday life, as it now goes on in their research.

Those researchers with little or no conceptual ability, but who have made it to the graduate level, also have no notion of what the constant comparative method, interchangeability of indices, theoretical saturation, theoretical sampling, sorting, memos and delimiting etc. are since one needs conceptual ability to understand these methods based on conceptualisation. Their research results, again, are QDA, based on received concepts, preconceived problems, models forcing the data collection and analysis and positivistic data collection techniques.

If the researcher can conceptualise then he/she will trust to emergence of a theory. It is part of their vision and realisation that concepts will emerge. Emergence of concepts often happens fast, even too fast, and the research must be slowed a little to check out best fit concepts and their saturation.

If the researcher cannot conceptualise, then he/she will not trust to emergence of theory. How could the researcher trust to emergence, when confronted with volumes of unwieldy data, which he or she cannot get out of, or more specifically, cannot transcend conceptually. For the unable, there are few or no patterns, no delimiting just endless description, uncontained except barely by a preconceived conceptual framework or a preformed model. They have no conceptual pick-up and its associated problems as they try to analyse the data. They miss many juicy concepts and subproblems associated with them as they endeavour to describe. They even miss the participant's main concern and its resolving. I get astounded at this lack of conceptual pickup as they tend to believe as normal that which is really a problem. For example in an organisation designed to enhance creativity, people are subject to confrontation sessions to make them think of creative solutions to the challenge. The researcher did not realise that this technique can easily scare, stultify and stun a creative mind.

This is why researchers who cannot conceptualise, reach out for, even need, the theory of the participants, however particularistic and low level it may be. They forget that the participants are the data, not the theorists. The participants, while having great involvement in resolving their main concern, seldom have a conceptual perception of it as a GT theorist does. And once they hear a grounded theory of their abiding concern, they use it as power to help resolve it. Relevant concepts have this enlightening effect.

This is why, also, nonconceptualisers turn to, and need computer software to engage in rote sorting based on forced, received categories. One author who cannot conceptualise, and does not realise it, sees GT as generating data rather than generating concepts, totally missing the point:

Proponents of grounded theory use the notion of data collection (Glaser, Strauss 1967) which is central to why I chose not to use an orthodox grounded theory approach. A grounded theorist collects data on social phenomena, codes for indicators, and properties of categories which are central to understanding of the phenomena in question. What I find problematic is that this view suggests that there always is a social pattern hidden in human interaction, and it is the role of the researcher to unveil this. Basically, grounded theory advocates state that it is possible to go out and find (collect) universal truths that are embedded in intricate social interaction. But social realities arise in human interaction, data is not lying around waiting to be collected. Data can be generated in interaction with others, and the generated data depends on whom one is interacting with, where and at what point in time. The same data can never be generated again. Through data generation however, it is possible to generate a description and an interpretation (i.e. a theory) by engaging in interaction with the actors under study.

So we see that with no ability to conceptualise, this researcher defaults to accuracy problems of description, particularly the popular ones of social construction of data by interviewers and the interpretation distortions by the interviewer. She had no way of transcending the data to get at the core pattern and subpatterns and indeed finds it hard to see patterns much less name them. She is subject to total description capture.

A researcher who can adequately conceptualise can use GT and have a good career. But remember, GT is merely a research option. If conceptualisation is difficult for the research, he or she can easily have a good career in one of the many very worthy QDA methods. I know many a very intelligent researcher who cannot conceptualise. They are linear describers, good at empirical generalisations, and have successful careers. Doing GT or not is usually a self selection phenomenon, although being able to conceptualise or not may have to, or should be, told to the researcher by a friend, colleague or supervisor.

It works both ways. Good conceptualisers should be made aware of their ability if they do not know, so they can move faster into conceptual work and skill development. I was never advised by a teacher how good I was at conceptualising which slowed my career 15 years. By the same token poor conceptualisers should be advised to 'not fight it', and put their efforts into other QDA methodology. This other-reflexivity is vital in the formative years. It is a very sensitive topic for most researchers, so be careful.

Conceptual Level

I have written at length in *Doing Grounded Theory* (1998, 135-139) on conceptual levels. So here I wish only to make a few additional observations. Bear in mind, categories are generated from the data and properties are generated concepts about categories. There are many examples of this in my readers. Once discovered, concepts leave the level of people. They become the focus of the research, to be later applied to people's social psychological behaviour. As the theory generates, and integrates through memoing and sorting, the conceptual level goes up, often from substantive to formal theory (Glaser 1995).

The goal of GT is to arrive at at least the third level of conceptual analysis. First is collecting the data, then generating categories, then discovering a core category which organises the other categories by continually resolving the main concern. From substantive theory one can go to a higher level, called formal theory. For example, becoming a nurse, a substantive theory, can be generalised to becoming a professional, a formal theory, and even raised to a higher formal level of becoming in general, a theory of socialisation. This is done by theoretical sampling and constant comparisons (Glaser 1995).

Many researchers do not understand or realise the nature, use and power of categories and their properties. Most fields of study are just properties of a substantiated category or two followed by extensive description. If you listen carefully, one hears of many properties of a category as an academic or professional talks with erudition about their field. The 'best' in a field knows the most properties of the category and their most intricate integration. For example students of non-political social movements just talk of the various properties of this category and a few sub-categories.

Properties vary categories. Systems are complex ways properties of categories relate to each other and vary one category in relation to other categories. Once the research is on a conceptual level, dealing with categories and their properties becomes the mode, description fades and abstraction of time, place and people take over. The concepts do not go away: ever!

Enduring Grab: Theory Bits

Concepts in general, whether conjectured, impressionistic or carefully generated by GT, have instant 'grab'. They can instantly sensitise people, rightly or wrongly, to seeing a pattern in an event or happening that makes them feel they understand with 'know how'. In a word, the person feels like he can explain what he sees.

It is impossible to stop the grab of theory bits. The person talking with them can show his skill and power. They can be applied 'on the fly', applied intuitively with no data with the feeling of knowing. They ring true with credibility. Use of concepts empower people, they compete in conversation well and in theoretical discussions. They are exciting handles of explanations, running fast ahead of the constraints of research. They can become stereotypical and routine. As enlightening as a concept is, it can cognitively stun others in the presence of users, as they stop thinking since all appears understood.

GT emphasises the productive use of conceptual grab by generating relevant concepts that work and are integrated into a theory. It keeps grab under control and makes its endurance secured by working it in application. Of course, many will do and use GT with no idea of this property of conceptualisation, but no matter. Even the concept 'Grounded Theory' is used freely to orient and legitimate QDA research to its consumers and colleagues. It has enduring grab. QDA researchers muzzle in on the grab of GT concepts to perk up their descriptions. This bit use works well in QDA.

Upon interviewing a Buddhist *swahmee* who studied philosophy of religion at University of California, Berkeley, he told me he did not get much from most of the course, but what he did get of a lasting nature were two concepts from a famous sociology professor of religion, Robert Bellah. That is all he really remembered. He said Bellah was a genius, but was referring to the two concepts.

Thus we have the enduring grab which carries with it the great respect of the concept generator. Some of these generators, whether grounded or conjectured, produce concepts that turn them into idols and theoretical capitalists, virtual owners of their concepts. GT allows many to claim this power modestly and with grounding, while at the same time it reduces the magic of a few conjectured concepts coming from a learned man or woman. GT puts morality into this power as it brings it into reach of many researchers, and takes it out of the hands of a few.

Listen to this description of a famous theoretician, Robert K. Merton, which lauds the 'grab' of his concepts which organise the patterns of much public opinion data. The grab of received concepts is used in fields have little or no conceptualisation. A conceptualiser, like Merton, has accumulated vast conceptual capital and acts like a theoretical capitalist. He controls the capital of production by requiring that his students use his received, conjectured concepts.

Merton has shown us how to relate opinion findings to the history of ideas and to general social theory. He has demonstrated the use of many conceptual tools, for example, 'reference groups' and 'local and cosmopolitan' in interpreting the puzzling variation of public judgements. His concept of 'status-set' has given theoretical relevance to the demographics included in every poll. His concept of 'status sequence' helped us understand the opinions of socially mobile people.

As a theorist, Merton, has identified and clarified a large number of the social mechanisms that constitute the present state of sociological knowledge. Several of them are highly relevant to the field of public opinion, for example, 'the self-fulfilling prophecy'. His much quoted paradigmatic essays *Social Theory and Social Structure* (Merton 1967) are brilliant in content and in style; many of their passages qualify as aphorisms.

In appreciation of these many contributions, the world association for Public Opinion Research is pleased to present the 2000 Helen S. Dinerman Award to Robert K. Merton.

None of these concepts are truly grounded and they pale in the flood of grounded theory concepts coming from dissertations the world over. It is only time before the enduring grab of grounded concepts yield awards to their author! The awards can easily make him a great man in some quarters. Student can be required to use these concepts to honour a 'great man'. Rightly or wrongly the enduring grab of these grounded, as opposed to conjectured, concepts organise the patterns in a volume of otherwise disparate data. GT makes sure the concepts are right and organised right as they are grounded in the data. GT can generate with ease many concepts like

Merton has conjectured with seemingly great thought. The magic and mystique of these conceptualisations is over.

The next sections build on these notions of enduring conceptual 'grab'.

Conceptual Conjecture

This paper is about grounding concepts in the data to which it will be applied. This insures fit, relevance and workability. In contrast conjectured concepts, from wherever, appear to be useful given their grab, hence apparent but forced fit and relevance. They are all over the literature, and many are woven into grand theory, based on logical deduction, to wit conjecture. Once applied they often do not work either on the conceptual level or data level. But they spawn many theory bits, to make the author or talker appear learned.

Conjectured, logically deduced concepts became more and more viewed as very 'airy', too abstract, reified, irrelevant and not workable in the 1960s. Lofland wrote about

> undisciplined abstraction leading to concepts which bear little relation to the social world that they are supposed to refer to, either because they are not apparently based in any empirical research or are wondrous elaborate edifices of theory based on very little empirical research (Lofland 1976).

Lofland calls for an empirical science "that gives rise to concepts, yet contains and constrains them by a context of concrete empirical materials" (Lofland 1976).

Ten years before this statement *Discovery of Grounded theory* (Glaser, Strauss 1967) was written in response to this empty, but grabbing conjectured conceptualisation. It also gave impetus to QDA research in order to make research 'get real' or 'grounded', with little or no conceptualisation. Barry Gibson (1997) puts it well:

> GT as a method was developed in opposition to the grand theories of the time and argued for all theory to be grounded

in observations of data. The researcher should approach the data with as few preconceptions as possible in order to see what is going-on. Preconceptions often mean little or nothing when derived from received grand theory concepts (Gibson 1997)!

At the same time that '*Discovery*' was written, Robert K. Merton wrote in his 1967 book "...theory, is logically interconnected sets of propositions from which empirical uniformities can be derived" (Merton 1967). This statement from a famous theorist such as Merton, was virtually a license to conjecture theory. The researcher at the time experienced great cross pressure between license for logically deducing theory and our demand that it can only be grounded to be relevant.

Reification was out, grounding was in, and the problem arose as to just how many researchers had conceptual ability to change to grounding. Our answer was more researchers than were heretofore allowed to. Anselm and I gave researchers the license to generate concepts on one's own and ignore the theoretical capitalists, idols and great men. They were always there for those who could not conceptualise on their own.

Research goal changes from theory based on unobserved to explain more unobserved, to GT theory generated from observation to explain the observed. In the standard appeal to future research of a GT article the author could conjecture a bit based on conceptual deduction from grounded concepts as he suggests next research steps; the only conjecture allowed which is a form of theoretical sampling.

Put simply, in putting a constraint on conjectural theory, based on the unobserved and thereby distrusted, GT gained theoretical leverage for social psychology in generating theory that could be trusted as fitting and relevant to the data. Social theory was rescued by GT from its growing disaffection by laymen and from being discounted as too airy by them. GT made theory accountable to others as it was right on and worked.

Conceptual Description

Conceptual description is a frequent occurrence among researchers trying to do GT. They even call it GT, but it is really a form of QDA. One concept is generated and then the researcher spends the rest of his time describing it and describing it with incident after incident. There is little or no constant comparative work to generate conceptual properties of the category based on the interchangeability of indices and conceptual saturation. The researcher just 'incident trips' with no more conceptual analysis (Glaser 1998, 162-165). The researcher just goes on and on over describing with no more conceptual analysis. Story after story is forced into the concept. It reads like story sharing at a party. It is conceptual grab by one concept gone wild.

There are two types of interrelated sources of conceptual description: the researcher's skill and the concept's source. It is done by researchers with limited ability to conceptualise and to relate concepts theoretically. The thrill of generating one concept is all they need and can handle. Close colleagues, who are use to QDA, can unawaredly pressure the researcher into lots of description. Some researchers cannot handle the tedium of conceptualisation by constant comparison while coding, collecting by theoretical sampling and analysing, writing up theoretical memos and saturating the concept. In actuality a researcher may get to two of three concepts which is even more strain on conceptual theorising for the conceptually unable. Thus we see many conceptual descriptions.

Mixed into these sources of conceptual description among researchers are the sources of the concept. One major source is to read through an interview 2 or 3 times for an overview of what is going on and conceptualising it. This overview impression source of a concept can be so grabbing that incident tripping (called description by others) takes over and that's it. Since the rigor of line by line study of the interview and then careful comparing incident to incident and then to concept, and constant theoretical sampling is abdicated, there is no control over the tendency to conceptual description. In QDA fashion it appears the way to explicate the concept.

Another source of concept that leads to incident tripping is the one incident concept. It is usually way over analysed and once the incident is conceptualised the tendency is to describe it *ad infinitum*. A one incident concept is not a careful generation of a pattern. It is not a pattern. It is a conjecture. Its name can have tremendous grab and since there is no more analysis, conceptual description ensues. This happens frequently with beginning researchers who may discuss at length what one incident means. They are not used to or trained to continually coding and analysing and therefore conceptually saturating the concept thereby discovering its properties and that it is a true pattern. The one incident may prove to be just that: one incident, and not relevant to much. In GT the researcher must keep moving through the data to see the incident over and over and constantly comparing and conceptualising. This is not easy. Researchers easily default to QDA.

To be sure, conceptual description can also result from a carefully generated concept. The concept can have so much grab and the researcher so thrilled, with no taste for the tedium of constant comparison, etc., that describing ensues at great length.

A colleague also advised me that there are fields with an overload of received concepts, such as his: business management, where one starts with the received concepts and tries to force many incidents into the meaning of the chosen concept. Conceptual description ensues. It is preconception to the max! Bengt Gustavsson, teacher and author of a GT book in Swedish (Gusatvsson 1998), says in a writing to me:

> to repeat, my main problem as a management teacher is to deconstruct all the fancy, but ill-grounded, conceptions in the management field, e.g., knowledge management, customer relationship marketing, virtual organizations employability, and intellectual capital. It turns out that although they are in vogue, nobody really knows what they stand for.

Fields like this may have many reified concepts (concepts with no empirical referents) so even conceptual description is hard. GT in these fields puts grounded concepts into direct competition with the field's conceptual jargon, which itself can cause conceptual description to undo the jargon.

The dosage mix between conceptual hypotheses and conceptual description is, of course, the prerogative of the GT researcher. It is his product.

Conceptual Foppery

Closely related to conceptual description but at the other end of the continuum is conceptual foppery. This occurs when every incident in sight is conceptualised with no theoretical meaning deriving from a clear focus an analysis of a main concern and its resolving. Dozens of one incident concepts are offered with no problem, no theoretical integration, no constant comparison, no realisation of prime mover of the people's predominant behaviour, no proven patterns, etc. No parsimony and scope are sought. The license to generate has gone wild! Too many concepts go every which way with no relation to 'whatever'! Conceptualisation in GT must be done as a careful part of its generating and emergence, with each concept earning its way with relevance into the theory.

Concept foppery is engaged in by researchers who can conceptualise one incident easily, but cannot compare many incidents. They do not seem to see patterns. The sensitivity of the concept is enough to imply patterns. They also dip into reification easily without knowing it. There are academic subfields in business and psychology where concept volume, grounded or not, is the thing with little or no regard for data.

Close to concept foppery is concept vagary. The concept rings true and is sensitising at first blush. But then it seems vague or sufficiently undetailed so the reader does not know what is being referred to or discussed. The grab starts to diminish. Theory bits are often quite vague upon examination. People use concept vagary like descriptive vagary, in order to not reveal sensitive information. It obfuscates. If vague concepts are submitted to conceptual description, the description becomes vague also.

GT, of course, does not produce and perforce does allow concept vagary if the category and its properties are carefully generated and saturated conceptually. By definition the concept fits with clarity. Properties of a category substruct it by showing its degrees, dimensions, aspects, types etc. These properties become the categories' clear definition.

Conceptual Power

Given our above discussion of conceptualisation, especially that of conceptual grab, most people feel the power of conceptualisation and its ability to transcend the descriptive, its ability to generate 'wise' propositions that explain behaviour in an area, especially its main concern, its ability to organise and make meaningful many seemingly disparate incidences, its ability to be used or applied as a wise academic and/or consultant.

GT gives the researcher this power. He/she becomes an expert in the substantive area of their study. The researcher is asked to guest lecture and to consult on the subject. For example one grounded theorist who did his dissertation on "enhancing creativity" in bureaucratic organisations gives lectures to many corporations on this subject as an expert.

Most GT researchers do not fully realise this power of abstractedness. They allude to the power, but cannot quite formulate it or precise it. Yet it is up to the GT researcher to use it and give it and show it to others not only in the substantive field from whence it was generated, but in other areas, and to laymen. The GT power gives control by its sensitising, enduring grab, its generalisability and its being abstract from time, place and people!

Listen to Wendy Guthrie allude to this power while not quite precising it:

> The veterinarian is undisputed in his ability to describe the way things work in his domain. He does not welcome an outsider telling him what he already knows. The explanatory power characteristic of grounded theory is where the difference lies. It gives practitioners a new conceptual understanding and control over actions like never before. Even when confronted by novel situations, conceptual theory yields powerful predictive ability enabling those with access to it to influence the direction ahead with recourse to appropriately selected strategies. Grounded theory elevates the theorist to an influential level. Description on the other hand, complicates and distracts (Guthrie 2000).

Guthrie is very close to seeing the power and control of GT. Others are not so close, but feel and see it strongly. Listen to Janice Morse,

...the identification of theory or a model that enables the case study to generalize to other cases. It is important to note that this linkage is done conceptually – in this case using the concepts of enduring and suffering – and it is this abstraction from the descriptive data that makes the study more powerful (Morse 1997).

So why not just go for the power of GT? Timidity is the answer, Morse says:

Qualitative researchers are theoretically timid. Some researchers may be more comfortable staying within the safety zone of their data. They may be unwilling to take the risk inherent in interpretation and move their analysis beyond the descriptive level. Theorising is also work: often researchers make the mistake of submitting their study for publication without making the effort to do the conceptual work necessary for the development of theory (Mores 1997).

She is no doubt right about timidity, but not doing the conceptual work is not quite correct. They simply do not know nor have training in GT, so they are at loggerheads on how to do conceptualisation. After learning GT, I have seen many a researcher lose the timidity that comes with knowing how to conceptualise and feeling its power.

Lastly, Morse does not realise the full power of GT. So she sees a continuum with no power valence. She says: "Qualitative research as a product may be classified according to the level of theoretical abstraction. This ranges from the most descriptive research to the most abstract, generalizable research, ..." (Morse 1997). The categories of her outline are neutral to the growing power of abstraction as QDA turns to GT. QDA and GT are confused, as always.

Barry Gibson, a well known GT researcher extols the conceptualisation of GT, but does not clearly extol the power of it. He says:

> As stated previously the procedures underlying grounded theory are not designed to yield themes within the data, but are aimed at developing a theory. By theory what is intended is a conceptual account of the 'main concerns' of those resolving a particular problem. Grounded theories are therefore conceptual communication concerning observation on how persons resolve particular problems in a particular area (such as health care or business organizations) (Gibson 1997).

He is quite correct but he does not say that these conceptual communications on accounting for the behaviours in a substantive area are quite powerful. So near and yet so far.

King, Keohane and Verba, political science researchers, actually turn to briefly bring out the power of concepts in the following: "Compelling concepts need not be part of a valid causal inference to be powerful, but to remain powerful, these concepts must be part of a research agenda that seeks to identify their systemic implications, revealing their link on a causal chain" (King, Keohane, Verba 1994). To be sure the power of conceptual grab is there and it does endure, not fade. But endurance is enhanced by the concept being integrated into a grounded theory that endures also.

In the section on conceptual grab above, we have seen the power of Robert K. Merton's concepts to organise with meaning public opinion findings and to relate them to general social theory. Exercising this power brings renown, even fame, since there are so few good conceptualises. GT, a rigorous conceptualising method, gives many an average researcher a chance at such renown.

This is a long paper, and obviously, could be longer since there are many more properties of conceptualisation. I have tried to discuss those most pertinent to GT.

References

Gibson, B. (1997). *Dangerous Dentaling. A Grounded Theory of HIV and Dentistry.* Queens University of Belfast (PhD Dissertation).

Glaser, B. (1998). *Doing Grounded Theory. Issues and Discussions.* Mill Valley, CA.

Glaser, B. (ed.) (1996). *Gerund Grounded Theory. The Basic Social Process Dissertation* (Reviews Eleven Dissertations). Mill Valley, CA.

Glaser, B. (ed.) (1995). *More Grounded Theory Methodology.* Mill Valley, CA.

Glaser, B. (1992). *Basics of Grounded Theory Analysis. Emergence vs Forcing.* Mill Valley, CA.

Glaser, B. (1978). *Theoretical Sensitivity. Advances in the Methodology of Grounded Theory.* Mill Valley, CA.

Glaser, B., Strauss, A. L. (1967). *The Discovery of Grounded Theory. Strategies for Qualitative Research.* Chicago (Reprint: Glaser, B. (1999). *The Discovery of Grounded Theory.* New York).

Glaser, B., Strauss, A. L. (1965). *Awareness of Dying.* Chicago.

Gustavsson, B. (1998). *Grundad Teori för företagsskonomer.* Lund.

Guthrie, W. (2000). *Keeping Clients in Line. A Grounded Theory Explaining How Veterinary Surgeons Control Their Clients.* University of Strathclyde, Scotland (PhD Dissertation).

King, G., Keohane, Verba, (1994). *Designing Social Inquiry. Scientific Inference in Qualitative Research.* Princeton.

Lofland, J. (1976). *Doing Social Life. The Qualitative Study of Human Interaction in Natural Settings.* New York, London.

Merton, R. K. (1967). *On Theoretical Sociology. Five Essays, Old and New.* New York.

Morse, J. (ed.) (1997). *Completing a Qualitative Project. Details and Dialoque.* New York.

AUTHORS

Peter Alheit, Professor
University of Göttingen
Institute of Education
Chair of Education
37033 Göttingen – Germany
palheit@gwdg.de

Agnieszka Bron, Professor
Institute of Education
Chair of Adult Education
44780 Bochum – Germany
agnieszka.bron@ruhr-uni-bochum.de

Etienne Bourgeois, Professor
Université catholique de Louvain
Department of Education / FORG
1348 Louvain-la-Neuve – Belgium
etienne.bourgeois@psp.ucl.ac.be
bourgeois@forg.ucl.ac.be

Bettina Dausien, Ph.D.
University of Bielefeld
Institute of Education
AG 2 Sozialisation
33501 Bielefeld – Germany
bettina.dausien@uni-bielefeld.de

Barney G. Glaser, Ph.D.
Sociology Press
P.O. Box 400
Mill Valley, CA 94942 – U.S.A.
BGlaser@linex.com

Barry J. Hake, Ph.D.
University of Leiden
Institute for the Study of Education
and Human Development
2300 Leiden – The Netherlands
hake@fsw.LeidenUniv.nl

Jon Ohlsson, Ph.D.
Stockholm University
Department of Education
10691 Stockholm – Sweden
jon.ohlsson@ped.su.se

Edmée Ollagnier, Ph.D.   Université de Genève
                         Faculty of Psychology and Education
                         FAPSE
                         1227 Carouge – Switzerland
                         edmee.ollagnier@pse.unige.ch

Michael Schemmann, Ph.D. Ruhr-University of Bochum
                         Institute of Education
                         Chair of Adult Education
                         44780 Bochum – Germany
                         michael.schemmann@ruhr-uni-bochum.de

Horst Siebert, Professor University of Hannover
                         Faculty of Education
                         Institute of Adult Education
                         30173 Hannover – Germany
                         eb@erz.uni-hannover.de

Piotr Sztompka, Professor University of Krakow
                         Institute of Sociology
                         31044 Krakow – Poland
                         ussztomp@cyf-kr.edu.pl

Linden West, Ph.D.   Canterbury Christ Church
                         University College
                         Neville House, 90-1 Northgate
                         Canterbury, Kent CT1 1BA – UK
                         lrw4@cant.ac.uk

Lena Wilhelmson, Ph.D.   National Institute for Working Life
                         Organisational Development and
                         Learning
                         11279 Stockholm – Sweden
                         lena.wilhelmson@niwl.se

Bochum Studies
in International Adult Education
edited by Agnieszka Bron and Michael Schemmann
Editorial Board: Joachim H. Knoll,
Agnieszka Bron, Michał Bron Jr., Linden West,
Edmée Ollagnier, Anja Heikkinen, Paul Bélanger

Agnieszka Bron; Michael Schemmann (eds.)
Language – Mobility – Identity
Contemporary Issues for Adult Education in Europe
With the first volume of Bochum Studies in International Adult Education we are launching a new series of publications from the Chair of Adult Education at the Ruhr-University of Bochum. BSIAE addresses not only researchers, university teachers and students of adult education but also those from related disciplines. While not explicitly addressing practitioners, except for providing them with up-to-date research overviews, each issue will also address politicans and policy makers.
Each volume will be organised around one topic or issue which is of interest, importance or of particular relevance for adult education in general. This particular topic will be considered from various points of view, i. e. comparative, historical, gender, socio-political and cultural.
The first volume of BSIAE intends to look closely at the topcis Language – Mobility – Identity and attempts to discuss these issues from the point of view of adult education. The intention of this volume is to create a compilation of different viewpoints and critical analyses on the three topics which together form an overview of their interrelation and their relevance for European development, adult education and adult's learning.
Bd. 1, 2000, 240 S., 20,90 €, br., ISBN 3-8258-4364-5

Agnieszka Bron; Michael Schemmann (Eds.)
Civil Society, Citizenship and Learning
Writing the story of democracy might seem like writing a story of success. In more and more countries all over the world democracy has been established as the leading form of government. However, democracy also has a less positive and optimistic side. Political scandals and corruption continue to shatter people's trust in its promises and institutions. This brings us to the topic of active democratic citizenship and civil society. Since the late 1980s these topics have continued to rise in importance in the fields of social and political sciences, and their influence has yet to reach a peak.
In comparison, civil society and citizenship remain relatively new topics for adult education, dating to the beginning of the 1990s. We also see that the respective national discourses within the different European countries differ immensely. Whereas the discourse on adult education and active democratic citizenship is quite lively in Great Britain or in Poland, in Germany there is only very little interest.
"Civil Society, Citizenship and Learning", the second volume of the Bochum Studies in International Adult Education, presents a variety of different perspectives on the topics of citizenship and civil society. The goal of this book is to give an overview of the European discourse on citizenship and civil society as well as on the discourse in some selected countries.
Bd. 2, 2001, 320 S., 20,90 €, br., ISBN 3-8258-5324-1

Texte zur Theorie und Geschichte der Bildung
herausgegeben von
Friedhelm Brüggen (Westfälische Wilhelms-Universität Münster),
Karl-Franz Göstemeyer
(Humboldt Universität Berlin)
und Petra Korte
(Technische Universität Braunschweig)

Ursula Reitemeyer
Perfektibilität gegen Perfektion
Rousseaus Theorie gesellschaftlicher Praxis
Bd. 4, 1996, 232 S., 30,90 €, br., ISBN 3-8258-2643-0

Lothar Böttcher; Reinhard Golz (Hrsg.)
Reformpädagogik und pädagogische Reformen in Mittel- und Osteuropa
Bd. 5, 1995, 320 S., 24,90 €, gb., ISBN 3-8258-2518-3

Hans-Eckehard Landwehr
Bildung – Sprache – altsprachlicher Unterricht
Eine Studie zur sprachtheoretischen Grundlegung pädagogischen Handelns bei Wilhelm von Humboldt
Bd. 6, 1996, 376 S., 35,90 €, gb., ISBN 3-8258-2811-5

Wolfgang Eichler
Bürgerliche Konzepte Allgemeiner Pädagogik
Theoriegeschichtliche Studien und Überblicke
Bd. 7, 1997, 384 S., 30,90 €, br., ISBN 3-8258-2997-9

Reinhard Golz; Wolfgang Mayrhofer (Hrsg.)
Luther und Melanchthon im Bildungsdenken Mittel- und Osteuropas
Bd. 8, 1997, 392 S., 25,90 €, br., ISBN 3-8258-3280-5

LIT Verlag Münster – Hamburg – Berlin – London
Grevener Str. 179 48159 Münster
Tel.: 0251 – 23 50 91 – Fax: 0251 – 23 19 72
e-Mail: vertrieb@lit-verlag.de – http://www.lit-verlag.de
Preise: unv. PE

Günter Dresselhaus
Das deutsche Bildungswesen zwischen Tradition und Fortschritt – Analyse eines Sonderwegs
Bd. 9, 1997, 176 S., 35,90 €, br., ISBN 3-8258-3356-9

Reinhard Golz; Wolfgang Mayrhofer (ed.)
Luther and Melanchthon in the Educational Thought of Central and Eastern Europe
Bd. 10, 1998, 232 S., 24,90 €, br., ISBN 3-8258-3490-5

Bernd Weber
Zwischen Gemütsbildung und Mündigkeit 1690 bis 1990
300 Jahre Annette von Droste-Hülshoff-Gymnasium Münster
Bd. 11, 1998, 440 S., 25,90 €, br., ISBN 3-8258-3866-8

Dietmar Engfer
Werteerziehung im öffentlichen Schulwesen?
Zwischen Ideologie und Desorientierung
Einfluß zu nehmen auf die Entwicklung von jungen Menschen, ihnen dadurch einen *wert*vollen Auftakt in die Freiheit der Selbstverantwortung zu ermöglichen, das ist sicher unbestritten das Ziel einer Erziehung in Elternhaus und Schule. Der Weg dazu wird immer häufiger mit dem schillernden Begriff der Werteerziehung beschrieben, der jedoch über Festreden, Richtlinien und Lehrpläne hinaus bald in den Erziehungsnebel der Praxis eines öffentlichen Schulwesens führt. Demgegenüber untersucht der Verfasser drei erfolgreiche inhomogene Schulerziehungskonzepte, die in die Lebensentwürfe ihrer Schülerinnen und Schüler eingingen. Dazu ließ die auf die marxistisch-leninistische Weltanschauung gegründete öffentliche Schule der DDR, die mit dem Untergang ihres ideologischen Staates ins Dunkel der Geschichte gestellt wurde, ohne ihre wertebezogene Erziehung vorurteilslos zu beleuchten. Ebenso blieb bisher der Erziehungserfolg der weltweiten anthroposophisch fundierten Waldorfschulbewegung zwischen pädagogischer Bewunderung und ständigem Indoktrinationsverdacht ungeklärt. Auch die auf christlicher Basis stehenden Schulen werden in einer pluralistischen Gesellschaft, die im Kruzifix nicht mehr ihre Grundlage symbolisiert sieht und im Religionsunterricht ein Relikt ausmacht, zunehmend kritisiert. Das hier vorgetragene wissenschaftliche Plädoyer gilt einer weltanschaulich pluralen Edukation, die nicht länger die Erziehungskongruenz der öffentlichen Schulen zum Ziel hat, für die aber dennoch ein kulturbezogener Konsens im unaufgebbaren gesellschaftlichen Dissens grundlegend ist.
Bd. 12, 1999, 432 S., 35,90 €, br., ISBN 3-8258-4157-x

Wolfgang Eichler
Der Stein des Sisyphos
Studien zur Allgemeinen Pädagogik in der DDR
Die Arbeit untersucht Ansätze zu einer neuen Grundlegung der Erziehungswissenschaft in der SBZ, die Suche der DDR-Pädagogik nach einer eigenen Identität in Systematisierungsversuchen der 50er Jahre, die Anfänge zur Herausbildung wissenschaftlicher Schulen im pädagogischen Grundlagenbereich während der 60er Jahre und die Bemühungen um die komplexe Entwicklung der Allgemeinen Pädagogik als Wissenschaftsdisziplin in den 70er und 80er Jahren. Dabei werden Versuche zur Entwicklung theoretischer Konzepte sowohl durch prominente Erziehungswissenschaftler der SBZ und DDR wie Max Gustav Lange, Werner Dorst, Hans Herbert Becker, Franz Hofmann und Gerhart Neuner als auch weniger bekannte Bestrebungen dargestellt. Es wird gezeigt, wie diese Arbeiten trotz Berufung auf den Marxismus und Verpflichtung auf die politische und erzieherische Praxis in der DDR immer wieder eingeschränkt, behindert, abgebrochen oder aufgegeben wurden, wie beachtenswerte Anfänge dem theoriegeschichtlichen Selbstverständnis verlorengingen. Zugleich wird sichtbar, wie stets erneut versucht wurde, dem dringenden Bedürfnis nach grundlagentheoretischer Selbstverständigung zu entsprechen, dem Anspruch auf die wissenschaftliche Bearbeitung der Erziehungswirklichkeit in ihrer Gesamtheit und gesellschaftlichen Vermittlung geltend zu machen und Allgemeine Pädagogik als Grundlagendisziplin des pädagogischen Wissenschaftsgebietes zu etablieren. Dabei wurde ein Lernprozeß konstituiert, der zwar mühsam und nicht hinreichend konsequent und effektiv, sich an gesellschafts- und persönlichkeitstheoretische Grundprobleme heranarbeitete und so etwas wie eine "Pluralität der Konzepte" (Cloer) hervorbrachte. Die Entwicklung der DDR-Pädagogik wird so mit ihrem eigenen Anspruch und mit den ihr immanenten Kriterien konfrontiert. Dem Betrachter von außen wird damit ein differenzierter Einblick in die Wissenschaftslandschaft der DDR-Pädagogik ermöglicht.
Bd. 13, 2000, 536 S., 35,90 €, br., ISBN 3-8258-4413-7

Stefan Meißner
Vom Schulstreit zum Marchtaler Plan
Die Wurzeln eines Erziehungs- und Bildungsplans in der südwestdeutschen Kirchen-, Gesellschafts- und Schulgeschichte der Jahre 1945 – 1967
Gegenwärtig ist im Schulwesen der Bundesrepublik Deutschland vieles in Bewegung gekommen. Die fortschreitende Computerisierung, Vernetzung und Beschleunigung in der Informationsgesell-

LIT Verlag Münster – Hamburg – Berlin – London
Grevener Str. 179 48159 Münster
Tel.: 0251 – 23 50 91 – Fax: 0251 – 23 19 72
e-Mail: vertrieb@lit-verlag.de – http://www.lit-verlag.de

Preise: unv. PE

schaft der letzten Jahre haben ein Nachdenken über die angemessene Bildung des Menschen ausgelöst, das sich im Schulbetrieb in angestrengter und mitunter hektischer Betriebsamkeit Ausdruck verschafft. Angesichts des raschen Wandels von gesellschaftlichen Normen und Plausibilitäten in den letzten fünfzig Jahren, der sich unter anderem im einem schwindenden Ansehen der großen christlichen Kirchen auswirkt, stellt sich für konfessionell geprägte christliche Schulen die Frage nach einer angemessenen und zeitunmittelbaren Umsetzung ihres Bildungsauftrags. Die vorliegende Studie versucht an diese Frage eine Annäherung am Beispiel der katholischen Bekenntnisschulen in (Süd-) Württemberg. Die Um- und Aufbrüche in diesem Segment des Schulwesens kulminieren in den Bemühungen um den "Marchtaler Plan", den Erziehungs- und Bildungsplan der katholischen Freien Schulen in der Diözese Rottenburg-Stuttgart. Das Ziel dieser Studie, die methodisch "gegen den Trend" bewußt die Verlangsamung sucht, ist es, nachdem dogmatisch orientierte Modelle konfessionell geprägter Schule im sogenannten "Schulstreit" gescheitert sind, die Optionen, die mit dem Konzept des "Marchtaler Plans" verbunden sind, in den Horizont der Schulgeschichte des ausgehenden zwanzigsten Jahrhunderts zu rücken. Aus dem historischen Vergleich können Euphorie und Verunsicherungen in der Gegenwart korrigiert werden.
Bd. 14, 2000, 272 S., 25,90 €, br., ISBN 3-8258-4524-9

Ilse Bürmann; Monika Fiegert; Petra Korte (Hrsg.)
Zeitalter der Aufklärung – Zeitalter der Pädagogik
Zu den Ambivalenzen einer Epoche. Mit Beiträgen von Ernst Cloer, Monika Fiegert, Alfred Langewand, Jürgen Oelkers, Horst G. Pöhlmann und Jörg Ruhloff
In sechs Beiträgen Ambivalenzen der Aufklärungspädagogik darzustellen ist das Ziel des vorliegenden Tagungsbandes. Indem die Spannungen und Polaritäten zwischen Verstandesaufklärung und traditioneller Lebensform, individueller Freiheit und gesellschaftlichen Zwängen, magischen Welterklärungen und kritischer Vernunft, Animalität und Vernunftfähigkeit zu immer neuen Klärungsversuchen herausfordern, stellt sich Aufklärung als ein unabgeschlossener Prozeß dar.
Bd. 15, 2000, 150 S., 20,90 €, br., ISBN 3-8258-4548-6

Marion Wagner (Hrsg.)
Wozu kirchliche Schulen?
Profile, Probleme und Projekte: Ein Beitrag zur aktuellen Bildungsdiskussion
Kirchliche Schulen sehen sich einer steigenden Nachfrage gegenüber. Diese Tatsache kann für die kirchlichen Schulen kein Grund sein, sich zufrieden zurückzulehnen, sondern gibt ihnen vielmehr Anlaß, sich der Frage nach dem unterscheidend Anderen der kirchlichen Schule zu stellen. Hanna Renate Laurien, Eckhard Nordhofen, Manfred Baldus, Volker Ladentin, Klaus Mertes SJ und Marion Wagner beantworten die Frage aus bildungspolitischer, pädagogischer, theologisch-kirchlicher und juristischer Sicht. Doris Sennekamp macht deutlich, warum Eltern für ihr Kind eine kirchliche Schule wählen. Frido Pflüger SJ und Rüdiger Kaldewey zeigen stellvertretend für viele, wie sich die von ihnen geleiteten Schulen den Herausforderungen der Zeit stellen.
Bd. 16, 2001, 184 S., 15,90 €, br., ISBN 3-8258-4880-9

Volker Steenblock
Arbeit am Logos
Aufstieg und Krise der wissenschaftlichen Vernunft
Mit dem *Logos*, dem argumentativen und auf Gründe gestützten Denken, beginnt der lange Prozeß der ihrer selbst bewußten kulturellen Arbeit von Philosophie und Wissenschaft. Durch den Aufstieg der modernen Wissenschaften steht die Logos heute im Zeichen der wissenschaftlichen Vernunft. Was wir von der Welt zu wissen glauben, ist von ihren Ergebnissen, und was wir für vernünftig halten, ist von ihrem Denkstil entscheidend geprägt.
Wissenschaftliche Vernunft zu entwickeln, hieß aber für den Menschen zugleich – und heißt es gerade heute: – einen Tiger zu reiten. Die wissenschaftlich-technische Revolution setzt zivilisatorische Prozesse in Gang, denen wir viel verdanken, die aber auch eine Lawine ausgelöst haben, deren mitreißender Kraft wir heute mehr denn je ausgesetzt sind. Globale Probleme, "Grenzen des Wachstums" und deren Widerhall in den theoretischen Produktionen der Philosophie und Wissenschaftstheorie bezeichnen eine *Krise der wissenschaftlichen Vernunft*.
Angesichts ihres "apokalyptischen Soges" gilt es, den Weg sowie die Risiken und Chancen dieser Errungenschaft auszuloten, die unsere Zivilisation antreibt. Eine "Arbeit am Logos" erscheint dringlicher denn je. Wie nachhaltig eine philosophische und gesellschaftliche Reflexion von Zielen und Zwecken das Machen des Machbaren begleiten, und womöglich, zunehmend steuern kann: hiervon wird abhängen, ob und inwiefern unsere Lebensverhältnisse noch das Produkt menschlicher Arbeit und Kooperation, inwieweit sie *Kultur* sein werden. Das szientifische Wissen muß, individuell und für alle, auf *Bildung* hin entwickelt werden.
Bd. 17, 2000, 264 S., 25,90 €, br., ISBN 3-8258-4967-8

LIT Verlag Münster – Hamburg – Berlin – London
Grevener Str. 179 48159 Münster
Tel.: 0251 – 23 50 91 – Fax: 0251 – 23 19 72
e-Mail: vertrieb@lit-verlag.de – http://www.lit-verlag.de

Preise: unv. PE

Roland Baecker
Reformpädagogische Praxis
Eine lern- und bildungstheoretische Auseinandersetzung über deren Möglichkeiten und Grenzen: dargestellt am Beispiel neuerer "Argumentationsfiguren" in der Erziehungswissenschaft
Dem "Offenen Unterricht" und der "Community Education" – zwei Argumentationsfiguren, die in der Auseinandersetzung um reformpädagogische Vorstellungen häufig bemüht werden – liegt die Idee einer "pädagogischen Haltung" als konzeptionelle Basis für Lehr-Lern-Prozesse zugrunde.
Das Konstrukt einer "pädagogischen Haltung" verhindert einen differenzierten Blick auf die realen Bedingungen, theoretischen Grundlagen und praktischen Möglichkeiten, selbstbestimmte und sich selbst organisierende Subjekte auszubilden. Das empirische Subjekt als reflexives, aktives und intentionales Wesen anthropologisch zu setzen und daraus die Konsequenz abzuleiten, selbstbestimmte und -organisierte Lernprozesse als das adäquate methodische Vermittlungsprinzip auszuweisen, ist nicht begründbar. Menschen sind als zu vernünftiger Selbstbestimmung fähige Wesen zu begreifen, d. h. sie sind prinzipiell in der Lage, vernünftige Selbstbestimmung bzw. Subjektivität (und damit sich selbst bildende Subjekte) auszubilden. Diese Subjektivität herzustellen, ist die Aufgabe von Bildungsprozessen: "Als Individuum ist der Mensch nur potentiell Subjekt, aktuell erst als Resultat der Bildung." Die unhinterfragte Setzung einer anthropologisch bedingten Subjektivität sowie die Förderung dieser durch selbstbestimmte und selbstorganisierte Lernprozesse bildet im Individuum dagegen tendenziell eine Fähigkeit zur 'schrankenlosen Lernbereitschaft' und bloßen Anpassung an die gesellschaftlich-funktionalen Prozesse aus. – Diese Form von Subjektivität, reduziert das Individuum auf eine "Selbstbehauptung ohne Selbst" und konterkariert damit letztlich die konzeptionellen Zielvorstellungen von Offenem Unterricht und Community Education.
Bd. 18, 2000, 360 S., 25,90 €, br., ISBN 3-8258-4911-2

Günter Dresselhaus
Weiterbildung in Deutschland
Entwicklungen und Herausforderungen am Beispiel des Zweiten Bildungsweges in Nordrhein-Westfalen
Weiterbildung ist ein zentrales Thema dieser Jahre. Viele beklagen die Qualität von Weiterbildung, aber kaum jemand weiß, wie sie verbessert werden kann. Dieses Arbeitsbuch beschäftigt sich mit den neuen Herausforderungen und mit den sich wandelnden Aufgaben, die angesichts der Dimensionen und Geschwindigkeiten von Veränderungen in unserer Gesellschaft künftig mehr oder weniger massiv an Einrichtungen des Zweiten Bildungsweges gestellt werden.
Der Autor beleuchtet zunächst die Entwicklungsgeschichte des ZBW in Deutschland, um hernach eine Bestandsaufnahme der jüngeren Entwicklung nach dem Zweiten Weltkrieg in Nordrhein-Westfalen vorzunehmen.
Bd. 19, 2001, 176 S., 15,90 €, br., ISBN 3-8258-5552-x

Günter Dresselhaus
Pädagogische Qualitätsentwicklung
Der Zweite Bildungsweg: Vorbild für neue Wege?
Dieses Buch von Günter Dresselhaus ist die Nachfolgestudie zu seinem Werk "Weiterbildung in Deutschland – Entwicklungen und Herausforderungen am Beispiel des Zweiten Bildungswegs in Nordrhein-Westfalen". Es beschäftigt sich im Wesentlichen mit den Herausforderungen, die künftig in noch stärkerem Maße an die einzelnen Schulen gestellt werden, sowie mit der interessanten Frage, warum im Rahmen einer erweiterten Selbstständigkeit von Schule dem Zweiten Bildungsweg eine Vorbildfunktion zukommen könnte. Im Zentrum der systematischen Darstellung stehen die Themen: Stärkere Eigenverantwortung von Schule, Schule als lernende Organisation, Evaluation – Zu ihrer Bedeutung für die innerschulische Entwicklung, Selbstorganisiertes Lernen.
Die Arbeit dürfte all denjenigen wertvolle Einsichten und praktische Hilfen bieten, die einmal erfahren möchten, mit welchen Instrumenten man im Zweiten Bildungsweg versucht, den Herausforderungen einer erweiterten Selbstständigkeit von Schule zu begegnen.
Bd. 20, 2001, 320 S., 25,90 €, br., ISBN 3-8258-5717-4

Junge Lebenswelt
Sozialisation jenseits der Schule
herausgegeben von Joachim H. Knoll
(Bochum / Hamburg)

Joachim H. Knoll
Jugend, Jugendgefährdung, Jugendmedienschutz
Der *rechtliche Jugendmedienschutz* reicht in Deutschland bis in die Gesetzgebung und Rechtsprechung der Weimarer Republik zurück und gilt im europäischen Vergleich als ein nahezu perfektes Regelungsinstrument. Die *Freiwillige Selbstkontrolle* der Medienanbieter wird heute als *Korrektiv und Ergänzung* des staatlichen Jugendmedienschutzes mit zunehmender Wertschätzung versehen. Da die neue Schriftenreihe Phänomene der außerschulischen Sozialisation beschreiben und kommentieren möchte, gebührt

L**IT** Verlag Münster – Hamburg – Berlin – London
Grevener Str. 179 48159 Münster
Tel.: 0251 – 23 50 91 – Fax: 0251 – 23 19 72
e-Mail: vertrieb@lit-verlag.de – http://www.lit-verlag.de

Preise: unv. PE

der Sozialisation durch Medien eine erhebliche Aufmerksamkeit, zumal wenn man Jugendliche Lebenswelt als Medienwelt begreift und sie auch solchermaßen beschreibt.
Im ersten Band wird Jugendmedienschutz im Spannungsfeld von gesetzlichen Vorgaben und der begründeten Sachkompetenz Freiwilliger Selbstkontrolle erläutert. Dabei wird das Verhältnis von Staat und Gesellschaft im Rahmen des Jugendschutzes ebenso behandelt, wie Werte- und Normfragen, die Leitlinien für einen pädagogisch begründeten Jugendschutz angesichts veränderter Selbstkonzepte Jugendlicher vorzeichnen können. Die Beobachtungen werden vor allem im Widerschein von Gutachten und Stellungnahmen des Verfassers konkretisiert und zwar im Hinblick auf Gefährdungen, die entweder tatsächlich vorhanden sind oder durch tradierte Vorurteile vermutet werden. "Gewalt" und "Pornographie" treten als Tatbestandsmerkmale der Jugendgefährdung besonders hervor. Daneben werden Grundfragen der sozialethischen Orientierung und der Altersdefinition Jugendlicher ausführlich erörtert. Der Verfasser setzt auf eine liberal verfaßte Selbstkontrolle, die er als Ausdruck gesellschaftlicher Selbstregulation versteht.
Bd. 1, 2000, 212 S., 17,90 €, br., ISBN 3-8258-4209-6

Pädagogische Beiträge zur sozialen und kulturellen Entwicklung
herausgegeben von Prof. Dr. Renate Girmes (Universität Magdeburg), Prof. Dr. Winfried Baudisch (Universität Magdeburg) und Prof. Dr. Arnulf Bojanowski (Universität Hannover)

Winfried Baudisch (Hrsg.)
Brennpunkte sozialer und beruflicher Rehabilitation
Kolloquium vom 8. 10. 1996 an der Otto-von-Guericke-Universität Magdeburg
Die Reihe "Pädagogische Beiträge zur sozialen und kulturellen Entwicklung" soll in relativer thematischer Breite wesentliche Fragen und Probleme der Sozialisation und Kulturation unter den aktuellen Bedingungen aufgreifen. So wird sie unter anderem schultheoretisch-curriculare Bereiche ebenso präsentieren wie ausgewählte Felder sozialpädagogischer und rehabilitationswissenschaftlicher Arbeit. Mit dem ersten Band sind Aspekte der sozialen und beruflichen Rehabilitation ins Zentrum der Betrachtung gerückt. Hilfe zur Selbsthilfe, Überwindung isolierender Lebensbedingungen, Erhalt und Verbesserung von Möglichkeiten einer beruflichen Ausbildung und Integration für Menschen mit Behinderungen sowie die bewußte Veränderung von institutionellen Angeboten der Rehabilitation hin zu Orten möglichst selbstbestimmter Gestaltung von Zielen und Wegen können als Brennpunkte dieses Geschehens herausgehoben werden, zumal sie durch veränderte Sozial- und Arbeitsmarktpolitik in ihrer Realisierung durchaus gefährdet sind. Die Beiträge dieses Bandes versuchen, nicht nur die aktuellen Problemlagen zu beschreiben sondern veränderte Gestaltungsspielräume zu erschließen. Dabei kommt sowohl die wissenschaftliche Betrachtungsweise rehabilitativer und sozialpädagogischer Gegenstände zum Tragen als auch die Sicht auf die Prozesse aus der Position der praktischen und arbeitsmarktpolitischen Verantwortung. In einer Reihe von Aufsätzen besteht ein deutlicher Bezug zu den rehabilitativen und bildungspolitischen Arbeitsbedingungen im Bundesland Sachsen-Anhalt. Das ist aus dem empirischen Bezug auf diese Region und dem Bemühen um ihre weitere Entwicklung erklärt. Dennoch wird sich die Schriftenreihe nicht auf eine landesspezifische Reflexion von sozialer und kultureller Entwicklung beschränken.
Bd. 1, 1997, 256 S., 25,90 €, br., ISBN 3-8258-3006-3

Renate Girmes (Hrsg.)
Modernisierungsdruck als Bildungschance?
Zu diesem Buch: Es gibt zahlreiche gesellschaftliche Veränderungen, die ein Überdenken und Neuorganisieren bestehender sozialer und pädagogischer Strukturen und Einrichtungen erforderlich machen: Die Schulen verändern ihr Gesicht, der Unterricht such neue Formen, die ökologische Frage hat sich in der Bildungsarbeit verschiedener Institutionen an Gewicht gewonnen, gesellschaftliche Veränderungen schaffen Modernisierungsverlierer, provozieren Lebenskrisen und machen neue Orientierungs- und Aktionsformen erforderlich.
Die Beiträge dieses Buches widmen sich der Gestaltung von Bildungsprozessen in den genannten Bereichen und zeigen auf verschiedene Weise, daß Bildung dann zur Chance wird, wenn man Offenheit und Aufgeschlossenheit für Neues als Voraussetzung jeden Sich-Bildens den anderen und sich selbst zugestehen und auch instituionell einräumen kann. Themen: Bildungschancen sehen lernen und nutzen wollen
Schulen als Bildungschance gestalten – Probleme und Wege
Unterricht neu denken? Chancen und Risiken einer zeitgerechten Methodik und Didaktik
Ökologischer Modernisierungsdruck als Ausgangspunkt vernetzten Denkens und Arbeitens
Gesellschaftlich-ökonomischer Modernisierungsdruck als Anlaß für die Individualisierung von

LIT Verlag Münster – Hamburg – Berlin – London
Grevener Str. 179 48159 Münster
Tel.: 0251 – 23 50 91 – Fax: 0251 – 23 19 72
e-Mail: vertrieb@lit-verlag.de – http://www.lit-verlag.de

Preise: unv. PE

Lernangeboten und Lernformen
Bd. 2, 1997, 280 S., 20,90 €, br., ISBN 3-8258-3159-0

Winfried Baudisch; Thomas Claus; Karin Haug (Hrsg.)
Wege aus der Isolation – zur Praxis der Enthospitalisierung
Die Schriftenreihe geht von einem weiten Verständnis kultureller und sozialer Entwicklung aus und findet unter anderem in der Betrachtung rehabilitationswissenschaftlicher Problemfelder einen ihrer Schwerpunkte.
Im vorliegenden Band stehen Fragen der Enthospitalisierung im Mittelpunkt, wobei dieser eher pragmatische Begriff den Anspruch auf grundlegende Veränderungen der Lebenssituation von LangzeitbewohnerInnen ehemaliger Landeskrankenhäuser für Psychiatrie umschreibt. Nach der politischen Wende 1989/90 wurde in den neuen Bundesländern sehr schnell und auf drastische Weise die defizitäre Situation in stationären Einrichtungen der Psychiatrie deutlich. Auch für Sachsen-Anhalt stellte sich die Aufgabe, LangzeitbewohnerInnen mit psychischen oder geistigen Behinderungen neue Lebensräume zu eröffnen und Chancen der aktiven Lebensgestaltung zu ermöglichen.
Die Initialphase des Enthospitalisierungsprozesses wurde wissenschaftlich begleitet. Die Mehrzahl der Beiträge ist aus diesem Evaluationsprozeß hervorgegangen. Bei der Drucklegung wurde das Ziel verfolgt, den Zusammenhang zwischen heilpädagogischer Theorie und praktischer Sozialpolitik herauszuarbeiten, Erkenntnisse aus bisherigen Enthospitalisierungsbemühungen anderer Länder zu bilanzieren, vor allem aber die Lebenssituationen und die potentiellen Kompetenzen der BewohnerInnen zu erhellen. Auf diesen repräsentativen Erhebungen basieren Vorschläge für die Führung des Prozesses, aber auch die Beschreibung erster Auswirkungen von neuen Lebensbedingungen unter gruppendynamischen Aspekten.
Bd. 3, 1999, 352 S., 25,90 €, br., ISBN 3-8258-3829-3

Winfried Baudisch (Hrsg.)
Selbstbestimmt leben trotz schwerer Behinderungen?
Schritte zur Annäherung an eine Vision
Die Schriftenreihe mit Beiträgen zur sozialen und kulturellen Entwicklung schließt von Beginn an pädagogische Problemlagen ein, die sich auf die Sozialisation von Menschen mit Behinderungen beziehen. Aspekte der sozialen und beruflichen Rehabilitation (Band 1) spielten dabei ebenso eine Rolle wie die Prozesse der Enthospitalisierung für Menschen mit isolierenden Lebensbedingungen (Band 3). Der neue Titel setzt diese inhaltliche Arbeitsrichtung fort, indem er sich speziellen Fragen der Förderung und Kompetenzentwicklung bei Menschen mit schweren (geistigen oder körperlichen) Behinderungen zuwendet und sie vor allem unter dem Aspekt der individuellen Lebensgestaltung diskutiert. Die theoretischen und empirischen Reflexionen beziehen sich dabei auf unterschiedliche Gegenstände und Lebensbereiche. Fragen des Dialogs in der Frühförderung, Sexualität und Partnerschaft als Menschenrecht auch für Behinderte, Kommunikationsentwicklung und Freizeitgestaltung durch Computernutzung, berufliche Integration in Werkstätten für Behinderte oder durch Programme der Befähigung zur Telearbeit sind als Schwerpunkte des Buches hervorzuheben. Sie bilden ihre theoretische Klammer in der Leitidee einer auf Selbstständigkeit und Selbstbestimmung von Menschen mit Behinderungen gerichteten Rehabilitationspädagogik, die den Widerspruch zwischen Anspruch und Möglichkeit nicht verdrängt, sondern thematisiert.
Bd. 4, 2000, 248 S., 20,90 €, br., ISBN 3-8258-5165-6

W. Baudisch; A. Bojanowski (Hrsg.)
Berufliche Rehabilitation mit behinderten und benachteiligten Jugendlichen im Berufsbildungswerk
Bd. 5, Frühjahr 2002, ca. 240 S., ca. 20,90 €, br., ISBN 3-8258-5504-x

Ruth Enggruber (Hrsg.)
Berufliche Bildung benachteiligter Jugendlicher
Empirische Einblicke und sozialpädagogische Ausblicke
Zur Bekämpfung von Jugendausbildungs- und Jugendarbeitslosigkeit hat sich in den letzten mehr als 20 Jahren eine große Vielfalt schulischer und außerschulischer, betrieblicher und außerbetrieblicher Maßnahmen zur Berufsbildung benachteiligter Jugendlicher entwickelt. Doch gelingt es mit den zahlreichen Angeboten auch, diese Zielsetzungen zu erreichen? Oder sind weitere Ziele und andere sozialpädagogische Konzepte für die Berufsberatung, Berufsvorbereitung und Berufsausbildung benachteiligter Jugendlicher gefragt? Welche Konsequenzen ergeben sich für die Professionalisierung des Personals? Die fünf Beiträge in diesem Sammelband suchen empirische Hinweise für mögliche Antworten auf diese Fragen.
Bd. 6, 2001, 224 S., 20,90 €, br., ISBN 3-8258-5518-x

LIT Verlag Münster – Hamburg – Berlin – London
Grevener Str. 179 48159 Münster
Tel.: 0251 – 23 50 91 – Fax: 0251 – 23 19 72
e-Mail: vertrieb@lit-verlag.de – http://www.lit-verlag.de

Preise: unv. PE